Speaking for the Dying

THE CHICAGO SERIES IN LAW AND SOCIETY

Edited by John M. Conley and Lynn Mather

Also in the series:

Just Words, Third Edition: Law, Language, and Power
by John M. Conley, William M. O'Barr, and Robin Conley Riner

Islands of Sovereignty: Haitian Migration and the Borders of Empire
by Jeffrey S. Kahn

Building the Prison State: Race and the Politics of Mass Incarceration
by Heather Schoenfeld

Navigating Conflict: How Youth Handle Trouble in a High-Poverty School
by Calvin Morrill and Michael Musheno

The Sit-Ins: Protest and Legal Change in the Civil Rights Era
by Christopher W. Schmidt

Working Law: Courts, Corporations, and Symbolic Civil Rights
by Lauren B. Edelman

The Myth of the Litigious Society: Why We Don't Sue
by David M. Engel

Policing Immigrants: Local Law Enforcement on the Front Lines
by Doris Marie Provine, Monica W. Varsanyi, Paul G. Lewis, and Scott H. Decker

The Seductions of Quantification: Measuring Human Rights, Gender Violence, and Sex Trafficking
by Sally Engle Merry

Invitation to Law and Society: An Introduction to the Study of Real Law, Second Edition
by Kitty Calavita

Pulled Over: How Police Stops Define Race and Citizenship
by Charles R. Epp, Steven Maynard-Moody, and Donald Haider-Markel

The Three and a Half Minute Transaction: Boilerplate and the Limits of Contract Design
by Mitu Gulati and Robert E. Scott

This Is Not Civil Rights: Discovering Rights Talk in 1939 America
by George I. Lovell

Additional series titles follow index

Speaking for the Dying

Life-and-Death Decisions in Intensive Care

SUSAN P. SHAPIRO

The University of Chicago Press
Chicago and London

The University of Chicago Press, Chicago 60637
The University of Chicago Press, Ltd., London
© 2019 by The University of Chicago
Published 2019
Printed in the United States of America

28 27 26 25 24 23 22 21 20 19   1 2 3 4 5

ISBN-13: 978-0-226-61560-8 (cloth)
ISBN-13: 978-0-226-61574-5 (paper)
ISBN-13: 978-0-226-61588-2 (e-book)
DOI: https://doi.org/10.7208/chicago/9780226615882.001.0001

Library of Congress Cataloging-in-Publication Data

Names: Shapiro, Susan P., author.
Title: Speaking for the dying : life-and-death decisions in intensive care / Susan P. Shapiro.
Other titles: Chicago series in law and society.
Description: Chicago : The University of Chicago Press, 2019. | Series: Chicago series in law and society | Includes bibliographical references and index.
Identifiers: LCCN 2018055504 | ISBN 9780226615608 (cloth : alk. paper) | ISBN 9780226615745 (pbk. : alk. paper) | ISBN 9780226615882 (e-book)
Subjects: LCSH: Terminal care—Decision making. | Terminal care—Decision making—Case studies. | Advance directives (Medical care) | Advance directives (Medical care)—Psychological aspects. | Terminally ill—Civil rights. | Right to die—Moral and ethical aspects. | Medical ethics. | Intensive care units.
Classification: LCC R726.8.S54 2019 | DDC 616.02/9—dc23
LC record available at https://lccn.loc.gov/2018055504

♾ This paper meets the requirements of ANSI/NISO Z39.48–1992 (Permanence of Paper).

For Nate and Ruth Shapiro
Nancy, Ken, and Fred

CONTENTS

ONE / Holding Life and Death in Their Hands / 1

Is This for Me? / 11

TWO / The Intensive Care Unit / 14

Personnel / 15

Rhythms / 17

Economics / 22

Conclusion / 24

THREE / Actors / 25

Patients / 25

Friends, Family, and Significant Others / 30

Health Care Professionals / 40

Conclusion / 44

FOUR / Decisions / 45

Informed Consent / 75

Venues / 79

Affect / 87

Conflict / 88

Conclusion / 99

FIVE / Prognosis / 101

Evidence / 112

Timing / 116

Mixed Messages / 119
Negotiation / 124
Accuracy / 129
Prognostic Framing / 132
Conclusion / 133

SIX / Decision-Making Scripts / 134

The Legal Script / 135
Cognitive Scripts / 142
Conflicts of Interest / 145
Law at the Bedside / 148
Conclusion / 151

SEVEN / Improvisation: Decisions in the Real World / 152

The Patient Should Decide / 153
Reprising Patient Instructions / 160
Standing in the Patient's Shoes / 171
Beneficence / 181
It's God's Decision / 189
What We Want / 193
Denial, Opting Out / 206
Conclusion / 212

EIGHT / Making a Difference? / 214

The Role of Physicians / 217
Opting for a Trajectory / 220
Outcomes / 223
I Thought the Law Would Take Care of This / 228
Does Any of This Matter? / 232

NINE / The End / 233

Implications / 236
Before It's Too Late / 238
When It's Too Late / 243
When "This" Happens to Me / 254

Contents / ix

Appendix A: The Research / 255

Appendix B.1: Patient Occupation / 275

Appendix B.2: Patient Age, Gender, and Marital Status / 277

Appendix B.3: Location and Purpose of Observed Meetings / 279

Appendix C: Relationship between Multiple Trajectories Traversed / 281

Appendix D: Decision Trajectory by Patient and Surrogate Characteristics / 283

Appendix E: Advance-Directive Status and Aspects of the
Decision-Making Process, Outcome, and Impact / 289

Acknowledgments / 291

Notes / 293

References / 305

Index / 317

ONE

Holding Life and Death in Their Hands

It is 6 A.M. The critical care resident checks on one of his patients before morning rounds and encounters ten angry family members encircling the unresponsive patient's bed, livid that he had been intubated (had a breathing tube inserted into his airway) and attached to a ventilator in the middle of the night. The patient, a seventy-six-year-old white man and former purchasing agent, had been admitted to the hospital for a relatively minor stent (drainage tube) procedure and to explore his eligibility for a liver transplant. He had previously designated his wife power of attorney for health care and documented that he did not want to be resuscitated or intubated.

The previous day, tests had revealed that the patient had liver cancer and would probably not be eligible for a transplant. Late that night the patient experienced breathing difficulties, and the medical team asked for his consent to be intubated and placed on a ventilator. At 3:25 A.M. the patient, alone in his room in the intensive care unit (ICU), had consented.

Two hours after the hostile encounter in the patient's room, the critical care team—an attending physician, fellow, and two residents—arrived for morning rounds. As he examined the patient, the attending physician spoke to the assembled family.

CRITICAL CARE ATTENDING: I'm going to look at his heart and lungs, and then I know you have concerns about the vent [ventilator].

WIFE: Pull the plug.

DAUGHTER-IN-LAW: This is not what he would have wanted.

CRITICAL CARE ATTENDING: Would he feel differently if he was able to potentially get a transplant?

DAUGHTER-IN-LAW: No.

CRITICAL CARE ATTENDING: If the cancer is confined to his liver, they wouldn't rule him out as a transplant candidate. It's a long shot, I'll be honest. But they haven't ruled him out yet.

WIFE: I thought they found fluid in his abdomen and so he can't get a transplant.

CRITICAL CARE ATTENDING: They haven't told us that he's definitely not a candidate.

WIFE: Just pull the damn plug!

CRITICAL CARE ATTENDING: See, we're in a bit of a bind. He told the nurses last night that he wanted to be intubated, and in effect retracted his living will. But sometimes when people are in distress they'll make decisions differently. You don't think this is what he wanted?

WIFE, DAUGHTER-IN-LAW, DAUGHTER, AND TWO SONS: [In unison] No.

DAUGHTER-IN-LAW: He talked about this at length with me in the last three months. He told me in detail what he wanted. It's not this.

WIFE: I think he was just frightened.

DAUGHTER-IN-LAW: Yes, I think he was scared. He thought he was just coming here for stents for his liver. Now he's on pressors and Levo [life-supportive medications].

CRITICAL CARE ATTENDING: We'll have to consult with our ethics committee to make sure that we're doing the right thing—that we're following his wishes.

DAUGHTER-IN-LAW: Yes, we understand.

CRITICAL CARE ATTENDING: We'll talk to Ethics and the nurses who were here as soon as possible to get their thoughts. Unfortunately, during the night, things sometimes are complicated because the primary team and the family aren't around.

The critical care team then consulted the chair of the hospital ethics committee to determine whether the patient's wife was permitted to reverse the patient's decision made just hours earlier. The physicians and nurses who had cared for the patient overnight and had secured his consent to be intubated were consulted as well. Physicians also reviewed instructions in the patient's power-of-attorney document. At 10:30 A.M. the critical care team removed life support and initiated comfort measures. The patient died around midnight.

It is unusual to hear the expression "pull the plug" in a hospital, let alone observe loved ones demand so quickly and decisively that physicians do so. More often families beg physicians to do everything possible, even when all hope is gone. The family of a second ICU patient shows the lengths to which loved ones may go to ensure that the plug remains securely in place. The immediate and unequivocal insistence of the first family to remove life support is matched by the unrelenting and fierce resistance to doing so by this second family. And the justifications for their decision look entirely different from those articulated by members of the first family, who stood in the patient's shoes and reprised his instructions and conversations.

The second patient is a fifty-five-year-old Middle Eastern man from a Christian denomination who immigrated to the United States in his late teens. He works in real estate. While doing pushups at home, he collapsed and had a seizure. He was taken to a small neighborhood hospital, which found that an aneurysm (a weak bulging in the wall of an artery that supplies blood to the brain) had ruptured. Initially talking and moving, the patient suffered another seizure and lost consciousness. He was airlifted to a second hospital, which administered life support and other interventions, but an exam suggested possible brain death. The patient's family transferred him to a third hospital, seeking a second opinion and a lifesaving intervention. Arriving at 1 A.M., the neurosurgeon on call explained to family members that an intervention was not appropriate and that another brain-death exam would be administered in the morning. The next morning the senior neurosurgeon on the case explained to the patient's family that the results were consistent with brain death.

NEUROSURGERY ATTENDING PHYSICIAN: The doctors have done an exam and I have reviewed all the scans. His brain is dead. His heart is only beating because we are giving it medication. He cannot think, cannot talk, cannot see, cannot hear.

SISTER: Give it more time to see if it comes back.

NEUROSURGERY ATTENDING PHYSICIAN: It cannot come back. It is destroyed. There is no blood going into the brain. . . . If there was a one in a million chance, I would do something. . . . Twenty to fifty percent of people with aneurysms do not survive. I do aneurysms, hemorrhages, brain trauma. This is what I do. If there is anything I could do, I would do it. If there was a one in a billion chance, I would do something.

WIFE: I believe in miracles.

NEUROSURGERY ATTENDING PHYSICIAN: I believe in miracles too. But I deal in facts. His brain is completely dead.

WIFE: They said something about a nuclear flow study [a scan that measures the amount of blood flow in the brain].

NEUROSURGERY ATTENDING PHYSICIAN: If you want that, we can do that.

WIFE: If there is even minimal flow, there is still hope. I was a doctor for four years. I know that things can happen. You don't always know what will happen.

About a half hour after the meeting ended, a senior neurologist arrived to perform a different kind of brain-death exam in the presence of the family. As he performed each step, he told the witnesses what he was doing. He shined a flashlight in the patient's eye and explained that he didn't see any reaction to light. He asked for permission to turn the patient's head to see if his eyes move. He explained that they didn't. He said that he will pinch the patient's fingers to see if he responds to pain. He noted that the patient didn't. He explained that he will put some cold water in the patient's ear to see if his eyes move. The neurologist inserted the water and said that it can take as long as a minute. Everyone in the room was riveted, staring at the patient's eyes, but they don't move. The patient's mother began shaking her head no. The neurologist put cold water in the other ear, again with no response. He then sat down beside the patient's wife and explained that, once again, the exam indicates brain death.

As they await the results from the nuclear flow study, fifteen family members begin filing in and out of the patient's room. Many are in tears. Others are screaming at the patient to wake up and commanding, "Don't do this to us!" As the hours tick away, visitors continue to implore the patient to wake up and open his eyes. "C'mon, it's time to wake up!"

The results from the flow study finally come back. The critical care attending physician escorts the family to a conference room. He hands a copy of the report to the patient's sister, who passes it to her brother and then to the patient's wife. They each slowly read the report. The physician explains that the report is absolutely clear; you can see it for yourself. "The scan shows that there is no flow to the brain. It is unequivocal. This confirms what we have known all day from the various tests that we have done—that he is brain-dead. Brain dead means that we can no longer treat him." Family members begin to protest that they need more time, and the patient's brother explains that they believe everything the physician said, but they need to be sure. They need to know that they have done everything that they can for him. As the resistance continues, the neurosurgery attending enters the room and declares, "I have just reviewed the last set of scans. The brain is entirely dead and the blood vessels in the brain are all empty." As the family files out of the room, the critical care attending tries negotiating with the patient's wife: the team will continue to treat the patient, but there will be no escalation of treatment, including resuscitating the patient if his heart should stop. The wife agrees.

The next morning the patient's sister arrives to rescind the do-not-resuscitate agreement, request that physicians give the patient Ambien (a sleeping pill touted on the Internet to reverse brain damage), ask for the name of the hospital's lawyer, and explain that the family hopes to transfer the patient to another facility and a better neurosurgeon. The nurse manager of the ICU responds that he will arrange a family meeting.

SISTER: We did that yesterday and we weren't happy with it.

NURSE: The patient is brain-dead. That means he is dead. Because he is dead. We cannot in good conscience send a dead patient to another facility. He is dead. He has passed. There is no blood flow to the brain.

AUNT: We don't believe it.

SISTER: People come back.

NURSE: But he has no blood flow to the brain.

SISTER: We know of another situation exactly. No blood flow and the guy comes back.

Some family members tell the hospital chaplain that the patient's fate is in God's hands and that they wish to give God every opportunity to restore the patient to health. God will decide. Others continue to argue with various members of the health care team that they do not believe the diagnosis. They cite anecdotal stories of individuals written off as brain-dead who are now alive and fully functional. Their goal is to keep the patient alive while they locate another specialist or institution that can perform a lifesaving intervention, a miracle. They will not give up until they find someone—whether at the Mayo Clinic or in London—able to do the intervention of which physicians in this hospital are incapable. They bring a lawyer to the hospital to ensure that physicians do not remove the patient's life support before they have an opportunity to transfer the patient elsewhere. Dubious that the family can arrange a transfer, the medical team nonetheless agrees to give them time to try to do so, although nurses and other physicians privately complain to one another about their discomfort and moral distress in treating a dead patient.

The next day, to the amazement of the health care team, an outside neurosurgeon agrees to treat the patient, and a local facility agrees to a transfer. (Just hours earlier an ICU nurse had confidently declared to his colleagues that, if any facility agreed to take a dead patient, he would quit his job.) ICU doctors prepare the brain-dead patient, his organs rapidly failing, for the risky ambulance ride to the new facility. A few days later, a death notice for the patient appears in the local newspaper.

Many of you probably cannot imagine yourself standing in the shoes of a member of either of these two families—deciding as they decided, as quickly or resolutely, or for the reasons they expressed. Some of you may not even realize how very likely it is that someday you too will stand at the bedside of a loved one facing wrenching life-and-death decisions on his or her behalf. And perhaps others of you are horrified to think that what happened to one or both of these patients could happen to you.

You are in good company. This book shares the very different stories of roughly two hundred other intensive care unit patients and how their families and friends negotiated medical decisions on their behalf. Like the first patient, many had preexisting medical problems, some of very long standing. Some patients were in the ICU for an elective procedure or second opinion; a few flew across the country when local physicians offered little hope. Others experienced complications—infections, respiratory problems, cardiac arrests, strokes—from unrelated medical procedures performed elsewhere in this or another hospital. And, like the second patient, for many the symptoms came out of the blue. They were at home, at work, in a public place, or engaged in sports when they collapsed, suffered a seizure or the worst headache of their life, or exhibited slurred speech, weakness on one side, or confusion. And others were transported to the ICU after a fall, accident, or assault.

The unfortunate patients in these stories are current or former doctors, nurses, lawyers, teachers, bus drivers, farmers, bookkeepers, construction workers, factory workers, business owners, musicians, performers, security guards, architects, salespersons, homemakers, honor students, and likely drug dealers. They are celebrities and street people. They are young and old, male, female, and transgendered, rich and poor, gay and straight, someone's parent and another's child. They are black and white, Hispanic and Middle Eastern, East and South Asian, Protestant and Catholic, Jewish and Muslim, Jehovah's Witness and Hmong, evangelicals and agnostics. Some live blocks and others thousands of miles away. Some are attended by round-the-clock vigils of family and friends; others languish alone in their room, day after day, without a single visitor.

The patients are as diverse—literally—as the American census.[1] Yet what they have in common is so much more fundamental than mere demographics or the circumstances of their visit. Whether comatose, nonresponsive, unconscious, sedated, or suffering cognitive deficits or dementia, they cannot speak for themselves. Denizens of intensive care units offering the highest-tech interventions that modern medicine has invented, they lack the capacity to direct their care—to embrace or refuse surgeries, procedures, medical devices, medications, or life-sustaining treatments that might cure their disease or relieve their symptoms, extend their lives or their suffering, restore their quality of life or destroy it, cheat death or sentence them to a fate worse than death. The biggest life-and-death decisions of their lives—literally—had to be made by someone else.

Hospital records will tell you that more than half didn't make it out of the hospital alive—nine in ten of them, because someone directed physicians to stop aggressive measures. They will document what procedures were performed or tally the many millions of dollars collectively paid for that care. This book will tell a different story. I look beyond the hospital bed and gaggle of white coats administering to unresponsive bodies secured with a tangle of lines, tubes, and monitors—activities methodically documented in the medical record and in many other books and articles—to the anxious faces of loved ones hovering nearby, and to waiting rooms and conference rooms and hallways. I tell the stories of these others, without the white coats, who also hold life and death in their hands, however reluctantly. It is easy to forget, in the drama of saving lives, that their stories are often the most decisive. After all, for every patient who died despite their doctors' best efforts, nine others did so at the behest of their loved ones.

Loved ones hold life and death in their hands because Americans' constitutional rights of autonomy and self-determination to make decisions regarding medical treatment are so sacred that they are extended by law to proxies or surrogates authorized to decide on patients' behalf when the latter cannot.[2] Intensive care units represent ground zero for surrogate medical decision making because of the gravity of the illnesses and injuries they attract and the aggressive interventions they offer. Two studies found, for example, that because so few ICU patients have decision-making capacity, 96–97 percent of decisions to withhold or withdraw life support were made by someone else.[3] Although impaired capacity may be commonplace in intensive care units, it is not uncommon elsewhere, especially near life's end. One study found that 70 percent of Americans aged sixty or over requiring decisions about care and treatment in the "final days of life" lack capacity to make these decisions.[4] Because these numbers are so large, most of us will someday be called on to act as a health care surrogate on behalf of another and perhaps need one ourselves.

These surrogates who make treatment decisions on patients' behalf often determine the trajectories of life's end: whether patients go to a health care institution at all and what kind; the level of risk or suffering to assume in the hope of a cure; the appropriate tipping point between length of life and quality of life; whether they receive routine treatment, cutting-edge interventions, aggressive care, life support, or hospice care, and for how long; whether they receive comfort care or heroic measures in their last hours; whether they die at home or in a hospital; the disposition of their bodies (organ donation, autopsy, cremation, etc.); and whether their wishes (if they ever expressed any) are honored, forgotten, or betrayed. And they choose between fidelity to patient interests and what is best for themselves or others. Surrogates also control many of the expenditures on health care near the end of life,[5] much of it, studies find, for unwanted treatment.[6]

Yet despite their critical role for so many near life's end, we know remarkably little about these surrogates, the decision-making process they follow, the choices they make, and the challenges they face. Other researchers have employed various methods to answer some of these questions. Many have presented hypothetical scenarios to healthy would-be patients and would-be surrogate decision makers. Some have abstracted data from medical records. Others have conducted retrospective interviews or surveys of varied informants—decision makers, family members, physicians, and others. And a few have collected snapshots of a meeting or a final decision. Some of the most powerful work has been done by journalists and documentary filmmakers who eschew the scientific method altogether. Typically cherry-picking a handful of compelling stories, too often about white middle- or upper-middle-class families, their accounts necessarily ignore the experience of many. In appendix A, I elaborate on these varied approaches and describe their blinders, limitations, and biases, which led me to look elsewhere to understand how surrogates navigate what could be the end of another's life.

This book offers a very different window on how these end-of-life trajectories take shape and change course—by systematically observing them, day after day, for more than two years. Early each morning, a medical social worker and/or I rushed off to a neurological or medical intensive care unit in a large urban Illinois teaching hospital serving a very diverse population of patients.[7] Like flies on the wall, we went along on critical care rounds and then hung out in the ICUs throughout the day to observe spontaneous encounters as well as formal meetings between health care providers and families and friends of patients who lacked decision-making capacity. After the meetings ended, we reconstructed (from memory) transcripts of what was said and documented characteristics of the meetings and participants, social dynamics, and emotional tone. We also examined patient medical records. Appendix A provides greater detail on our method and on its strengths and limitations.

More than 2500 patients passed through the two ICUs during the research period, some of whom lacked the capacity to make medical decisions throughout their ICU admission. We observed those who spoke on their behalf. These surrogate decision makers faced a host of medical decisions, ranging from whether to undertake surgery or other medical procedures to whether to withhold or withdraw life support or donate the patient's organs. We observed not just the big final decisions documented by so many of the other researchers and storytellers, but also the ongoing conversations and smaller incremental decisions that shaped and constrained the bigger choices surrogates ultimately faced. In all, we observed more than a thousand encounters regarding 205 patients, involving more than 700 of their family and friends and almost 300 different health care providers.

These observations yield rich, detailed accounts of the dialogue between health care providers, families, and others, day after day, as diagnoses and prognoses change; treatments succeed and fail; new interventions become necessary or are exhausted; new medical teams rotate on and off the service; significant others appear and disappear; and families' understandings, goals, and expectations change. We observed how participants make and remake treatment decisions on behalf of patients: the questions they ask, the stories they tell, their statements about the patient, the rationale or justifications they offer, the conflicting understandings or priorities they negotiate, how they make sense of technical or incomplete information and mixed messages they receive, how they balance their obligations to the patient with their own self-interest and the interests of others, how financial considerations or religious and other values come into play, how conflicts erupt and are managed, the role of advance directives and of law in the deliberative process, and how health care providers instigate, frame, and shape the decision-making process. In short, what and how did participants decide? And why do some decision makers authorize one aggressive intervention after the next while others do not—even on behalf of patients with similar problems and prospects?

In this book I tell their stories, drawing on the most extensive observational study of surrogate decision making undertaken to date. The transcripts that I will share throughout the book take you to the private bedsides, hallways, and conference rooms to hear, in their own words, pulsing with raw emotion, how physicians really talk to families and how loved ones respond, inquire, ignore, regale, justify, plead, or disagree. Their words will often be more instructive than my own, and I encourage you to spend time with them. Still, however exhaustive the portrait I share, this book does not—and cannot—report on all of the many sites and settings in which end-of-life decision making unfolds. But it does open an expansive window on that private world and exposes an extremely diverse collection of participants.

The window opens on the ICU itself, where you will become familiar with the rooms, technology, actors, sights, sounds, rhythms, and routines. Looking behind the privacy curtains, you will meet health care personnel, patients, and especially their significant others. Drawing on examples from the experience of hundreds of patients and families, you will learn of the misfortunes that brought patients to the ICU and the worlds from which they traveled. You will see the arrangements, if any, that they made in advance to prepare for medical decision making on their behalf. You will get to know the friends and family who visit or maintain the occasional vigil at the bedside, the complex tangled family trees from which some travel, the sometimes challenging or contentious struggles to determine who gets to speak on behalf of the patient, and how decision makers come to understand their role and responsibilities.

Now familiar with the setting and the actors, the book turns to the medical decisions themselves that physicians and significant others negotiate. You will hear physicians describe in their own words the varied medical interventions appropriate near life's end; the risks, benefits, uncertainties, and other considerations they disclose as they discourage or seek consent to these procedures; and how loved ones respond and the ways the dialogues unfold—with emotions, misunderstandings, and conflicts on display. Considerations of prognosis—the likelihood that the patient will recover, become disabled, or die—course through these conversations and often play a significant role in how surrogates respond. The book explores prognosis—how it is avoided, framed, conveyed, even negotiated with loved ones—and reveals the silences, accuracy, consistency, and biases to which prognosis is often subject.

The central question of the book can now be addressed. How do loved ones and others make decisions on the patient's behalf? I present the legal and bioethical norms about surrogate decision making and the difficulties of following these norms in the real world, even as so many participants don't even know that they exist. One of those difficulties results from the impossibility of truly knowing another's wishes, another from the conflicts of interest that arise at the bedside and are inevitable when loved ones, who have the most to gain or lose, are entrusted with life-and-death decisions. Yet another reflects the cognitive biases that compromise the judgments of physicians and decision makers alike.

Given that decision-making norms are often unknown or difficult to follow, I reveal how surrogates and other friends and family improvise and the decision-making criteria they fashion, sometimes in collaboration with health care providers, sometimes in opposition to them. Again in their own words, I show how loved ones struggle with and justify the excruciating medical decisions they are called on to make on behalf of the patient—from standing in the patient's shoes or maximizing what's best for the decision maker (as did the two families who opened this chapter) to avoiding decisions altogether (whether because they are in denial or because they are waiting for the patient to regain the ability to decide or for God to do so), and much more. I uncover the characteristics of patients and families that gravitate to one decision-making strategy or another and what difference choice of strategy makes in the likelihood the patient will survive, the length of hospitalization and likely suffering, or the emotional distress experienced by loved ones. I also provide systematic evidence that advance directives—living wills and health care proxies—touted to enhance patients' autonomy and to empower their decision makers and ease their burden make almost no difference in the two ICUs.

So what does or could make a difference? The book concludes with lessons learned and proposes steps that readers—whether would-be patients, would-be surrogates or family members, health care providers, health care institutions, legal professionals, or policy makers—might undertake before it is "too late" and even after.

Is This for Me?

If you are still reading this, you may be questioning its relevance. After all, like a significant majority of Americans, you hope to die at home—not in an intensive care unit or even a hospital. But, if you are like more than two-thirds of Americans, your life will not end at home.[8] Most Americans will spend time in a hospital near life's end. Almost three-quarters of Medicare enrollees are hospitalized at least once (on average, for eight days) in the last six months of life, 40 percent of enrollees in an intensive care unit. One in five Americans will die in a hospital and one in seven in an ICU.[9]

Intensive care units are not only places to die, of course. Misfortunes throughout the life course often require critical care. Many ICU patients are neither elderly nor chronically sick. Half of all the patients admitted to the two ICUs were fifty-seven years old or younger (with average life expectancies of another twenty-five years).[10] For 43 percent of the patients observed, their visit to the ICU came out of the blue. Like many of you, these unlucky patients did not foresee themselves confined to an ICU either.

Moreover, even if you are determined or fortunate enough to escape intensive care throughout your life, this may not be true of those you love. Many of you will spend time in ICUs, not on beds or gurneys, but in waiting rooms and at bedsides, charged with excruciating life-and-death decisions on behalf of another or supporting, challenging, or bearing witness to those who are. Given the prevalence of visits to intensive care units, it is almost inevitable that each of us will eventually find ourselves at the ICU bedside of a loved one. That day may not be too far off, given the relatively young ICU population. Research has consistently found that choosing life or death for another is one of the most difficult decisions of a lifetime and the source of guilt or remorse that can haunt families decades later. This book foreshadows what some of you may encounter at those bedsides as patient, surrogate, or witness and offers an opportunity to question, reflect, and converse with your friends and family before it is too late. Perhaps the most generous final gift one can leave to a loved one is that of information, reassurance, and trust that may help avoid the helplessness, paralysis, guilt, or self-doubt that plague so many families after the patient loses the ability to speak.

Lessons from the ICUs are especially relevant to those of you who serve, counsel, or care for people as they near life's end and their families—physicians, nurses, chaplains, social workers—as well as those training to do so. Some of you may feel that you already know what happens at the ICU bedside. But this knowledge comes from the idiosyncratic prism of your own experience: the kinds of patients or clients you serve and the length and depth of these relationships; the medical problems, prognoses, and treatment decisions unique to your specialty; your own bedside manner; your personal values; and the ways that you interact with patients and their families, present information, offer options or support, and provide or avoid advice. You may not realize just how different these prisms are for some of your colleagues, especially those who serve a highly diverse population of patients—differences that may shape the understandings (and misunderstandings), priorities, challenges, crises, and options faced by the patients, families, and clients that you inherit from or share with them. Drawing on observations of almost three hundred health care providers, this book takes you along on their rounds and into their offices and conference rooms as they negotiate life-and-death decisions with those who speak for their patients or clients. Helping families negotiate the end of life is rarely the favorite part of a health care provider's job description. This book shows how others undertake these responsibilities and provides new insight into what families are going through.

For those of you who provide legal counsel, helping clients anticipate the challenges of infirmity or death, drafting documents to protect their interests, or responding at times of crisis, this book will provide a cautionary tale about the efficacy of legal solutions to the challenges near life's end and some suggestions about how you might play a more supportive role.

Finally, scholars, bioethicists, and those who work on health care policy are well aware that surrogates represent a critical black box in understanding outcomes at the end of life and efforts to change the American way of death. If seven in ten Americans who need medical decisions in the final days of life lack the capacity to make these decisions, surrogates play an enormous role in controlling the trajectories of life's end—decisions made; the alignment or misalignment of patient preferences and treatment;[11] resources expended, conserved, or squandered; and pain and suffering mitigated or exacerbated. This book shares rich new data from an extremely diverse population that help shine a light into that black box.

In short, whether providing, receiving, directing, bearing witness, or seeking to improve intensive care, this book is or will someday be about you.

TWO

The Intensive Care Unit

The elevator door opens. Two figures in scrubs push a gurney laden with tubes, monitors, and machines through the door. They wheel the gurney into one of the rooms in the intensive care unit. The curtain is drawn and a nurse hurriedly reconnects the wires, tubes, lines, leads, electrodes, probes, cuffs, pumps, monitors and other machines to permanent fixtures and connections in the room. A respiratory therapist attaches the breathing tube to a ventilator and calibrates the settings. New bags of fluids, medications, blood, and nutrition are hung and attached to machines administering the proper dosages. Catheters carrying bodily fluids from the bladder, chest, or brain are secured to drainage bags on the bed or more high-tech devices. Lines connect to bright monitors flashing numbers, ratios, and trend lines in greens and reds. A computer displays electronic medical records in which some of these numbers and settings are recorded and orders for future tests, medications, and procedures entered and displayed. A cacophonous symphony of pulsating alarms, beeps, chirps, hums, wheezes, whirs, gushes, swooshes, sucking, and computer keystrokes fills the air.

In time the room will likely fill with more technology. Perhaps a high-tech pulsating rotating bed. Perhaps a special kind of continuous bedside dialysis machine for kidney failure called CVVH (continuous veno-venous hemofiltration). Perhaps a video electroencephalogram (EEG) that monitors electrical patterns in the brain, along with a video camera to record movement. Or a device to monitor intracranial pressure in the brain. Perhaps pneumatic compression stockings to prevent blood clots in the legs. Or cooling blankets. Bags containing new medications will be hung and the settings adjusted on the intravenous infusion pumps that deliver the drugs. Ventilator settings will be recalibrated. Lines will be changed out to prevent infection. Invariably, new interventions will be implemented and additional bodily functions monitored as complications develop. And some rooms will collect more personal items as well: religious icons, comforters, photographs of better times, children's drawings, greeting cards, or collages signed by well-wishers.

Mounted on the wall outside each room, a dispenser supplies hand sanitizer. Some entryways announce that a patient is in isolation, with stacks of disposable gowns, masks, and gloves that those entering the room must don and overflowing receptacles inside the door in which they are discarded upon leaving. Some rooms are equipped with anterooms and pressurization to isolate patients with communicable diseases.

Panning out from the room, one sees a long corridor lined with twenty-odd rooms just like this one. When these beds are filled, spillover ICU patients are housed in another intensive care unit in the hospital.[1] A large nursing station spans the other side of the corridor, with binders holding paper records for each patient room, telephones, computers, banks of monitors that display data transmitted from each room, and other monitors with big screens that allow teams of physicians to cluster around them to read and discuss X-rays, MRI, and CT scans together. The ICU floor also houses offices for administrators, staff workrooms, several conference rooms and smaller family meeting rooms, and on-call rooms where physicians try to catch some sleep between crises. Stationed along the wall are racks of food trays for those few patients able to eat, crash carts with emergency equipment to resuscitate patients who are "coding" (in cardiac arrest), and "cows," wheeled carts securing laptop computers that are pushed through the corridor during critical care rounds. The floor is bright and sterile; flowers are not permitted in the ICU. Waiting rooms and restrooms for family and other visitors are located outside the entrance.

Personnel

A large cast of characters populates the ICU. A nurse, such as the one who opened the chapter, is assigned to every two patients. Nurses work twelve-hour shifts, usually three days a week. Patients invariably receive care from many different nurses. Daily and nightly charge nurses supervise the nursing team; nurse managers oversee the ICU floor.

Like nurses, critical care physicians are always on-site in the ICU, twenty-four hours a day, seven days a week. In the medical ICU they are usually internists or pulmonologists (lung specialists); in the neurological ICU they are usually anesthesiologists, neurologists, or, on rare occasions, neurosurgeons. Many other medical specialists pass through the intensive care units as well—specializing in trauma, thoracic (chest), and general surgery; orthopedics; infectious diseases; palliative care; oncology (cancer); immunology; nephrology (kidney); hepatology (liver); gastroenterology (stomach); hematology (blood); cardiology (heart); ear, nose, and throat; psychiatry; physiatry (rehabilitation); interventional radiology; ethics; and even the occasional ob-gyn.

If the physician's coat is waist length, he or she is a medical student; if knee length, a resident (also called a member of the house staff), fellow, or attending physician (a faculty member and the most senior physician on the case). For most of the period of the study, the neurological ICU had one team and the medical ICU two teams. Each critical care team was made up of an attending physician, five or six residents (including a couple more assigned for night coverage or "night float"), and possibly a fellow or occasional medical student. Medical students, fellows, and residents rotate through the ICU, the latter on usually one- or two-month rotations. Attending physicians generally change every two weeks.

Each critical care team includes a pharmacist who participates in rounds and consults on selecting and procuring appropriate medications, dosages, and avoiding drug interactions. Because pharmacists rarely rotate, they often know more about the patients and their histories than anyone else on the team. The unit also houses respiratory therapists, who assist in the management of ventilators.

Each ICU is also assigned a social worker and an interfaith chaplain (some ordained clergy, some certified lay chaplains; some employed by the hospital, some volunteers). Social workers focus primarily on discharge planning but also secure advance directives (living wills and powers of attorney for health care), locate family members, resolve insurance issues, and respond to challenging family dynamics or interpersonal conflicts, ethical problems, and the like. Chaplains address some of the same challenges but also visit with families (or the occasional lucid patient). They read scripture or pray with patients and families, listen to their stories, bear witness, try to assuage their grief and provide comfort, and counsel them. Some become very close with families; on a few occasions, families have asked them to officiate at memorial services. Chaplains often visit with patients and families of different religious faiths than their own. When patients require official religious interventions—last rites, for example—or families request it, a local priest is called or a chaplain of the appropriate faith assigned elsewhere in the hospital is paged. Social workers and chaplains rarely participate in the meetings between families, physicians, and other health care providers that we observed (2 percent of the meetings included one or both).

Various outsiders pass through the ICU: the patients, of course; their friends, family, and significant others; and—rarely—family doctors, "civilian" clergy visiting their parishioners or congregants, lawyers, public guardians, and personnel from outside agencies (nursing homes and long-term care or rehabilitation facilities) to which patients are discharged.

Rhythms

The ICU operates 24/7, with nurses, physicians, respiratory therapists and others on-site day and night and others available on call. The day begins very early each morning, around 5 or 6 A.M., as medical residents arrive to confer with night nurses and night-float residents and check in on their patients and work them up for presentation during morning rounds. The residents include those from the critical care team that staffs the ICUs as well as those in the various specialties, described earlier, who are also treating the patient. At around 7 A.M. a new shift of nurses arrives, meets with the night shift, and then begins attending to the two patients to which each nurse is assigned.

Sometime between 7 and 8 A.M. the attending critical care physicians in each ICU will arrive and critical care morning rounds begin for each of their teams. Numerous participants attend critical care rounds: the attending physician, possibly a fellow, five or six residents or interns (some coming off the night shift and others beginning their day shift), a pharmacist, often a couple of medical students, and sometimes the nurse treating a particular patient under consideration. Everyone wears a white coat. Underneath, most nurses and residents wear scrubs; most attendings and some nonsurgical residents (e.g., neurologists) wear shirts and ties or blouses. Most residents carry sheaves of paper, folded lengthwise so that they fit in the pockets of their white coats, listing vital statistics for each patient that they consult as they report on an assigned case. Anywhere from one to three or four team members are pushing cows—the carts carrying laptop computers with secure Wi-Fi connections to the hospital electronic medical record system. Physicians and the pharmacist standing around each cow are reporting data from the electronic medical records, and some are writing electronic notes and medication and treatment orders and paging other physicians online as the tangle of white-coated team members snakes through the narrow ICU hallway.

Each attending physician has a unique way of structuring rounds. A few first meet with the team in a conference room where all new X-rays and MRI and CT scans for each patient are examined on a big screen. Most attendings just begin outside the door of the first patient. (First, for some, is the sickest patient; for others, the first door on the end of the hall.) The resident responsible for each patient will pull the paper out of the pocket of his or her white coat; provide an overview of the patient's medical history, current status and problems, overnight events, upcoming procedures, gossip or family dynamics (sometimes); and then begin reporting various numbers pertaining to each organ system, medication dosages, ventilator settings, and the like. Someone will pull up the patient's scans on a laptop on one of the cows or the team will make its way over to one of the big computer monitors at the nursing station to study the patient's recent X-rays, MRIs, and CTs (if it hadn't done so earlier).

The attending physician will respond to the reporting resident with Socratic-like questioning—some of it to clarify the patient's condition and treatment options, some of it to teach the entire team more general principles. (From this process, by the end of the study I knew more about some common ICU medications, diagnoses, procedures, and test results than newly minted interns and could perform a better neurological exam.) For some attendings, this questioning is gentle and friendly; for others, critical, impatient, or anxiety-producing. Although team members are often distracted during the presentation of others' patients—sending or answering pages, preparing their own presentation, checking up on their own patients, writing up orders or notes in the electronic medical record, texting their friends, or googling something on the laptop—they sometimes interject questions or offer differing opinions. Almost every day during rounds, two of the anesthesiology residents will receive an emergency page regarding a cardiac arrest or respiratory distress elsewhere in the hospital where they are needed to intubate the patient. They grab their bag of equipment and literally race out of the ICU mid-sentence.

After anywhere from five minutes to an hour or more, the hallway presentation of a given patient will end. In the medical ICU, and for some attendings in the neurological ICU, the entire team will then enter the room, all of them first washing their hands and slipping on gloves and, if the patient is in isolation, donning gowns and masks. Encircling the bed, the team then examines the patient, checks the monitors, tinkers with ventilator settings, tries to communicate with the patient, and converses with anyone visiting in the room. (Some of the anesthesiologist attendings in the neurological ICU will simply move on to the next patient without entering the patient's room.) Upon leaving the room, the team will pause, address additional questions, and come up with a treatment plan for the patient for the day.

While critical care rounds proceed, rounds of many of the specialty teams—neurology, oncology, infectious diseases, nephrology, and others—will cross their paths.[2] Critical care physicians and these specialists generally know about the activities and treatment plans of the other. Their notes in the electronic medical record are accessible to one another. And often residents from the two teams will confer with one another each day on their shared patients. Sometimes the specialist team will stop and confer with the critical care team about a particular patient. At times, the cluster of teams clogging the hall; conflicts between them over diagnosis, prognosis, and appropriate treatment; and the large egos and even larger disdain for the other specialty convey the feel of an imminent gang rumble.

Anywhere from an hour and a half to seven hours after they began, critical care rounds will end. The length depends on whether the attending is just beginning an ICU rotation (requiring longer presentations), the personality of the attending, his or her predilection for teaching, the number of patients, how sick or complicated the patients are, whether the team enters the patient's room, how many family members seek to converse with the team, and whether the attending writes his or her notes during or after rounds. With the exception of the early departure of the night-float residents and those peeling off to attend emergencies, rounds run nonstop without bathroom or any other breaks. Regulations forbid physicians from ingesting coffee, water, or any other food or beverage in the ICU, although infractions are not unheard of.

After rounds, the residents will go off to their patients to administer the treatment plan developed. Some residents will work up new patients admitted to the ICU over the course of the day. Some attendings, fellows, or residents will have more extensive conversations or scheduled meetings with patient families. Each will write up his or her notes in the electronic medical record. And some attendings and fellows will leave the ICU for a few hours to see outpatients in a hospital clinic.

Throughout the day, others pass in and out of the patients' rooms. Chaplains will drop by to meet with patients and families. Social workers will visit to discuss insurance issues or discharge planning. X-ray technicians will take images at the bedside. Other teams will perform procedures at the bedside, providing wound care or inserting feeding tubes, tracheostomies (breathing tubes inserted directly into the trachea or windpipe), chest tubes, or special catheters. The palliative care team will meet with families contemplating removing life support or transitioning from aggressive to comfort care. Members of the ethics committee will stop by to meet with families in conflict with physicians or with one another or struggling with decision-making responsibilities. Members of the critical care team will join some of these palliative care and ethics consultations that they ordered. Representatives of the regional organ transplant organization will visit as well when notified that a patient is likely to experience brain death or when families ask about organ donation. They will go through the patient's chart to determine whether he or she is a candidate and then arrange to meet with the family. We observed these family meetings run by the organ transplant representatives, palliative care team, and ethics committee and report on them in later chapters.

Cleaning crews, food service workers, security guards, and others pass through the ICU throughout the day as well. Orderlies will transport patients in and out of the ICU for scans, tests, or surgical procedures, or to a step-down unit or to what is called the "floor," which provide less intensive care.

The intricate, well-choreographed dance of the cast of characters in the ICU is periodically interrupted by extremely loud, insistent alarms announcing a cardiac arrest somewhere in the unit. Everyone stops in their tracks as hospital staff race to determine which patient is coding, and then nurses, physicians, anesthesiologists, crash carts, medications, and other people and equipment descend on the room. Medical personnel fill the room while others stand anxiously in the hall. Someone puts a board under the patient. A nurse jumps on the bed and begins aggressive chest compressions; another administers medications; a physician shouts orders to everyone in the room. Someone may be cardioverting (shocking) the patient, though this seems to happen a lot more often on television than in real hospitals. The anesthesiologists arrive and intubate the patient. The "code" may continue for quite some time, sometimes with positive results, sometimes not. If the patient codes a second or third time, another round of resuscitation is administered, while physicians may search for a family member to seek guidance on whether to stop what is becoming a futile and what many consider an inhumane exercise.

Around 4 or 5 each afternoon, the critical care team will reconvene and conduct more abbreviated rounds on their roster of patients. Residents will then sign out their patients to those on night float, and nurses will do the same. Attendings will go home but remain on call, receiving calls throughout the night when questions and problems arise, sometimes occasioning a midnight visit to the ICU. As the workday ends, more visitors will filter into the ICU. Around 9 P.M., when visiting hours end, visitors are encouraged to go home. A few persistent family members will stay with the patient through the night; a few will take up residence in the waiting room outside the ICU; and the rest will return home, to repeat the drill again the next morning.

ICU Differences

The neurological intensive care unit houses patients experiencing brain trauma, tumors, hemorrhages, strokes, seizures, and spinal cord injuries. Patients in the medical ICU suffer from organ failures, sepsis and other infections, respiratory distress, other cancers, bleeding, and so on. The rhythms and routines are mostly the same in each ICU. But there are a few important exceptions. The medical ICU is a closed unit; critical care physicians have day-to-day responsibility for the ICU patients. The neurological ICU is an open unit; specialists (who generally work outside the ICU)—usually neurologists or neurosurgeons and sometimes oncologists or orthopedists—have primary responsibility for patient care and the on-site critical care physicians serve as their consultants. As a result, members of the critical care team in the neurological ICU are a little more reticent about initiating conversations with the significant others of patients and more likely to defer to the primary team, especially when their views conflict with those of the specialists. Since the primary team in the neurological ICU is off-site, there are fewer opportunities throughout the day for spontaneous conversations between visitors and these specialists, which are common in the medical ICU. Also, because critical care physicians sometimes have a different (typically more realistic and usually more pessimistic) perspective about patient prognosis than specialists (who are more mindful of the patient's preexisting problems than of the life-threatening complications that have landed them in the ICU), significant others may get a less rosy picture in the medical ICU and more mixed messages (between primary and critical care physicians) in the neurological ICU.

Second, as noted earlier, all critical care teams in the medical ICU enter the room and examine the patient during rounds. This is up to the discretion of the attending in the neurological ICU; although most of the neurologist attendings examine each patient, not all of the anesthesiologist attendings do. As a result, there are more opportunities for familiarity, small incremental updates, and chitchat between physicians and families in the medical than the neurological ICU. Third, fellows (post-resident, pre-attending physicians) play a much larger role in the medical ICU than the neurological ICU. Each team in the medical ICU included a fellow throughout the study, and fellows played a significant role, especially in communicating with patient families. Fellows rarely participated in direct patient care in the neurological ICU, which therefore lacked an important resource for communication with families. In short, for several reasons (closed unit, primary team on-site, going into the patient's room during rounds, fellows available to meet with families), the medical ICU afforded more communication opportunities.

Fourth, medical ICU patients are somewhat more likely to lack decision-making capacity. The roster of neurological ICU patients includes post-surgical patients who often regain consciousness after a few hours as well as others recovering from subarachnoid hemorrhages (a kind of brain hemorrhage) who are conversant, but for whom protocols require that they be monitored in the ICU for at least two weeks until the statistical window of risk from secondary sequelae has closed. Some of these patients have decision-making capacity, so they are excluded from the observational study. Because more neurological ICU beds are filled with patients who do not qualify for the study, it took much longer to reach the goal of one hundred patients in the neurological ICU than the medical ICU.

Finally, because neurological intensive care units treat many patients with brain injury or disease, it is much more likely that these patients will experience brain death than those in the medical ICU. This is relevant in at least two ways. First, families tend to have difficulty understanding impairments of consciousness and brain death, a challenge exacerbated by Internet and media accounts that suggest that brain death can be survivable,[3] which leads to some more difficult conversations in the neurological ICU. Second, most of the meetings regarding organ donation occur in the neurological ICU, since organ donation is more desirable when patients are brain-dead. (Because the heart is still beating, all of the organs are still viable for transplant.) All of the encounters observed regarding organ donation occurred in the neurological ICU.

Economics

Intensive care is very expensive. Hospital care consumes about a third of all U.S. expenditures on health care. ICU charges make up about half of all hospital charges (although ICUs treat only about a quarter of hospital patients). That's more than $500 billion annually and close to $70,000, on average, per patient for a hospital visit that includes a stint in the ICU.[4] In this book you will read relatively little about the economics of intensive care, the cost of treatment, who is paying for it, or how health care providers and patient families talk about it. That is because, remarkably, I heard little about it, even when I was hanging out alone with physicians and nurses. I heard the occasional question by family members about whether a proposed treatment was covered by insurance or a rare comment about their financial precarity, concern about treatment cost, or insistence that they had the means to bankroll a heroic intervention or to discharge the patient to a location of their choice. I almost never heard from families of patients with no insurance about how treatment costs would be paid, although I did observe some of their encounters with social workers who were trying to enroll the patient in Medicaid or looking for discharge options for patients without insurance.

Similarly, physicians rarely spoke about the costs of treatment to families or to one another, even for treatments they considered futile. It wasn't clear that physicians were always aware of the relative costs of alternative treatments under consideration. One day on rounds in the neurological ICU, physicians reached a stalemate in a debate over the merits of one routine drug over another. The team pharmacist eventually weighed in, suggesting that, if they were truly undecided, one cost hundreds of times more than the other. The physicians were astounded, so much so that several were still talking about it days later. Physicians did occasionally talk with families about drugs that were so expensive that they were not on the hospital formulary and explained that they were awaiting permission to get access to the medications. But physicians seemed clueless or uninterested in the costs of routine treatments and provided no sense, even when debating alternatives with residents and other members of their team, that cost factored into their treatment decisions or recommendations.

The electronic medical record provided no information about treatment costs either. It disclosed the insurance status of patients but included no billing information whatsoever. Undoubtedly, those in hospital administration with access to billing records were preoccupied with financial considerations, but there was little evidence that this concern percolated to medical providers in the ICU.

Throughout this book, when discussions about costs come up in the observed encounters, they will be shared. The relative absence of such talk, given the considerable costs of intensive care, came as a great surprise. Nonetheless, just because participants in ICU treatment decisions rarely talk about economics, that does not mean that these decisions do not have enormous economic consequences. Some implications are considered in chapter 8.

Conclusion

A significant part of the ICU day finds individual or teams of health care providers conversing with patients and families. Whether during rounds or in spontaneous or scheduled meetings, caregivers provide medical updates, gather information, discuss goals of care, and describe and seek consent for upcoming medical procedures. The next chapter introduces the major participants in these conversations in the two intensive care units: patients, families and significant others, and physicians.

THREE

Actors

Patients

Back inside the ICU room, underneath the pile of high-tech detritus, a person lies inert, nonresponsive, the face barely recognizable in a snarl of tubes and bandages, defaced by medical afflictions or treatments that have caused some to swell, others to become gaunt or jaundiced. The drama to unfold concerns these patients, although few play much of a role.

More than 2,500 patients passed through the two intensive care units during the period of the study. This book follows 205 of them under the care of the critical care team, who lacked decision-making capacity, generally spent more than a few days in the ICU, whose friends or family interacted with health care providers, and who met other criteria described in detail in appendix A. The appendix also shows that, compared to the population of all patients in the two ICUs, the 205 patients followed in the research were sicker, slightly older, and more likely to lack decision-making capacity for most of their time in the ICU, and they had longer ICU stays. On other demographic characteristics—gender, race/ethnicity, neighborhood income, and the like—the two groups were indistinguishable.

As the first chapter described, patients follow numerous paths to the ICU. About half of the 205 patients followed in the observational research had significant preexisting medical problems—cancers (22 percent), organ failures (20 percent), neurological disorders (6 percent), and the like. Some were admitted to the ICUs for treatment, others for complications from a medical intervention, and others for the sequelae of problems that accompany serious illness, old age, poverty, or homelessness. Other patients had seemed perfectly healthy just hours earlier, at home, work, or play, when

Table 3.1 Reason for ICU Admission

Reason for ICU admission	Percentage	Median age	White	Black	Other
Trauma	8%	47	8%	11%	7%
Stroke	9%	76	11%	4%	7%
Hemorrhage	20%	68	17%	24%	30%
Respiratory distress	22%	65	23%	20%	15%
Pneumonia	5%	70	4%	2%	15%
Sepsis*	22%	64	23%	24%	7%
Other	14%	69	14%	13%	18%
Out of the blue	43%	68	39%	53%	44%
Total	(205)	67	(133)	(45)	(27)

*Sepsis is a life-threatening complication of an infection.

an accident, trauma, undiagnosed medical problem, or medical emergency waylaid them. For 43 percent, the visit to the ICU came out of the blue.

The patients in the observational study were desperately ill, although some fared better than others.[1] Table 3.1 displays some patient characteristics and the reason for their admission to the ICU. Trauma patients are considerably younger than other ICU patients and more likely to be black; stroke patients the oldest and most likely to be white. White patients are also most likely to have preexisting medical problems that landed them in the ICU.

ICU patients spent anywhere from one to one hundred days in the ICU during their hospitalization. Those included in the observational study spent a median of twelve days in the ICU;[2] those excluded spent a median of three days. Not surprisingly, observed patients whose families sought aggressive interventions remained in the ICU longer (14.5 days) than those whose families sought to limit or stop aggressive care (8 days). About a quarter of the observed patients visited the ICU on more than one occasion during their hospitalization, bouncing between the ICU, a step-down unit (which provides less intensive care and cannot accommodate ventilators), or what is called "the floor" (regular hospital rooms); others returned quickly to the ICU after discharge to a rehabilitation facility or nursing home.

Patients included in the observational study lacked the capacity to make their own medical decisions. On admission to the ICU, almost half of the patients were comatose and only a little more than a quarter had a normal neurological response. Only 3 percent of patients remained consistently responsive throughout their ICU admission. About one in ten lost capacity, and 3 percent regained it during their ICU stay; the remainder lacked capacity throughout. Most were comatose, nonresponsive, or heavily sedated; a few suffered from confusion or dementia; and a couple who appeared to lay observers to have capacity were treated by physicians as though they did not.

Capacity determinations are made by the physicians, although the ICUs do not have a specific protocol for making such judgments. Patients receive a daily Glasgow Coma Score (or "GCS," as one hears on television medical dramas)—a neurological assessment of consciousness reflected in eye, verbal, and motor responses. But even patients with a perfect GCS score may still be compromised by dementia, confusion, or other cognitive or emotional problems that render them unable to make complex medical decisions.[3] Some patients are heavily sedated; others are unable to speak, though perhaps capable of understanding. Physicians would talk to and question patients to determine whether they were capable of making their own medical decisions or at least participating in these conversations. There were no specific medical or legal criteria reflected in their inquiry; rather they looked to see whether patients understood their condition, the medical choices they faced, and the risks and benefits of treatment. In a few instances physicians ordered psychiatric consultations to assess the patients' decision-making capacity or of what sorts of decisions they were capable (for example, whom they trust as a decision maker, if not the decision itself).

As described in later chapters, some physicians and family members tried, often unsuccessfully, to converse with or take direction from the patient, sometimes removing the patient from sedation temporarily to elicit a response. Patients on ventilators or incapable of speech were asked to blink, nod their head, squeeze someone's hand, or provide a hand signal (thumbs up, show two fingers). Participants tried to interpret words the patient mouthed. Occasionally patients were offered paper and pencil (though invariably the writing was illegible) or an alphabet or communication board (to which they blink or gesture when someone points to a desired letter or word). For others, grimaces, facial expressions, rapid eye movements, opening of the eyes in response to a particular voice, gestures, agitation, recoiling, and other body language or lack thereof was subject to interpretation.

Others at the bedside directed comments to patients without expecting a response. Some physicians routinely addressed patients during their examination on the chance that they might understand, even if unable to communicate. Some family members spoke to patients, some aware that the patient couldn't hear or understand them and others certain of the opposite.

WIFE: [*After deciding to remove life support*] My greatest wish is for him to open his eyes and for me to look into his eyes and connect with him one last time. But I guess that isn't likely to happen. . . . [Patient], you are a good sport and such a good friend. I will never find such a good friend. We have had a wonderful life. We were married for forty-nine years. You were not only my lover; you were also my friend. . . . [Patient], we are taking care of you. [Patient], I am going to be okay. I will find a way to be okay.

Both physicians and family members would occasionally ask to move a conversation out of earshot of a comatose patient. A daughter changed her mother's hearing-aid batteries, "just in case." Even I found myself engaged in a long, awkward soliloquy with a deeply comatose patient when his daughter introduced me to the patient, explained that he likes to have company, and asked me to talk with him until she returned to the room. Like the family whose story opened the first chapter, some family members pleaded with the patient to wake up and join the conversation; others insisted on waiting to see if the patient regained capacity and was able to make decisions for him or herself (more about this in chapter 7). And then there were patients who were entirely ignored—neither spoken to, interrogated, or speculated or talked about. Physicians and significant others simply negotiated a series of medical interventions, as if they were to be performed on an inanimate object.

The ICU patients are very diverse. Appendix A documents that, on a variety of demographic characteristics, they mirror census figures for the nation as a whole. As in the U.S. population, slightly more than half are female and 35 percent are nonwhite—although these Illinois ICUs have disproportionately more blacks (22 percent) and disproportionately fewer Hispanics (6 percent). ICU patients reside in zip codes whose median household income ranges from the first (poorest) to the ninety-ninth (richest) percentile in U.S. census data. Overall, their place of residence is slightly more affluent than that in the nation as a whole, reflecting the higher cost of living in the large metropolitan area in which the hospital is located. Still, the median poverty rate of their place of residence is at least as high as that of the nation as a whole. Appendix A also shows remarkable similarity in access to and type of health insurance among Americans in general and ICU patients in the study; about a quarter of the latter under the age of sixty-five have no health insurance.[4] As noted in the appendix, data on patients' religion were unavailable for a substantial number of patients. Of those whose religion was known, 44 percent were Protestant, 37 percent Catholic, 15 percent Jewish, and 5 percent of another religious faith.

Of course, the ICU patients observed are older than the U.S. population overall (or even than the ICU patients excluded from the study). They range in age from fifteen to ninety-eight,[5] their median age sixty-seven. Black patients are substantially younger (median age fifty-six) than white (seventy) or Hispanic, Asian, and patients of other ethnicities (sixty-three). Most patients live in the vicinity of the hospital, almost two-thirds within twenty miles; only 11 percent reside more than one hundred miles away. Almost three-quarters are still living on their own, 16 percent with a caregiver, 3 percent in an assisted living facility, and 8 percent in a nursing home.

Much of what one would like to know about the patients was not documented in hospital records. One learns about them unsystematically from conversations at the bedside, stories shared, introductions or disclosures made, photographs or mementos on display, or questions asked of family members by physicians. Some of these portraits will emerge as the chapters unfold. A fifth of the patients are retired. Appendix B.1 shows that they come from all walks of life—some from the streets, others from positions of power or celebrity. One in six of those whose occupation is known have worked in health care.[6] The distribution of current or former occupations displayed in the table in the appendix fails to do justice to the rich variety of roles they play. Stories shared throughout the book reveal more about the textures of their lives.

About half of the patients were married, 34 percent widowed or divorced, and 16 percent never married. Appendix B.2 shows that overall, fewer than half of all patients were in their first marriage, though marital status varied considerably by patients' age and gender. The majority of patients under forty had never married. Female patients were considerably less likely to be currently married (43 percent) than their male counterparts (59 percent) and two and a half times more likely to be divorced or widowed. Hospital records do not indicate the patients' childbearing status or family structure. However, a child participated in meetings with health care providers for three in five patients, and a few significant others disclosed that they were the unmarried heterosexual or same-sex partners of the patient.[7]

Whatever the implications of these demographic trends for quality of life or other social indicators, they wreak havoc in the intensive care unit when patients lack capacity to make their own medical decisions. First marriages are no panacea, of course. Nuclear families can be messy enough—with disagreements, secrets, distrust, resentments, betrayals, estrangements, power struggles, coalitions, black sheep, and favorites. But when step-, half-, ex-, or soon-to-be-ex- spouses, parents, children, siblings, grandparents, or grandchildren, unmarried partners, and intimate friends all show up at the bedside, the challenges multiply. Not only is greater resentment and distrust among members of these hybrid or fractured family trees more likely, but they are even more likely to bring to the bedside distinct or competing interests, values, memories, promises, shared histories, senses of entitlement, and financial entanglements with the patient. Who is allowed to speak for the patient? Who is permitted to participate in the conversation? How is consensus possible? Is it necessary? The answers to these questions are often negotiated patient by patient and physician by physician, day by day.

Friends, Family, and Significant Others

Some patient's rooms are always empty, others always full of visitors. A few patients arrive in the ICU as John or Jane Does and may not be identified for several days until police match their fingerprints or follow up on random scraps of paper in their pockets, or until a friend or relative notices that they are missing. The identities of other patients may be clear, but there is no one competent to make decisions on their behalf. Some have no families but do have dedicated circles of friends who are at the bedside. Other patients got sick or were injured away from home and all of their significant others may be out of town and communicating with the hospital by phone. Some may live only a few miles from the hospital, but their next of kin do not visit and are rarely available even by phone. Others have large extended families and networks of friends, groups of which are at the hospital day and night. Some receive the same visitor day after day; for others, different associates filter in and out of the room. Over time, out-of-town relatives will come and go, or entirely different branches of the family tree may appear and then vanish. As the patient's illness becomes more hopeless, a larger or different group of significant others may visit.

And then there are a sizable number of patients from fractured or dysfunctional families and social networks with little overlap. They may be in the midst of a divorce; be involved in multiple or sometimes secret intimate relationships; have estranged parents, children, siblings, or former spouses; be close to individuals who distrust or refuse to speak to one another; have abusive partners (who physicians or others believe are responsible for their illness or injury); and so on. On occasion patients will be given aliases so that one set of family members can prevent contact by other friends or family members. Other members will avoid the ICU at times that they know their estranged relatives are likely to visit.

These cleavages, fractures, and random visitation patterns are burdensome for physicians who seek to communicate with families, because it often means that different significant others will not only have very different relationships with and priorities for the patient, but also different understandings of what is going on.

Even less is known about the subjects of this book—these friends and relatives who interact with physicians, visit patients, speak for them, decide for them, or hold their lives in their hands—than about the patients themselves. One learns about them by observing how they act, how they look, what they say or disclose, what others say about them, and what others ask of them. As a result, more is known about some than others.

Some of these significant others rarely leave the hospital.[8] A few participate in round-the-clock vigils at the patient's bedside. Others visit daily or stop by early every morning to listen in on morning rounds or drop in after work, a few in the middle of the night. Clad in pajamas, jeans, uniforms, scrubs, aprons, tailored suits, furs, construction clothes, and company-name-embossed caps, carrying briefcases, backpacks, and lunch pails, one gets a superficial glimpse of the lives sandwiched between their moments at the bedside. A few have traveled from out of town, taking up residence in or near the hospital. Some friends and family visit only when summoned by doctors; they seem awkward and nervous, unfamiliar with the sights, sounds, rhythms, and personnel of the ICU. Some elderly spouses and parents are unable to travel to the hospital and send other representatives to act on their behalf. A handful of loved ones could not visit because they had been deported, were in prison or under house arrest, were hospitalized (one even giving birth in the middle of her sister's ICU saga) or in rehab, were serving as a caregiver for someone else, or simply were starting a new job. Some did not visit at all and communicated with hospital staff over the phone, even providing informed consent for potentially life-threatening interventions from afar or participating in family meetings over a speaker phone. Members of this last group are underrepresented in the observational study because they did not participate in face-to-face meetings on-site that could be observed.

Some significant others seem ill at ease at the patient's bedside but can be found, day after day, in the ICU waiting room, some of them taking

over a section of the room, rearranging the chairs, and marking their terri-
tory with coolers, food, blankets, pillows, laptop computers, Bibles, maga-
zines, toiletries, prayer rugs, and other implements for the long haul. Some
waiting-room denizens—especially women—befriend the loved ones of
other patients. In some especially poignant moments, one can be seen
sporting a T-shirt emblazoned with the face of the desperately ill son of
another, or the mother of one is observed walking down the hall arm-in-
arm with or embracing the mother or wife of another. Medical crises are
great levelers, breaking down the walls of race, class, education, religion, or
language that normally separate us.

Seven hundred forty individuals participated in one or more encounters or family meetings with hospital staff regarding the 205 patients in the
observational study. (That number does not include scores of other visitors
who passed through the ICU over the course of the patient's admission
but did not interact with staff.[9]) Not surprisingly, these participants are not
evenly distributed across the patients. For more than half of the patients,
three or fewer individuals participated in meetings with hospital staff at
one time or another. This number ranged from only one family member
(16 percent of patients) to eight or more (7 percent of the patients); one
patient had twenty-five friends or family participating in various meetings
at some point during her ICU admission.

Some significant others play a very marginal role in ICU interactions,
dropping in on rare occasions or only when serious decisions are required;
about a quarter of them participate in not even a quarter of the meetings
with health care providers. Others consistently participate, day after day;
almost a third of the significant others are involved in at least 75 percent
of the observed encounters. Of course, it is relatively easy to have a perfect
attendance record when there are few meetings to attend. Some families
request, or patients require, many more conversations with health care providers than others. Although half of the patients occasion no more than six
encounters, for a few there are more than fifty. More than fifty significant
others (5 percent of them) attended ten or more meetings. Roughly half of
them participated once or twice.

Who are these individuals? Most (about a third) are the patient's child.
Fourteen percent are the patient's spouse, 17 percent a sibling, and 7 percent a parent. Almost a quarter are members of the extended family—
especially in-laws, nieces, nephews, and grandchildren. Only 4 percent are
friends of the patient. Participants are disproportionately female (60 percent); this is true even if one eliminates spouses from the pool of those

who bear witness at the hospital. By far, daughters represent the largest group of visitors at the bedside. Since so many participants are the patients' offspring, they are younger on average than the patients, ranging from about five to ninety-three years old; half appear to be younger than forty-eight. On other demographic characteristics, they mostly mirror those of the patient.

Nine percent of these meeting participants claim to have a medical background; less than 1 percent say that they have legal training. From watching them converse with physicians, most seem to get the big picture medically. Ten percent display a thorough understanding of the medical information conveyed, and two-thirds seem to grasp most of the details; about one in five appear to comprehend the major points, though not the details, and one in twenty display major gaps in understanding. Over the course of the ICU admission, as participants are deluged with test results and fixated on numbers and trend lines on the patient's bedside monitors, a number experience difficulty seeing the forest for the trees.

A handful of participants themselves appear to suffer from serious illness, dementia, cognitive impairments, extreme emotional distress, mental illness, or substance abuse. Four percent speak a language other than English (two-thirds of them Spanish); for 2 percent of the meetings, either an interpreter or family member translated for the others. Whatever the challenges participants faced, it is striking how many of them truly rose to the occasion and navigated the difficult shoals of the ICU with seriousness, intelligence, courage, selflessness, and grace.

Of course, a significant other rarely interacts with ICU staff alone, especially in prearranged family meetings. So this dry census of the 740 individual participants provides little sense of the dynamics of these encounters. Although the circle of friends and family surrounding the patient may be similar demographically, some participants will be young and others old; some male and others female. Some close to the patient or to one another and others estranged. Some largely silent and others overbearing. Some consensus builders and others hostile and aggressive. Some volatile or emotional and others without affect. Some secular and others deeply religious. Some conversing in esoteric medical jargon and others clearly out of their element. Some deeply involved in the day-to-day developments and others showing up only at the eleventh hour. Some arriving with their minds made up, some open to persuasion, and others unwilling to take responsibility for any decision.[10] These dynamic interactions will be revealed as the chapters unfold.

Decision Makers

As noted earlier, patients in the study lacked decision-making capacity for some or all of their ICU admission. An ICU stay occasions numerous treatment decisions of which these patients are not capable. The law in most states anticipates this problem. On the one hand, durable powers of attorney for health care or health care proxies allow competent adults to name their medical decision maker in the event that they lose capacity in the future, empowering these legally designated decision makers to make the same medical decisions on their behalf as the patients themselves. On the other, surrogacy laws in most states specify which member of the family tree should serve as the default decision maker when the patient has named no one.[11]

To name a durable power of attorney for health care in Illinois, all one needs is a free form, available online and in hospitals and doctors' and lawyers' offices, and two witnesses. Neither lawyers nor notaries are required. By law, hospitals are also required to offer competent patients the opportunity and resources to complete advance directives, yet only 22 percent of the ICU patients in the observational study or their families produced a document. Another 24 percent of the patients or their loved ones claimed that such a document existed elsewhere but never produced a copy, despite daily reminders by the ICU nursing staff.[12] Experience and empirical data suggest that as many as a quarter of these reports are erroneous and that the alleged documents do not actually exist.[13]

In short, in the two ICUs more than half of the patients observed had not named a legal decision maker. (This was true of more than two-thirds of the ICU patients excluded from the observational study, who tended to be younger and less critically ill—perhaps explaining their disinclination to designate someone to make decisions on their behalf.) Most states have default surrogate consent laws that go into effect when patients fail to name a legal decision maker. In Illinois, as in most other states, these laws create a hierarchy—usually beginning with the guardian of the patient, and then the spouse, adult child, parent, adult sibling, adult grandchild, close friend, and so on—from which the default surrogate decision maker is to be selected. Different states have different rules about the composition and order of the rungs of the hierarchy and about who decides when there are multiple parties on the same rung; most states, including Illinois, specify that the majority rules. As described in chapter 6, in some states, these default decision makers face constraints in their authority that do not apply to decision makers named in a health care proxy or medical power-of-attorney document.

Table 3.2 describes the relationship of the ICU patients to their legal or default surrogate decision makers, most of whom are their spouse or child and female. The far-left-hand column of the table represents the person or persons atop the hierarchy of default surrogate decision makers—at least in theory, as you will see. Persons on the far-right-hand column were hand-picked by the patient before losing capacity. Persons in the middle column claim that they were handpicked by the patient; usually the health care team goes along with such an assertion, even though a legal document was not produced and may not even exist.

The table shows that the differences between default surrogates and those actually or allegedly chosen by the patient are not dramatic. Patients who bother to prepare a durable power of attorney for health care are a bit more likely to designate women over men as their decision maker as well as their siblings, more distant relatives, and friends—persons farther down the default hierarchy had they failed to prepare the directive. Parents play a more prominent role as default surrogates for younger patients, who are less likely to have a spouse or adult child. Spouses are more common surrogates for patients with alleged documents elsewhere, perhaps because they are the ones who (erroneously?) report their status to the medical team.

The preponderance of women at the bedside noted earlier is not just because they are more willing to bear witness to the medical crisis of a loved

Table 3.2   Identities of Surrogate Decision Maker

	No power of attorney	Alleged document elsewhere	Document in hospital	Total
Spouse	37%	51%	37%	40%
Child	31%	35%	33%	32%
Parent	16%	2%	4%	10%
Sibling	6%	4%	11%	6%
Other family	1%	2%	6%	2%
Friend	0%	0%	4%	1%
Other	10%	6%	4%	8%
Total	(110)	(49)	(46)	(205)
Female	65%	65%	70%	66%
Male	31%	35%	30%	32%
Both	4%	0%	0%	2%

one. It seems the patients also prefer that women speak on their behalf. Patients who name a legal decision maker are more than twice as likely to pick a woman—wife, daughter, mother, sister, or female friend—over a husband, son, father, brother, or male friend.

Although the legal rules for selecting surrogate decision makers appear straightforward enough, they proved problematic for at least one out of every seven ICU patients, often resulting in the wrong person making medical decisions, for part if not all of the admission. Imagine a lush tree enveloped in thick fog. One cannot see how big the tree is, how many branches or even leaves it has, or where the one visible leaf is located, even whether the leaf is attached to this or a neighboring tree. That is, until some of the fog begins to dissipate.

This metaphor reflects the most common challenge in determining the appropriate decision maker for ICU patients. The patient arrives in the ICU alone or perhaps accompanied by a single person. The person claims to have been designated power of attorney by the patient but never produces the documentation. Or the person claims to be or is understood to be a spouse, child, sibling, or parent, and hospital personnel assume that he or she tops the patient's hierarchy of family members and significant others. But as the fog lifts, it turns out the spouse is an unmarried partner, the child or parent is acting for the patient's spouse who is housebound or busy at work, the sibling is actually a cousin, or there are many others on the same branch of the family tree as the visible leaf and still other stepchildren or estranged family members clinging to other branches of the family tree— perhaps even higher branches—who don't show up at the hospital until the patient's condition begins to worsen or until they get wind of the crisis that others had tried to hide from them.

I observed numerous variations on this theme: Persons making medical decisions at the outset of the ICU admission are displaced after their identity is revealed or more of the tree is exposed. (Sometimes it takes considerable effort to identify someone closer to the top of the hierarchy and who is available or willing to serve in their place.) New family members arrive from out of town or crawl out of the woodwork. Those atop the hierarchy and privileged to act as default surrogate only show up in the eleventh hour or refuse to step up to the plate when decisions become more difficult. The appropriate surrogate cannot speak or understand English or is too sick, demented, or too young to take on such an onerous responsibility. A couple of times the patient regains capacity long enough to fire the decision maker or appoint someone new. Or even the physician in charge does not read the document or understand the legal rules and empowers the wrong family member as decision maker, at least until a new physician takes over the case and recognizes the mistake. So sometimes the decision-making process looks more like a relay race—with the baton of responsibility passed from one runner to another—than a marathon.

Identification and commitment of the surrogate decision maker usually follows one of several paths:

- conventional: most often, the person named as power of attorney or who tops the default hierarchy serves throughout the ICU admission;
- unearthing: decision making begins with the apparent default surrogate and then decision-making responsibility shifts as the family tree is fully exposed (sometimes requiring involvement of hospital staff to do some sleuthing to find a replacement). Rarely, a copy of the power-of-attorney document is eventually produced and reveals that it does not apply to medical decision making, and therefore the default surrogate has authority but not the purported legal power of attorney.
- silencing: the default decision maker (e.g., elderly spouse or young adult child) is convinced to turn authority over to someone else;
- competition: jockeying for power among various would-be decision makers;
- refusal: of the legal or default decision maker to serve;
- stepping up to the plate: a reluctant family member takes responsibility when no one else will serve;
- power behind the throne: the default or legal decision maker serves, but someone else is calling the shots from the sidelines.

As decision-making responsibilities are newly shared or handed off as the family tree is clarified or as new members arrive at the bedside, sometimes irreversible life-and-death decisions made by others have already been implemented. Moreover, the newly arrived surrogates were away from the bedside when information was shared, diagnoses and prognoses offered and revised, clinical trials succeeded or failed, learning curves sharpened, and patient suffering witnessed; they are often ill equipped to assume the mantle when so much has happened in their absence. So, even as compliance with legal rules improves over time, the quality of the decision making can worsen. The latest loved one to step up to the plate may offer more intimacy or fidelity but may also be impaired by less information or experience.

Even durable-power-of-attorney-for-health-care documents were not immune from challenges. Especially when members of the patient's family of origin were passed over for someone else designated power of attorney

—a friend of the patient, a romantic partner, a new spouse—the former sometimes bridled at the authority vested in the latter and their perception that these interlopers didn't know the patient as well as they did. And physicians, who are far more accustomed to negotiating medical details with spouses, parents, and children, often deferred to or took direction from them, either forgetting that someone else had legal decision-making authority or never bothering to examine the document in the first place and thus failing to realize that they were approaching the wrong persons for consent to medical procedures. In several instances the legal decision makers named by the patient eventually disappeared or stayed silent, perhaps uncomfortable with asserting their authority over distraught family members who never accorded them much legitimacy.

Though most of the time the correct person was making decisions on behalf of the patient, for many patients decision making was a collective, consensual process in any case—either of the family's own volition or because physicians (trying to heal the family as well as the patient, or else fearful of conflict) encouraged surrogates to wait until everyone was on the same page before proceeding. I witnessed considerable generosity and respect from those atop the family tree toward others, even just friends of the patient, including them in the decision-making process. But not always. I also observed bullying sons who dismissed the concerns of their sisters or asserted their authority over others; domineering children who tried to exclude, berate, or manipulate an elderly parent or a new partner of the patient, a granddaughter power of attorney who created ruses to conceal meetings with physicians from the patient's children; parents who tried to exclude the patient's ex-spouse (at the bedside to support his young children, who were struggling as default decision makers); and so on. Though crisis and tragedy brings out the best in many families, it reproduces the dysfunction of others.

Construing Their Role

Legal or default surrogate decision makers displayed the same level of understanding as other participants in encounters at the bedside but were more likely to be found in the ICU on a regular basis. Sixty-one percent of the legal or default surrogates and about a quarter of the others visited the patient frequently. Eighteen percent of the former and 41 percent of the latter rarely visited.

For some surrogates, especially of younger patients or of those whose illness or injury came out of the blue, this was their first time in an intensive care unit or facing life-and-death decision making. Others explained that "they knew the drill" only too well. Some took direction from the health care staff, especially the nurses assigned to care for their loved ones whom they frequently encountered at the bedside, sometimes the social worker or chaplain. As later chapters will illustrate, they studied the monitors attached to the patient, dutifully recording every grimace or blink of the eye, listened as physicians rounded at the bedside, asked and answered questions, and met with the health care team when requested to do so. A minority were more proactive, requesting or demanding meetings with physicians to consider their goals for the patient's care, sometimes soliciting a second opinion. About one in five asked physicians for advice, though more often physicians offered it unsolicited. Some scoured the Internet for information and then implored physicians to implement or prescribe whatever they unearthed.

Not quite half of all families relied on the expertise or cited the experiences of their friends and family. Many contacted or relied on members of their social network with health care experience—physicians, nurses, X-ray technicians, nursing home employees—whose experience was invariably tangential or irrelevant. Some drew on their own—usually more benign—experiences as a patient. Many referenced the end-of-life experiences of the patient's siblings, a grandparent, a parent, a spouse, a child, an acquaintance, or even a pet. A few described a friend or relative with an entirely different medical problem from which the surrogates tried to extrapolate. Others spoke about medical crises the patient faced and overcame in the past. Many of the stories reprised had happy endings and convinced the surrogate that the outcome would be the same again.

> The same thing happened to me. The doctors said I wouldn't survive and here I am. So we'll just keep going.

> We've seen her like this and we've seen her come out of this.

A handful cited optimistic prognoses that went terribly wrong.

> They said he would need a ventilator for three days. He needed it forever.

Some surrogates took direction from how the patient had navigated the critical illness of a loved one. Others learned from mistakes they had made at the end of life of another and were resolved not to make the same mistake again. And, as described earlier, many surrogates listened to the stories, advice, inferences, and priorities of everyone at the bedside and sought consensus before weighing in on a serious medical decision. But, for most—even those who knew the drill—acting as a surrogate requires constant improvisation as new opportunities, bad news, unexpected challenges, family dysfunction, unusually supportive or difficult physicians, and unimaginable sadness confound them. It is one of life's most demanding roles, and many acknowledge it.

Health Care Professionals

Two hundred eighty-one health care practitioners participated in observed meetings with surrogate decision makers and other friends and family. Three quarters were physicians, 17 percent nurses, and the rest a mixture of representatives of the regional organ-donation organization, chaplains, social workers, and others.

ICU nurses are among the most unflappable and technically skilled of any in the hospital. Mostly white and female, they range in age from their twenties to their fifties. Aside from their clinical responsibilities, nurses play an important backstage role in the ICU. They confer with physicians about the status of their patients and the needs of and challenges presented by patient families and significant others. Because they spend so much time in the patients' rooms attending to their needs, they interact with visitors, update them on patient status, counsel and support them, and help prepare them for the medical decisions they face—important work largely invisible to observers in the ICU (who cannot wander in and out of patient rooms unaccompanied by the critical care team).

But, at least in these two ICUs, nurses play a very small role in encounters between physicians and families in which medical decisions are negotiated. Nurses participated in only 9 percent of the thousand-plus encounters observed in the ICU study, a few of whom you will hear from in subsequent chapters. Probably the biggest reason for their infrequent involvement is logistical: it is difficult to cover the other patients when nurses attend a family meeting. But undoubtedly there are cultural and structural reasons as well. Though largely absent from these meetings, nurses were deeply concerned about decision making on behalf of their patients. Some needled physicians who they felt were not properly advocating for their patients, and others probably did the same to belligerent family members or those in denial. Several threatened to call in the ethics committee, and a couple followed through. And quite a few sought out my colleague or me to express their opinions, unease, or frustration regarding the decision-making process. The last chapter considers strategies to give nurses a greater role in surrogate decision making.

The patients' family doctors or primary care physicians are even less visible in the ICUs. Family doctors have been largely supplanted by hospitalists, physicians specialized in the care of hospitalized patients. Over the two-plus years of the study, ten primary care physicians participated in 14 (1 percent) meetings between ICU physicians and families. Whatever the value of hospitalists, they do not have firsthand knowledge of the patient's medical history or preexisting relationships with the patient or family, which can facilitate surrogate deliberations. As you will see in later chapters, some of the oncologists on staff have been caring for patients undergoing cancer treatment long before their ICU admission and have forged long-term relationships with surrogates and families. Drawing on this familiarity and trust, oncologists sometimes play a distinctive role in family meetings. Such preexisting relationships are rare among the other specialists described below.

A little more than half of the hospital physicians observed were members of the critical care team. Other specialists who participated most frequently included neurosurgeons, neurologists, palliative care physicians, and oncologists. Only rarely (<3 percent of meetings) did an ethics consultant participate. A third of the physicians observed were attending physicians, 10 percent fellows, and the remainder residents and a handful of medical students. Medical students are generally in their mid-twenties, residents in their late twenties to early thirties, fellows in their mid-thirties, and attending physicians in their late thirties to early sixties. Overall, the physicians observed were 47 percent female (27 percent of attending physicians) and a third nonwhite (24 percent of attending physicians), mostly East and South Asian and African American.

Few members of the ICU staff disclose their religious preference; the majority appeared to be Protestant, Catholic, or Jewish. Surveys find relatively low levels of religious identification or participation among U.S. physicians.[14] In the two ICUs observed, with the exception of one or two physicians, one hears very little conversation initiated by physicians about God, religion, miracles, or religious objections to medical interventions or lack thereof. However, some awkwardly respond to religious comments initiated by family members or ask whether the family would like to speak with a chaplain. One critical care fellow talked a lot about God—usually to suggest that physicians are not omnipotent or to ensure that families received spiritual support. And one specialist attending physician (who did not participate in many encounters in the ICU) did express reluctance a few times to authorize the withdrawal of life support, usually because the request was premature but also because of apparent religious or moral qualms.

> That would require an active response, if you know what I mean [*the family member didn't*] . . . and that is something that I am not comfortable with.

But, in every instance, the specialist referred the matter to the ethics committee and ultimately offloaded the patient to another physician who complied with the surrogate's goals of care for the patient.

Because of rotation schedules that influence the amount of time physicians spend in the ICU, whether physicians have primary responsibility for patients or serve as consultants, whether fellows are on hand to take responsibility for conducting meetings, as well as individual predilections to communicate with families, some physicians participated in far more conversations with family members than others. One critical care fellow in the medical ICU participated in 160 observed encounters (more than one in six of all those observed); one critical care attending physician in the medical ICU participated in 97 meetings, and his counterpart in the neurological ICU, presiding over the most encounters there, took part in 70 meetings over the course of the study. The most meetings for any of the residents in either of the ICUs was 15. Overall, the median number of meetings in which the observed health care staff members participated was only 2, but for critical care attending physicians, the number was over 18. In short, the findings and stories shared throughout the book draw on the perspectives and experience of a diverse group of health care providers.

In future chapters, as their conversations are reprised and you read their stories, you will learn a great deal about these physicians: how they think about life and death, hope and suffering, optimism and pessimism; how they attend to and advocate for their patients and support or struggle with the patients' friends and families; how different medical specialists interact; and how hierarchy among doctors plays out at the bedside. You will see the extraordinary physical and emotional toll they endure and when sweetness, compassion, delight, impatience, insensitivity, and arrogance can be found. Here I will make only a few general observations.

First, most physicians are very professional. They treat patients and families without judgment and with respect and show a commitment to communicate openly and transparently. Few are defensive, and most admit when they don't know something or when they are wrong. They doggedly struggle to improve their patient's lot, tinker with new interventions, and try to push the envelope medically. But most, especially the critical care physicians, are pragmatic and recognize when they have exhausted potential remedies and it is time to change course. Although many have strong opinions and will share them with families, most defer to the patient's surrogates, even when physicians find them misguided. Despite stereotypes to the contrary, even among one another, out of earshot of patients or family, physicians rarely speak about the risk of lawsuits or threat of lawyers. As noted in chapter 2, they rarely talk about the cost of various medical treatments either. On rare occasions, though, physicians reflect privately with their colleagues on the cost of the futile treatments they are administering and how these resources could be used more productively.

Physicians differ most on attributes that I would call their "bedside manner." Some are warm and empathetic, even shedding the occasional real or ersatz tear; others are cold, distant, or brusque. Some seek out conversations with family members; others avoid them. Some are blunt and direct; others equivocate or try to sugarcoat bad news. Some are articulate and easily understood, others confusing and convoluted. Some are patient and generous, others hurried or distracted. Some speak in jargon; others calibrate their disclosures to the sophistication of those with whom they speak. Some possess people skills; others appear clueless at times. Some have a sense of humor; others are humorless. A few are condescending, others humble. Some are directive and readily offer advice; others resist doing so even when families implore them. Some are optimistic by nature, others less hopeful. Some welcome confrontation; others back away from manipulative or abusive family members. Many experience tension between placating the family and protecting their patient, but some draw the line sooner than others. Some are dedicated teachers; others just want to get through their clinical responsibilities.

Although female physicians were often more empathetic and patient than male doctors, other elements of bedside manner were not distributed in any predictable ways. Some of the most humble and gentle physicians were the most senior and distinguished men. Both some of the best communicators and some of the most condescending were the most junior residents (also men).

But there is no such thing as a "good" bedside manner, because these qualities are not valued consistently by loved ones at the bedside. What is cold or arrogant to some family members is professional to others. What some consider humble, warm, or solicitous, others find weak or second-rate. For example, a handful of physicians managed to be among both the most disliked and the favorite of different patient families, usually because of their directness and honesty—dispiriting to the former, refreshing to the latter. The chemistry was not always optimal between a given physician and family member, and the end of the rotation of an attending physician was sometimes occasion for celebration or dismay by patient families.

Conclusion

The population of patients, families, and physicians who passed through the two intensive care units is unusually heterogeneous compared to many hospital studies or those focusing on the end of life (often restricted to middle- or upper-class whites). The fact that more than a third of the patients in this study are nonwhite and collectively hit both the first and the ninety-ninth percentile nationwide on income are two of many stunning indicators of their diversity. Data presented in this chapter and especially in appendix A show that the patients mirror demographic trends nationwide. This fortunate occurrence is important because there is every reason to believe that people from different walks of life—racially, religiously, educationally, economically, and by age and family status—have prepared differently for the possible loss of decision-making capacity, and have different values and priorities about life's end.

As argued earlier, one distinctive feature of this narrative is that it relies on what people actually do, day after day, when confronted with the potential end of another's life, not what they say they do or what physicians claim they do. But this narrative is also distinctive because it recounts this process in exquisite detail for a large and extremely diverse group of patients and families. You will see many differences in the coming chapters, some clearly related to the diverse backgrounds of the denizens of these ICUs and others surprisingly unrelated to these characteristics. When stories do not ring so true in the coming pages or you witness surrogates authorizing what you find unfathomable, remind yourself that you are meeting some patients and families for the first time—unlike your own or those of your friends—whose sagas have never been recounted before by other chroniclers of life's end whose perspective was far less diverse. This book opens the curtain onto a window much wider than other accounts have been able to expose before and reveals a richer and more variegated landscape below.

FOUR

Decisions

A patient's two sons and two of their friends sit uneasily in a conference room in the medical intensive care unit. A critical care attending, fellow, and resident, and the patient's primary care physician surround them. The critical care attending opens the conversation, describing several life-threatening problems compromising the patient and the medical interventions that have all failed. Concluding that it is unlikely that the patient will survive, the physician explains:

> The reason I brought you all together is to talk to me about what you think her wishes would be at this point, whether she would want us to continue treating her, or whether she would want us to switch the goals of her care to making her comfortable, making sure she's not suffering at all—or somewhere in between. Ideally, I would have this conversation with her, but because she is not able to participate in any meaningful way where I could be sure that she understood what her options are, I am turning to you guys to see what you think she would say if she were able to sit here with us in this room and tell us what she wants.

This chapter visits conference rooms like this one or hospital rooms, waiting rooms, or hallways, as friends and family consider medical interventions on behalf of patients who cannot speak for themselves, direct their medical care, or participate in the decision-making process. Others must decide on their behalf. Without providing a crash course in critical care medicine or in the countless esoteric interventions available for the diverse medical problems threatening patients in the two intensive care units, this chapter describes the most common decisions their surrogates face and the contexts and rhythms of medical decision making. Descriptions draw on extended examples from the study that introduce the sorts of dialogues that physicians and families compose with one another as they negotiate the decision-making process. These transcripts transport you into the intensive care units to see firsthand how physicians frame the decision-making process and how differently the patients' loved ones fashion or respond to the choices before them. Though reflecting only a small sampling of interactions from more than a thousand observed encounters, these transcripts set the stage as the book unfolds.

The various pathways to the intensive care unit described in chapter 1 usually result from one or more decisions, often made by patients themselves, to undertake an elective procedure, to get a second opinion, to pursue aggressive treatment, to dial 911. Some ICU patients arrive from the emergency room, some from the operating room, and others from another part of the hospital after something has gone wrong. Patients admitted to the neurological intensive care unit may be returning from spinal surgeries or operations to resect (i.e., remove) a brain tumor. Others have received pharmaceutical, mechanical, or surgical procedures to remove a blood clot in the brain; interventions to repair a ruptured aneurysm in the brain; or surgeries to remove part of the skull to relieve pressure on the brain or evacuate blood or bullets therein. Patients admitted to the medical intensive care unit may have recently undergone biopsies or other surgical procedures, chemotherapy, stem cell transplants, or dialysis. Some will have been resuscitated after a cardiac arrest. Many patients in both ICUs will arrive intubated with a breathing tube and on a ventilator. Indeed, it is the need for a ventilator that often occasions their transfer to an intensive care unit.

An observational study from the mid-1990s of a medical-surgical intensive care unit found that, on average, 178 different "activities" or interventions are performed per patient per day;[1] undoubtedly even more are carried out today. Fortunately, decision makers do not weigh in on all of these interventions. But they face many decisions over the course of an ICU admission, some routine, others momentous. Even minor or routine decisions may shape the course of those to follow. By a very conservative count, more than half of the decision makers in the study were consulted or initiated a conversation about at least four major interventions or changes in goals of care while in the ICU. On average, a meeting to discuss goals of care or a potential intervention was held twice every three days the patient was in the unit.

Figure 4.1 depicts the decision-making process, presenting the most common interventions contemplated in an intensive care unit: intubation

and ventilation, tracheostomies, feeding tubes, surgery and other procedures, dialysis, cardiac resuscitation (code status), and palliative care or
withdrawal of life support. Many surrogates will also consider or be asked
to consider goals of care for the patient: whether to pursue aggressive, even
heroic, measures or to refuse, stop, or remove life support and transition to
comfort care. A few, especially if the patient faces brain death, will contem-
plate organ donation as well. Although some of these interventions were
offered, decided, or implemented before the patient arrived in the ICU (especially surgeries, dialysis, and code status), the figure depicts only those
contemplated in or on the way to the ICU and presents them in the order
in which they are often first broached—going clockwise from intubation.
Of course, not all decision makers face the full complement of decisions or
experience them in clockwise fashion. Some decisions preclude or neces-
sitate others or require that previous decisions be revisited. As hours turn
to days and then to weeks, some surrogates travel back and forth along the
face of the clock as interventions succeed and fail, patients face new medical challenges, their prognosis changes, or the goals of care evolve.

The big white circle in the center of the figure represents the total num-

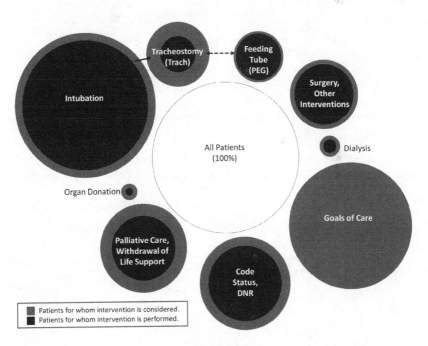

Figure 4.1. Decisions

ber of patients in the study. The size of the other circles is proportionate to the number of patients to whom the intervention applies: the larger the circle, the more common the intervention. The light-gray circles represent the number of patients for whom an intervention is considered on one or more occasions, the dark-gray circles, the number for whom it is performed (goals of care reflect a conversation and not an intervention, so it has only a light-gray circle). The difference between whether an intervention is contemplated or implemented (the size of the light-gray rings around each intervention) reflects not only whether surrogates consent to the procedure, but also whether it is ultimately not needed (because the patient has improved or died), as well as whether the patient is stable enough for it to be performed.

Intubation

The most common major medical intervention ICU patients share is intubation, the insertion of an endotracheal tube (ETT) also known as a breathing tube, down their throat and into their windpipe and is then connected to a ventilator, also known as a respirator. The procedure is undoubtedly familiar to many of you from hospital dramas, and the intensity depicted on the screen mirrors that performed emergently in the ICU. Almost two-thirds of patients in the study arrived in the ICU already intubated and on a ventilator. By the time they were discharged from the ICU, another 22 percent (86 percent in all) had been intubated at some point. And conversations about possible intubation transpired for 66 percent of the remaining patients who avoided intubation; they did not receive a breathing tube either because it ultimately was not needed or because it was refused. Decisions about intubation and ventilation are thus ubiquitous in the intensive care unit; 96 percent of decision makers in the study considered them at some point.

When patients without decision-making capacity develop respiratory distress, physicians turn to their surrogate decision maker for consent to intubate them. Although many of these conversations are urgent, physicians sometimes anticipate the need for artificial ventilation down the road and have time to talk through the issues with patients and/or their families.

CRITICAL CARE RESIDENT: Your husband is severely ill. I wanted to talk to you about whether you want us to put a breathing tube in.

WIFE: I don't have any medical expertise. You're the doctor. Do you think he needs to be intubated? Would it help him?

CRITICAL CARE RESIDENT: I do think it would help him. If we intubate him, I think it will help his infection heal. His lungs will get a rest and the blood that is going to his lungs right now could go to other places in his body to help heal the infection.

WIFE: Well if you think he needs this, then let's do it. I mean, I don't want him to die. [*Nervous laughter*]. Do you think he might?

CRITICAL CARE RESIDENT: Yes, it's possible that without the breathing tube that might happen.

WIFE: How long would it be in?

CRITICAL CARE RESIDENT: We don't know. We'll just have to wait and see.

WIFE: Would it hurt him?

CRITICAL CARE RESIDENT: We don't know that either, unfortunately. We give him medications so that he'll forget. And we give medications for pain.

WIFE: Is he with it right now?

CRITICAL CARE RESIDENT: He's confused, more so than when we were upstairs.

WIFE: Well, you're the doctor. If you think that he needs this, then let's go for it.

CRITICAL CARE RESIDENT: Do you think that your husband would be comfortable with that decision? Because upstairs I know we had talked about not doing this.

WIFE: That's why I asked if it would hurt him. I think that he's just fearful. But let's do it; it sounds like we need to.

. . .

CRITICAL CARE RESIDENT: Have you ever talked about these things before?

WIFE: No, not until today. He was fine before.

CRITICAL CARE FELLOW: [*Enters the room and sits down, still wearing her scrub cap*] Hi. I'm [name]. I'm so sorry to put this all on you so suddenly. It was really urgent, actually past when we'd normally intubate. I know it's hard. I'm a doctor. I can understand why he would want DNR/DNI [a do-not-resuscitate/do-not-intubate order]. But he really needs this.

WIFE: Yes, do whatever needs to be done.

In this example, the patient had recently indicated that he did not want to be intubated (reflected in a DNI order), a decision his wife overrode. Many patients, when still competent, even still healthy, also express a desire to avoid intubation or life on a ventilator. The commonplace and ambiguous cry "No machines!" frequently refers to ventilators. Many family members reprise this instruction and refuse to authorize physicians to intubate the patient. And yet, when the patient is gasping for air, some surrogates have difficulty refusing an emergent request to intubate the patient, as the wife of a second patient explains:

DAUGHTER: You know, he never wanted to be on a ventilator. But she [the patient's wife] was alone, and it was midnight and she just had to make a decision.

WIFE: I knew he didn't want it, but it seemed like the only option.

. . .

DAUGHTER: He'll fight. He didn't want the tube, so it's good he has the restraints.

Over the course of their ICU stay, some patients no longer need ventilation and are extubated (have their breathing tube removed), though some of them subsequently develop respiratory distress and require reintubation, as illustrated in the following example. The encounter occurred during critical care rounds. The patient was having difficulty breathing. The critical care attending physician examined the patient and listened to his lungs. He began to speak to the wife, who was in the room and holding up a cell phone. The physician was yelling so that his comments would be heard over the speaker phone, broadcasting to the patient's daughter, halfway across the country.

CRITICAL CARE ATTENDING: He doesn't sound good. I don't hear him moving air through his lungs. He is needing to use other accessory muscles to breathe. I am afraid that he will aspirate or go into respiratory failure. He needs to be intubated.

WIFE: What do the X-rays show?

CRITICAL CARE ATTENDING: This is a clinical decision. The X-rays won't show his current distress until much later.

WIFE: [Looking very frustrated and almost afraid that she will get in trouble with the patient's children, she nervously glances at her notebook.] Could it be because he is tired from the extubation? Perhaps that is why he is having so much difficulty breathing.

CRITICAL CARE ATTENDING: No. We extubate patients when they are ready and able to breathe on their own. Ten percent of extubations require reintubation. Your husband is one of this 10 percent. It's like an appendectomy, where you expect that some of the appendixes removed will be healthy. If you don't have this 10 percent number, it means that physicians have been too conservative and left people on the ventilator who didn't need it.

CRITICAL CARE ATTENDING: [To the daughter on the phone] Do you have any questions?

[Because she is not in the room, the daughter doesn't have a sense of urgency. She is being very deliberate and very fixated on future procedures, when the real issue is that *the patient must go back on the ventilator emergently. She asks various questions that imply that she thinks there is a choice between intubation and these procedures down the road.*]

CRITICAL CARE ATTENDING: We will intubate now and do [the other procedure] in a few days. . . . If we don't intubate him soon, it will be a matter of life and death later today.

[*The daughter asks several more questions about the other procedure, to which the critical care attending responds.*]

WIFE: I need to talk to his daughter on the phone.

[*The critical care team stands there, somewhat annoyed. The phone is still on speaker phone, so all can hear what they say.*]

DAUGHTER: I think they should do the [other procedure]; maybe he'll do better if he is less sedated.

[*Eventually the critical care team calls an "airway" (protocol to intubate a patient). A resident runs to get an anesthesiologist to help with the intubation. The wife leaves the room. Numerous physicians descend on the room.*]

Tracheostomy

CRITICAL CARE ATTENDING: Do you know what a tracheotomy is?

MOTHER: No.

CRITICAL CARE ATTENDING: Because this is going to be a long course—with his lungs and pancreas and kidneys— A tracheostomy is a procedure that we think about after a week or so to move the breathing tube in his mouth over here [*points to his own neck*]. It sounds worse than it is. It makes the patient more comfortable, because it uncovers the face. And if the patient is comfortable, he needs less sedation. It is also better because we can remove and replace the ventilator easily without having to put the tube down his throat each time [*mimes the motion*]. It is something we recommend. And it doesn't have to be permanent. If we are able to remove it, he will just have a little scar. You can think about it. And the surgeons who do it can talk to you about it too.

[*Mother doesn't respond and changes the subject.*]

. . .

CRITICAL CARE ATTENDING: We ask the question, "Can we do more?" many times each day. Right now, he is getting the maximal therapy. The tracheostomy is what we are thinking about now. It is done right here at the bedside. We can have the surgeons talk to you.

MOTHER: He can't breathe on his own?

CRITICAL CARE ATTENDING: No.

MOTHER: But how will he talk?

CRITICAL CARE ATTENDING: There are things we can do to help him talk. Besides, it doesn't have to be permanent.

. . .

MOTHER: So when he have the trach, it's not comfortable?

FIRST CRITICAL CARE RESIDENT: No, the trach is more comfortable. The tube is the one that's not comfortable, what he's got right now.

MOTHER: Okay. And you'll let him talk when he got the trach?

FIRST CRITICAL CARE RESIDENT: Eventually he could talk with it, but at least initially we'll need to keep him sedated because he gets so agitated.

MOTHER: Alright. But he'll be able to move his feets when he got the trach?

FIRST CRITICAL CARE RESIDENT: Yes, he'll be able to follow commands once we take him off the sedation.

MOTHER: But this isn't permanent? They say it was gonna be in there the rest of his life.

SECOND CRITICAL CARE RESIDENT: No, it can be long term, but it's not permanent. Once he doesn't need it, they can remove it.

Throughout their ICU admission, the critical care team will attempt breathing trials and efforts to wean patients off the ventilator so that they can be extubated. But many patients repeatedly fail these tests and require intubation for a prolonged period of time. Unfortunately, intubation is safe for only a couple of weeks (the number varies by physician). After that, risks of infection, narrowing of the windpipe, and injury to the vocal cords dictate that the breathing tube be removed. For patients who still require ventilatory support or are unable to protect their airway (by coughing, gagging, or clearing their throat), the breathing tube is replaced with a tracheostomy (sometimes called a tracheotomy) tube that goes directly into a hole in their neck into their windpipe and that connects to the ventilator. The surgical procedure is relatively benign, performed either at the bedside or in the operating room by thoracic or ear-nose-and-throat specialists with mild anesthesia. The "trach"—as it is called—has many advantages: the patient is more comfortable and requires less sedation than with a breathing tube; it is easier to clear secretions; it is easy to reattach the ventilator if the patient has difficulty breathing (rather than necessitating reintubation); it will eventually allow the patient to talk; and the procedure is reversible, leaving only a small scar. A tracheostomy was considered for half of all intubated patients.

Tracheostomy is often the first medical intervention that decision makers face in the ICU.[2] Because physicians anticipate the need for a tracheostomy down the road, they often open the conversation well in advance to allow families to mull over the decision and then revisit it again as the time nears.

CRITICAL CARE ATTENDING: He will probably need a tracheostomy.

WIFE: That tube in the neck [*wife points to her neck*]?

CRITICAL CARE ATTENDING: Yes, we place a tube directly into the windpipe. It will make him more comfortable; now, he is agitated by the breathing tube down his throat. It will make eating easier. You can talk with him. It lowers the risk of infection and is better for his vocal cords because the tube won't be right on the vocal cords. This is a decision that we don't generally make until the breathing tube is in for two to three weeks. I'm not recommending that we do that now, but it's something to start thinking about.

As a result, almost half of these conversations continue over three or more meetings; for two patients, we observed more than eighteen meetings each on the subject. As the examples reveal, these conversations vary in how technical the questions and answers tend to be, the extent to which they explicitly address risks and benefits, whether physicians frame the conversation around consent or simply announce that this is something they will do, and how difficult families find the decision.

Many decision makers easily consent to the procedure, even imploring physicians to perform it right away and not wait a few weeks. Others plead for delay, hoping to avoid an unwelcome scar (for which, I suspect, they fear they may be blamed). Although the tracheostomy procedure is relatively benign, for others it represents a symbolic turning point that occasions more difficult (or numerous) deliberations than the procedure alone would ordinarily warrant. For some families, it signals that the patient will remain ventilator dependent, requiring long-term institutional care, and will not be coming home.

CRITICAL CARE ATTENDING: The issue that we're running into now is that we don't think that she's going to be able to wean off the ventilator anytime soon. If she would want to continue pursuing treatment, then she would need what's called a tracheostomy, which is a surgical procedure where they put a tube directly connected to her windpipe, and she would go to a long-term care facility where they specialize in weaning people off ventilators—

GRANDDAUGHTER: How long are we talking? Months? Years?

CRITICAL CARE ATTENDING: Well, not years because— I think that it could take

her days to weeks, up to a month or two. If she weren't able to get off the
ventilator by that point, I don't think she'd ever be able to.

GRANDDAUGHTER: What if she wouldn't want a trach?

CRITICAL CARE ATTENDING: Then we would shift to what we call comfort care.
Now, I know that she wanted full support and care, and she wanted to go on
a ventilator.

GRANDDAUGHTER: Well, but that's only if it was temporary. She was willing to
go back on the ventilator because they were hopeful that she would be able
to get off of it again.

Since the alternative to a tracheostomy for patients unable to breathe on
their own is extubation and likely death, the conversation often occasions
consideration of the bigger picture.

CRITICAL CARE RESIDENT: So, as we discussed yesterday with [Sister] and
[Mother], there are two options. One is to replace the breathing tube down
her throat with a tracheostomy tube that goes in her neck. It will remain connected to the ventilator, the breathing machine. She will then go to what is
called a long-term acute care facility that has ventilators, where she will stay
for the rest of her life. Because ventilators are very complicated and complex,
she will not be able to go home. But you will be able to visit her there and
she will have the opportunity to spend more time with her family. The second option would be to remove the breathing tube and give her medications
so that she will feel no pain.

CRITICAL CARE ATTENDING: We would give her the medications first, before we
removed the breathing tube, so that she would be comfortable and will feel
no pain.

CRITICAL CARE RESIDENT: But the medications would be very strong and she
would be very sleepy. So she probably would be unable to communicate
with you. Of course, we don't have a crystal ball. She would most likely pass
away in the hospital, either here in the ICU or, if she is still alive after a few
hours, we would send her to another unit in this hospital, where she will
pass away. So those are the two options. There is no right answer. The only
right answer is what she wants. So the question is, what would she want?

For 43 percent of the patients, a tracheostomy was considered; a quarter of
all patients received one. Nine percent of decision makers refused to consent to the procedure; for the other patients, a trach was no longer needed
or appropriate.

Feeding (PEG) Tube

CRITICAL CARE RESIDENT: The other thing I wanted to ask you about is a feeding tube. Right now he has a tube in his mouth for feedings. That tube can't stay in there either, though, so when patients get trachs, they also usually get feeding tubes called PEGs that go straight into the stomach. So if he needs the trach, we usually do the PEG at the same time.

WIFE: Okay.

CRITICAL CARE RESIDENT: And just like the trach, that's not permanent. If they're able to take him off the trach, they can just take out the feeding tube also.

"A PEG and trach are like Bert and Ernie."[3] That is how one critical care attending described to his team the ubiquitous pairing of these two procedures. Usually, when physicians consider replacing the breathing tube, they also recommend that the tube down the patient's nose (or occasionally their mouth) that provides nutrition be replaced with a feeding tube—a percutaneous endoscopic gastrostomy (PEG) tube (sometimes called a G-tube)—that typically goes directly into their stomach. Like tracheostomies, procedures to insert a PEG tube are generally safe and performed (usually by gastrointestinal surgeons at the bedside or an operating room) with mild sedation; they too can be removed when no longer needed. Although there are situations when patients who have difficulty swallowing but not breathing require a PEG tube alone, most ICU patients with a trach also need a PEG. Sixty-one percent of the time that a trach is considered, a PEG is as well; when a PEG is considered, 83 percent of the time a trach is too.

Most conversations about PEG tubes occur simultaneously with those about tracheostomy. Consideration of PEG tubes typically occasioned far less discussion or deliberation than that occasioned by trachs. For a few decision makers, however, a feeding tube elicited reflection on the symbolic meaning of food, especially as a proxy for quality of life.

CRITICAL CARE ATTENDING: I'm concerned that when you give her medications, they don't always go to the right place. What percentage of the time would you say that she gets her medications without aspirating [going down her windpipe, often leading to pneumonia] them?

DAUGHTER: I would say about 90 percent.

CRITICAL CARE ATTENDING: I would guess that it would be less actually. The reason I ask is because I think that if she can't reliably get medications, then she would need a PEG tube so that she can get what she needs reliably. Otherwise she's going to continue getting pneumonias.

DAUGHTER: I just don't think there's enough quality of life here [*gestures toward the patient*] if she can't eat.

CRITICAL CARE ATTENDING: If she continues to get pneumonias, that's not great for quality of life either.

DAUGHTER: I want to keep feeding her until I can't any more.

A PEG tube was considered for 34 percent of the patients, typically discussed on two or more occasions, and placed in 31 percent of the patients.

Surgical and Other Interventions

Almost half of the decision makers considered one to as many as six surgical or other procedures throughout the ICU stay. These varied interventions respond to specific medical problems that threaten only a subset of ICU patients. Stripping away the medical jargon, they generically involve variations on the themes of:

- procedures to drain or tap and sometimes measure fluids from the brain (external ventricular drains [EVDs], bolts, or ventriculoperitoneal [VP] shunts), abdomen (paracentesis), or in or around the lungs (thoracentesis or chest tubes);
- procedures to examine (and sometimes repair) inside an organ, typically the lungs (bronchoscopy), heart, or blood vessels in the brain (angiogram), using catheters, tubes, scopes, or cameras;
- procedures to embolize (i.e., stop) bleeding, typically in the brain, stomach, or liver;
- surgical procedures to decompress, debride, wash out, excavate, remove, excise, or repair dead tissues, abscesses, foreign material, clots, tumors, ruptured blood vessels, and the like;
- procedures to insert or replace catheters, lines, stents, or filters that prevent blood clots from traveling to the lungs (IVC filters);
- invasive diagnostic tests such as a biopsy or spinal tap (lumbar puncture); and
- administration of paralytic drugs (as a lung-protective strategy), drugs to medically induce a coma, or drugs to increase blood pressure (pressors).

In the following example, a critical care fellow seeks consent to the administration of a paralytic drug.

CRITICAL CARE FELLOW: As you know, his situation has gotten significantly worse. He was having respiratory distress even while on the ventilator. We were concerned that there may have been a blockage in the tube, but the anesthesiologist took a look inside and there is none— Now that we know there is no blockage, that means that the respiratory distress is a result of the severity of his pneumonia. He has what is called Acute Respiratory Distress Syndrome, ARDS. I don't know if anyone has mentioned that term to you.

SISTER: No.

CRITICAL CARE FELLOW: Basically, it's a very severe form of respiratory failure. Now his breathing rate is very rapid, which we believe is causing damage to his lungs. There is something we would like to do to get him to stop breathing so fast. It's a medication that is what's called a neuromuscular blocker. It's different than medications like morphine or Ativan, which he's getting now for sedation. This medication basically relaxes his muscles, including the muscles that he uses to breathe, so that the ventilator would be doing all of the work for him. He would not be able to move at all while he's on this medication. And actually, the medication usually takes time to wear off, even after we turn it off. So if we are able to turn it off, he probably wouldn't be able to move still for a few days. Sometimes it can take weeks to regain mobility. He would be very weak and probably have a lot of numbness.

SISTER: Will he be in a coma?

CRITICAL CARE FELLOW: Yes.

SISTER: So he won't be able to hear us or anything?

CRITICAL CARE FELLOW: He may be able to hear you, but he definitely would not be able to move or respond to you. It basically paralyzes his muscles.

BROTHER: His heart too?

CRITICAL CARE FELLOW: No, that's a good question. The heart is a soft muscle, so it doesn't paralyze those kinds of muscles.

BROTHER: Okay, 'cause I know the heart is a muscle.

CRITICAL CARE FELLOW: Right.

SISTER: So this will help the pneumonia?

CRITICAL CARE FELLOW: No, this is not a treatment for his ARDS or pneumonia. This medication is just something to buy us time. We're hoping that it will buy us time so that the pneumonia has time to respond to the antibiotics.

BROTHER-IN-LAW: There's nothing else to do, though, not the trach or anything?

CRITICAL CARE FELLOW: No, because there was no blockage in the tube, the trach would not help. We really only consider this medication when we're all out of other options.

BROTHER: So, with him on the ventilator, that's something that we'd look at day to day and decide if there's still a chance of him coming out of this?

CRITICAL CARE FELLOW: I'd say minute to minute, not day to day. He is at a very critical point right now. We're hoping that this will buy us some time.

BROTHER: Yeah, well, it's been a rough morning for him; they moved him and he got real agitated, and then this—

BROTHER-IN-LAW: When would you do this?

CRITICAL CARE FELLOW: Right away. He needs this now.

BROTHER: Well, let's go ahead full force.

CRITICAL CARE FELLOW: Okay. And just to be clear, there is no guarantee that this will help. It may, but there's a good chance that it will not. This is a last-ditch effort to save him.

BROTHER: Do patients come out of this, with this medication and everything?

CRITICAL CARE FELLOW: Some do. Most do not, though.

BROTHER: Well, we gotta do everything we can for him. Let's go ahead and do it, not waste any more time.

CRITICAL CARE FELLOW: Okay. Do you think this is what he would want?

SISTER: Yes, absolutely. If there's a chance he could come out of this, he would want it.

BROTHER-IN-LAW: I agree.

BROTHER: If he was asked what he would want and there was a chance of him being a normal person again, I think he'd say go for it.

FIANCÉE: Right.

SISTER: Should we ask his son?

BROTHER: No, I'm calling the shots too. I'll call him.

CRITICAL CARE FELLOW: And does he have a daughter also?

SISTER: Yes, I've been keeping her updated.

CRITICAL CARE FELLOW: This would be a good time for them to come in. . . . I think you should tell your family to come in today. I don't know if he's even going to make it to the end of the day. I'm hoping that he will, but he might not.

SISTER: Even with the medication?

CRITICAL CARE FELLOW: Right. The medication is just to buy us time, really.

FIANCÉE: So this could really go either way today, he could be perfect, he could do worse. We don't want worse.

CRITICAL CARE FELLOW: I would say that I would be very surprised if he got better today. We're hoping that he stays stable. But there is a good chance that he will die.

BROTHER: Okay, well, let's do everything we can. I mean, if you told us there was nothing left to do for him, then we'd give up.

CRITICAL CARE FELLOW: We're definitely not at that point yet. We're closer to it than we were this morning, but we're not there yet. We will definitely let you know if it gets to that point.

In a second example, another critical care fellow seeks consent for drugs (pressors to raise blood pressure) *not* to be administered. The patient is a thirty-two-year-old man with alcoholic cirrhosis that has resulted in liver failure, among many other problems. In this example, even more than the first, the physician follows a somewhat circuitous route to get all parties to appreciate the decision at hand.

CRITICAL CARE FELLOW: So, I know how much you love him. But I'm very concerned that despite the most aggressive treatment we're giving him, we won't be able to keep up. You all love him and have known him for many years. So we look to you now to give us a sense of what you think [Patient] would want, how he would want to live. Up until now, we've been treating him with the most aggressive support possible, and we're wondering if you think he would want us to continue doing that, since we can't fix his liver, which is causing all these problems. Some families in situations like this will say, if his blood pressures were to drop, we don't want to put him on medications to keep them up. That's what I would recommend here. We would keep doing everything else and continue giving him the transfusions, but if his blood pressures were to drop, that's essentially his body saying he's leaving us. So instead of giving him medications to prolong things, we would just let him go. He's fought very hard, but unfortunately we're doing everything we can, but we just can't keep up.

SISTER NO. 1: So you're saying you're not going to give him medications if his blood pressure goes down?

CRITICAL CARE FELLOW: That's what I wanted to talk to you all about. I'm here to answer your questions so you can make that decision as his family. Some families would say that they wouldn't want to put him on blood pressure medications at this point because it wouldn't change the outcome. Another route is to just focus on making him comfortable, so stop treating him so aggressively and instead focusing on giving him pain medications and medications for anxiety to make sure he's comfortable. That's called withdrawal of care.

[*Silence*]

CHAPLAIN: Doctor, is he dying?

CRITICAL CARE FELLOW: Yes, I think that he is dying. Because he is so young, we've been doing everything we could to treat him as aggressively as medically

possible. But I think his body can't fight anymore. I can't know for sure because only He [*critical care fellow raises her arms toward the ceiling*] makes those
decisions. I wish we could control everything, but God is the one who decides
these things.

SISTER NO. 2: Is he feeling pain?

CRITICAL CARE FELLOW: Yes, I think he is in pain. When I examined him this
morning it looked like he was in pain and so I had his nurse increase his
medications for pain and anxiety.

SISTER NO. 1: So you are suggesting that we stop his blood pressure medications?

CRITICAL CARE FELLOW: He's actually not on blood pressure medications right
now. But I think that his blood pressure will probably drop, and I am suggesting that we not escalate care by adding blood pressure medications because they would only help him temporarily. When he was infected, the
blood pressure medications helped him, but now it wouldn't help because
of all the underlying problems.

SISTER NO. 2: I don't think we should do the blood pressure medications.

WIFE: [*Nods in agreement.*]

MOTHER: [*Nods in agreement.*]

SISTER NO. 3: [*Nods in agreement.*]

SISTER NO. 1: It is up to his spouse.

MOTHER: [*Nods.*]

WIFE: If he didn't get blood pressure medications, would he die, and that would
be it?

CRITICAL CARE FELLOW: Not yet, but if his blood pressures were to drop, which
I think will happen, and we didn't give him medications, then yes, he would
die.

SISTER NO. 2: What would happen if you stopped all the medications?

CRITICAL CARE FELLOW: All the medications?

SISTER NO. 2: All the medications and treatments for the bleeding.

CRITICAL CARE FELLOW: He would leave us.

SISTER NO. 2: If you stopped everything, would he die immediately?

CRITICAL CARE FELLOW: I'm going to be honest with you. Doctors are very hard
at predicting these things. But based on how much blood he's losing, I think
that it would be not immediate, but pretty soon after. It's very rare that we
give patients this medication. Usually we only give it to patients who have
had a massive trauma.

SISTER NO. 1: So the question is whether we would stop the blood pressure
medications.

NIECE: He's not on blood pressure medications.

SISTER NO. 2: Yes, that's what the doctor said. We'd decide whether to start him on the medications.

CRITICAL CARE FELLOW: Right, he's not on any blood pressure medications at this point. But I think that his blood pressure probably will drop and he would require blood pressure medications.

SISTER NO. 3: Would you be able to do anything?

CRITICAL CARE FELLOW: We can do something, but I am recommending that we do not. We could give him medications to raise his blood pressure, but I don't think that is a good option, since it would only have a temporary effect and it wouldn't affect his overall problem, which is really his liver.

SISTER NO. 3: How is his heart?

CRITICAL CARE FELLOW: His heart is stressed. But it's still working hard enough to keep his blood pressures up so far. I think that's because he's so young. But I don't think that it will be able to keep up for much longer.

SISTER NO. 3: And how are his lungs?

CRITICAL CARE FELLOW: He needs ventilator support because he can't breathe on his own, but he is oxygenating well.

NIECE: How are his kidneys?

CRITICAL CARE FELLOW: His kidneys are not functioning well; they're not able to keep up. One way that we measure that is by how much urine he's able to make, and he's really not able to make much at all right now. That could be because of the blood loss or because of all the fluid in his abdomen, but his kidneys are not able to do their job. . . . Why don't I give you some time to talk this all over. You can talk amongst yourselves or I can stay here in case you have questions, or you can talk alone and come find me if you have questions.

WIFE: How much time will you give us to talk?

CRITICAL CARE FELLOW: As much time as you need. The most important thing is that you make a decision that you all agree with.

MOTHER: [To Wife] You have to say something.

WIFE: Not everyone is here, so I don't know if we can make any decisions without them being here.

CRITICAL CARE FELLOW: I know there are a lot of people who love [Patient] and not all of them are here. I can give you time if you want to call your other loved ones. Just come get me if you have any questions.[4]

Most of the procedures generically listed above require informed consent. Some are performed at the bedside, others in the operating room (OR) or interventional radiology (IR). Some are relatively benign, others very risky. Refusing them may lead to risk of infection, inability to deliver food or medication, increased pain or suffering, unnecessary or inappropriate treatment, prolonged hospitalization, impairment or diminished quality of life, brain damage, or death. Consenting to these procedures sometimes carries equally serious risks. Two-fifths of all patients received one or more surgical or other intervention.

Dialysis

Critical care interventions, along with medical problems that cause multisystem organ failure, are hard on the kidneys. Patients present with both chronic and acute renal failure. Some become overloaded with fluid. One patient in the study gained eighty pounds of fluid in a week's time and was barely recognizable. For these patients, dialysis, or more often, an ICU variation on dialysis called CVVH that runs slowly and continually, filtering the blood at the bedside, is appropriate.

CRITICAL CARE ATTENDING: Hi, I'm [name], the pulmonary critical care attending in the ICU. I'm not sure how much you've been told, so I'll just start by giving you an update. [Patient] has what we call multi-system organ failure. He's on the ventilator, on life support. We think he needs that for two reasons: a pneumonia and general fluid overload in his body. The second thing is that his blood pressure is low and he's requiring medications to keep it up. We think that's from the infection in his bloodstream. And then his kidneys are still making urine, which is good, but they're not clearing the toxins out of the bloodstream. Part of the increase in those numbers is artificial because the chemo is killing cells and so those toxins are entering the bloodstream. But his kidneys are not adequately clearing the toxins from the bloodstream. So those are the main things going on right now.

SON: Yes, we're up to speed on all that.

CRITICAL CARE ATTENDING: The main decisional point today is whether or not to do dialysis. Now, the issue is whether that's something you think he would want at this point. Being on those two machines—dialysis and the ventilator—portends a very poor prognosis. There is a very, very small chance that the dialysis would allow him to get off the ventilator. But it would basically be trading one machine for the other. And that's the best-case scenario: being on dialysis for the rest of his life, in the hospital. I don't think he will ever go home. I don't know what you've been hearing from Oncology, but the bottom line is that he's going to die.

SON: We understand that.

CRITICAL CARE ATTENDING: What have they been telling you?

SON: They haven't given us any false hope or anything. They said that the chemo may give him a month to live.

CRITICAL CARE ATTENDING: Yes, it's a very aggressive tumor. There's just no cure for his lymphoma.

SON: We know that. And he was aware of that too when we all made the decision to go forward with this last round of chemo. They said that it'll be another seven days or so before we know whether the chemo was effective.

CRITICAL CARE ATTENDING: The dialysis is a decision that needs to be made today though. If we don't initiate it early on, it could be too late to do it later on after there's already more damage.

SON: And you're saying there may already be damage to his kidneys?

CRITICAL CARE ATTENDING: He is making urine still, but his kidneys are not functioning properly. They're not clearing toxins from his bloodstream, which will start causing more problems for him. Best-case scenario, he'd have to be on dialysis for six weeks. There's a small chance we could get him off the ventilator, but that's basically trading one machine for the other. He'd be on the dialysis machine instead of the ventilator. The advantage of that, though, is that he may be able to interact with you and talk with you. . . . At this point, we can go full force and do everything—dialysis and other interventions. Or you could just decide to make him comfortable.

CVVH was broached with 14 percent of the ICU patients' decision makers, usually discussed over two or more meetings. Nine percent of all patients subsequently received dialysis.

Goals of Care

In the dialogue that opened this chapter, the attending physician asked about the patient's goals for her care. Goals of care, though rarely defined in the medical literature, most often include a patient's (or surrogate speaking on his or her behalf) desire to "(1) be cured, (2) live longer, (3) improve or maintain function/quality of life/independence, (4) be comfortable, (5) achieve life goals, and (6) provide support for family/caregiver."[5] In the setting of an intensive care unit, reflection on goals of care typically involves choices between aggressive or even heroic interventions; time-limited trials of aggressive treatments; continuing, but not escalating, treatment; withholding or withdrawing interventions; or initiating interventions to make the patient comfortable, even if they result in the patient's death.

Although conversations about goals of care are frequently abstract, they are often triggered by concrete decisions. As several previous examples, including the last one, demonstrate, deliberation about specific interventions sometimes reflects on goals of care, as participants consider the alternatives. Discussion of code status and do-not-resuscitate orders (described in the next section) is often framed within a broader discussion of goals of care as well. As interventions succeed and fail and as the patient's prognosis changes, goals of care may be addressed repeatedly throughout an ICU admission, often beginning with support for aggressive interventions and ending with the embrace of comfort care. Less frequently, physicians and surrogates are surprised by a patient's resilience or positive response to treatment, and goals shift to more aggressive interventions.

Conversations about goals of care are very common in the ICU, especially when a patient's prognosis of regaining functional status or of surviving the ICU stay is low. More than eight in ten patients were the subject of at least one conversation about goals of care. Because goals of care are often revisited, more than half were the subject of three or more separate conversations (5 percent had ten or more). For about half of the patients for whom goals of care were considered, these conversations occurred within the first two days of their admission to the ICU and for 86 percent within the first week. But for 5 percent of patients, the issue was not even raised until after two weeks in the ICU, and for two patients not until after five weeks.

Health care providers are about three times more likely to initiate conversations about goals of care than are the patient's friends and family.

CRITICAL CARE ATTENDING: So, as I said, we're pretty much giving [Patient] very heroic support right now, but he's still deteriorating. Even since he's been in the ICU, he's deteriorated quite a bit. The fact that he's still with us shows how strong of a person he must be. It's remarkable for anyone to be able to withstand so much disease and such aggressive treatment. I think that the chances that [Patient] could get back to the person that we want him to be are very slim. A lot of times we talk with families and make the decision that if the chances of survival are very low, that we change the goals. Right now, our goals have been to do everything we can to help [Patient] and get him better. We're treating him very aggressively with the ventilator and the blood pressure medications and the antibiotics to fight the infections. In many cases we talk with the families and decide together—we never decide on our own, we always work together—that the goals should be to make the patient as comfortable as possible. The treatments he's receiving are unnatural and they're essentially prolonging his life until he passes. If we hadn't intubated him when he arrived in the ICU, he would have passed then. So we often decide that what we're doing, keeping all these tubes in him, is unnatural, and it's not changing the overall outcome. So we remove the tubes so that he's a little closer to the [Patient] you know and love, and we try to maintain his dignity. We do everything we can to treat him respectfully as a human being and allow him to pass more naturally. We would increase his pain medications so that we could make him comfortable.

But on occasion, family members seek to address (or even see) the big picture before physicians do and press physicians to consider whether treatments are futile or contrary to the patient's wishes.

BROTHER-IN-LAW: I'm just a layman, but I do have common sense. Let me tell you what I'm thinking. He has problems with his kidneys, his heart, and his brain—three of the most vital organs. I don't see how he will improve in all of them. He may be a bit more stable, but he is not improving.

CRITICAL CARE ATTENDING: There is a 95 percent likelihood that he will not make it.

SISTER: [Gasps] Oh my God! [This is actually an exclamation that she can't believe they are dithering if the odds are so bad.]

CRITICAL CARE ATTENDING: That statistic comes from the fact that not just one organ is involved, but all three. I realize that this is worse than we had been talking about before. But he has not been improving, and each day that he doesn't improve is worse. One of our reasons for optimism was that he was more responsive initially, but he has not been for the last few days. And if he had an infarct [stroke], that is another problem. But your brother is a little different than this statistic might suggest. First, we are treating his kidneys and they seem to be improving. Second, his heart is doing okay. We are not doing anything to help his heart and it is functioning on its own.

. . .

SISTER: This is like a house of cards. When I spoke with [Cardiologist] yesterday, he told me that we can't even treat his heart problems now. He is not stable enough. So we will still need to deal with that eventually. On Monday you said to be optimistic. Then it was Tuesday, and then Wednesday, and now it is Thursday. I didn't see him when he was more responsive; we were still flying in. But when we got here, he did react the way you might react to someone you know. He seemed to recognize us. Now there is nothing. He just stares.

CRITICAL CARE ATTENDING: That may be partly because of the sedation. We give him a vacation from sedation early every morning so that we can examine him and assess his mental status. But you don't see that. . . . I think we need to give it another twenty-four or forty-eight hours. I think when we talk next time we should also include Neurosurgery. But I will tell them that you are concerned about us providing futile care.

BROTHER-IN-LAW: You've hit the nail on the head. We don't want that.

DAUGHTER NO. 1: If everything were to go swimmingly well, what is the very best outcome that could result from this kind of injury?

NEUROSURGERY ATTENDING: I don't have a crystal ball.

DAUGHTER NO. 2: I know. But what would be the very best that you can imagine?

NEUROSURGERY ATTENDING: She would be able to feed herself. She would be able to converse and interact. She should be able to understand talking and speak herself.

DAUGHTER NO. 1: See, I just don't think this is enough. We want an outcome that would be—

DAUGHTER NO. 2: Appropriate.

DAUGHTER NO. 1: I am afraid that we would make her better enough to be where she won't want. I don't want to sentence her to a fate worse than death. We have been thinking about the kinds of things that give her pleasure in life. We would want her to have pleasure in her life and worry that she won't be able to do these things.

. . .

NEUROSURGERY ATTENDING: It is just too early to know how she will do.

DAUGHTER NO. 1: What do you need more time for?

NEUROSURGERY ATTENDING: We need to do some tests.

DAUGHTER NO. 1: What kind of tests?

NEUROSURGERY ATTENDING: Well, we know about the stroke. We need to know the cause of the stroke—whether it was caused by the arteries in her neck or by her heart.

DAUGHTER NO. 1: But what's the purpose of the tests?

NEUROSURGERY ATTENDING: Well, if we don't know what caused the stroke, then she could have another stroke. Do we want her to have another stroke?

DAUGHTER NO. 1: Well, I don't know that it matters if she has another stroke if we don't think she would want to live the way she is now.

Code Status

Code status refers to the interventions to be performed if patients stop breathing or their heart stops beating. "Full code," the default status, instructs that patients be resuscitated, which may include some combination of chest compressions, electric shocks, medications, and intubation. When patients are first admitted to the ICU, they or their surrogate decision maker will be asked about code status. If they do not want cardiac resuscitation (CPR) or intubation, they may instruct physicians to enter a DNR/DNI (do-not-resuscitate/do-not-intubate) order. Most patients begin their ICU stay full code. Eleven percent of those in the study arrived in the ICU with preexisting DNR and or DNI orders, some of which surrogates subsequently altered or rescinded.

In the ICUs, because so many patients need intubation and ventilation, usually early in their admission, conversations about preferences for intubation generally occur separately from those about cardiac resuscitation. But as patients become more critically ill, as blood pressures drop precipitously and the likelihood that their heart may stop beating or that they will not survive a resuscitation attempt increases, physicians broach the subject of code status with their families once again.

CRITICAL CARE RESIDENT: Your mother is very sick. She has pneumonia and her cancer is very advanced. We're still giving her antibiotics and blood pressure medications and we've got her on the breathing machine. There is less than a 1 percent chance of getting off. One thing that we need to discuss is the possibility that your mother's heart could stop and she could pass here in the ICU. If that happened, she would be dead, but if you wanted us to, we could try to bring her back by shocking her heart and doing compressions like you see on TV, what we call aggressive measures. Have you ever talked to your mother about what she would want in this situation? Probably not; most people don't.

SON: No.

CRITICAL CARE RESIDENT: If I could ask her, I would. But she can't tell us right now, so you guys, as her next of kin, have to make the decision for her. Well, you can discuss amongst yourselves what you would want us to do if that were to happen, and, most importantly, what you think she would want. Do you think she would want us to try to bring her back or do you think she would want us to let her go peacefully?

[Family members begin talking to one another in Spanish.]

FEMALE COUSIN: She was lying like that for a week once before, but she recuperated.

CRITICAL CARE RESIDENT: And that's what we're hoping for. But if something were to happen, we need to know what you'd like us to do. Either way, we'll keep the machines going that we have her on. We'll definitely do that.

[*Family members talk to one another in Spanish.*]

CRITICAL CARE RESIDENT: Do you have any questions? The questions I would
want answers to if this was someone in my family would be, what are the
chances that you'd be able to bring her back? I'd say slim to none. It's never 0
percent, because there's always a chance. But it's very low. Another question
I would have is, what would happen if you were able to bring her back? To
be honest, the compressions would cause a great deal of damage to her body
and it would actually make her worse. She won't recognize you guys. If we
were able to bring her back, I don't think that she would ever be able to leave
the hospital. And the other question I would have is, would this cause her
more pain and suffering? And the answer is yes, it probably would. So those
are some things to think about.

Perhaps because many patients and families think about the efficacy of
CPR from depictions on television dramas, where the procedure is considerably more successful and less traumatic and brutal than in the ICU,
physician depictions—in order to disabuse them of this assumption—can
be rather indelicate.

CRITICAL CARE RESIDENT: Well, the first thing I would recommend is that we
make her DNR, do not resuscitate. If her heart were to stop, this is what
would happen. A code alarm would go off really loudly on the entire unit.
About twenty doctors' pagers would go off and they'd all rush to her room.
We'd clear everyone else out of the room, lower her bed, and pound on her
chest. At that point, she'd be dead, and I think that the chances of her coming back are very, very small. Close to zero.

CRITICAL CARE ATTENDING: We need to make a decision about what you want
us to do if her heart should stop. Do you want us to break her ribs by doing compressions of the chest and to shock her? Knowing that this would
not improve her outcome? In fact, it would make her even worse. [*He very
vigorously imitates giving compressions.*] And how long do you want us to do
it? Five minutes, ten minutes, forty-five minutes? It's not like what you see
on TV.

These characterizations do not always have the desired effect of persuading
families to eschew CPR.

Code status was discussed for 62 percent of patients, for half of them
over three or more meetings. Code status was ultimately changed for a little
more than half of the patients who arrived in the ICU full code. A handful

of patients seesawed back and forth several times between full code and DNR/DNI.

Palliative Care

CRITICAL CARE ATTENDING: His kidney functioning is worse today. He's just spiraling downward. He's on 100 percent oxygen. The medications aren't working. We tried stopping that medication for his heart, but then he started deteriorating, so we had to put it back on. Now he has this pain in his abdomen, which I'm concerned means that his bowel is possibly dying. His heart is not pumping enough blood, and so that's causing this bowel ischemia, which basically means that it's not getting enough blood flow and so it's starting to die. That will become immensely painful. With everything that's going on, I just think it's time to focus on just making him comfortable. At this point, the treatments that we're giving him are as bad as the disease itself. I think we should consult our palliative care team and just try to keep him comfortable. That sliver of a chance that he could overcome all these things is gone now. He's going to die, and it's inevitable that he's going to die during this hospitalization. I don't have any hope that he can make it through this, and so I think the best thing is just to make him comfortable. I think at this point we're probably hurting him more than we're helping him. I'll contact the palliative care team—well, I'll have them meet with you either way.

When decision makers shift goals of care from aggressive treatment to interventions that make the patient comfortable, conversations typically continue about the process, mechanics, logistics, and timing of stopping or withdrawing treatment and implementing comfort care. Some of these conversations—and the process itself—are conducted exclusively by the critical care team. Often, however, palliative care specialists are brought in as consultants to meet with the family. And if the surrogate decides to withdraw treatment, the palliative care specialists often disconnect life support apparatus (ventilators, lines, tubes, monitors, etc.), administer medications to keep the patient comfortable and not gasping for air, and manage further care for patients still alive a few hours after life support was withdrawn. In rare circumstances, the palliative care team arranges for the patient to go home and receive hospice care there. More often in the ICU, where patients are too vulnerable to leave the hospital, they are transported to a separate palliative care unit, which provides comfort care and family support for as long as the patient is alive (usually hours to days).

CRITICAL CARE FELLOW: When we spoke before, we said that we would meet again after we gave her some time to see if she would improve and discuss other options. The three over there are from Palliative Care. Would you like me to start by giving you an update?

SISTER: Yes.

CRITICAL CARE FELLOW: We are still continuing to ventilate her. Because of the infection in her hip, her blood pressure is very low and it is difficult for us to keep it higher. We are giving her medications—pressors—for that. You can pretty much only give three pressors for low blood pressure and she is now on three pressors.

SISTER: Yes, [Nurse] told me that.

CRITICAL CARE FELLOW: The infection is causing her blood to be very acidic. The CVVH helps to remove some of the acid in her blood, but it can barely keep up. I know we hoped that she might improve in the next twenty-four hours or so, but I am sorry to say that she is actually worse than yesterday. But I want to be honest with you. I know you discussed these issues when you met with [Critical Care Attending] yesterday. I am sorry that I wasn't there, but I had to be in clinic. I understand that you decided to wait and see if there was any improvement. But she is worse. We are losing her. Even if we were able to get her to improve, she will just get another infection. I wish we could remove her hip, but we can't. Do you have any questions?

. . .

SISTER: The word that keeps coming into my mind is "imminent." I just keep thinking about imminent. How imminent is her death? Of course, we want her to be with us. But it would be wonderful if she died on her own and we didn't have to make a decision.

CRITICAL CARE FELLOW: I don't think of it as a decision. I think of it as giving her peace and doing what she would want for herself in her final days.

PALLIATIVE CARE ATTENDING: You know, you really are not making a decision. We are keeping her from letting her body decide. We are doing everything available to medical science to keep her alive. We are preventing her from letting her body stop.

CRITICAL CARE FELLOW: We have machines making her breathe, medications to keep her heart from stopping, her heart from dying, CVVH to make her kidneys work. We are not allowing *Him* [*points up*] to decide.

PALLIATIVE CARE ATTENDING: Yes, machines for breathing, to maintain her blood pressure, for her kidneys.

PALLIATIVE CARE FELLOW: I'd like to make a point. We shouldn't think about this as stopping care. We are not stopping care. We are changing care. We are changing care to providing her comfort.

SISTER: What specifically is involved?

PALLIATIVE CARE FELLOW: Well, we remove all her lines that are not absolutely necessary. We remove the tubes through her nose that are uncomfortable. I don't know what the policy is here [in this ICU], but we usually turn off the monitors, because they just cause more anxiety.

CRITICAL CARE FELLOW: That's what we do here.

PALLIATIVE CARE FELLOW: We continually monitor the patient and look for any signs that she might be in pain—a furrow in her brow, touching her chest, as though she is trying to push something away [*fellow imitates the gesture*]. And we adjust her medications so that she is in no pain.

CRITICAL CARE FELLOW: Actually, many of the medications that she would be given for comfort, we are already giving her: fentanyl for pain, Ativan for anxiety. And, so, if she has any memory, there would be no memories of this.

SISTER: Can she hear us?

PALLIATIVE CARE FELLOW: We don't know, but you should assume that she can hear you.

SISTER: That's what [Nurse] said.

PALLIATIVE CARE ATTENDING: Now is an opportunity to say goodbye, to tell her that you love her and you respect her. To say that although you want her to be with you, that it is okay to release. It's important to tell her to release.

SISTER: That's what we have been telling her, that we love her. She is on so much support for her breathing. One of my biggest fears if you remove the breathing tube is that she will feel that she is suffocating.

PALLIATIVE CARE FELLOW: We give patients medications to ensure that they do not feel that they are suffocating and that they can breathe comfortably—morphine, for example.

PALLIATIVE CARE ATTENDING: Actually, it might be more comfortable for her to get rid of the breathing tube. One of the things they do to all medical students is that they make you simulate being on a breathing machine. It is actually one of the most uncomfortable, unpleasant things I have ever experienced—that feeling of puffs of air being forced into you against your will. That is one of the reasons that we have to sedate patients so heavily when they are on a ventilator.

SISTER: Oh, I didn't know that.

. . .

CRITICAL CARE FELLOW: I just want you to know that you can have as much time as you need. It can be tomorrow. Or later. Perhaps you want other people to have a chance to be with her. We are around all the time. Just let us know if you have any questions or want to talk with us some more.

Families of 59 percent of the patients considered palliative care and withdrawing life support; a little over a quarter of them met with the palliative care service. Surrogates for 43 percent of all patients instructed physicians to withdraw life support.

Organ Donation

More than half the patients in the study died in the ICU or palliative care unit. Conversations about organ donation or donating the patient's body to science came up for 11 percent of all ICU patients, often at the initiative of a family member. Federal regulations require hospitals to notify the regional organ-donation organization when death is imminent so that the patient can be evaluated for possible organ donation. Many patients, even those who are registered organ donors, are not appropriate candidates because of their medical problems. But some are, especially those suffering brain death, from whom the largest number of organs is available for harvest. When a patient is a potential organ donor, protocols dictate that only representatives of the regional organization—and not hospital staff[6]—meet with families to discuss organ donation. In the two examples below, the patients had completed organ donor cards, but many of the meetings surrounding organ donation concerned patients who had not done so.

[*The organ-donation representative shows the patient's wife a piece of paper from the secretary of state's office stating that the patient is an organ donor.*]

WIFE: Yes, but he had some reservations because he was afraid that they may not wait long enough before they retrieve your organs.

ORGAN-DONATION REQUESTER: They do nothing until the patient is pronounced dead or brain-dead.

WIFE: His sisters want to donate his organs. I am overwhelmed. It's not been even twenty-four hours. He was such a healthy, active man. He parachuted, scuba dived. It's hard to believe. The kids, especially the younger one, are having trouble accepting this.

ORGAN-DONATION REQUESTER: How old are they?

WIFE: Seventeen and twenty-two.

ORGAN-DONATION REQUESTER: I have kids roughly the same age.

WIFE: I don't think that we are ready to withdraw care so quickly.

ORGAN-DONATION REQUESTER: Perhaps it makes sense to wait a little bit, perhaps until morning. If the patient is declared brain-dead, one is able to use the most organs—the heart, liver, pancreas, lungs, kidneys, etc. Most likely eight lives will be saved by this donation. If the patient was a runner and scuba diver, he probably has a really good heart.

WIFE: He was not a runner, but he didn't drink or smoke. We're a Christian family.

ORGAN-DONATION REQUESTER: I have checked on the patient's condition, and it is possible that he will be brain-dead by the morning.

WIFE: We don't want to donate skin.

ORGAN-DONATION REQUESTER: That is fine. This is not an all-or-nothing proposition. We will do what you want when you want to do it.

WIFE: I understand that they will fill up the body cavity.

ORGAN-DONATION REQUESTER: No one will be able to tell that they donated organs. The procedure takes roughly eighteen to twenty-four hours. We need to test the patient and collect all the relevant cross-matching information. Then we need to find out who will get the organs and notify all of the surgeons. The actual surgery will take about five hours and will be performed at this hospital.

WIFE: What happens with the funeral home?

ORGAN-DONATION REQUESTER: We will contact the funeral home when it is time to pick up the body. Throughout this process, the family can go home or they can stay with the patient, right up until surgery.

WIFE: I think my husband's spirit is gone; all that's left is his body. I have a grandson with a genetic defect; it would be nice if some day someone did this for him.

A second example of a very tearful meeting, facilitated by a different requester, shows a less ambivalent family embracing organ donation as a redemptive end of their troubled young son's life.

MOTHER: [*Holding patient's driver's license*] My son is an organ donor.

. . .

ORGAN-DONATION REQUESTER: How would you like to start out? Do you have any questions?

MOTHER: How does it work?

ORGAN-DONATION REQUESTER: Basically there are two ways. You can wait for the brain to herniate—which will result in brain death—or you can withdraw care.

MOTHER: I know the pressure in his brain keeps going up and that it is dangerously high. What does herniated mean?

ORGAN-DONATION REQUESTER: [*Explains that it is when part of the brain tissue is pushed from its normal position inside the skull.*]

AUNT: How do you know if he is brain-dead?

ORGAN-DONATION REQUESTER: There are some tests we do. . . . We will need to take him off some sedation and paralytics first.

MOTHER: Will he feel any pain?

ORGAN-DONATION REQUESTER: No. He's gone. You can donate more organs with brain death—especially the heart and lungs—than you can if you withdraw care.

MOTHER: Then that's what we want. We want to wait for brain death. We want to be able to donate as many organs as possible.

ORGAN-DONATION REQUESTER: It might take a bit longer to wait for brain death than to withdraw care.

MOTHER: That's okay. [*With pride in her voice*] He would want this.

ORGAN-DONATION REQUESTER: [*With genuine emotion*] You are so gracious. This is such a gracious thing to do.

MOTHER: He hasn't had much purpose the last few years. This would give his life purpose.

[*Mother, stepfather, and aunt begin to cry. Requester and observer have tears in their eyes.*]

For 6 percent of all ICU patients, families met with these organ-donation representatives (all but one of them in the neurological ICU); for another 1 percent, families refused to meet. Family members initially agreed to organ donation after all of these meetings; conflict subsequently developed among the extended family of a quarter of these patients and the decision to donate was rescinded.

Differences by Intervention

As noted earlier, the difference in figure 4.1 between considering an intervention and implementing it (the size of the light-gray rings around each decision) reflects whether the intervention is still appropriate as well as whether the surrogate consents to it. But can one explain the size of the entire circle—whether an intervention is considered at all? Holding a conversation about the procedures on the top of figure 4.1 depends upon the patient's medical needs. One doesn't discuss dialysis, for example, if the patient's kidneys are functioning normally. Decisions represented on the bottom of the figure are more appropriate the sicker the patient is, but there is no medical necessity to discuss goals of care, code status, palliative care, or withdrawing life support; the default is full code and aggressive care. When surrogate decision makers are unavailable or appear resistant to abandoning the default, physicians may not initiate these conversations or may do so infrequently. Observing in the ICUs, day after day, one gets the sense that physicians raise or avoid these exchanges more for some surrogates than others, seemingly based on stereotypes or experiences over prior medical decisions. Moreover, as noted earlier, some surrogates initiate these conversations even before physicians raise them.

Are there differences by patient or family characteristics in the likelihood that these decisions are broached or considered? Statistical analyses query whether the likelihood of a discussion of goals of care, code status, or palliative care/withdrawal of care varies by patients' age, race/ethnicity, affluence of their place of residence, having significant others who cannot hear or understand English, or severity of illness.[7] Not surprisingly, all of these three conversations are significantly more likely the more severe the patient's illness. Goals of care and changes in code status are also more likely to be broached the older the patient—a reflection in part, perhaps, of the efficacy of CPR for elderly frail patients or the disinclination to "give up" on younger patients. Discussion of palliative care or withdrawing life support is significantly more likely for white than for nonwhite patients.[8] There are no significant differences by the affluence of the patient's neighborhood—a proxy for income or social class—or by the existence of participating family members who are deaf or cannot understand English.

Informed Consent

The legal doctrine of informed consent is omnipresent in ICU decision making. Rooted in laws pertaining to battery and negligence as well as principles of autonomy and self-determination, the doctrine enunciates patients' right to decide whether to undertake a medical intervention in light of the risks, benefits, and alternatives.[9] Although the law varies across the fifty states regarding the kind of information that physicians must disclose,[10] generally patients or those who act on their behalf are to be told the medical condition that warrants the proposed treatment or procedure, the nature and purpose of the procedure, reasonable alternatives, the risks and benefits of each alternative (including unusual but serious risks) and their likelihood, and the consequences of not receiving the treatment. Physicians are also expected to assess the decision maker's understanding of these disclosures and provide opportunities to ask questions.

Few of the ICU physicians I observed would consider initiating a major medical intervention without first consulting the patient and, when the patient lacks capacity, the patient's surrogate decision maker.[11] Consultation occurs, not because legal statute and case law require it, because physicians would face liability for proceeding without consent, or even because hospital protocols demand it—all of which are true—but because it is how procedures and interventions happen. Indeed, we observed the use of the legal phrase "informed consent" on only two occasions out of more than a thousand meetings. Legal requirements have become institutionalized in day-to-day practices; many follow them without considering why.

That said, one observes considerable variability in the formality and comprehensiveness of the conversation, who is consulted, by whom, how often, for what sorts of interventions, what is disclosed, in what context, the extent to which the decision maker's comprehension of the options is assessed, and the ease with which the decision maker may refuse the intervention. In short, one observes some variation in whether consent is sought and considerable variation in whether it was truly informed.

Variability is exacerbated by the social organization of the ICU. In the course of a day, the patient will be treated by a critical care attending physician and several residents, medical students, and fellows, as well as a coterie of junior and senior specialists.[12] Over the course of a week or month, all of these physicians may rotate off their service, to be replaced by still others; and most will be replaced by a different team of physicians each night. More than one set of physicians or specialists may broach the subject of a prospective procedure or intervention and begin a dialogue on the theme of informed consent. Since the specific details of these conversations are not documented in physician notes in the medical record, the parade of physicians will not know exactly what was disclosed by another ahead in line. Indeed, competing specialists sometimes provide mixed messages to decision makers, casting very different perspectives on risks and benefits, alternatives, consequences of doing nothing, prognosis, or even the seriousness of the problem for which the procedure is offered as a corrective. On occasion, these mixed messages result in consents that are given and then rescinded (or vice versa) after a different specialist paints a more or a less rosy picture. Depending on who happens to be visiting the patient at a given time, these partial conversations may be initiated with different members of the patient's network each time. And because the conversation is a continuing one and the need for the intervention initially uncertain, no one iteration may cover all aspects of the ideal type informed-consent process. Having discussed the matter many times before, the actual formal consent may, in fact, be quite superficial and pro forma, often conducted quickly over the phone.

For example, conversations about tracheostomies typically begin after the patient has been intubated for about a week. As reflected in some of the examples earlier, these conversations, which often occur during critical care rounds, will address the rationale for the tracheostomy, the risks and benefits, and the alternatives, sometimes even the big picture in which this seemingly minor intervention plays a role. Each day, if a family member happens to be in the room when the team sees the patient on its rounds, physicians may revisit the impending decision and offer a progress report on the patient's ability to be weaned from the ventilator (therefore, no longer requiring the breathing tube or a trach). Ultimately, though, the procedure will be performed by ear, nose, and throat (ENT) specialists or general surgeons along with anesthesiologists—physicians who may have had no prior contact with patients or their families. These physicians will secure written consents separately for the surgery and administration of anesthesia (usually just hours before the tracheostomy is performed). Any one of these conversations may fall well short of informed consent. However, a fly on the wall, over the course of the week, might well be sufficiently informed and have ample opportunity to ask questions.

Because of this iterative process and because so many interventions are contemplated or performed in an ICU, a substantial number of meetings were observed—about a quarter of the total—in which consent for a given procedure was broached or discussed (if not actually solicited or given), even if it was not the major topic of the conversation. Not surprisingly, consents were even more common for the interactions that were not observed (about a third of them)—often because they occurred over the phone or in odd places or times, the sole purpose of which was to secure written consent for an imminent intervention. For 99 percent of the patients in the study, at least one conversation about consent to a procedure or to a change in the goals of care occurred.[13]

The deficiencies in informed consent derive not only from the iterative, multiplicative process. Some disclosures—even if one aggregated all of them, as experienced by a fly on the wall—are very cursory or described very technically. On some occasions the physician omits a discussion of risks and benefits, treatment alternatives, or the consequences of doing nothing. For example, over the course of two days physicians asked the parents and sister, uncle and cousin of a twenty-one-year-old woman, her body riddled with untreatable end-stage cancer, whether they thought she would want a tracheostomy and a few months of institutional care before she died or would prefer comfort care. (A slice of these conversations was reprised earlier in this chapter as an example of a dialogue over tracheostomy.) After several extensive discussions, all agreed—tearfully—that the patient would not want the trach. After the last of these meetings, the family assembled in the patient's room, the patient woozy from sedation, intubated, and unable to speak. The resident rolled a chair over to the patient; her family encircled her bed.

CRITICAL CARE RESIDENT: [Patient], can you open your eyes? Is it okay to talk to you?

[*Patient nods yes very slightly.*]

CRITICAL CARE RESIDENT: Do you understand what I am saying?

[*Patient nods yes.*]

CRITICAL CARE RESIDENT: Are you in any pain?

[*Patient very slightly shakes her head no.*]

CRITICAL CARE RESIDENT: There is something we want to discuss with you. The cancer in your abdomen and around your lungs is pressing against your lungs and making it difficult for you to breathe. That is why we have you on the breathing machine. Unfortunately, we don't believe that you will ever be able to get off the breathing machine. We want to know whether you want us to put a tube in your neck so that we can remove the tube down your throat. It would connect to the breathing machine. You won't be able to go home because the machine is too big and complex. You would go to a special facility that would manage your breathing machine. But your family can visit you there and you will be able to spend time with them there. Is that something you want?

[*Patient nods yes very slightly. Everyone in the room seems stunned.*]

CRITICAL CARE RESIDENT: Do you have any questions?

[*Patient shakes her head no.*]

CRITICAL CARE FELLOW: I know that it is difficult for you to ask questions. But we can anticipate some of the questions you might want to ask and we could answer them.

[*Patient shakes her head no.*]

Of course, the patient was not told that she would die soon in either case, that the question was really about her goals of care (whether to die comfortably now or continue aggressive care until she dies in an institution) and not simply about the kind of tube that would help her breathe, nor was she given an alternative to the tracheostomy. Perhaps the patient thought she was simply choosing between an uncomfortable tube down her throat or a more comfortable one in her neck. Perhaps she even thought that assenting to the trach was what her family, silently hovering around her, wanted. Because she had been sedated throughout most of her hospital stay, she had no context, no history, no awareness of what she had been going through or what she faced going forward. Few would consider this informed consent. The deficiencies of this conversation highlight why intubated patients are rarely consulted about medical decisions.

On occasion, physician disclosures appear manipulative, designed to convince decision makers to concur with their treatment preferences.[14] For example:

·   characterizing the proposed treatment as a "very violent," "absurdly painful," or "brutal" process;
·   saying it will require "pounding on her chest, breaking her ribs, shocking her, things that would cause her pain and suffering";
·   explaining that "it's not a very pleasant way to spend your [i.e., the patient's] last time"; or
·   pointing out "that is not something you would want to be there for; it would be very difficult to watch her go through all that."

Or physicians simply announce a treatment without giving decision makers an opportunity to object: "We can take things day to day. But we won't resuscitate her if her heart stops."

As foreshadowed in chapter 2, one theme that was not heard in physician descriptions of or recommendations for proposed interventions or solicitation of consent concerned the cost of the treatment. On rare occasions, families asked about the cost or insurance coverage of a proposed treatment; they will be considered in chapter 7. Except for a few occasions when physicians sought to use a medication that was so expensive that it was not available in the hospital without special pleading, they did not otherwise offer unsolicited information about treatment cost in their disclosure of the benefits and burdens of treatment. Observations of the interactions among physicians during rounds—out of earshot of patients and loved ones— found few instances in which physicians weighed with one another the costs of alternative interventions or possibly recommending none at all.

Venues

Some physicians solicit consent for medical interventions over the telephone, typically in an emergency, when a procedure is imminent, or when decision makers are out of town or unable to visit the hospital. Hospital protocols require that telephone consents be witnessed by two medical professionals, often a physician and a nurse. For example:

[*Telephone call placed by resident:*]

CRITICAL CARE RESIDENT: So, you would like to press on at this point?

DAUGHTER: [*Presumably says yes.*]

CRITICAL CARE RESIDENT: There are two diagnostic procedures we would like to do. The first is to look at the pleural fluid around her lungs. We want to check to make sure there's no infection there. We'd have to drain that fluid because the antibiotics we're giving her wouldn't help with that. We'd use a long needle to do the procedure. The risks involved are the risk of bleeding, the risk of infection, and the third risk is that we'd puncture her lung. But we would use an ultrasound machine so we could see where the needle was in relation to her lung. The second procedure is to look at the fluid accumulating in her abdomen. That one also involves a needle and the risks are bleeding, infection, and hitting the bowel or liver. But again here we also use an ultrasound machine.

DAUGHTER: [*Presumably asks how long it takes to get the results back.*]

CRITICAL CARE RESIDENT: We'd get the preliminary reports a few hours later. The final reads usually take three days.

DAUGHTER: [*Presumably asks how the tests would be helpful.*]

CRITICAL CARE RESIDENT: She's on a broad spectrum of antibiotics now, but it would help us figure out how to best treat her infections.

DAUGHTER: [*Presumably asks about the patient's status.*]

CRITICAL CARE RESIDENT: Yeah, she's still requiring blood pressure medications and the ventilator.

DAUGHTER: [*Presumably asks if the patient could breathe on her own without the ventilator.*]

CRITICAL CARE RESIDENT: I think she would make efforts to breathe on her own. I don't know if she'd be able to keep her oxygenation up. If we were to withdraw care, we'd give her morphine to make her breathing more comfortable. It would minimize her struggle to breathe, take away what we call that air hunger.

DAUGHTER: [*Gives consent for the tests.*]

CRITICAL CARE RESIDENT: Okay, I'll be here until 5. I'm going to put you on hold so I can have you give consent over the phone to her nurse too, so she can serve as a witness.

Like the dialogues reprised throughout this chapter, most conversations about medical decisions or goals of care occur face-to-face, often, as noted earlier, over two or more encounters.[15] Physicians initiate most of them. Some conversations begin during daily rounds by the critical care team or other specialists, the team of physicians encircling the patient's bed and chatting with visitors who happen to be seated in the room. The series of conversations sometimes concludes in the patient's room as well, when specialists performing the procedure drop by with consent forms for surrogates to sign. Longer, more substantive conversations are often conducted in family meetings held in small conference rooms (or occasionally, waiting rooms), many spontaneous and others prearranged. Family members—clad in jeans, sweats, uniforms, casual or corporate attire—sit in a semicircle of sofas and armchairs, hospital staff either seated or standing, depending on the availability of extra chairs. Their conversations are often disrupted by sobbing, the persistent, irreverent ring tones of cell phones (selected in happier times), the beep of the physicians' pagers, or hospital staff filing in and out of the room to answer pages or attend to other patients. Occasionally meetings begin in one place and move to another, whether to discuss matters out of earshot of the patient or to review X-rays, MRIs, or CT scans with families on large monitors.

Conversations about medical decisions and goals of care conducted in all venues ranged in length from a couple of minutes to more than an hour and a half; the average meeting lasted almost fourteen minutes, a quarter more than twenty minutes. When the patient's medical condition was especially precarious, there might be a series of meetings within hours of one another, either to get the views of additional medical specialists or family members or to respond to new information or to the failure of a previously authorized intervention.

Meetings encompassed anywhere from two to almost thirty participants; half the encounters had fewer than five members. Most meetings included two or more family members and two or more members of the hospital staff (although meetings included as many as eight staff members and as many as twenty-five associates of the patient). Hospital staff participants were largely residents, fellows, and attending physicians; only rarely did nurses, chaplains, social workers, or interpreters attend.[16] Typically, the most senior physician ran the meeting; ICU physicians usually deferred to specialists of the same rank. About two-thirds of the meetings were conducted by attending physicians, 14 percent by fellows, and 21 percent by residents.[17] Fewer than one in ten of the meetings were made up of multidisciplinary participants from different teams of specialists. Representatives of the hospital ethics committee were involved in patient care only when consulted by staff or a family member; they participated in less than 3 percent of the meetings.

The following dialogue illustrates a large, multidisciplinary meeting conducted in a big conference room in the neurological intensive care unit.

The meeting included four physicians (neurologists and neurosurgeons, all of whom stood, including a very pregnant physician), the patient's husband, four daughters, one son, two sons-in-law, and two granddaughters. Because the meeting lasted an hour, even an excerpt of the transcript is quite long. You may want to skim through it. But the excerpt is included to convey the twists, turns, and detours that arise with multiple participants offering different perspectives.

FIRST NEUROLOGY ATTENDING: I've been studying the EEGs [electroencephalogram that detects electrical activity in the brain] every day since [Patient] first arrived at the hospital. They have been improving. In fact, except for the times that she is having a seizure, her EEG looks very normal—like yours or mine. However, she is having seizures very frequently and some last a long time. Her brain is very active. We try to quiet it down to see if the seizures will stop and we tried to do so with pentobarb [pentobarbital] and then with some other medications, but she continues to seize. In examining the MRIs and other scans, I see one epileptogenic lesion that appears to be the source of her seizures. It is probably the scar tissue that has developed from the resection [removal of brain tumor] in December, or it may be a small remnant of the tumor. However, I believe that if we removed the lesion, there is a good chance that her seizures will stop and she will be back to the way she was at Christmastime. Basically, I see three options that are available: to continue the medications (that are not controlling her seizures), withdrawing care, or going back to the operating room and removing the lesion. When I was in Cleveland [at the Cleveland Clinic], we did this procedure many times—more often with thirty-year-olds than with seventy-eight-year-olds—but many of them did really well after the surgery and returned to their former functioning.

SECOND NEUROLOGY ATTENDING: I have spoken with the neuro-oncologists and they say that the pathology on the tumor looks mostly benign, but it is a little suspicious and wanted to send it to New York for a second opinion. They haven't done it because they need your consent and hadn't yet approached you for your consent. So it may not be entirely benign.

DAUGHTER NO. 1: Why didn't anyone say anything about it? Are you telling us that she still has cancer? Will she need chemo? . . . The surgeon came out and told us that it was as clean as a baby's bottom—those were his exact words.

NEUROSURGERY ATTENDING: . . . The thing about brain cancer is that it is not encapsulated. No matter how much you are able to remove, there are going to be a few cells that remain. Depending on how aggressive the cells are, it may be a matter of twelve years or six months that the tumor may come back.

FIRST NEUROLOGY ATTENDING: After a surgery like this, it is the surgeon's job to give the patient optimism and hope, to tell them that everything went well. Because the patient needs that optimism and you don't really know if a new problem will develop. Then if you encounter problems later on, you address them or deal with them.

. . .

FIRST NEUROLOGY ATTENDING: Here are some of the ictal spects [brain scans initiated during a seizure] that they did today. We inject some dye and expect it will go to the areas with a lot of blood flow in the brain, to the epileptogenic focus—in other words, the hot spots, where there is a lot of activity, the areas of seizure. [*The neurology resident puts a sheet of paper with a bunch of black circles from the scan on the table.*]

DAUGHTER NO. 1: What part of the brain is involved?

NEUROSURGERY ATTENDING: This is the nondominant side of her brain, in her temporal region. So it won't affect her speech or her mobility. It will affect her associations.

FIRST NEUROLOGY ATTENDING: It may affect her ability to see on one side. [*He holds his hands to block his peripheral vision on one side.*] In fact, this may already have happened from the original surgery, if she noticed it. Did she complain that she had trouble seeing off to the side?

HUSBAND: No.

FIRST NEUROLOGY ATTENDING: That's why she won't be allowed to drive, because you need to see if something is coming at you. We've done all we can do. We are offering this as an option.

DAUGHTER NO. 1: I don't understand it. Just a couple of days ago, we spoke to the neurosurgeons and they told us that the chance that she would have a meaningful functional recovery was in the single digits. Now you are telling me that her EEG is normal and, if you can stop the seizures, she can return to the way she used to be. How can that be?

FIRST NEUROLOGY ATTENDING: First of all, her EEGs originally looked worse. Now the EEGs are improving. Also, those statistics are based on everyone who has seizures. But many of those patients have more significant brain injuries—they have had permanent damage to their brain, which is not true of your mother.

SON-IN-LAW: Tell us exactly how the surgery would be done.

NEUROSURGERY ATTENDING: We take the MRI we just did and the MRI that was done at the end of December and the ictal scans and line them up to make a computer projection for guidance of exactly where we expect the epileptogenic lesion to be. We bring the computer projections into the operating room. We will use the same incision that was used for the original surgery;

remove the same piece of bone that was cut away before. Although once we get in, we may need to remove more if the lesion is in a slightly different spot. We have in the operating room dozens, sometimes as many as a hundred probes like in the EEG. Some are flat. Some are more like wires. We insert them throughout the area to detect where the seizure activity is coming from. If necessary, we also use the information from the MRI and from the ictal scan. If I find a single lesion, I remove it. If I find many lesions, I will close the brain up and stop the surgery.

SON-IN-LAW: [*Mouths "close the brain up."*] How long does it take?

NEUROSURGERY ATTENDING: All morning. We may save a few minutes because the bone has already been removed.

SON-IN-LAW: When would you do it?

NEUROSURGERY ATTENDING: Monday. I have another procedure scheduled. But I will cancel it and give you the slot. I will need to know fairly soon because I have to line up the technicians and get all of the equipment ready and notify the other patient that I will have to postpone the surgery.

DAUGHTER NO. 1: Why didn't you offer this fifteen days ago?

FIRST NEUROLOGY ATTENDING: Because we always take the most conservative treatment first. Ninety-nine percent of seizures are stopped with a pentobarb coma and the other medications help most of the rest of patients. We would always try those first.

NEUROSURGERY ATTENDING: If we came in and said that we were going back to surgery immediately, you would have questioned our judgment. We have tried everything we can. There is nothing more we can do. That is why we offer this as an option.

DAUGHTER (UNSPECIFIED): Can the lesion that is causing the seizures come back?

NEUROSURGERY ATTENDING: Yes.

DAUGHTER (UNSPECIFIED): How long will it take to recover and go through rehab?

FIRST NEUROLOGY ATTENDING: She won't need rehab to learn how to talk or to walk. She already knows that. She will only need conditioning, strengthening her muscles from lying in bed for so long.

DAUGHTER (UNSPECIFIED): When will she wake up?

NEUROSURGERY ATTENDING: After the surgery, we will need to give her time to come off the sedatives, just like with the pentobarb. I would think she would begin to wake up after seventy-two hours or so. Then it may be necessary to give it a few weeks to see how much she regains.

DAUGHTER NO. 3: What if you do the surgery and eventually she wakes up and looks at us but she is not herself? It is going to be a lot more difficult doing something with her looking at you.

NEUROSURGERY ATTENDING: Let me say this: No matter what. No matter when. You can always do less. You can always do less.

HUSBAND: I have two questions: If this was your wife or mother, what would you do?

SON-IN-LAW: I have the same question.

HUSBAND: I don't want to hear from you two [*glaring and pointing disparagingly at the second neurology attending and the neurology resident*]. I've already heard what you have to say.

SECOND NEUROLOGY ATTENDING: [*Protesting*] But the EEG is better now.

HUSBAND: Second, no one has said anything about the staples. When we went to [the original neurosurgeon who did the tumor resection]'s office around Christmas to remove the staples, his assistant removed a few of them. I could tell that something was not right. My wife was not herself; she was not behaving right. She got very nauseous and we went to the restroom. When we came back I told the assistant that something was wrong.

DAUGHTER NO. 4: [*Starts to speak, but her father takes her hand and tells her to shut up.*]

HUSBAND: Then they sent us up to the hospital and she had a big seizure and then I am told that she had another one when I was out of the room. I have to believe that the staples caused the problem.

NEUROSURGERY ATTENDING: The staples could not have played a role. They are very small and just go into the scalp. They don't penetrate very deep. And they are very wimpy. You or I could bend them in our hands. It is just a coincidence. Actually you are lucky that it happened this way because you were so close to the hospital. If this had happened in your home, it would have been much more difficult.

FIRST NEUROLOGY ATTENDING: But I think you want to know what we would do if it was our wife or our mother. If it was my mother, I would think of this in the context of a long full life.

DAUGHTER NO. 1: [*Shakes her head in agreement.*]

FIRST NEUROLOGY ATTENDING: But I think I would want her to have the chance. I would give her the chance. Of course, if she had brain cancer that would take her life in a year or two, I might think differently and want her to die this way rather than have her endure a painful death from cancer.

SON-IN-LAW: I want to go around the room and find out what each of you would decide if it was your mother. First, [*calls on the second neurology attending*].

SECOND NEUROLOGY ATTENDING: I can't really answer that question because it is so subjective. It depends so much on who your mother is and what she would want, based on many years of life together. My guess is that there wouldn't be agreement, even among the doctors in the room.

HUSBAND: Now I don't want you to misconstrue or misinterpret this question. But I have worked my whole life accumulating money to support my family. I love my wife dearly, but how much will this cost? Medicare has already paid all this money for her first surgery. They aren't going to pay for a second one.

NEUROSURGERY ATTENDING: Whatever rate Medicare paid for her first surgery, it will pay for the second surgery.

DAUGHTER (UNSPECIFIED): Do you know, Dad?

HUSBAND: Maybe 80 percent. I don't care.

SON-IN-LAW: Plus the supplemental.

DAUGHTER NO. 2: Have the seizures caused brain damage?

SECOND NEUROLOGY ATTENDING: Probably not at this point. [*Second neurology attending and neurosurgery attending begin to discuss whether they have indicators of her brain function.*]

NEUROSURGERY ATTENDING: Both EEGs and MRIs are indirect indicators of brain function. People with dementia and those with very impaired brains may have normal EEGs, while people who function entirely normally may have abnormal ones.

SECOND NEUROLOGY ATTENDING: We don't know. We just don't know. The science is not that precise.

DAUGHTER (UNSPECIFIED): What are the odds that the surgery will be a success?

NEUROSURGERY ATTENDING: I won't know until I get in there. One cannot know the odds. But we wouldn't offer this surgery if we didn't think it might help.

DAUGHTER NO. 2: Can't we wait until the tumor is evaluated in New York?

SECOND NEUROLOGY ATTENDING: Unfortunately, we don't have that luxury. The longer we allow her to have seizures, the more likely that her brain will sustain damage. This is a decision that we need to make now.

SON-IN-LAW: What are the risks of the surgery?

NEUROSURGERY ATTENDING: She will not die on the operating table. This is a relatively safe surgery. But there are the risks of most brain surgeries—the risk of anesthesia, blood, the possibility of a stroke, etc.

HUSBAND: I had a sister who had epilepsy. I guess that's like seizures.

SECOND NEUROLOGY ATTENDING: Yes, it's the same thing.

HUSBAND: She bit her lip all the time.

SECOND NEUROLOGY ATTENDING: Aside from the first few seizures, most of your wife's seizures have been very subtle. They can only be seen on an EEG.

SON: Is she suffering at all?

NEUROSURGERY ATTENDING: No. She isn't feeling any pain and she doesn't know what is going on.

DAUGHTER NO. 2: So what is the window for us to make a decision?

NEUROSURGERY ATTENDING: I'm really sorry, but I probably need to know by 5.

HUSBAND: No one is going to rush us to make a decision!

DAUGHTER NO. 2: But if we need to get the slot for the surgery, we need to decide now.

HUSBAND: We really want to talk with [Primary Care Physician] before we make any decision.

NEUROSURGERY ATTENDING: I will call him right now and give him the information so that he can call you.[18]

Affect

In the previous example, the patient's husband and one of her daughters displayed anger; indeed, the former was a bit of a bully. It is not surprising that these encounters would be rife with emotion, given the participants' shock, desperation, fear, frustration, disappointment, sadness, loss of control, and exhaustion, coupled with emotional baggage from former encounters, a ticking clock, struggles for power, and challenges communicating, getting straight answers from one another, and building consensus. Tears represent the most common expression of emotion; in almost one in five of the observed encounters considering medical decisions or goals of care, one or more family members cried—some barely tearing up and others wailing uncontrollably. In 2 percent of the encounters, we observed a physician cry (whether from empathy, sadness, intimidation, frustration, or exhaustion), and a tear came to my eye from time to time as well. Anger was less common. In about one in ten meetings a family member showed anger or abrasiveness; in 4 percent of the meetings a physician did the same. And in about one in twenty meetings, a family member expressed or displayed distrust of members of the health care team. Certainly other emotions were in play—fear, guilt, remorse, despair, anxiety, affection, compassion, hope, joy, pride, relief, resentment, shock, betrayal, and so on—but not all can be reliably identified by observation alone. Needless to say, many of these encounters were riveting because of the intense display and interplay of emotions by the participants.

Conflict

Notorious court cases and news stories about end-of-life decision making depict family members at one another's throats or struggling with hospitals or physicians over their right to make medical decisions on behalf of their loved ones. In day-to-day encounters in the intensive care unit, conflict is in surprisingly short supply. Although family members occasionally invoked their own legal credentials when frustrated with the health care team, only once did a lawyer show up at the hospital because of a dispute over medical decision making (for thirty-five minutes in the brain-death example that opened this book).

Conflict was especially rare among the patient's significant others. For only 4 percent of the patients and in 2 percent of the observed encounters in which medical decisions or goals of care were addressed did one or more members of the patient's social circle express serious disagreement, hostility, impatience, disrespect, or resistance toward another. Given the number of patients living in fractured families, the absence of significant conflict is especially striking.

One source of tension concerns the speed and rhythms of decision making. The following dialogue, in which some family members were more decisive or reticent than others, is the most common sort of conflict observed among significant others. This meeting was conducted in a large conference room, in which one of the patient's sons (no. 1) and the son's wife were joined by four physicians. The patient's daughter and another son (no. 2) participated by speaker phone from California.

SON NO. 1: [Wife] and I are here with a bunch of doctors.

FAMILY PHYSICIAN: Hi [Daughter, Son No. 2]. It's [name]. I was just telling [Son No. 1] that [Patient] is at a point where we can either keep treating her aggressively or just make her comfortable.

SON NO. 2: I think that she's got a nominal existence at this point. She's got no quality of life in my opinion. It's not what I would want. It's not torture, but I think we're just prolonging her suffering. I think we should stop everything and just give her a morphine drip.

FAMILY PHYSICIAN: Well [Son No. 2], there's a fine line; I mean, we can't euthanize her.

SON NO. 1: [Patient] didn't want a feeding tube. We know that. But she needs nutrition to survive. So the mathematics of that seems to point in a certain way.

PALLIATIVE CARE ATTENDING: Hi, this is [name] from the palliative care team.
. . . If you choose to switch to comfort measures, we would take care of her
and make sure that she doesn't experience any pain or discomfort. It's too
difficult to judge how long she would survive after switching to comfort
measures, but if she were still stable after a couple of days, we could look
into transporting her back home with hospice care. I will add that I don't
know her well, certainly not as long as [Family Physician] has, but it seems
to me that this is an appropriate decision and one that is in line with her
wishes.

SON NO. 1: Okay, so are we all in agreement?

SON NO. 2: Yes.

DAUGHTER: Well, no. I mean, what about the IVIG [intravenous therapy]? Without that, she's going to suffocate. She needs that for her lungs.

SON NO. 2: [Daughter], the point isn't to keep treating things. We're just going
to make her comfortable.

DAUGHTER: You didn't see her yesterday when they took off the mask. She was
gasping for air and she was suffering! It was horrible!

SON NO. 1'S WIFE: [Daughter], I was there with you yesterday and I saw how
uncomfortable she looked. And for what it's worth, she's not like that today.
She doesn't have the mask on at all today and she looks very comfortable.
It's not at all like yesterday.

DAUGHTER: I just want to treat the pneumonia. It's such a severe pneumonia. If
we can just get that under control then at least she won't die of suffocation.

SON NO. 2: [Daughter], if it's not one thing, it's gonna be another.

DAUGHTER: I don't want her to suffocate. I think it sounds horrible to die
from suffocating. And I can't imagine dying from a urinary tract infection.
I mean—

FAMILY PHYSICIAN: [Daughter], I understand what you're saying, but then you
face this bigger question, and not just in this situation but in general, which
is: What is it okay to die from? A GI [gastrointestinal] bleed?

PALLIATIVE CARE ATTENDING: This is [name] from the palliative care team. I
want to tell you that we have excellent medications that make it so that you
don't have that sense of air hunger or suffocation. Everyone stops breathing
when they die, unfortunately. It's just a reality. But we have medications that
make it so that even though your body isn't taking in oxygen, you don't feel
that. It's very comfortable. And we know this because we have patients who
experience this while they're conscious. So, she won't feel like she's suffocating, okay?

DAUGHTER: Can't we just give her the antibiotics to just treat the pneumonia?

PALLIATIVE CARE ATTENDING: How long is the antibiotic course?

CRITICAL CARE ATTENDING: Seven days. [*To critical care resident*] What day are we on?

CRITICAL CARE RESIDENT: Yesterday was day 1.

SON NO. 2: [Daughter], that's another six days of just prolonging things.

SON NO. 1: [Daughter], it doesn't matter if they treat the infection medically. All that's important to you is that she's not feeling like she's suffocating, right?

DAUGHTER: Yeah, I guess so.

SON NO. 1: Well she's not gasping for air anymore, and she's comfortable. So we don't need to finish giving her all the antibiotics.

DAUGHTER: What about physical therapy? Could she still get physical therapy? Her neck causes her so much pain. The neuropathy [weakness, numbness, or pain caused by nerve damage] is really painful and her neck muscles are shortened and so they need to be stretched. Can they still have physical therapy help her muscles get a little exercise? Otherwise she's going to be suffering.

PALLIATIVE CARE ATTENDING: Hi, this is [name] again. I just want to say that our team focuses on symptom control. We manage symptoms, whether that be through medications, physical therapy, or anything else that I'm not thinking of at this moment. So yes, I think that if physical therapy makes her more comfortable, then that is in line with our goals.

SON NO. 1: Okay, so then we'll do comfort care with IVIG and physical therapy.

PALLIATIVE CARE ATTENDING: That works for me.

FAMILY PHYSICIAN: I think that's a good plan.

SON NO. 2: Me too.

DAUGHTER: Can I ask an unrelated question? What is an infection in the blood?

FAMILY PHYSICIAN: Sepsis is an infection in the bloodstream that can be from a variety of sources. In her case, it's probably from the urinary tract infection. It can also be from the decubitus ulcer [bedsore] that she has, though; we're not certain.

DAUGHTER: What kind of risk is that for a normal person?

FAMILY PHYSICIAN: High. And when someone has other medical problems and is weak, it's very hard to fight it. She's had sepsis several times, but this time I don't think that she's in a state to fight it.

DAUGHTER: Oh.

SON NO. 1: So will she stay here, or will she be transferred somewhere else?

PALLIATIVE CARE ATTENDING: We will probably transfer her to the palliative care unit—

SON NO. 1: When will she go there?

PALLIATIVE CARE ATTENDING: Either today or tomorrow. It really just depends on whether we have a bed.

DAUGHTER: I have a question. I know that she's having trouble with her tongue, but if she's able to, can she eat?

PALLIATIVE CARE ATTENDING: Yes, absolutely. If she can eat or if she wants the taste of food in her mouth, then that's certainly fine.

. . .

SON NO. 2: Okay, I think we have a plan of action. [Daughter], are you okay with this decision?

DAUGHTER: [*Crying; her voice is very shaky.*] Well, obviously not. But I said you can do it.

SON NO. 2: It's one thing to make the decision, but it's another thing to be okay with it. I don't want you holding this over our heads years from now.

SON NO. 1: [Son No. 2], she's already there, okay? Just leave it.

PALLIATIVE CARE ATTENDING: This is [name] again. For what it's worth, it sounds like you are respecting her wishes by doing this. Based on what she expressed about not wanting a feeding tube or intubation, I think that this is what she would have wanted, a peaceful death.

SON NO. 1'S WIFE: [Daughter], I talked to my dad about this last night, and he told me all the details of when we went through this with my mom. I'd heard everything before, but now that this is all happening, he wanted to tell me about it again. And when I was talking to him, he was crying and had a really difficult time just thinking about it. What I'm saying is that it's always going to be hard because these decisions are never easy.

CRITICAL CARE ATTENDING: I think it's important to acknowledge here that the choice is not between life or death. That's already been decided. She is dying, and there's nothing we can do to stop that, unfortunately. You're just choosing what the dying process will be like. And I think that by doing this, you are giving her a dignified death. Of course these situations are always difficult, but it's always better in situations like this because you're a close family.

SON NO. 1: [Daughter], about four or five months ago, [Patient] gave [Son No. 1's Wife] a copy of *On Death and Dying*, written by Barbara Ross's mom. She believed in the importance of having a dignified death. [*He starts to get a little choked up.*]

DAUGHTER: You guys can stop lecturing me about dignified death. The thing is, I really didn't realize until a couple days ago that she was dying. I thought if we could just treat the infection then we could address the neuropathy.

[*The family physician whispers something to son no. 1's wife. She then leans over and whispers something to son no. 1.*]

SON NO. 1'S WIFE: [*Quietly*] This is going in the wrong direction.

[*Son no. 1 looks to the family physician and nods in agreement.*]

FAMILY PHYSICIAN: [Daughter], I'm sorry to cut you off, but [Critical Care Attending] and the ICU team have to get back to work. I'm available by phone if anyone has any further questions.

CRITICAL CARE ATTENDING: This is [name] from the ICU team. I just want to reiterate that I think this is an appropriate decision. These are really the best situations, where the family is so engaged.

Clearly the patient's daughter was not ready for this decision. Nonetheless, her mother was transferred to palliative care after the meeting and died two days later.

It was not uncommon for different family members of other ICU patients to decide about and make peace with a given treatment or goal of care at different speeds. Sometimes surrogates were the most decisive; sometimes they were the most deliberate, taking the longest time to feel certain about or comfortable with a decision, while other family members impatiently pushed them to take action. Unlike the example, most surrogates managed this potential conflict not by railroading the most reticent, but by delaying decisions until everyone was on the same page.

Even when family members agree about goals of care and appropriate medical decisions, conflicts over seemingly trivial issues can bubble up from other sources simmering under the surface. The following encounter, which almost led to fisticuffs, was the most hostile of any that the medical social worker or I observed. The meeting began with a calm consensual conversation between the critical care attending and fellow and the patient's husband, mother, father, and brother. They spoke about the patient's wishes and the family members all readily agreed that the patient would have wanted them to stop treatment and make her comfortable and to donate her organs as well. They began discussing the logistics and then:

BROTHER: How long would she last after they take the machines off?

CRITICAL CARE FELLOW: Probably hours up to a whole day.

CRITICAL CARE ATTENDING: [*Nods*]

CRITICAL CARE FELLOW: But even doctors who specialize in withdrawal of care are very bad at guesstimating these things, so it's really hard to say.

CRITICAL CARE ATTENDING: I will add that she is very young and she's been fighting so strong this whole time, so it may not be very quick.

BROTHER: I think we should call some people and see if anyone wants to come in first.

HUSBAND: You know what, [Brother]? No. Everyone who was gonna come in already came, okay? And as for [woman's name], that thing she sent out was fucking bullshit.

BROTHER: I agree, but—

HUSBAND: No, let's just fucking get this over with. I'm fucking tired of this.

FATHER: Watch your mouth.

HUSBAND: You fucking stay out of this. You shut up, okay? Just shut up. [*At this point the husband is shouting.*]

FATHER: I said, watch your mouth.

HUSBAND: I'll fucking pop you in the face, all right? I'll fucking knock you out.

FATHER: [*Leans forward and sticks out one side of his face toward husband.*] Yeah, go ahead and hit me.

HUSBAND: You wanna fucking go at it? [*Husband lunges at father.*] I have a lot to say to you. But I won't. I will knock you out, both of you [*motions to brother*]. [*The husband gets up and leaves. As he's walking out the door, he turns back around.*] At the same fucking time, too.

CRITICAL CARE FELLOW: We'll leave you guys here to talk. You don't have to make any decisions today. Just let us know what you want to do.

BROTHER: Okay.

[*At this point the husband grabbed his jacket and a piece of Kleenex and stormed out of the ICU. The father asked for directions to the chapel. Eventually the family and some friends returned to the patient's room, visited and prayed together. The patient's life support was removed, and six hours after the volatile meeting, she died.*]

Of course, encounters between the significant others of patients and hospital staff represent a small sampling of occasions under which the former interact. Clearly some save their conflicts for more private venues. Undoubtedly some family members stay away from the hospital altogether, certain that their competing views will receive no respect. And some surrogates order hospital personnel to refrain from sharing information with certain members of the family. Some even give the patient an alias so that unwelcome relatives cannot locate the patient. Others arrange to visit at separate times, especially when significant rifts pre-date the hospitalization.

Occasionally we learn of these disputes playing out away from the hospital when a participant mentions them to hospital staff. The following dialogue during rounds provides an example. In this case, the patient's elderly wife visited the ICU during the first days of the patient's hospitalization but thereafter remained at home, her son, daughter, and son-in-law taking shifts in a twenty-four-hour vigil in the patient's room and running interference with hospital staff.

CRITICAL CARE ATTENDING: The trach and PEG are scheduled for tomorrow. They will be done at the bedside— Our social worker has recommended that we get a [Language] translator so that we can provide a more detailed update to his wife. So far, we have been talking to your "committee." . . . By law, she is the next of kin and serves as his decision maker. Of course, if she wants to defer to your committee to make decisions, that is perfectly fine. But that is her decision.

SON-IN-LAW: Actually, his son has been talking to his wife. We have to proceed slowly because it takes time for things to sink in with her. And we are concerned about her health. She is of the old school and has said that she is not sure she wants to make a hole in his neck connected to more tubes. It seems we are at a fork in the road [*uses his hands to make a "V"*]. We have been moving forward and seeking out aggressive care. But, frankly, she may want to go down a different fork and not want to be so aggressive.

CRITICAL CARE ATTENDING: Well, I did talk with you about DNR. I am not pressuring you to make a decision. But I will remind you about it perhaps not every day, but every other day.

SON-IN-LAW: We haven't really discussed this. For now I think the standing rule works for us. Is there a kind of holding pattern we can pursue in the meantime?

CRITICAL CARE ATTENDING: Let's discuss this in the hall, just in case he can understand.

[*We go out to the hall.*]

CRITICAL CARE ATTENDING: I'm not sure I understand you. There are two options at the fork in the road: aggressive care, and palliative care, in which we deescalate treatment.

SON-IN-LAW: No, no. We don't want palliative care. We don't want to deescalate his care. We need more time for her to come around.

CRITICAL CARE ATTENDING: You can't wait. We are trying to help you move forward.

SON-IN-LAW: We appreciate that. We want to move forward too.

CRITICAL CARE ATTENDING: Either you let us move forward or we deescalate care. Those are our options.

SON-IN-LAW: Can't we postpone the trach for a little while?

CRITICAL CARE ATTENDING: We need to do it now. Do you want me to cancel it for tomorrow?

. . .

SON-IN-LAW: Could we wait until next week? My mother-in-law will need some time for "saturation"; we are more "soaked."

In another example of conflicts outside the hospital that participants report to hospital staff, the out-of-town parents and siblings of a patient felt that her husband (and surrogate decision maker) was responsible for the injury that landed her in the hospital. When he telephoned them to say that he planned to donate the patient's organs, they threatened to call the authorities if he followed through on his plans. Adding in conflicts reported on but not observed, the incidence of conflict among the patient's significant others still remains remarkably low. Even if external conflicts are profoundly underreported, their impact on encounters between surrogates and physicians is seldom perceptible.

Though still relatively rare, conflicts between medical staff and the patient's significant others were more common, affecting 7 percent of patients and erupting in 3 percent of the observed meetings about medical interventions or goals of care. Tensions arise out of everything from interpersonal differences to perceptions that medical staff are not trying hard enough or paying enough attention to the patient or to family members to anger that physicians will not do what the family demands (e.g., prescribe a particular drug, enter the patient in a clinical trial, keep the patient in the ICU indefinitely, etc.). But conflicts are especially significant when physicians and families disagree about appropriate goals of care for the patient. Most often, families await a miracle and insist that heroic treatment be continued or escalated, while health care staff argue that the patient will not survive and is needlessly suffering. Some disagree about prognosis; in a few cases they even disagree about whether the patient is alive or dead. Far less often, conflicts play out on the flip side, when physicians consider it premature to give up aggressive interventions and families seek comfort care; these conflicts are often resolved by offloading the patient to a different physician or specialist or to the ethics committee.

The following two encounters from the neurological intensive care unit reflect more explosive examples of conflict between health care staff and families. In the first example, the floor nurse manager of the ICU and the charge nurse come over to the critical care team on rounds and ask whether someone would please speak to the patient's daughter. The daughter accuses us of killing her mother to steal her organs. A critical care resident joins the two nurses, the daughter, and a friend of the daughter's in the patient's room.

DAUGHTER: [*Irate*] You are trying to steal my mother's organs. And look at the bruises on her legs.

CRITICAL CARE RESIDENT: I don't see any bruises.

DAUGHTER: [*Incensed*] What do you mean that you don't see the bruises? [*Angrily*] There used to be three bruises on the legs and now there are more. Where did they come from?

CRITICAL CARE RESIDENT: I don't know, but in the course of doing a neuro exam, they sometimes push on the legs.

DAUGHTER: Why will there be no CT [scan]?

CRITICAL CARE RESIDENT: It is no longer necessary because there have been two brain-death exams and both found her brain-dead.

DAUGHTER: I got these calls at church about the CT scan and it got me to thinking about things one way and now you tell me that it is another way. You take me here and then you go there. You misled me.

CRITICAL CARE RESIDENT: I didn't make the call; it was someone from Neurosurgery. I don't know why they ordered the CT scan.

DAUGHTER: [*Getting angrier*] Were any of you around over the weekend when this happened?

CRITICAL CARE RESIDENT: No.

NURSE FLOOR MANAGER: No.

CHARGE NURSE: No.

AUTHOR: I was only there on Friday.

DAUGHTER: Oh, when we saw the CT? I remember you. Why was the sedation turned off?

CRITICAL CARE RESIDENT: It is not necessary because your mother feels no pain because she has no brain function. According to the hospital protocol, we have done all that we need to do to declare her brain-dead.

[*This just makes the daughter even angrier.*]

DAUGHTER: [*In frustration*] I'm in this all alone.

NURSE FLOOR MANAGER: The reason why we can't do the CT is that you must take her from the room to have a CT and the process of disconnecting the ventilator would cause her to die.[19] She is too unstable to leave the room. But there have been two tests already done. She is brain-dead. According to Illinois law, that means that she is dead. That means that she has passed; she is gone. There is no more blood flowing into her brain. Perhaps there is another test that can be performed in the room. Perhaps we can do an EEG. We'll order that. I understand that you want to have closure. It can be very confusing to see her breathing and the monitor showing that her heart is beating. But she is breathing only because of this machine and her heart is beating only because of these medicines. Her brain is gone. Her brain cannot tell her lungs to breathe or her heart to beat; it's only a chemical reaction. She has passed over; she is gone. She is gone.

[*Daughter begins to cry uncontrollably.*]

NURSE FLOOR MANAGER: I am sorry. I am so, so sorry.

[*Daughter runs out of the room and stops along the hall, crying hysterically.*]

The second example occurs during rounds.

CRITICAL CARE ATTENDING: Any questions?

DAUGHTER: How was his X-ray?

CRITICAL CARE ATTENDING: It is better.

DAUGHTER: Does he still have the collapsed lung?

CRITICAL CARE ATTENDING: It shows slightly on the X-ray, but it is actually better.

DAUGHTER: What about the CT?

CRITICAL CARE ATTENDING: I don't believe that it was done.

NURSE: It wasn't done.

DAUGHTER: So, tomorrow morning.

CRITICAL CARE ATTENDING: It was my understanding that you had asked us to try to wean the vent [see if the patient can breathe with less ventilation]. One of the physicians came in last night to do it and I understand that you refused to allow it.

DAUGHTER: I wasn't here. I thought that they were doing some kind of respiratory treatment and my brother noticed that his blood pressure went up to 250 so he asked him to stop.

CRITICAL CARE ATTENDING: No, this is something completely unrelated. One of the team came in to change his ventilator settings.

DAUGHTER: As you know, Doctor, there are several studies that say that it is better to wean the ventilator when the patient is awake, including one in the *Lancet*. My brother asked the doctor whether it would be better to do this in the morning and he agreed. I have been waiting all morning for someone to come and start the trial.

CRITICAL CARE ATTENDING: We didn't know that you wanted us to start the trial. I know these studies. But they apply to people who sleep and are awake like you and me. It doesn't apply to people in comas.

DAUGHTER: But we notice that he is more responsive during the day.

CRITICAL CARE ATTENDING: Yes, people in comas have sleep and wake cycles, but it is completely different, not the same thing as those for you and me. It really makes no difference when you attempt to wean the ventilator for someone in a coma. But weaning the ventilator is unrelated to his need for a trach. He cannot protect his airway [cough, gag, etc.]. Once we get in a trach, he may be able to breathe without the vent. But he needs to protect his airway. It would be negligent for us to remove his breathing tube.

DAUGHTER: I'm not asking you to remove the breathing tube. We just want to have this trial. We were supposed to start this last week but it never happened. We have discussed this with three different doctors and you are the only one setting up barriers.

CRITICAL CARE ATTENDING: I can't teach you fifteen years of medical judgment.

DAUGHTER: I find that very insulting.

CRITICAL CARE ATTENDING: You need to be able to trust your doctors. If you don't trust your doctors, then you should take him to another facility. . . . So we will have someone come in and change the vent settings.

[*Seven minutes later the critical care attending returns to the room with the neurosurgery attending.*]

NEUROSURGERY ATTENDING: Do you mind if I come and talk to you?

DAUGHTER: Of course not. You are welcome at any time.

NEUROSURGERY ATTENDING: As you know, we are starting the EVD [drain from the brain] challenge. We have raised the setting and we will see how it goes.

DAUGHTER: It's at least twenty-four hours before you know anything?

NEUROSURGERY ATTENDING: Yes, something like that. I thought we agreed yesterday that we would see if we could wean the ventilator.

DAUGHTER: Yes. The doctor who came last night told us that it would be better in the morning. So we have been waiting for someone to come this morning and start the process.

CRITICAL CARE ATTENDING: We explained that the weaning could be done at any time. But we also explained that weaning from the vent is separate from the necessity that he have a trach.

DAUGHTER: [*Angrily*] All of the doctors but you agreed since last week that we would try to wean my father from the vent. Why do you always have to create roadblocks?

[*Critical care attending quietly walks out of the room.*]

. . .

NEUROSURGERY ATTENDING: I know that this must seem like a bumpy road, but you need to find a way to get along with the critical care team for the good of your father. My duty is to him, not to the critical care team and not to you. I have complete faith in [Critical Care Attending], and you will need to find a way to communicate with her.

Because families deal with many health care providers over the course of a day, let alone over the entire ICU admission, conflicts tend to ebb and flow with the interpersonal style of the parties. Even the most contentious family members, suspicious of and antagonistic toward almost everyone treating their loved one, usually had a few physicians or nurses they trusted or with whom they could share a civil dialogue. This variability in conflict or civility toward particular physicians was in evidence in several of the dialogues shared earlier. But variability is in the eye of the beholder; as noted earlier, physicians who engendered the most hostility overall were most trusted by others (for example, because of their bluntness).

Conclusion

A prominent study of surrogate decision making on behalf of older Americans around their time of death surveyed informants about treatment decisions in the "final days" of life and asked about the goals of care reflected in "those last decisions."[20] The interviews did not define "final days" or "last decisions," nor did they inquire over which specific decisions surrogates deliberated. Of course, the set of "last decisions" is far more limited when death occurs at home than in an intensive care unit offering a diverse smorgasbord of high-tech interventions. Surrogate decision makers in the ICU face many decisions in what for some patients are their final days, weeks, or months and what for others may not even be their final decade.

As depicted in figure 4.1, almost half of all surrogates faced decisions—often more than once—about five different kinds of interventions or goals of care; a third or more considered every intervention except dialysis and organ donation. Because intensive care units provide aggressive treatments intended to extend life and cure or arrest disease, the range of decisions surrogates face necessarily spans the spectrum from heroic interventions to comfort care. Surrogates move back and forth across this spectrum as interventions succeed and fail, treatment options begin to run out, perceptions of patient pain or suffering change, the prognosis changes or becomes more precise, additional health care providers become involved in the case offering different perspectives and mixed messages, hope turns to despair, families become physically and financially exhausted, some family members disappear and others come out of the woodwork, surrogates become more realistic with more day-to-day ICU experience, and consensus within families builds.

This book explores how families navigate this spectrum and make different judgments about the treatment options they face. But concentrating on a "last decision" obscures this variability. For many patients, the last decision is over code status or palliative care. But a decision to eschew cardiac resuscitation, for example, is quite different when it is made after first administering several rounds of CPR and after weeks on a ventilator, a trach and feeding tube, dialysis, multiple surgeries, a host of invasive interventions, a medically induced coma, multiple drugs to elevate blood pressure, wound care for bedsores, and the like, versus after a few days on a ventilator following a single surgical intervention. Although both patients died when their heart stopped and no one tried to restart it, one endured more pain, suffering, and indignity; one faced the promise of a longer life and possible recovery, while another's life was cut short, perhaps needlessly; one risked a fate worse than death or, at best, a compromised quality of life; and one consumed considerably more resources. The decisions that transpire in the middle between a first intensive intervention and a final decision to stop are what truly differentiate the trajectories surrogates take and with which they all struggle.

This chapter introduced the sorts of dialogues that physicians and families construct around medical decision making. One theme underlying many of the examples is the extent to which many physicians seek to frame the exchange as not being about a decision at all. On the one hand, many ask instead, "What would the patient want?," "Is this something the patient would have wanted?," "Would the patient be comfortable with this?," or "Would the patient want us to continue?," or instruct families that "the only right answer is what the patient wants." So the family is providing an answer rather than making a decision. On the other hand, some physicians assert that the decision (between life and death) has already been made. Either the surrogate is choosing how the decision will be implemented (e.g., fashioning the dying process) or is preventing the patient's body from "deciding" (by authorizing technology that forces the heart to beat, the lungs to expand, etc.). Of course, many families reject this framing and express anguish and uncertainty about the decisions they face.

A second theme is the extent to which physicians frequently provide relatively soft recommendations about decision making. Though some certainly give advice (and others have strong opinions that they keep to themselves), many others refuse to advise, even when families implore them to. Or they present the decision generically, indicating that "some families" see the issues one way and others rather differently. Moreover, whenever possible, physicians raise decisions well in advance so that surrogates and other family members have more time to ruminate on a decision, revisit it, ask questions, seek advice, or build consensus. Except in medical emergencies, surrogates are told to take as much time as they need. In the following chapters, we see how they use this time.

FIVE

Prognosis

The patient is a seventy-three-year-old African American woman with a previous stroke and brain hemorrhage. She was staying with her nephew and developed a headache, then began slurring her speech and became unconscious. She was taken to a nearby hospital, where physicians found that an aneurysm had ruptured in her brain. She was transferred to the ICU. Upon arrival, the patient was put on a ventilator and other life support, and neurosurgeons inserted a drain to remove blood from her brain. The patient has a large family. The patient had designated her niece, a nurse, power of attorney.

For the first two days the family had routine encounters with a neurosurgery resident as well as the critical care team. On the third day, they scheduled a family meeting with the neurosurgery attending who explained that there was still a lot of blood in the brain and that, with all the blood, it was difficult to sort out what was going on and how bad the problem was. He commented that, in another week, he may know better, but it is hard to give a prognosis at this point. He then suggested that they get another opinion from a neurologist who does medical treatment (rather than surgical treatment) of brains and then offered, "My advice would be to wait." The niece asked the family members whether they should wait and everyone shook their heads yes. The neurosurgery attending then paged the critical care attending—a neurologist—who appeared in the patient's room twenty minutes later. He began by asking the women—the patient's niece, daughter, and two sisters—to introduce themselves.

NEUROLOGIST: [Neurosurgery Attending] said that you would like my opinion of a prognosis. I am on the critical care team and have been treating her all week and reviewing all of her scans and tests. Based on what I see, the chance of a meaningful recovery—by which I mean that she can talk and interact, maybe in a wheelchair—is probably about 1 in 10.

[*The younger of the two sisters was visibly taken aback; the others didn't seem to react.*]

NEUROLOGIST: If you'd like, I can show you the scans of her brain. As [Neurosurgery Attending] told you, she has a lot of blood in her brain. It's hard to get the blood out. We have a drain in her head, but that only does so much. It's hard to know how the blood will resolve. At two weeks out, we can get a better sense of her prognosis. At three months, you get a very good idea of how she will be at a year. If she looks like this at three months, there is about a 1 in 1000 chance that she will make a meaningful recovery. It's your decision how long you want to wait and see what will happen. If you want to do everything for her, you will need to embolize [seal off] the AVM [abnormal blood vessels in the brain], but this doesn't have to be done immediately if you're not sure what you will decide. You can wait to do that later. If you want to give her more time, she will also need a trach and a feeding tube. The longer that she has a breathing tube, the higher the chance of infection because it's hard to suction secretions out through a long, narrow straw. If you told me that you were going to wait for three months, I'd do a trach now. If you want to give it two weeks, then it's reasonable to wait to do the trach.

[*The neurologist then shows the CT scans on a computer in the room.*]

NEUROLOGIST: The white portions are blood, and the little black dot in the middle is probably the aneurysm. Each click of the mouse on the computer moves up from the brainstem to the top of the brain. [*He shows on his own head.*] There is a lot of blood.

NIECE: I can't keep your mother like this for three months, especially given what she said.

NEUROLOGIST: What did she say?

NIECE: "No respirator, no machines, no feeding tube."

YOUNGER SISTER: She told us too; these were her instructions.

NEUROLOGIST: Did she say absolutely not or just if there is no chance of recovery?

OLDER SISTER: No chance of recovery. It's all written down. It's in her chart at home.

NEUROLOGIST: So it sounds like you are thinking of giving it two weeks. . . . That is a reasonable thing to do. I want to warn you that she could die in these two weeks, from infections, pneumonia, a blood clot that could go into her lungs, etc. By two weeks, do you mean two weeks from now or from the injury?

NIECE: From now, I guess.

That evening the neurosurgery attending called the niece at home and indicated that the chair of the neurosurgery department felt that there was a chance that the patient's prognosis would improve if they did a small procedure to remove part of the skull and then remove the blood clot. He asked for her consent to the procedure. After discussion with other family members, the niece agreed. The procedure was performed, but the patient's condition did not improve. Two days later the neurosurgery attending recommended they perform the surgery to seal off the abnormal vessels in the brain, and the niece refused. Three days after that the niece decided to make the patient DNR. The next day neurosurgery informed the niece that a rupture of the vessels and subsequent fatal brain hemorrhage was imminent and offered a different procedure to prevent it; the niece refused. At a family meeting three days later, the niece informed the team that the patient would not have wanted them to go so far and that, although it is sooner than she originally said, she wanted to end treatment. Four days later, when family members were available, physicians removed the patient's life support and the patient died.

Prognosis embodies a forecast—"the kind of future that awaits the patient"[1]—on which medical decisions frequently rest. Although some patients or families will insist on pursuing every available treatment or refuse undertaking any interventions regardless of their expected outcome, most consider the likely course of a disease or injury with and without proposed medical interventions. They choose among future scenarios foretold by health care providers.[2] If only it were so easy. As this chapter elaborates, prognoses in the intensive care unit can be elusive, vague, equivocal, conflicting, inaccurate, or misinterpreted. Some have different meanings to different actors, while others are subject to negotiation.

Physicians apparently dread prognosis. In a classic study, Nicholas Christakis summarized their norms regarding prognostication: "(1) do not make predictions, (2) keep what predictions you do make to yourself, (3) do not communicate predictions to patients unless asked, (4) do not be specific, (5) do not be extreme, and (6) be optimistic."[3] Christakis found that, in an average encounter of 14.6 minutes, physicians devoted 3 seconds to prognosis. Even when physicians were supplied with accurate prognostic information, they reportedly shared it with patients or families only 15 percent of the time. A different study found that not even one in five patients with advanced cancer (who were less than six months from death) reported ever receiving a prognostic estimate from their physician.[4]

And when physicians do prognosticate, their predictions tend to be tainted by error and bias, almost always in the direction of excessive optimism.[5] These findings do not bode well for informed medical decisions.

Of course, these patterns conceal important sources of variability, which include:

· the availability of therapeutic options (the more options, the more prognosis is avoided);
· how well physicians know the patient and family (the better they know them, the more prognostic error and excessive optimism);
· whether the physician is speaking to a patient or a family member (more optimistic with patient); as well as
· physician specialty.[6]

Perhaps for these reasons—few options, no preexisting relationships, inability to speak with the patient—prognosis is more common conversational fare in the ICUs we observed. For 84 percent of these ICU patients, some version of prognosis was broached at least once during their ICU stay. It came up in about half of the encounters—80 percent of the longer or prearranged meetings—and was initiated almost twice as often by health care providers as by patient family and friends. But "version" is the operative word here.

Physicians prognosticate or are asked for prognoses about many things. The likelihood of survival is certainly one of them. Physicians initiate conversations about survival especially when they want families to reconsider their goals of care for the patient. For example:

CRITICAL CARE ATTENDING: . . . I want you to know that the most important thing here is that [Patient] is dying. There is nothing we can do to stop that. She is not going to recover from this. She has widely metastatic breast cancer. It's spreading, and it's killing her. Without the ventilator and all these machines, her natural condition would be that she would die. We're keeping her alive with all this technology, but there is no way for us to change what's ultimately going to happen, which is that she will die from this. It's a horrible, horrifying disease, and it affects young people who have families, children. It is a huge tragedy. But what we are doing could be causing [Patient] pain and suffering, without any real chance of a positive outcome.

A different critical care attending quoted in chapter 4 was even more direct: "That sliver of a chance that he could overcome all these things is gone now. He's going to die, and it's inevitable that he's going to die during this hospitalization. I don't have any hope that he can make it through this, and so I think the best thing is just to make him comfortable."

For almost a third of patients, a prognosis indicating less than a 50 percent chance of survival is offered at least once over the ICU admission; for 18 percent, one or more physicians indicate that the chance of survival is next to zero. Positive prognoses about survival are far less common, offered at least once for 7 percent of patients—although a quarter of these patients receive negative prognoses as well.

NEUROLOGY ATTENDING: She probably had the massive stroke that she is suffering from at the outside hospital when she became unresponsive. It is a terrible, devastating kind of stroke involving the brainstem from which it is unlikely that she will ever improve. She is in what we call a locked-in state. She can hear you. She can feel your hand when you touch her. She can probably understand what you say to her. But she can't respond. All she can do is blink her eyes. It will be this way forever. She will probably survive this for a very long time. There is a chance that she will bleed into the stroke—in which case, that would be the end. The decision that you or she will have to make is whether she wants to continue to live this way and treat the condition aggressively or whether she wants comfort care instead.

NEUROSURGERY ATTENDING: The nature of her injury is not life threatening. This disease will not result in death. Even if we removed her respirator and stopped feeding her, she will not die from it.

Family members also ask about the chances of survival.

BROTHER-IN-LAW: I know that doctors don't like to give probabilities. But given his age and other factors, what is the probability that he will survive?

CRITICAL CARE ATTENDING: It is near zero.

[*The brother-in-law looks shocked and covers his face with his hands. The patient's brother looks extremely distraught and forces back tears.*]

BROTHER-IN-LAW: So there is no hope?

CRITICAL CARE ATTENDING: I said it was *near* zero. The chance of death with ARDS [acute respiratory distress syndrome] is 40–70 percent. The chance of death with his renal failure is 20 percent. He also has problems with his heart. And we don't know about his brain. We will have to wait an exquisitely long time to know the condition of his brain.

BROTHER-IN-LAW: So all of these risks are additive?

CRITICAL CARE ATTENDING: Yes.

. . .

BROTHER-IN-LAW: If he continues to remain stable today and tomorrow, is there more reason for hope?

CRITICAL CARE ATTENDING: I would say we would need to wait even longer. I don't expect him to survive through the weekend. Remember, earlier today I told you that I didn't even know if he would survive for an hour.

Where survival seems unlikely or in lieu of asking about it directly, family members will ask how much time the patient has left. Unlike the previous example, they often receive evasive answers.

SON: My next question is, how long do you think he has? I mean, he's got these infections, and the respiratory problems and everything on top of the leukemia. Now, I understand that you guys don't like to give timelines, and I know you don't have a crystal ball or anything. It would be great if we had one. But I really just want to get a sense of what his timeline is, whether it's weeks, months, or what.

ONCOLOGY ATTENDING: So, in the best of circumstances, the chances of getting healthy patients who walk into my office with AML [acute myeloid leukemia] who had a previous blood disorder like your father's into remission is less than 50 percent. The chances of it going away entirely are only about 20 percent. But those statistics are for patients who are totally healthy otherwise. Your father, like you pointed out, has a lot of medical problems. He's got the pulmonary issues, the infections, the renal problems. The chances for your father's leukemia going into remission are very low. I've talked about this at length with your mom, but he is in no condition to receive any treatment for his leukemia. He can't receive treatment until a number of things happen. The first is that we cannot treat anyone on a ventilator. So he would need to be weaned off ventilation and gain pulmonary strength. He would then be transferred to the hematology service for inpatient rehabilitation. It would take a lot of rehabilitation for him to get to the point of being able to get treated. We're talking months, if that was even possible. He's extremely debilitated right now. The next issue is that I think that the chances that your father will get a serious complication in the next couple weeks is very possible. Now, patients can live weeks to months with untreated AML, up to six months to a year in the very best of situations—but that is very rare. If we did treat your father's leukemia now, he would experience the risks and the harms of chemotherapy without appreciating any of the benefits. And again, I think that the chances are very high that he will get a life-threatening infection in the coming days or weeks. Unfortunately, I just don't think that [Patient's Primary Oncologist] or I will be able to cure him.

A second example comes from a conversation with the son of a different patient. There will be back-to-back examples throughout the book involving sons, daughters, siblings, spouses, and physicians. Unless noted otherwise, they are always related to different patients.

SON: I have a question. How much time does she have left in her?

CRITICAL CARE FELLOW: That's so hard to answer. Doctors really stink at that. It is so hard to predict. Sometimes a patient is doing really well and we are wrong, and sometimes they are not doing so well and we are surprised to see that they do well. Her lungs are so sick. There is really nothing more that doctors can do for her. As you know, [Oncology Attending] has done everything she can.

HUSBAND: When she's in the danger zone and I'm definitely gonna lose her, I gotta know so I can come and be here with her all the time. I wanna spend that last week here with her. But if she could maybe get better, I'll keep comin' every other day so I can see her and try to do some small jobs on the side. I do some remodeling on the side so I can work here and there. She said today, you gotta go make some money. [*Laughs*] Yeah, I am poor as poor as poor. I had to ask some friends for help with gas money to get here today. It's thirty bucks in gas to get here, and then I gotta pay for parking. By the time I'm done, it costs me fifty bucks every time I come out here.

The critical care fellow (a different one than in the previous example) responded with suggestions about getting a parking validation rather than addressing the husband's concern about prognosis. Note that none of the physicians in these examples responded with an estimated time frame.

Far more bedside conversations and family meetings explore patients' likely functional abilities and quality of life if they survive. Some are initiated by physicians.

NEUROLOGY ATTENDING: . . . He will have a hole in his stomach, a hole in his neck, sitting in a chair and blinking.

DAUGHTER: Blinking in response to something?

NEUROLOGY ATTENDING: No. Actually, that is the very best he could experience. He may not make it. At this point, it is still a crap shoot.

CRITICAL CARE FELLOW: The swelling has continued and it's even worse today. She's not even responding when we touch her eyes, and she's not responding to pain any more either. Her brain is really not functioning any more. She's not going to be able to interact with you again or function at all. I know that when it's your family member and you love them, you want to be able to do that again. But that's not going to happen with her. It's really hard to hear, and I really hate to have to tell you any of this. I really wish I didn't have to tell you this. But I have to. The medical team does whatever it can to give quality. At this point I don't see that there would be any quality of life if we were to continue supporting her.

NEUROSURGERY RESIDENT: He had a very large hemorrhage and it did a lot of damage, especially in a seventy-eight-year-old. He is manifesting only the most primitive responses and reflexes. It is unlikely that he will have a meaningful recovery, where he will recognize his family and interact with them. The hemorrhage is in his dominant hemisphere, which controls the opposite side of his body. In almost all cases, that part of the brain controls his movement, his speech, his ability to understand speech.

CRITICAL CARE RESIDENT: . . . I think it's important that you understand that we're not sure if he will survive this, but if he does, it's not clear how much functioning he'll have. I can tell you that his level of functioning will not be the same as it was before. His brain functioning may not recover. He may be on a ventilator for the rest of his life. He may need to have dialysis for the rest of his life. I can tell you for certain that his quality of life will not be the same as it was before.

NEUROSURGERY ATTENDING: The prognosis is not great. It is unlikely that he will return to his previous level of functioning. The range is between waking up and dying. It is likely that he will be somewhere in the middle.

Family members also ask about functional prognoses. Some ask whether the patient is likely to be able to return to his or her previous lifestyle or quality of life.

GRANDDAUGHTER: I think what it really comes down to is a quality-of-life issue. I mean, lying in a bed in a facility is not an acceptable quality of life for her. The only exercise she gets is trying to get out of bed all day. She's just languishing there. She only wanted aggressive care if she was going to be able to go home and be able to live her life. She really wants to live, but not if it means lying in bed on a ventilator in a facility.

CRITICAL CARE ATTENDING: I would say that the chances that she would be able to end up going home and returning to what most people would consider a somewhat normal life—and this would include dependence and major care-taking needs—are very slim. Even in the most optimistic scenario, she'd be looking at probably weeks to a month or two at a facility before being able to go home. But even with the tracheostomy and full support, there is still a good chance that she will not survive this. I would say the chances are less than 50 percent—probably significantly less, in fact. Her prognosis is very grim. But I'm not 100 percent confident—it's not a 0 percent chance. It's not black and white. . . . The difficult part is that it sounds like we know what she would want if we knew definitively one way or the other if she would be able to ulti-mately recover from this. I don't believe that she will be able to, but I could be wrong. I am not certain, and so it makes following her wishes a little trickier.

Some echoed the daughter quoted in the last chapter who asked about the best possible outcome for her mother, if "everything were to go swim-mingly well."

SON: Let me ask this a different way. If he had the most remote possibility of the best possible recovery, what would that recovery be?

NEUROSURGERY RESIDENT: Could he respond if a loved one was in the room? No.

SON: So you are telling me that even in the best of cases, he would be just a body?

NEUROSURGERY RESIDENT: Yes. He would only have the most primitive brain functions.

Others ask about specific abilities.

PATIENT'S SISTER'S FIANCÉ: Will he ever be able to talk?

NEUROSURGERY RESIDENT: No. The location of his stroke is mostly on the left side of his brain. That is a very bad place to have a stroke. It controls what we call his executive functions—his ability to think and to talk.

PATIENT'S SISTER'S FIANCÉ: Does he understand what we're talking about right now?

NEUROSURGERY RESIDENT: No. Maybe for a second he does, but he has no memory, so he couldn't track what is being said.

PATIENT'S SISTER'S FIANCÉ: Will he ever walk?

NEUROSURGERY RESIDENT: Probably not. He cannot move the right side of his body. He has limited movement on the left side of his body.

PATIENT'S SISTER'S FIANCÉ: Will he get better?

NEUROSURGERY RESIDENT: Probably only slightly. He will need care until he dies. He will have a very low quality of life.

PATIENT'S SISTER: If unexpectedly she were to improve and wake up, would she recognize us? Would she understand what we were saying to her?

CRITICAL CARE ATTENDING: If there were a miracle and she woke up, she probably wouldn't be able to speak. She wouldn't be able to walk. I don't know that she would be able to comprehend anything.

PATIENT'S FATHER'S NEW WIFE: I don't know much about the brain; what do the involved parts control?

NEUROSURGERY ATTENDING: There will probably be some right-sided weakness. Some memory loss. The things that were problems for her before will continue to be problems. She has a young brain and they recover better than older ones.

PATIENT'S FATHER'S NEW WIFE: Will she see?

NEUROSURGERY ATTENDING: Probably.

One might readily empathize with the challenges faced by physicians, being called on to foretell a very uncertain future. But to get a perspective on their omissions or lack of prognostic expertise, the following example stands in sharp contrast with what I heard, day after day, in encounters between families and critical care physicians or other specialists. It comes from a report prepared by a rehabilitation attending physician asked by critical care physicians to evaluate an ICU patient and provide a functional prognosis.

. . . At best, I think she may be able to get to the point where she can sit up in chair and do some upper limb activities such as wash face or scratch herself. Self-feeding will not be a goal. At best she will be able to transfer from bed to chair with one-person assist. She may be able to stand and take a few steps in walker, but I doubt she would be at all a functional ambulator. She may be able to gain continence, but her mobility will make functional toileting a challenge, though not impossible with dedicated caregivers. She will need twenty-four-hour care and her endurance for daily activities will be limited. . . . My prognosis is what I consider the best possible outcome; however, given her past medical condition, there is only about a 10 percent chance of her achieving the above functional level.

Neither my colleague nor I observed anything even marginally as comprehensive or specific in conversations between health care providers and the patients' loved ones.

In conversations surrounding functional prognosis, participants asked, worried, or opined about quality of life, disability, or fates worse than death. Disability scholars warn that, however difficult these conversations, there is more than meets the eye. They question prevailing stigma and stereotypes about the disabled that suggest "that functional impairment leads to an unacceptable, unsatisfying life." Instead, they argue, "the problem of disability" is "one of denial of civil, social, and economic rights and not one of biology and health," asserting that "even on 'quality-of-life' measures, a life with disability can be rewarding."[7] A considerable body of research by other scholars finds that "across a wide range of health conditions, [disabled] patients typically report greater happiness and [quality of life] than do healthy people under similar circumstances, a phenomenon that has been referred to as 'the disability paradox.'"[8] And still other research demonstrates that, as patients' health declines, their values and standards shift; they tend to tolerate more adverse outcomes and prefer longer life in poor health over death,[9] a shift about which proxies may be unaware.

These sources of misunderstanding about the experience of disability or impairment are compounded by psychological processes that make healthy adults very bad predictors of how they will feel about future events, especially their ability to adapt to adversity, a phenomenon labeled "impact" bias or "affective forecasting."[10] Research has found that people "overestimate the intensity and the duration of [their] emotional reactions—[their] 'affect'—to future events. . . . On average, bad events prove less intense and more transient than . . . predicted. . . . People adapt to serious physical challenges far better and will be happier than they imagine."[11] Moreover, people tend to predict that the duration of negative affect will be longer for others than for themselves.[12] So overestimates about negative impact may be even greater when predictions are being made by a surrogate on behalf of someone else. In short, there are numerous reasons why decision makers may hold exaggerated negative assumptions about the patient's future quality of life or of fates worse than death, assumptions rarely contested by physicians at the bedside.

Evidence

Numerous studies find that many physicians (among many of the rest of us) suffer from statistical illiteracy or innumeracy—for example, misunderstanding probabilities.[13] Yet, in numerous examples cited earlier, numbers play a significant role in conversations about prognosis. In one out of six discussions about prognosis, the statistical likelihood of one outcome or another is elicited or offered. Like the neurologist who opened this chapter, some physicians convey relatively precise probabilities.

NEUROSURGERY ATTENDING: We wanted to update you on the latest information on your mother's status. The prognosis is fairly poor. The chance of recovery is small but not zero. There is probably a 5 to 7 percent chance of her being able to recover enough to interact with you. It could take three to six months, perhaps a year, to see any improvement.

Others hedge their bets, offering statistics that convey what the forecast is not.

CRITICAL CARE FELLOW: As I say, it's not like she only has a 1 or 2 percent chance of recovery. She has a real chance of recovery. But perhaps it is more likely that she won't make it.

CRITICAL CARE ATTENDING: He's in a very critical situation. Then again, it's not 0 percent or 1 percent.

Many assiduously avoid disclosing 0 percent or 100 percent probabilities but present numbers very close to these absolutes or speak of miracles.

NEPHEW: Have you seen patients in her situation survive if you do the aggressive treatments?
CRITICAL CARE FELLOW: Yes, I have. But it is extremely rare. It is very unlikely that she will survive all this. In medicine there's never a 0 percent chance. There's also never a 100 percent chance. But I'd say she's as close to zero as it gets.

SISTER-IN-LAW: Is there a chance that she might come out of the coma?
CRITICAL CARE ATTENDING: We have no crystal ball. We never say never. I've never seen it in my experience. There is nothing that can be done to regrow the damaged nerve tissue—no stem cells, no drugs.

CRITICAL CARE ATTENDING: She did survive. But the biggest problem is that we don't think she's going to have any meaningful neurologic recovery. Zero out of a hundred patients with her infection—zero out of a thousand—end up recovering in their brains. I've talked to the infectious disease doctors and they agree that the chances that she'll recover are very, very low. It is unlikely that her brain will recover. The chances aren't zero. It may be one in a hundred million. I don't know. But we all don't expect her brain to recover. This would be her best state.

DAUGHTER-IN-LAW: As a doctor, what's your recommendation? Is there any chance he could come out of this?

CRITICAL CARE FELLOW: I really can't give a percentage. I wish I could. That would be really helpful to know. But unfortunately, all I can say is that he's extremely critical. Most patients in his situation are at the end. But every once in a while there's a miracle. So there's that couple percent chance that there would be a miracle, but I can't say what the chances are exactly.

As demonstrated earlier, a few physicians qualify statistical prognoses by noting that they vary by the patient's age or existence of other medical problems.

BROTHER: Does he have a chance here?

CRITICAL CARE ATTENDING: If he didn't have a chance, we'd be telling you that. His pneumonia is causing something called acute respiratory distress syndrome. It's a mouthful; we call it ARDS. Of all patients with ARDS, about 70 percent make it; 30 percent don't. There are different factors that make the chances higher or lower. Older patients are less likely to make it. He's a bit older, so he's got that going against him, but we see patients who are quite a bit older than him. There's also the issue of whether other organs are failing. If there's also liver failure, renal failure, those things decrease your chances. So far, the rest of his organs are okay.

And some add the caveat that statistics can only apply to populations, not individuals for whom the outcome is either zero or one hundred.

CRITICAL CARE ATTENDING: For all comers, there is a 30 percent chance of mortality. But that's the studies in the literature. He's not a statistic. Either he lives or dies. He may be less than 50/50 [chance of survival].

CRITICAL CARE ATTENDING: She will not recover to be the way she was. I can't give you any numbers—5 percent, 10 percent, 3 percent. Every individual is unique and your family member is unique to you. What happens on average isn't relevant to you.

But despite the caveats, equivocation, and euphemisms, numbers have considerable power and sometimes echo through conversations long after they were first offered.

DAUGHTER: But her prognosis is terrible. You [*referring to the critical care attending*] said it yourself yesterday. You said it was zero.
CRITICAL CARE ATTENDING: I think you are misinterpreting what I said. I didn't say that she would never breathe without the ventilator. I said that if we removed it yesterday or today or probably tomorrow, there was no chance that she would breathe on her own. But it is our hope that she will breathe on her own in the future.
NEUROSURGERY ATTENDING: Let me tell you something. We have a lot of patients in this hospital on ventilators. If we removed them all, 50 percent of the patients would die. That doesn't mean that in a few days or a week or a few weeks they would die. Just that they are too vulnerable right now.

This reference to the "zero" prognosis came up repeatedly in subsequent conversations about the patient.

Other physicians eschew statistical evidence and instead cite their experience to support their prognostic estimates.

GODDAUGHTER: Is there any chance of recovery?
NEUROLOGY ATTENDING: The chance of improvement is not zero, but it is very unlikely. I see a thousand strokes a year and have a lot of experience with this.

NEUROSURGERY ATTENDING: Ninety percent of what I do is aneurysm repairs. I see a lot of patients and a lot of them come back to the clinic and I see how they do over a period of time. This is not based on the literature or academic studies; this is based on my own experience. Just this week, I saw a forty-year-old patient who was here just a month ago and she was in a coma. And now she is walking and talking and just a little confused. She is probably 90 percent back. Many patients make great recoveries. It just takes a little time.

Earlier that day the neurosurgeon had boasted to a colleague about this patient, a physician doing a residency in emergency medicine, who had recovered enough to question one of her medications when he examined her later in the clinic. A risk of relying on personal experience, of course, is that it draws on a biased sample of healthier patients. Patients who are unable to come to the clinic—whether because they died or are on ventilators or are too sick to travel—have experienced worse outcomes than those the physician sees in the clinic.

Many physicians avoid responding to queries about prognosis altogether. Some directly state that they do not know.

CRITICAL CARE ATTENDING: I don't believe in making many predictions anymore because we are so bad at it. He may not survive and if he does, he may not wake up. It can be six months to a year to know the extent of his recovery.

WIFE: And what would his quality of life be if they were able to get the tube out and he just came home and didn't get treatment?
ONCOLOGY ATTENDING: I really can't say at this point. It's too hard to tell. I'm not trying to be evasive, I really just don't know. We'll just have to wait and see medically how he's doing.

DAUGHTER: What is the best you could expect?
NEUROSURGERY ATTENDING: I can't really answer that because it varies too much for each individual. But he won't wake up and be himself.

WIFE: Doctor, are you telling me that he won't come back?
NEUROSURGERY RESIDENT: Will he be the same? No, that's very unlikely.
SON: What are the odds that he will improve from this?
NEUROSURGERY RESIDENT: I can't give you numbers. I don't know.
SON: What is your experience?
NEUROSURGERY RESIDENT: I can't tell you. Perhaps [Neurosurgery Attending] or [Neurology Attending] can tell you.
SON: Do you have other patients who have both a bleed and strokes?
NEUROSURGERY RESIDENT: Yes. There are always one or two on this hall at all times.
SON: What is your experience with them?
NEUROSURGERY RESIDENT: I really don't have much experience. But logically, you have to assume that it is worse to have both strokes and a bleed. The strokes are permanent; you can't improve from them.

Others invoke the metaphor of the crystal ball.

NEUROSURGERY ATTENDING: I wish we had a crystal ball. But we just don't, especially with neurological disease.

NEUROSURGERY ATTENDING: Everything is on a continuum and what that means is that she is in the middle between lack of electrical activity on the one extreme and a full recovery on the other. She is not brain-dead. Her brain is working. There is electrical activity. I have no crystal ball and cannot predict what amount of recovery is likely. We would like to see her move all her extremities and be interactive, but I can't say whether that would be possible.

Timing

The classic study of prognosis, cited earlier, found that physicians (especially older ones) believe that unfavorable prognoses should be conveyed in stages or "small chunks." They call "the practice of unduly rapid or excessively comprehensive prognostication 'terminal candor' or 'truth dumping.'"[14] These concerns are evident in the ICU as well. For example, one morning, during rounds, the critical care fellow (who had been on a long rotation in the ICU) admonished the attending physician who had just rotated onto the team.

CRITICAL CARE FELLOW: I feel uncomfortable with what you said to the family. Rather than backing me up and talking about the big picture, you brought up the issue of a tracheostomy and discussed all the benefits of a trach [which implied that the patient had some hope of recovery].
CRITICAL CARE ATTENDING: I had only met the family once before, so I wanted to build trust with them first [before presenting a bad prognosis].
CRITICAL CARE FELLOW: I had built trust and built a relationship with the family, and then yesterday I was blunt with them about my prognosis. I wanted you to back me up and agree that the prognosis was grim, but instead I feel like you gave them hope.
CRITICAL CARE ATTENDING: I didn't give them hope. But, tomorrow on rounds, I will say how poor her prognosis is and tell the family that I therefore do not recommend tracheostomy.

Prognosis in the ICU often follows a temporal trajectory, though usually it is driven less by civility, sensitivity, or the desire to establish trust and more by uncertainties about how well the patient will respond to treatment, on the one hand, and sometimes rapid changes in the patient's condition, on the other.

CRITICAL CARE RESIDENT: I don't think it's time to throw in the towel just yet because she is showing signs of improvement. We'll have a better sense in the next twenty-four or forty-eight hours of which way she's going. If she starts to get worse, then we can talk about comfort measures. But I think that's a little premature at this point.

The accuracy of or willingness to offer prognosis tends to increase over the course of the patient's treatment. This is especially the case for injuries to the brain, which may require time for blood to drain, swelling to subside, seizures to end, new pathways to develop, the patient to regain consciousness, and so forth before prognosis about functional abilities or even survival is likely to be meaningful. As a critical care attending explained in an earlier example, as he summed up the chance of survival associated with each medical problem faced by a desperately ill patient: "And we don't know about his brain. We will have to wait an exquisitely long time to know the condition of his brain." Some physicians suggested that neurological prognoses should wait for the patient or disease to "declare" itself; another spoke of giving the disease the "tincture of time."

NEUROLOGY ATTENDING: Things have changed since yesterday. His new scans and clinical exam are worse than they were yesterday. I think it was reasonable yesterday to give it some time and wait and see how things develop. We have given it the "tincture of time," and the situation is not looking good.

Families in the neurological ICU, where most patients are treated for brain injury or disease, therefore often faced excruciating medical decisions that had to be made long before all of the relevant prognostic data were in.

DAUGHTER: We have been on a roller coaster. First we think that he has suffered a devastating injury. Then yesterday we are told that it might not be that bad—maybe it's a small stroke. I went home yesterday feeling hope. Then at 9 at night, I get a phone call from [Neurology Resident] telling me that he is doing poorly and may not live through the night, and we spend the night thinking that he will die, and then we come in today. It's hard to know what to believe. I am very upset about this thing.

NEUROLOGY RESIDENT [*Different from the one who phoned the night before*]: Can I comment on this? As we explained yesterday, it takes a while—at least seventy-two hours, usually three to five days—for this sort of stroke to reach its peak amount of injury, where the bleeding continues and the brain keeps swelling. He has not reached that point yet. Yesterday, your father looked much worse clinically than his CT scan looked. That is not uncommon; usually it takes some time for the scan to catch up. But we did another CT scan last night and a second one early this morning and they are looking worse. That is why our prognosis has changed over the course of the last day.

CRITICAL CARE ATTENDING: The brain is very slow to heal. It will take six months to a year to see how much he will recover.

AUNT: Time will tell.

CRITICAL CARE ATTENDING: That's right. He could be pretty much the same or could have a significant improvement. Though most likely, there will be some disability with such a significant injury.

NEUROSURGERY ATTENDING: I know that [Different Neurosurgery Attending] last week told you that it was necessary to give it more time. In our experience, at six months you can be 90 percent sure about the quality of life that the patient will have long term. But now that it has been three weeks and there has been no improvement, I don't think she has a chance of recovery.

Perhaps in part because of limited prognostic information regarding brain injuries, negative prognoses were far less common in the neurological ICU (15 percent) than in the medical one (45 percent).

Because prognostic information shared with families changes over time—whether because of the unexpected efficacy of treatment, unforeseen complications, time for the brain to declare itself, greater clarity about the patient's medical status, or because bad news is staged—family members who visit the hospital or participate in family meetings only sporadically will have very different understandings of the likelihood that their loved one will survive and with what functional limitations or disabilities from those who participate consistently. This creates yet another source of conflict among friends and family, as they deliberate about medical decisions on behalf of the patient. But it is not the only reason different significant others draw different conclusions about the patient's chances. The consistency of the prognostic information they receive provides another source of tension.

Mixed Messages

However violent the prognostic roller coaster or equivocal, evasive, or delayed the forecasts conveyed in these examples, decision makers face even greater challenges making sense of the likely future scenarios from which they must choose. Few receive scenarios from only a single prognosticator, as the excerpted examples perhaps mistakenly suggest. Over the course of days or weeks in the ICU, prognoses will be delivered by multiple sources across specialty, rank, or team. A prognosis offered at night may come from more junior practitioners than one offered during the day. And some prognosticators will have preexisting, sometimes long-term, relationships with patients and their loved ones—compromised by the excessive optimism engendered by familiarity—while others will have made their acquaintance just hours or days earlier and will be more disposed to candor.

The choir of prognosticators brings to the bedside different levels of professional experience, different kinds and amount of contact with the patient, preoccupation with different body parts (some more treatable than others), different sources of information and methods for coming up with prognosis, different time horizons, more or less familiarity with the academic literature, and different personalities or values.[15] For some, a recent miraculous save is most salient in coming up with a forecast; others are chastened by a recent devastating loss.[16] It is no wonder that they do not all sing in the same key.[17] Unfortunately, the cacophony of voices rarely perform all at once where they are potentially subject to harmonization. Instead, prognosticators wander in and out of the ICU, following the rhythms of their schedules, giving solo performances throughout the day and night. Decision makers must reconcile their mixed messages. However confusing or equivocal any single prognosis, surrogates must also evaluate these contradictions. It is only human nature that many hear the sunny major chords more clearly than the nagging minor ones.

Even when different specialists agree on the prognosis, families may distill conflicting information from conversation. For example, a social visit from a patient's long-term oncologist left the patient's sister in tears. She complained to the nurse that the critical care team was telling them that her brother was probably going to die and the oncologist was saying that he would make a full recovery. Confused and distraught, the family wanted to reconsider the patient's do-not-resuscitate status in light of the oncologist's optimism. Furious, the critical care resident called the oncologist, who told her that the sister had misunderstood his comment that, although the patient is very, very sick, she shouldn't give up hope because he has seen patients come back from situations like this. The resident then met with the family.

CRITICAL CARE RESIDENT: So I just spoke to [Oncologist] to get an understanding of what his perception was of the conversation he had with you earlier today. Why don't we start by you telling me what you understand from that discussion?

. . .

SISTER: I wasn't here yesterday, so I wanted to know where we were at. I asked him, through my tears, if he is going to make it. He was very optimistic. He said that his organs are all okay and that he's seen patients come out of this before. The last thing he said to me was, "Keep the faith."

PATIENT'S PARTNER: I just don't understand, because he was apparently telling her that this is something they expected to see.

CRITICAL CARE RESIDENT: When I just talked to [Oncologist], he said that [a different attending oncologist] is the one who is on service, but he has been following [Patient] for a while, and so he wanted to say hello. He said that it was more of a social visit. What he said he was trying to purvey was that [Patient] is very, very sick, but that each of his individual organs aren't failing at this point. His kidneys are still doing well, which is something that often isn't the case when someone is in his condition. It's something we watch for, if the patient needs dialysis. So that's good. And his liver is functioning okay. And when we take him off the sedation a little bit, he responds appropriately, so his brain functioning seems to be fine. So from that perspective, I think what he was purveying to you is that his organs are not at a point where any of them have permanent damage or are unrecoverable. But he is still critically ill. I think that's what he was trying to purvey to you, and if it came across differently or if it seemed to conflict with the messages that we've been conveying to you as his primary team, then I apologize for the miscommunication. He said he didn't mean to instill any false hope.

Because ICU patients have so many things wrong with them—many of them complications from an initial medical problem or its treatment—they face many different prognoses on top of that pertaining to their original medical problem.

CRITICAL CARE ATTENDING: I wanted to get you guys together today to tell you about where she's at, take stock of things, and figure out what the next steps should be. So why don't I go ahead and tell you how she's doing from a medical standpoint? She came to the hospital last week for diarrhea and dehydration, which was likely related to the infection in her gut, the colitis. She also has a systemic infection called sepsis. We've been treating her with antibiotics, but her body is not responding to the infection. Because of her altered mental status, we had to intubate her, and so she's on a respirator. She's had two or three small heart attacks since being admitted. Her kidneys are—actually, her kidneys are okay. But she's still requiring medications to keep her blood pressure up. Despite everything that we have been doing for her, she has continued to not get better. We get very concerned when patients don't respond to such aggressive treatments; it's a very poor prognostic sign. And this is all in the background of the underlying cancer, which is not treatable. I am very pessimistic that she will survive this—and that's not even taking into account the cancer. I don't have a crystal ball, but—

Although critical care specialists, who treat the sequelae of complications, take a more holistic perspective, other specialists may have a narrower view of a single or the original problem. The latter may have many promising interventions still up their sleeves; the problem is that the patient, wracked by the new complications, is too sick to receive them. These differing perspectives create a systemic source of potential inconsistency in the prognoses offered by different teams.

Medical specialties also differ in their likelihood to offer a prognosis at all; as noted earlier, research finds that those with more therapeutic options (e.g., infectious diseases) are more likely to neglect prognostication than those with fewer (e.g., neurology). Specialties differ in the nature of the message they deliver as well as its frequency.

"How do you know which one is the oncologist? He's the one holding the IV over the casket."

This joke, told by a chaplain in the ICU, illustrates a common source of mixed messages. Some specialties bring a greater optimism to prognosis than others. Many of the examples of family frustration over mixed messages involved the oncology team, which tended to be more upbeat, on the one hand, and with preexisting relationships with the family, engendering greater trust, on the other.

SISTER: [Oncology Attending] was very positive about the leukemia and the transplant and everything.
CRITICAL CARE ATTENDING: Well, that's his job.
SISTER: But he's very honest also. I've known him for six months now.

CRITICAL CARE ATTENDING: I've worked with him for a long time. The combination of the disseminated TB [tuberculosis] and the AML [acute myeloid
leukemia] is very difficult.

CRITICAL CARE ATTENDING: What happened was that he got esophageal cancer.
This is not the cancer you want to get.
WIFE: But the oncologists were optimistic.
CRITICAL CARE ATTENDING: You go to oncologists to be hopeful.

But conflicting prognoses were also offered by other specialists as well,
even those who attend to the same body part (e.g., neurologists vs.
neurosurgeons). Recall from chapter 4 the daughter who referred to the
neurosurgeon's statement that the tumor site was as clean as a baby's
bottom. The more downbeat neurologist then responded that it is a neurosurgeon's job to give the patient optimism and hope, to tell them that
everything went well; then if you encounter problems later on, you deal
with them.

CRITICAL CARE ATTENDING: Just this morning, I spoke with [Neurology Resi-
dent]. He told us that the family didn't want all of us to be talking about
prognosis. He told us to focus only on critical care issues. He said that Neurology and Neurosurgery would talk with each other and decide who should
speak to you about prognosis. He also said that the family might prefer to
have us talk to your primary care physician about these issues, and he can
communicate with you.
DAUGHTER: I didn't know that. I'm glad to hear that you are talking to one
another. We can't get a consistent story. Some give us hope. Some tell us to
withdraw care. We don't know who to believe.

DAUGHTER: With time, will he be exactly the same as he is now?
NEUROSURGERY ATTENDING: No, not necessarily. But it could be months or
years to see any improvement, if at all. He will be severely handicapped—in
his vision, his speech, his ability to understand language. It is especially significant when the bleed occurs on the dominant side of the brain. I don't
want to give you false hope or despair.
ETHICS COMMITTEE ATTENDING: [Neurology Attending] said something different about prognosis. She said that she didn't expect his condition to improve
from what it is now. I think this is important to address if the family are
trying to determine what the patient would want, since this is in light of the
patient's likely prognosis. [Neurosurgery Attending does not address this.]

Occasionally even physicians from the same discipline, especially with different rank or experience, will disagree.

CRITICAL CARE ATTENDING: He is very, very sick.

MOTHER: Is it hopeless?

CRITICAL CARE ATTENDING: No. If it was, we wouldn't be doing this. To be honest, some doctors are less optimistic than I am. I have had patients who are worse who have done well and patients who were better who didn't make it. We will continue to be aggressive.

NEUROSURGERY ATTENDING: On Saturday, before we went back into surgery, she was in a deep coma. She was posturing. It looked very bad. Today she is doing much better. It's just too soon to know how much she will recover. We need to give it more time.

MOTHER: What the resident told us last night was very concerning.

NEUROSURGERY ATTENDING: Please, I have to ask you to do me a favor. Don't talk to anyone but me. They are just around at night to make sure that medical issues are handled. They don't have the longitudinal perspective, the experience that I have.

CRITICAL CARE FELLOW: Her electrolytes are back to normal. Tomorrow, we'll do the apnea test [brain-death exam] to see if she can breathe on her own. If she can't, it means she's left us.

MOTHER: I don't understand. The doctor came in and said her heart is still beating, she's still making urine, and she just had a bowel movement.

CRITICAL CARE FELLOW: Which doctor said that?

MOTHER: I don't know his name, but he's twenty-eight, just like my daughter.

CRITICAL CARE FELLOW: Those are automatic functions that are not controlled by the brain. You don't have to think about that stuff, it just happens. Your heart beats on its own without you having to think about it. We need this test to see what's going on in her brain, to see if she's still with us.

AUNT: Okay, that's enough. You can leave the room.

[After leaving the room, the critical care fellow commented in exasperation, "That must be {Critical Care Resident} who suggested that the patient was still alive. I'm going to kill him."]

On the flip side, I observed a number of encounters in which physicians held their tongue or equivocated about prognosis because they knew that their assessment conflicted with that of a more senior colleague whom they did not want to antagonize.

Negotiation

Not all surrogates believe the prognostic information shared by physicians. One interview study found that 88 percent "expressed doubt in physicians' ability to prognosticate"; another study found physicians and surrogates disagreed about prognosis 53 percent of the time.[18] Family members formulate their own prognostic estimates as well. A different interview study found that not even 2 percent of "surrogates reported that their beliefs about the patients' prognoses hinged exclusively on prognostic information provided to them by physicians." Rather, surrogates also considered "perceptions of the patient's individual strength of character and will to live; the patient's unique history of illness and survival; the surrogate's own observations of the patient's physical appearance; the surrogate's belief that their presence at the bedside may improve the prognosis; and the surrogate's optimism, intuition, and faith. For some surrogates, these other sources of knowledge superseded the importance of the physician's prognostication."[19] Not even half of the surrogates in that study based their forecasts at least in part on prognoses or other information provided by physicians. Moreover, some surrogates draw on Internet research, social media postings, and conversations with friends and associates to develop their own lay understandings of prognosis. In short, not only do some physicians disagree among themselves or provide inconsistent assessments of prognosis, but the prognoses of surrogates and physicians may also be at odds.[20]

As families struggle to evaluate, harmonize, or reconcile the mixed messages they receive from various physicians over the course of the patient's admission, some therefore also attempt to negotiate the prognosis itself. A minority want to ensure that what they consider relevant data figure into the prognosis physicians offer. More simply do not want to hear bad news and seek a different prognosticator or more optimistic or equivocal forecasts, or none at all. Some seek to shape the evidence on which the prognosis is constructed.

DAUGHTER: This is what I would like to get out of this meeting. [Neurosurgery Attending] said that it is like throwing a rock through glass. Whatever you do, the glass is still broken. We understand that the parts of the brain that were damaged will not come back. We want to know what his functional status will be. Will he be blind? Will he be able to speak? I also want them to describe other patients they have had just like this who took the unpopular course at this fork in the road [i.e., pursued aggressive treatment] and tell us what happened to them. Tell stories of what happened.

ETHICS COMMITTEE ATTENDING: Stories are not the same thing as statistics.
DAUGHTER: Exactly. I want to hear stories. But I would also like to hear best estimates of the likelihood that various outcomes will happen.

Others insist that physicians are missing or discounting relevant information in making their forecast.

CRITICAL CARE ATTENDING: I defer to Neuro on these issues because that's not my area of expertise, but they have said that the chances that she'll recover neurologically are very small to none. I know that she's been nonverbal for some time now. But she's not even interactive, and Neurology does not think that she will ever return to that level of functioning.
BROTHER: Well, right now she does not seem interactive, but when I was here at 3 A.M. she was blinking her eyes and demonstrated some hope for rebound. I visit her every day. Not as much here as I did when she was at [Outside Hospital]. . . . I come every day though, like I promised I would, around 2 or 3 A.M., and stay for at least an hour. If I was just seeing her for the first time now, I'd agree with them. But it goes up and down a bit, and I don't think that she's done.
CRITICAL CARE ATTENDING: Yes, it does wax and wane. But Neurology does not think that it's going to improve from here.
BROTHER: When we were back in [East Coast City], I took her to [Outside Hospital], where she was diagnosed. There was a woman there who was part of the PT/OT [physical/occupational therapy] team. She did a lot of work with her back then, and her husband is a doctor there. He wasn't her primary doctor but he was very familiar with her disease. They both know her very well and I've spoken with them recently and they're not convinced that she won't make a bit of a rebound neurologically. . . . All I can say is that I still see the fight in her. If I didn't, I would say it's enough. But last night when she was blinking and everything, I felt like she was still fighting.

As will be elaborated in chapter 7, some reject the prognosis because it doesn't allow for miracles or divine intervention in the outcome. Others reject the prognosis because it does not square with previous experiences of the patient, other loved ones, acquaintances with serious illness, or media accounts.

DAUGHTER: Nine years ago she had a heart condition and a CABG [coronary bypass] operation, and the family was told that her prognosis was very grim and that she had weeks to a month to live. But she has now lived nine years.

So we're a bit wary about dire prognoses and want to give her more of a chance now.

MOTHER: I was in the same position as her. I was in the ICU for three weeks. I didn't have an infection but all my organs had shut down. I had dialysis, just like her. I was on all these machines. The doctors said I wouldn't survive. I don't know how it happened, but they just kept going and here I am. So we'll just keep going now.

One family refused to believe their patriarch was brain-dead because an uncle injured in the Iraq War had been declared brain-dead and subsequently recovered. And some do not want to hear bad news.

WIFE: Is [Critical Care Attending] nice?
CRITICAL CARE RESIDENT: [Critical Care Attending] will tell it to you straight.
WIFE: Can you tell him not to? I just want to hear some good news.
CRITICAL CARE RESIDENT: I don't think he would change his style. He just thinks it's really important to be honest about what he thinks.
WIFE: I don't know if I want him to be honest, though.

SISTER: Well, is there another doctor on the floor or just him?
CRITICAL CARE RESIDENT: The way it's set up, there are two teams, one led by [Critical Care Attending] and another one. The teams rotate every two weeks.
SISTER: Well, are his two weeks almost up? Because I don't want him to see me anymore if all he's going to do is talk about funeral services. He can talk to me about labs and all that—I understand that stuff. But I don't need him trying to take away hope. If he wants to come in and tell me reasons to have hope, that's great. But at this point, he keeps coming in and making me upset every time. I don't want to keep hearing that she's going to die.

Others—families as well as physicians—try to negotiate a better prognosis with one another.

SON: Yes, we need to keep fighting. So there are a lot of things that are problems, but he's neck-and-neck with them so far.
CRITICAL CARE ATTENDING: I wouldn't say that, no. I don't mean to take away your hope or optimism, but I also need to be honest with you. He is either going to survive this or he's not. My opinion is that he will not. But that's just my opinion. I can't know what's going to happen. But I would not say that he's neck-and-neck with it.

SON: [Thoracic Attending] was optimistic about him getting off the ventilator. He was on trach collar for two hours before he left for [Long-Term Acute Care Facility].

CRITICAL CARE ATTENDING: I didn't know that.

FRIEND: It was two and a half.

CRITICAL CARE ATTENDING: Two hours isn't very long. If he was at FiO2 [oxygen level] of 15, that's pretty good. But 30, not so much. It doesn't change things now though. Right now, it is what it is.

SON: But if we can get back to that point, then there's hope.

CRITICAL CARE ATTENDING: Being back in the ICU is a setback.

SON: Right, but it's reversible. He can get back to that point and then eventually get better.

CRITICAL CARE ATTENDING: Yes, that could happen. But what I think is more likely is that he will encounter complications—some serious infection— before his lungs are able to recover.

SON: Well, can he get a lung transplant?

CRITICAL CARE ATTENDING: Absolutely not.

WIFE: Why not?

CRITICAL CARE ATTENDING: First of all, he is far too unstable for a transplant.

SON: But once he gets a little better?

CRITICAL CARE ATTENDING: No. There has never been a patient who has received a lung transplant who has been on a ventilator—not one in the history of lung transplantation.

SON: Well, is there any way to repair the damaged lung tissue?

CRITICAL CARE ATTENDING: No. Just time.

SON: It's just too sensitive to repair it?

CRITICAL CARE ATTENDING: Kind of. That's the simplest answer I can give you.

SON: What about any surgical interventions that could maybe help with the scarring?

CRITICAL CARE ATTENDING: No, just time.

WIFE: I don't really know what I'm talking about, but what about a bone marrow transplant? Would that help?

CRITICAL CARE ATTENDING: No. Totally separate.

. . .

SON: When he was going to transfer to [Long-Term Acute Care Facility], [Thoracic Attending] was very hopeful.

CRITICAL CARE ATTENDING: I understand that. This is my specialty. I would've been more pessimistic.

SON: But if he could get to that point before, he can again, right?

CRITICAL CARE ATTENDING: It's unlikely, but yes, it's possible.

SON: Well, the pneumonia is not permanent, right?

CRITICAL CARE ATTENDING: Right.

SON: And the scarring is not permanent. Is anything permanent?

CRITICAL CARE ATTENDING: No, nothing is permanent per se. It's just that when you look at the big picture of what's going on, he has a lot of things working against him. . . . I don't mean to take away your hope. You need to have hope. But I also can't do anything to lessen your fears and anxiety about this. He is very, very sick.

In a second example of a negotiated prognosis, a different critical care attending physician tried to reframe the prognosis as more upbeat in order to encourage a family to reconsider or delay a decision to withdraw life support.

CRITICAL CARE ATTENDING: Two weeks probably isn't enough time. It probably will take more time to see improvement. But what if we thought she might improve in three months? We have every hope and expectation that she will recover in three months.

DAUGHTER NO. 1: Where would she go?

CRITICAL CARE ATTENDING: Either a nursing home or rehab, though probably a nursing home. You have to be able to do three hours of rehab to go to a rehab facility—that's a national policy. But she might start out in a nursing home and then go to rehab.

DAUGHTER NO. 1: But you said there are no guarantees.

DAUGHTER NO. 2: She can't go to a nursing home.

CRITICAL CARE ATTENDING: What if it was 99 percent certain that she would recover? Would that be acceptable?

DAUGHTER NO. 2: But you said there are no guarantees.

CRITICAL CARE ATTENDING: What prognosis could you live with?

DAUGHTER NO. 3: She's suffered too much already.

CRITICAL CARE ATTENDING: Her head is getting better, but, just like her head, it takes time for the rest of her to get better. It is necessary to give it time.

DAUGHTER NO. 2: Not if she has to go to a nursing home.

CRITICAL CARE ATTENDING: We have patients in which continued care is futile. But this case is not futile. We expect that she will improve.

The negotiation of prognosis may serve decision makers well if it adds methodological rigor, transparency, or nuance to the forecast or helps to reconcile mixed messages. When negotiation instead serves as a mechanism of denial or to lessen anxiety, the resulting forecast may undermine the decision-making process.

Finally, some physicians and family members simply disagree on how to characterize the end point. The physician and *New Yorker* staff writer Atul Gawande reprised a conversation with the son of an eighty-two-year-old patient who had a stroke during cardiac surgery. The son recounted, "I'm looking into his eyes and they're like stones. There's no life in his eyes. There's no recognition. He's like the living dead." He reported that his father eventually regained his ability to talk but made no sense, whereupon the surgeon told him, "We're going to put this in the win column." "I [the son] said, 'Are you fucking kidding me?'"[21]

What counts as a win so often goes undefined in encounters at the bedside. With so much unfamiliar medical jargon bandied about, it is easy to take for granted the meaning of seemingly commonplace language. For example, variations on the word "recover" were uttered more than 250 times in the observed encounters. Only once did a family member ask what a physician meant by the word.

CRITICAL CARE ATTENDING: I would say that for her to recover would be in the miracle range. Her prognosis is grave.
SON: Define recover. Do you mean return to her normal life?
CRITICAL CARE ATTENDING: To have a pretty full recovery, to resume her normal activities, yes.

On a handful of occasions, physicians clarified on their own that "recover" meant the ability to recognize, talk, or interact with family members. One offered what physicians consider a "good" outcome: "One in which the patient may need help dressing, bathing, wiping, or feeding himself—but he can talk and can interact." Not quite the return to "normal life" envisioned by the patient's son quoted above and undoubtedly by many others who authorized medical procedures because they might lead to the "recovery" of a loved one who would thereby return to practicing law or medicine, driving a bus, caring for a child, running a business, living independently, and so on. Little did they know that, at most, the patient might eventually talk or interact.

Accuracy

Because many physicians apparently believe in self-fulfilling prophecy, they fear that a downbeat prognosis that saps the patient's hope or willingness to fight will thereby harm the patient.[22] Such quasi-magical thinking is one explanation for the disinclination to prognosticate and for the excessive optimism—and therefore error—that plagues those who do. But in the ICU, where patients lack the capacity to understand downbeat forecasts and thereby give up hope, prophecies are less likely to be self-fulfilling. Although ICUs may be prone to pessimism,[23] their prophecies are undoubtedly more accurate than in other settings because physicians are freer to speak what they consider the truth without thereby upsetting or undermining the patient.

Because prognoses delivered in the ICU are often vague, equivocal, contingent, probabilistic, incremental, changeable, and conflicting, it is difficult to assess their accuracy. Some patients do better than the most positive forecast offered during their admission, and others do worse than the most negative prognosis. But many fall within the wide range of outcomes projected. And of course, since almost half of the decision makers ultimately authorize a do-not-resuscitate order or request that life support be withdrawn, there is no way of knowing whether these patients would have otherwise survived and with what kinds of disabilities.

Nonetheless, it is possible to compare prognoses about survival with outcomes for patients whose decision makers opted for aggressive treatment throughout their admission. (Prognoses about functional abilities cannot be evaluated with ICU data because they pertain to the patient's status long after discharge from the ICU.) Among patients who received only positive prognoses, none died in the ICU, half were discharged home or to a rehabilitation facility, and half went to a skilled nursing or long-term acute care facility. Among those receiving only equivocal fifty-fifty prognoses, none died in the ICU, 40 percent were discharged home or to rehab, and 60 percent went to nursing or long-term care. And among those receiving only negative prognoses, 38 percent died in the ICU, 15 percent went home or to rehab, and 46 percent were discharged to a nursing or long-term acute care facility. Six months after discharge, 67 percent of those with good prognoses, 40 percent of those with equivocal prognoses, and 31 percent of those with negative prognoses were still alive; their functional abilities are unknown. Painting with a broad brush, the prognoses predicted reasonably well; across the board, patients with better prognoses had better survival outcomes.

But there were some striking exceptions, especially with younger patients—what some would call miracles—which left hospital staff almost giddy when they received reports on former patients or when these patients returned to visit the ICU. The most dramatic case came up earlier in this chapter—the patient with a near zero likelihood of survival who was not expected to survive an hour, let alone the weekend. The patient was a twenty-one-year-old man, ejected from the car in a motor vehicle accident, who suffered a traumatic brain injury and developed life-threatening complications in the ICU. Two weeks after this devastating prognosis was offered, the patient woke up and began following commands. The critical care attending who had delivered the prognosis, no longer on rotation in the ICU, came racing to the unit to see for himself: "It's awesome; I'm amazed." A month after the prognosis, that physician was back on rotation in the ICU. He told his team that he was "stunned and blown away" by the patient's continued progress. "He is probably the sickest patient I have ever treated. It's a miracle. I never would have bet that he would get better. Just his kidneys alone should not have recovered." Less than seven weeks after the prognosis, the patient was transferred to rehab. His mother, with a mischievous smile that conveyed relief that her son's personality was returning along with his body, observed that her son still had a temper. A little more than ten weeks after the prognosis, the patient was back home, walking and talking and planning for his future.

A second "miracle" that astonished hospital staff concerned a thirty-four-year-old man who was shot in the head. Inoperable, the bullet remained lodged in his brain, migrating from side to side. A neurosurgery resident told his mother:

> In terms of his prognosis, I am not omniscient. We have no way of knowing for sure what will happen. But the chance of mortality is about 90 percent. Even if he doesn't die, he probably will not wake up. . . . If he were to wake up—which is very unlikely—he would require twenty-four-hour monitoring. He would not have any control of his bodily functions. He would not be the person he was.

Physicians conducted numerous meetings with the family to consider changing their goals of care for the hopeless patient, but his mother insisted on continued aggressive treatment. Six weeks after admission to the ICU, the patient was transferred to a skilled nursing facility. Four months after the shooting, the ICU social worker reported to the team that she had just spoken with the nursing home. The patient had woken up, walked out of the nursing home, and moved back in with his mother. Despite some visual challenges and limitations in short-term memory, the patient reportedly could dress himself and do his own cooking. Two weeks later we learned that he had been kicked off Medicare because he was no longer considered disabled enough. The story spread like wildfire. ICU staff shook their heads in stunned disbelief.

There were certainly other surprises, both good and bad. The prognostic "mistakes," though rare, evoke some disquiet about how much a decision maker should rely on prognostic forecasts—especially those about the brain—and how quickly life-ending decisions that rely on these projections should be made.

Prognostic Framing

A large body of work in psychology and behavioral economics examines the effects of how probabilistic information is framed on how judgments and decisions are made. For example, whether risks are presented as frequencies (1000 of every 10,000) or as percentages (10 percent) and whether they are presented absolutely (mortality is 5 percent vs. 10 percent) or relatively (mortality is reduced by half) is shown to affect responses, especially among those with less numeracy, but even among physicians.[24] Presentation of risks relatively or as frequencies tends to have more impact than their presentation as absolutes or percentages. Research also finds that we tend to overweight improbable outcomes and underweight those that are almost certain.[25]

The most-studied framing bias finds that people tend to respond differently when choices are presented as gains or as losses.[26] The typical example involves money. Daniel Kahneman asks:

> Which do you choose? (a) Get $900 for sure OR (b) 90 percent chance to get $1000.
> Which do you choose? (c) Lose $900 for sure OR (d) 90 percent chance to lose $1000.

Most people opt for (a) and (d); they are risk averse when probabilities were presented as gains and risk seeking when presented as losses. A classic example shows the same pattern when people are asked to choose between survival and death.[27] Numerous studies find that physicians and even statisticians sometimes succumb to such bias as well. They are more likely to gamble or take bigger risks when faced with loss or death. As Kahneman observed, "People who face very bad options take desperate gambles, accepting a probability of making things worse in exchange for a small hope of avoiding a large loss. . . . The thought of accepting the large sure loss is too painful, and the hope of complete relief too enticing, to make the sensible decision that it is time to cut one's losses."[28] Findings from these studies have been somewhat uneven and their designs subject to criticism, especially for drawing on hypothetical vignettes with little resemblance to real medical encounters. Still, their insight that alternative ways of framing prognostic information may lead to different medical decisions is compelling. Decision making is vulnerable to bias first in how physicians understand prognostic information themselves and then in how they convey it to those at the bedside. Do physicians pick a frame to encourage a desired response? Perhaps those with more numeracy and self-awareness do from time to time. But it was never apparent, nor did they talk with one another about this.

Whether prognosis is framed as risk of survival or of death, whether as a relative or absolute risk, whether as a frequency or percentage, those who receive the forecast may draw very different conclusions. Even where the likely outcome is objectively identical, some may embrace—even plead for—further treatment; others quit while they are "ahead," depending on prognostic framing. Many of the mixed messages about which ICU families complain may simply reflect how prognosis was framed rather than conflicting forecasts or their underlying data.

Conclusion

The psychological and behavioral economics literature that examines cognitive biases in decision making has uncovered many other sources of bias beyond the framing effects and impact bias reviewed here. They will be presented in later chapters that examine how surrogates make medical decisions. Insights about these biases shore up the conclusion evident in the data presented throughout this chapter that prognosis—however important in deciding the course of medical treatment on behalf of another—leaves much to be desired. Forecasts can be elusive, unavailable at critical decision points, vague, ill-defined, changeable, inconsistent, conflicting, inaccurate, pessimistic, misunderstood, manipulable, self-fulfilling, and also vulnerable to bias. And for each decision maker clamoring for more, better, or unequivocal prognostic information, others eschew any information at all or do so unless it is hopeful. Prognosis plays a critical role for some decisions and not for others.

SIX

Decision-Making Scripts

The patient is an eighty-two-year-old Catholic woman of color who had a massive ruptured brain aneurysm. She has a husband, six daughters, and a son. Neither the patient nor her husband is a native English-speaker, so the patient's daughters, some of whom have health care experience, generally spoke on her behalf. The patient's aneurysm was repaired surgically, but she remained in a coma. As her ICU stay dragged on and the patient developed kidney failure and other complications but showed no improvement in her brain functioning, the family requested last rites and began the wrenching process of talking about possibly removing life support. The neurosurgeons dismissed their concerns, indicating that they were premature and that the family needed to give it a few more days. In the meantime, they explained, it was necessary to insert a feeding tube and replace her breathing tube with a more permanent tracheostomy tube. The family refused and requested withdrawal of life support.

In an effort to buy some time, physicians asked for an ethics consultation. A member of the hospital ethics committee reviewed the patient's file and discovered a document naming a daughter power of attorney for property and financial matters. The ethics consultant informed the patient's physicians that this document was not valid for medical decision making. Moreover, the consultant explained, without a durable power of attorney for health care, decision making was subject to the Illinois Health Care Surrogate Act, which limits removal of life support only to patients who meet qualifying medical conditions. This patient did not, so her default surrogate decision maker was not permitted to authorize the withdrawal of life support. The family was informed of this unexpected development and went ballistic: "What do you want? You want her to lie there? You want her to suffer?" Having reached the point of demanding the unthinkable, they could not reverse course and sentence their wife and mother to a life of suffering.

Depending on your age, you can probably evoke indelible images of Karen Ann Quinlan, Nancy Cruzan, Terri Schiavo, or Jahi McMath. We know their names and faces because private family tragedies were transported to U.S. courts to resolve irreconcilable conflicts about medical decision making on behalf of these young women, who were unable to speak for themselves. Bodies of law and of bioethics have responded to the complex questions raised by these and countless other tragedies and provide guidance about patients' rights and about the responsibilities of and criteria to be followed by those who act on their behalf. Many Americans, even health care providers, are unaware of some or all of the legal guidance. Still, medical decision making in intensive care units as well as in community hospitals, nursing homes, and even private residences plays out in the shadow of these legal and ethical norms.

This chapter presents the official scripts for surrogate decision making enunciated in laws and court opinions as well as in bioethics treatises. It describes the challenges following these scripts—evidentiary, philosophical, biographical, cognitive, psychological, interpersonal, and empirical. The next chapter presents the real-world scripts that surrogates improvise and enact in the two intensive care units.

The Legal Script

In an assortment of cases that range from the doctrine of *parens patriae* to the nineteenth-century law of lunacy;[1] child custody; the removal of organs from, sterilization of, or forced medication of the incompetent; and especially the termination of life support and the right to die,[2] legislatures and courts have enunciated standards by which surrogates decide for others and evidentiary rules to guide their judgments. Surrogate decision making is grounded in constitutional rights of autonomy, self-determination, privacy, and bodily integrity.[3] These principles are reflected in the doctrine of informed consent and the right of competent patients to undertake or refuse medical treatment. These rights extend to incompetent patients as well, "on the premise that the right of self-determination in matters of medical treatment should not be lost or impaired when one is no longer able to personally exercise that right."[4] For example, the Illinois Health Care Surrogate Act states:

The legislature recognizes that all persons have a fundamental right to make decisions relating to their own medical treatment, including the right to forgo life-sustaining treatment. Lack of decisional capacity, alone, should not prevent decisions to forgo life-sustaining treatment from being made on behalf of persons who lack decisional capacity and have no known applicable living will or power of attorney for health care.[5]

This statement about decisions being made on behalf of patients without capacity is expressed in the passive voice. The question, of course, is how is this right exercised when patients are unable to do so? This is where law often steps in.

Because state and federal constitutions, statutes, court decisions, regulations, and policies secure and specify these rights of self-determination, legal scripts for surrogate decision makers vary somewhat from state to state in the United States.[6] Although the procedures and forms may look different, state statutes permit individuals to prepare advance directives—living wills or instructional directives that specify treatment preferences and durable powers of attorney or proxy directives that appoint a health care agent should they lose capacity in the future. A number of states also authorize Physician Orders for Life-Sustaining Treatment (POLST or other acronyms that vary from state to state), which are portable medical orders for specific interventions prepared by health care providers for frail or seriously ill patients about whom providers "would not be surprised if they died in the next year."[7] Illinois, the site of the research, did not adopt POLST until after the conclusion of the study.

Most states have default surrogate consent statutes that specify who should make health care decisions when incapacitated patients have not appointed a health care agent or medical power of attorney.[8] As described in chapter 3, most of these states specify a priority list—usually beginning with a spouse or guardian and followed by an adult child, parent, adult sibling, and so on, sometimes including close friends as well—that dictates who may act as surrogate decision maker;[9] a few states instead require a consensus of interested persons. Many state statutes also dictate how to resolve disagreements among surrogates of equal priority. As illustrated by the example that opened this chapter, about a quarter of the states—including Illinois—also place limitations on decision making by these default surrogates, most often permitting them to forgo life-sustaining treatment only if the patient meets a narrow set of qualifying medical conditions (usually terminal illness or permanent unconsciousness)—limits that do not apply to patient-appointed agents. And almost all states specify decision-making standards that agents and/or surrogates should follow.[10] Laws in Illinois have all of these elements.

State decision-making standards usually specify a hierarchy of criteria that decision makers—agents, surrogates, or proxies, labels that vary from state to state and which I use interchangeably[11]—should follow, privileging patient self-determination over patient welfare or other interests. The patient's explicit directions, verbally or especially specified in advance-directive documents, usually top the hierarchy.[12] Where patients have provided no explicit instructions or their directions do not exactly apply, legal norms dictate that surrogates should engage in "substituted judgment," choosing as the patients would choose, if competent and aware of all the relevant facts and circumstances, including the fact that they are not competent. It is as if patients were to awaken miraculously from a coma or attain lucidity for a few moments, knowing that they will soon lapse back into their former state.[13] Surrogates are instructed to stand in the patients' shoes[14]—taking account of prior statements, actions, instructions, personal value systems, character, goals, religious and moral beliefs, fears, attitudes, and lifestyle—to try to replicate what patients would have wanted. Still giving voice to patient autonomy, when actual wishes are unknown, these substituted judgments infer probable wishes.

Where even probable wishes are unknown, contradictory, or cannot be inferred, legal rules call for a "best-interest" standard—to advance the patients' interests, promote their well-being, and choose, after weighing the benefits and burdens, a course of action with the greatest net benefit. In some formulations, a best-interest standard reflects what a "reasonable person" would choose under the circumstances.[15] In either case, best interests are considered objective or generic, evaluating, for example, not what the specific patient might find burdensome, but what a typical or reasonable patient would. The best-interest standard straddles the bottom of the hierarchy of decision criteria because, when surrogates are unable to give voice to patients' subjective preferences, it gives priority to patient welfare over autonomy.

Surrogates draw on varied sources in reprising, reconstructing, replicating, or inferring patient wishes, some of which are more accurate, credible, or reliable than others. In evaluating these sources, courts and commentators have asked about the patients' statement being reprised—how specific it was; how unequivocal it was; how spontaneous or deliberate it was; how consistent it was; in what context it was made; to whom it was made; whether it was a statement made about the patients themselves or about someone else; how casual or offhanded it was; how sincere it was; whether there are reasons to discount or disbelieve the statement; how often they made it and over what period of time; how recently they made it; whether their views have changed over time; whether their statements are consistent with their behavior; how many different sources of independent evidence are available; how directly the evidence bears on the decision to be made on the patients' behalf; how great the inferential leap is; and whether most of their significant others made the same inference about the evidence. As one can imagine, evidence of patient wishes available to surrogates falls short on many of these criteria.

Some state courts therefore specify not only the standards that surrogates should use to make medical decisions for another, but the strength of the evidence necessary to draw these conclusions as well. Among those courts that address this issue, many demand the highest evidentiary standard in civil law, requiring "clear and convincing evidence." The clear-and-convincing-evidence standard falls between the requirement in criminal cases that a defendant must be guilty "beyond a reasonable doubt" and the lesser requirement in most civil cases of a "preponderance of the evidence," that the claim is more probably (e.g., more than 50 percent) true than not. Evidence that is clear and convincing is highly or substantially more probable to be true than untrue.

Evidentiary Challenges

Even when surrogates struggle through patients' convoluted biographies to discern their true preferences, it is unlikely that these ruminations will reach the bar set by the clear-and-convincing-evidence standard.[16] Some patients leave rather vague legacies of ambivalence, meaningless or imprecise words, mixed, ambiguous, or contradictory messages, and silences that can be interpreted in disparate ways by different interpreters with unique relationships and histories with the patients and with different interests. As Bart Collopy eloquently observes:

> [A]lthough discussions might, in theory, promise an instructional lode for proxies, they often produce a blurring web of conditionals and subjunctives. Patients tell proxies what they would want or not want, *if* they were to face certain treatment options, *if* their physical and mental condition were such and such, *if* their prognosis was of this or that sort, or *if* the potential benefits and burdens were at some or other balance. All of this may be spun out in a mix of suppositions and projections into the future, scenarios sewn together from patients' own limited experience, from reliable infor-

mation and hearsay, from careful calculation and gambles about what will or will not happen, from apprehension and doubt and the specters of the patient's worst fears. The resulting evidence available to a proxy may run a wide gamut: preferences quite settled and certain, choices still "in process"; glimpses of a patient exploring, thinking through possibilities, creating scenarios; or the more perplexing stuff of a patient grown tentative, muddled, or even stymied.[17]

Fortunately, few surrogate decisions end up in court (where these evidentiary standards have been articulated in a handful of states); evaluation of such standards rarely arises at the bedside. Nonetheless, except where the most abundant, direct, specific, consistent, compelling, triangulated, and unwavering evidence is available, the law is asking surrogates to choose among various versions of the patient, to reconstruct an identity from ambiguous and fragmentary pieces, to decide whether the priorities and values the patient treasured as a young or middle-aged adult trump those expressed in the past year or maybe only the past few weeks.

Indeed, the law is asking others to do that of which competent patients may be incapable. Is it even possible for patients to know how they would decide before they faced the situation and experienced the many changes that led up to it?[18] Surveys that ask adults about treatment preferences across a number of medical scenarios find that 12 percent of respondents say they don't know their preference in *any* of the scenarios, and 18–46 percent of the remaining respondents don't know about a particular scenario.[19] If would-be *patients* cannot make a substituted judgment for their future selves, how can they expect someone else to make it on even more slender evidence? And how can patients expect their surrogates to do it while in shock, at the most painful moment in their lives, often with the clock ticking?

Surrogates making substituted judgments encounter many additional challenges. For one, they face a moving target: patients change their minds all the time. Ezekiel and Linda Emanuel observe that "there are few, and conflicting data, to suggest that a patient's preferences are durable and thus that views expressed at one point in time reflect the patient's true wishes months or years in the future."[20] Their preferences—about spending or saving money, taking risks, need for independence, tolerance of limitations or impairment,[21] what gives them pleasure, whom they trust or love, what they value, their religiosity or faith, and so on—change, especially as they age, experience illness or disability, or approach death.[22] Some decision makers may interpret these changes as consequences of impairment or of

undue influence rather than legitimate shifts in patient values and preferences and therefore refuse to honor them. Indeed, patients may themselves
fail to appreciate in advance how impairments that undermine their competence may simultaneously alter other judgments and preferences.[23]

Numerous studies document the substantial instability of patient preferences over time, even over short periods of time.[24] Across all these studies
and all sorts of patients, researchers find that end-of-life treatment preferences change, on average, between 20 and 40 percent over relatively short
periods of time (anywhere from twelve hours to four months).[25] And 80
percent of these patients are not even aware that their preferences have
changed.

Moreover, who is the patient whose preferences must be replicated?
Where does one look for substituted judgments when patients' minds are
literally changed?[26] When illness and injury to the brain transform or alter
identity, whose autonomy and interests are to be honored: the person before the onset of disease or injury, or the person after?[27] The legal scholar
Rebecca Dresser argues that competent and incompetent patients may well
have profoundly conflicting interests. Why, she asks, "should a patient who
is now a different person be burdened by a treatment decision consistent
with the former person's preferences? Compelling justification is lacking
for according greater respect to the wishes of the earlier person (no longer
in existence) than to the interests of the existing one."[28] The substituted-
judgment standard, she therefore asserts, is actually a "past preferences
principle." But, if one is convinced that surrogates should articulate the
"present preferences" of the incapacitated patients for whom they now
speak, how do they identify these preferences?

These challenges in getting substituted judgment right are borne out
in empirical research. Remember *The Newlywed Game,* an American television game show in which recently married couples were asked often em-
barrassing questions to see how well they knew one another? (The couple
whose answers most corresponded might win a washer and dryer or an
exotic trip.) Modeled after the game show, a large body of research presents
hypothetical medical scenarios to potential patients and their potential
surrogates to see how well the latter predict the treatment preferences of
the former.[29] Other studies focus not on specific wishes or treatment preferences, but on general goals of care or preferences about the process by
which patients want end-of-life decisions to be made.

Without going into great detail, the results of dozens of studies suggest
that some of the assumptions underlying the use of substituted judgment
may be illusory. A meta-analysis of 16 of these studies (encompassing 151

scenarios and 2595 patient/surrogate pairs) found that, overall, surrogates accurately predicted patient preferences 68 percent of the time, varying somewhat by the type of health problem or medical intervention offered in the scenario.[30] Indeed, in several studies, surrogates did no better than chance (and occasionally did worse). Some studies even shared the patient's written treatment preferences with the surrogate and/or invited conversation on end-of-life issues between patient and surrogate before they completed the questionnaire—typically to no effect.[31] Nor did the surrogates named by subjects as their preferred decision maker do any better than others enlisted to play the surrogate role. Moreover, neither frequency of contact, similarity in age or gender, nor type of relationship affected the accuracy of surrogate predictions.

Studies also found substantial discrepancies between subjects and surrogates in their assessment of the subjects' satisfaction and quality of life. They also found that spouses and children tend to underestimate the subjects' functional status. Both these assessments are essential to the surrogate's ability to make either substituted or best-interest judgments.

Even *Newlywed Game*–type studies of hospitalized or critically ill patients or those facing life-limiting diseases and their actual surrogates regarding preferences for treatments that these patients have or will likely face yield only slightly better predictions.[32] Not only are the predictions often wrong, but surrogates also get patient preferences about how they want decisions made wrong.[33] Studies also find differences between these medically vulnerable patients and surrogates in their perceptions of the patients' health or their quality of life—for example, in their willingness to give up months of life in their current state of health for a shorter life in excellent health (what researchers call "time trade-off scores").[34] Many surrogates also got wrong patients' willingness to live in a nursing home. Although they were reasonably accurate predicting those patients who indicated that they were unwilling to live in a nursing home, they correctly predicted only 37 percent of those patients willing to do so. Among patients who indicated that they were very willing to live permanently in a nursing home, surrogates said that 14 percent would rather die.[35] Adding insult to injury, despite their errors in predicting patient preferences, surrogates tend to be confident in their ability to make end-of-life decisions on behalf of their loved ones.[36]

Most of these studies conclude that the disparities between preferences and predictions cast doubt on the capacity of surrogates to reproduce substituted judgments. As one overview of the empirical evidence observed, ". . . the imaginative capacity required for accurate prediction of a patient's wishes may be beyond most people."[37] Another concluded that surrogate decision making—"far from having scientific accuracy and objectivity—in most cases represents a complicated form of guesswork, suffused by the decision maker's biases."[38]

Of course, *Newlywed Game* research designs are a far cry from real-world end-of-life decision making. Unlike the participants in these games, surrogates rarely formulate substituted judgments alone, but rather consult with various friends and significant others, whose input might provide richer insights about the patient's likely preferences and collectively yield more accurate substituted judgments. Moreover, dispassionate paper-and-pencil answers from usually young, healthy research subjects to hypothetical questions without life-and-death consequences reported over the course of a few minutes about scenarios few have ever faced provide a limited test of the capacity of surrogates to render substituted judgments.[39] Indeed, in these studies, would-be patients are undoubtedly guessing about their future preferences just as much as their would-be surrogates. And if as many as half of respondents don't know their own treatment preference for a particular scenario, about what is their would-be surrogate guessing? There must be an actual patient judgment that substituted judgments are trying to replicate.

Some bioethicists and philosophers would be untroubled by these empirical findings: they reject the notion that the task of a proxy is merely to follow "a straightforward process of gathering evidence of the patient's preferences and values and then mechanically translating these preferences and values into treatment decisions."[40] Rather, choosing a proxy is an act of trust,[41] and the role of the proxy is not to reproduce instructions about life's end—which cannot be set out in advance—but to continue "the life stories of those who have lost narrative capacity."[42] For these bioethicists, substituted judgment is not second-best to adherence to actual wishes, but an imaginative narrative ideal to which decision makers should aspire.[43]

Cognitive Scripts

Substituted judgment is much more than a parlor game. There are many additional reasons surrogates get the "wrong" answers, reasons that illuminate the complex medical, cognitive, psychological, normative, interpersonal, epistemological, and social-organizational contexts in which end-of-life decisions are made. As the social psychologist Angela Fagerlin and her colleagues observe, "Because substituted judgment is inherently a matter of interpersonal perception, it is troubling that policy development guiding end-of-life decision making has proceeded uninformed by basic social psychological research on judgmental bias and accuracy."[44]

Evidence of framing effects, presented in the last chapter, represents one insight from such research in social and cognitive psychology. Recall that the way prognostic information is framed affects how decision makers proceed. Presentation of risks relatively or as frequencies tends to have more impact than as absolutes or percentages. Or, as illustrated in the last chapter, research suggests that we tend to be risk averse toward gains and risk seeking with regard to losses. As a result, when things are bad (or framed as bad)—as they often are in an intensive care unit—people tend to take "desperate gambles, accepting a high probability of making things worse in exchange for a small hope of avoiding a large loss."[45] A second psychological process considered in the last chapter—impact bias or affective forecasting—suggests that people tend to overestimate the long-term impact of negative events such as impairment or disability.

Much of the work on the social science of judgment and decision making focuses on "simplifying shortcuts of intuitive thinking,"[46] otherwise known as heuristics. As Daniel Kahneman explains, "When faced with a difficult question, we often answer an easier one, usually without noticing the substitution."[47] Although these shortcuts often lead to efficient, appropriate solutions, some are vulnerable to systematic errors, known as heuristic or cognitive biases. This literature is vast; just that on medical decision making by physicians, patients, and surrogates consists of thousands of articles and hundreds of empirical studies exploring dozens of potential biases.[48] Like the framing and other effects, heuristic biases that go unrecognized may distort substituted judgments or lead to decisions that actually undermine rather than serve patient autonomy.

Illustrations of a few heuristic biases salient to medical decision making provide a sense—by no means exhaustive—of how surrogates may be unwittingly swayed by their intuitive shortcuts. The "false consensus effect" observes that we tend to overestimate the extent to which others share our beliefs, opinions, and choices. Surrogates therefore may project their own choices onto the patient, erroneously assuming that the treatments they would want for themselves mirror those that the patient would want.[49]

A number of heuristics pertain to the ordering or ease with which options are presented or come to mind. For example, the "availability" bias asserts that we overweight phenomena—whether more recent or memorable—that come easily to mind. Even physicians appeared vulnerable to this bias, as they reflected on a recent loss or miracle in another patient while formulating a course of action for a current patient.

Other heuristic biases suggest why surrogates may grasp at hopeful straws. For example, we tend to underestimate the likelihood of highly probable events (e.g., death or significant disability) and overestimate that of less probable events (e.g., a full recovery). "Optimism" bias suggests that we believe that we are at less risk of experiencing a negative outcome than other people, or what some call the "Lake Wobegon effect" (referring to the fictional radio town where all the children are above average).[50]

"Omission" bias reflects our preference for inaction and the status quo. We consider harms of commission worse or more blameworthy than those of omission. One hears in the ICU such comments as, "We hope God takes him tonight so that we don't have to decide." We regret our actions more than inactions. This insight might help understand how difficult it may be for surrogates to change course or to authorize the cessation or withdrawal of treatment. "Sunk-cost" effects reflect our disinclination to stop a course of action once a substantial investment has been made—yet another reason, perhaps, that it is difficult for surrogates to change course, even when it has become hopeless.

These and countless other heuristics that I have not described cut in different ways. Some will cause surrogates to overreact, others to decide uncritically, still others to feel reluctant to rock the boat. Many will goad surrogates to embrace aggressive interventions long after they are likely to be effective, others to eschew them even when they offer realistic hope. And all of this happens out of the consciousness of the struggling surrogate.

Because these heuristics are usually invisible, I cannot point to a particular conversation as indicative of a given bias. But as you take in the examples of surrogate decision making in the next chapter and observe responses that appear unexpected, irrational, or counterproductive or see health care providers trying to reframe the thinking of loved ones at the bedside, be mindful that heuristics may be at work.

Of course, competent patients are undoubtedly subject to many of the same heuristic biases as their surrogate decision makers (though probably not projection). And so are health care providers who inform and counsel decision makers through the lens of their own heuristic shortcuts and biases. Cognitive psychology exposes that much is going on under the surface as decision makers struggle with their unenviable task. It draws a picture of the surrogate as a marionette, unaware of the strings pulled by their own psyches or cognitive shortcuts that may influence their perceptions of the wishes or best interests of as well as the decisions they make on behalf of the incapacitated patient.

Conflicts of Interest

As if constructing substituted judgments or formulating the best interests of another was not formidable enough, surrogates must proceed encumbered by weighty baggage imposed by the interests of themselves and others.[51] Perhaps the greatest irony of relationships of trust (of which serving as a surrogate is a prime example) is that the most able and desirable trustees—who offer familiarity and intimacy, caring and commitment, esoteric knowledge, inside information, expertise, hands-on experience, and political, financial, and social capital—are also the least likely to be disinterested.[52] They may face challenges in putting the patients' interests ahead of their own. Those who can best serve another also have the most reason to betray them.

When intimates serve as surrogates, their interests are inevitably entangled with those of the patient, and they therefore have the most to gain or lose by discretionary decisions they make on the patient's behalf.[53] This tug-of-war is most palpable when family members serve as surrogates. The compelling case for entrusting them with this profound responsibility, especially with making substituted judgments, reverberates from presidential commissions to court opinions to empirical data. Nancy Rhoden summarizes the argument:

[B]ecause of the nature of the family as an association, its members are in the best position to reproduce the preferences of an incompetent patient. Numerous courts and commentators have emphasized that family members are best qualified to make these decisions, because of their knowledge of the patient's likely preferences and their special bonds with the patient. Not only are family members most likely to be privy to any relevant statements that patients have made on the topics of treatment or its termination, but they also have longstanding knowledge of the patient's character traits. Although evidence of character traits may seem inconclusive to third parties, closely related persons may, quite legitimately, "just know" what the patient would want in a way that transcends purely logical evidence. Longstanding knowledge, love, and intimacy make family members the best candidates for implementing the patient's probable wishes and upholding her values. Family members also care most. . . . Moreover, no patient is an island. The family is the context within which a person first develops her powers of autonomous choice, and the values she brings to these choices spring from, and are intertwined with, the family's values. A parent may understand a child's values because she helped to form them, a child may grasp a parent's values because the parent imparted them to her, and a couple may have developed and refined their views in tandem. Whereas an objective third party will view the patient purely in isolation, a close family member will view the patient as a son, or father, or spouse. If an incompetent patient has lost her actual power of self-determination, it makes sense, when trying to identify the choice the patient would make if she could, to defer to the family as one of the groups from which the patient's former power to make rational choices arose.[54]

But these virtues also make it difficult for family members, however well-meaning, to distinguish or separate their interests from those of the patient. One finds in the literature a litany of reasons that loved ones may defy the patient's wish for heroic treatment—because they suffer as the patient does (perhaps even more so if the patient is comatose or unaware of his mental incapacity or undignified treatment) and because of the extraordinary emotional burden, disruption in their lives, and caregiving responsibilities the patient has imposed on them, all of which may be relieved by his death; some may even do so out of anger or because they dislike the patient. Other relatives may insist on aggressive, heroic, or futile treatments to keep the patient alive—out of guilt, fear of being responsible for his death, fear of loss and concomitant feelings of attachment or love, the relative's "own fear of dying, or a religious view that life must be prolonged at all cost, . . . a perverse satisfaction in seeing the patient suffer,"[55] even compensation from a lawsuit that is typically greater when the patient is alive than dead.[56] And, of course, financial interests frequently roil family systems. Expensive custodial and medical care may be imposing substantial financial burdens on loved ones. Other families may be luckier but mindful that decisions on the patient's behalf may drain or deplete the inheritances they expect down the road,[57] bequests to which they may feel especially entitled as compensation for all of this wrenching surrogacy the patient has put them through. And even when surrogates have silenced their own self-interest, their obligations to other family members (the patient's children, for example) may force them to choose between the interests of the patient and others. Surrogates may not even be aware of how their own interests and those of others are distorting their judgments.[58]

Ironically, after all this angst from trying to reproduce the patients' wishes and to do so disinterestedly, it turns out that many patients do not care if their surrogates do so or even prefer that they do not; nor do many seem troubled by these conflicts of interest. Some patients do not want to be an emotional burden to others, don't want health care expenses to bankrupt the family, and don't want their loved ones to become their nursemaids, saddled with caregiving responsibilities. And, perhaps echoing the bioethicists described earlier, other patients believe that their loved ones can better respond to the nuances of treatment decisions in real time than would following their abstract wishes expressed weeks or even decades earlier; they are untroubled or even grateful if surrogates ignore their prior wishes.[59] And still other patients are at best ambivalent about exercising their autonomy in the first place.[60]

A diverse collection of studies has found that, when asked, a substantial number of patients indicate that they feel the wishes or needs of their surrogates or other family members ought to trump their own. A large study of critically ill hospitalized patients found that 78 percent of them indicated that, if they were to lose decision-making capacity, they preferred that their family and physician make resuscitation decisions rather than that their own previously stated preferences be followed.[61] Two other studies found that around half of respondents felt that their surrogates should have "a lot [of]" or "complete" leeway to override their advance directives; a third study found that more than half of the respondents wanted the preferences of their surrogates to apply, even when the surrogates had expressed preferences that were the opposite of their own.[62] Of course, since few patients document their desire to give loved ones such decision-making leeway, substituted judgments must also incorporate these sentiments—though they may be no easier for surrogates to identify than treatment preferences themselves. Nor will it be easy to distinguish between surrogates acting out of their own self-interest and those who claim they do so because the patient wanted them to.

This concern expressed by some patients about the impact of medical decisions on their surrogates and other loved ones is echoed by some bioethicists. The most extreme argument comes from the philosopher John Hardwig:

> Our present individualistic medical ethics is isolating and destructive. For by implicitly suggesting that patients make "their own" treatment decisions on a self-regarding basis and supporting those who do so, such an ethics encourages each of us to see our lives as simply our own. . . . To be part of a family is to be morally required to make decisions on the basis of thinking about what is best for all concerned, not simply what is best for yourself.[63]

Hardwig goes so far as to propose that substituted judgment should apply only when "the treatment decision will affect only the patient, or . . .

when the patient's judgment would have duly reflected the interests of others whose lives will be affected. In other situations, proxy deciders should make decisions that may be at odds with the known wishes of a formerly competent patient." He concedes, though, that "it is presently illegal to make proxy decisions in the way I think is morally appropriate."[64]

Although Hardwig (as well as others who share his perspective) reflects a minority view, his argument brings us full circle to the concept of autonomy that animates legal scripts about surrogate decision making. In contrast with legal norms of self-determination, Hardwig asserts that autonomy comes with moral responsibilities toward others, and he appears ready to snatch it away from those unwilling to factor in the needs of others. Even scholars who reject Hardwig's normative position concede that autonomy and self-determination for many patients is not about accurately identifying and implementing their wishes, but rather about the right to give discretion to those they trust.[65] For them, all these *Newlywed Game* scenarios are beside the point. Surrogate decision makers—whether consciously or unwittingly—undoubtedly land somewhere between these two extremes. In any case, their decision-making process proves difficult to script.

Law at the Bedside

As required by the federal Patient Self-Determination Act of 1990, when patients are admitted to most American hospitals, the patients or the persons who accompany them are asked whether they have or whether the patient would like to complete an advance directive—a power of attorney for health care and/or a living will. For the majority of patients in the two ICUs in the study, as for most Americans, the answer to both questions is "no." As noted in chapter 3, about a third of all the patients who passed through the two ICUs or their spokespersons reported an advance directive or completed one during hospitalization. Despite continual prodding of family members by ICU staff to bring in copies of these reported directives, few ever appear in the patient's chart; in some cases it is not clear that they exist. Only one in ten of the patients have any documentation in their medical records of their wishes or of their legally designated medical decision maker.[66] Even fewer of these documents are ever reviewed by any of the physicians treating the patient. Indeed, some do not know where the documents are located.

In short, the majority of the incapacitated ICU patients were served by default surrogate decision makers. Chapter 3 described the challenges of navigating the legal hierarchical order from which the default surrogate is selected, especially for fractured, blended, or unconventional nuclear families. Some patients arrive at the hospital unbefriended or as a Jane or (usually) John Doe.[67] Others arrive with a "spouse" who later turns out to be an unmarried partner (ranked far down the hierarchy), a soon-to-be-ex-spouse, a cognitively challenged spouse, or an abusive spouse (who may in fact be responsible for the patient's injuries). Certain members of the family may be difficult to locate or unwilling to take on the responsibility. Sometimes a relative will appear days or even weeks into the admission and reveal that the wrong person has been making decisions all along. And many patients have multiple family members sharing the same rung on the hierarchy, though little else, as they jockey for position and clash over what is in the patient's best interest. Although on rare occasions social workers or even police officers will be enlisted to sort out the tangle, the responsibility usually falls on doctors and nurses who lack adequate training, time, or interest to conduct extensive forensic genealogical investigations to identify the proper default surrogate.

The legally specified priority order of default surrogate decision makers will select poorly for some patients—and with potentially disastrous consequences. Perhaps for this reason, as noted earlier, some states, such as Illinois, limit the authority bestowed on these default surrogate decision makers, whom patients did not themselves select. Because the majority of decision makers in the ICU study are default surrogates and many patients do not meet the qualifying conditions (in Illinois, terminal illness and imminent death or permanent unconsciousness) that permit forgoing life-sustaining treatment, these legal limitations have potentially profound implications. This was demonstrated in the account that opened this chapter of the eighty-two-year-old patient whose family was not permitted to authorize the removal of life support when someone from the ethics committee discovered that she did not have a proper health care power-of-attorney document. Although similar medical scenarios—in which default surrogates request that life support be withdrawn—occur repeatedly in the two ICUs, I only encountered one other instance in which such a decision was refused when a physician observed that the patient had not appointed a legal power of attorney for health care and did not meet the qualifying conditions of the Illinois Health Care Surrogate Act (in this case as well, only because a member of the ethics committee was involved and flagged the problem).

The potential havoc wreaked on the ICU by surrogacy laws for patients who did not name a power of attorney is rarely realized because health care providers are not always cognizant of the legal requirements or of the legal status of the patient's surrogate. Recall that few medical records contain copies of advance directives and that physicians do not always consult these records. Many health care providers conceptually understand the difference between a power of attorney and a default surrogate, but few seem to know whether the person from whom they are seeking consent for a procedure or discussing a DNR order or transfer to palliative care is one or the other. Sometimes the patient has named a power of attorney, but physicians assume that it is the next of kin (with whom they consult and to whom they defer), never realizing that it is actually the patient's friend or lover. Often physicians' conversations, written notes, and even medical orders refer to the default surrogate simply as the "power of attorney" or even just "POA"—a generic linguistic shorthand that confers on the decision maker enormous legal power and discretion that a more accurate label would not.

Moreover, few physicians show any awareness that Illinois law dictates that default surrogate decision makers and powers of attorney face a different menu of options and medical decisions. On a couple of occasions, I observed an attending physician, who had been burned by cases like the one that opened the chapter, review the legal rules for their team. I attended a grand rounds on this very subject—with dozens of physicians in attendance. And yet the subject rarely comes up. Conversations between medical staff or with families do not refer to the qualifying conditions or to the legal requirements that must be met before life support can be withdrawn; physicians did so for not even 2 percent of the patients in the study. Generally, if a family requests the withdrawal of life support, physicians comply, whether or not the appropriate legal document exists. Among ICU patients who were the least severely ill and therefore the least likely to meet the qualifying conditions of imminent death or permanent unconsciousness, the percentage of surrogates who withdrew life support was the same for patients with and without powers of attorney.

The hospital houses a complex network of specialists—nurses, social workers, chaplains, the ethics committee, the department of risk management, and the hospital legal counsel's office—responsible for implementing or responding to legal and other regulations regarding medical decision making when patients are unable to speak for themselves. However, because physicians are intrinsically involved in making surrogate medical decisions, they are the most important figures in implementing legal rules that govern who can make the decisions, about which medical interventions, under what conditions, with what criteria. It is a daunting responsibility for actors untrained in law and often unfamiliar with the legal requirements, some still struggling to learn medicine, who participate in the making and unmaking of dozens of decisions a day, often under tight time constraints in emergency situations, with individuals who may be hundreds of miles away, asleep, in shock, inaccessible, or unable to understand English or medical jargon.

Moreover, there are few incentives to comply with the legal rules, even if more physicians knew them and knew that it was their responsibility to ensure compliance with them. Indeed, there may be disincentives when compliance makes getting consents for treatment more protracted or difficult and provokes anger and pain in patient families when the enforcement of legal rules constrains the decisions they can make for their loved one (as it did for the family whose story opened this chapter).

Law casts an uneven shadow over the ICUs. On the one hand, one finds bursts of activity, day after day, by nurses, chaplains, and social workers to document patient wishes and the legal status of their surrogate decision maker. On the other hand, one finds a dearth of physicians who consult these records or even know where to look for them, know the difference between a power of attorney and a default surrogate or why the distinction matters, know the legal status of their patients' decision makers, or discuss treatment options in light of the appropriate legal rules.

The next two chapters will review the role of health care providers in counseling families about decision-making criteria. Here they seemingly play a more active role in disseminating the legal and bioethics norms about patient autonomy and best interest that were reprised at the beginning of this chapter. However, it is not clear whether they are sharing these norms (or even aware of them) or simply articulating their own common-sense notions of fidelity to their patients.

Conclusion

In this chapter I have, with a few exceptions, ignored the extensive and insightful legal, bioethical, and philosophical literature that critiques or seeks to modify the legal scripts surrounding surrogate medical decision making. I do so because my purpose is to see whether or how the official dialogue is reproduced or modified at the bedside, guiding, empowering, enriching, constraining, confusing, undermining, or proving irrelevant to the scripts that real-world surrogates draft as they speak on behalf of their loved ones. I now turn to these voices and will return to the policies in the last chapter.

SEVEN

Improvisation: Decisions in the Real World

WIFE: Last night they asked me if I would want them to zap him or put him on
the ventilator. What kind of ventilator were they talking about?
CRITICAL CARE FELLOW: The one he's on now.
WIFE: That? You mean some people wouldn't let their loved ones live for just
that?
CRITICAL CARE FELLOW: Yes, well, your loved one's injury was very acute. Some
patients have had long-term problems and they choose not to continue.
WIFE: But why wouldn't they just let them go on the ventilator so they can
breathe?
CRITICAL CARE FELLOW: Sometimes it's against the patient's religious beliefs.
WIFE: That's amazing. I can't believe someone could do that. Hey, did you guys
hear that?

The legal and bioethical scripts described in chapter 6 are hard to find
in the intensive care unit. In more than two years of observation in the
two ICUs, neither my colleague nor I ever heard the words "substituted
judgment," let alone "autonomy" or "self-determination." Because "best
interest" is part of our everyday lexicon, we did hear this expression, and
we often observed efforts to stand in the patient's shoes. Although participants in bedside conversations occasionally described or asked how the
speaker knew about the patient's wishes, never did these conversations
consider the more nuanced evidentiary standards weighed in court opinions. We observed the spirit if not the letter of the law in action—usually
because it accorded with commonsense notions of fidelity or empathy,
and occasionally because a physician knew the rules. But often, neither
the spirit nor the letter of the law played out at the bedside; rather, surrogates fashioned decision-making standards drawing on their own interests,

fears, suspicions, experiences, religious beliefs, or worldview. Some formulated standards at the instigation of or in collaboration with health care providers, others in opposition to them. As the wife, in disbelief, quoted above suggests, different criteria lead to very different decisions and outcomes.

Decision making in the two ICUs followed one or more of seven trajectories.

1 The Patient Should Decide
2 Reprising Patient Instructions
3 Standing in the Patient's Shoes
4 Beneficence
5 It's God's Decision
6 What We Want
7 Denial, Opting Out[1]

Some surrogates followed a single trajectory; some navigated several simultaneously; and others traversed different trajectories serially, as physicians, loved ones, or developments at the bedside persuaded them to change course. This chapter describes these real-world decision-making trajectories and how they were constructed. The next chapter will show which surrogates traversed the trajectories and the outcomes of their decisions.

1. The Patient Should Decide

Patients in the study lacked decision-making capacity for some—if not all—of their ICU admission. Nonetheless, whether in order to respect their autonomy or to avoid difficult decisions or responsibility for them, surrogates and even some physicians felt that the patients themselves should or would make medical decisions. This preference for patient input had several manifestations. Some surrogates—and occasionally some physicians as well—delayed decisions in the hope or expectation that patients would regain capacity in the future and could make the decision themselves or at least provide some guidance. This waiting game was rarely successful. Some delays closed the window on potentially promising treatment options or provided an opening for new complications to develop, worsening prognosis or exacerbating pain and suffering. Numerous encounters involved desperate negotiations between families pleading for more time and physicians insisting that further delay would irreparably harm their patients.

CRITICAL CARE RESIDENT: She's doing significantly worse. I wanted to talk to you about what you think she would want at this point, if she would want us to keep poking her and treating her aggressively.

DAUGHTER: I am not going to make this decision for her. It's just not fair to her. It's her life. If that's what she wants, that's fine. But she has to say that. We'll wait until she is awake to express her wishes.

CRITICAL CARE RESIDENT: I'm just concerned that she's not going to be able to wake up enough for that to happen.

. . .

DAUGHTER: I've seen her like this; you haven't. She opens her eyes for a minute or two at a time. She's just tired now. I think she's going to wake up and be able to express herself. We can wait a few days and see.

PALLIATIVE CARE ATTENDING: I just hope she's not uncomfortable.

CRITICAL CARE RESIDENT: She's significantly worse now. She hasn't asked for pain medications since yesterday. That's very uncommon; usually she asks for them frequently.

DAUGHTER: We're going to wait until she wakes up and tells us. I've told you this and you keep coming and asking again. I'm not angry, but I'm very annoyed, because I keep having to repeat this. Last time, crystal clear: We know she's at the end of life. She knows that too. I am going to wait until she wakes up so she can make her own decision. I'm not going to make it for her. It's her decision. We're going to do everything to sustain her until she makes a decision. My father is aware of the situation and he agrees with doing everything for her. So we'll wait until she wakes up and tells us what she wants. I don't see any problem with waiting a few days. It just gives her more of a chance.

PALLIATIVE CARE ATTENDING: Hopefully we can keep her comfortable until then.

MOTHER: I wasn't aware until you just said all those things that that's where we were at. We were hoping that she would wake up enough that we could communicate with her. I thought that there was a chance that that would happen. Is that a fair response?

CRITICAL CARE ATTENDING: Yes. I mean, it's your response— But I don't think she will ever come off the ventilator. And I don't know that she will ever wake up enough to communicate in any way. We may not ever be able to take off enough sedation that she can wake up without being in so much pain that we need to put the medications back on. I can't see into the future, so I can't know for sure. But that's what I think.

Some of these patients died while surrogates insistently waited for them to regain capacity; for others, surrogates eventually shifted to an alternative decision-making strategy.

Other families and physicians tried to include compromised patients in the decision-making process.

DAUGHTER: He's been talking. He said good-bye and all those good things. He said that he will get to see his mother and father in heaven. We all got to say our good-byes. It's a beautiful thing. [*She seems almost happy.*]

CRITICAL CARE RESIDENT: He's been talking?

DAUGHTER: Oh yes. As recently as ten minutes ago. He started out by saying that he hopes he goes tonight.

CRITICAL CARE RESIDENT: I thought we were going to withdraw care—

SON NO. 2: Not before. But we made our peace tonight.

. . .

SON NO. 1: We don't want to be selfish. But he told us. He helped us make the decision.

Occasionally, this involved discussions with conversant patients suffering from some dementia or cognitive impairment. Even if not capable of true informed consent regarding complex, nuanced treatment options, these patients might be queried about whom they most trust as a decision maker, asked whether they assent to a treatment decision, or invited into conversation about their general preferences or goals. For example, a fifty-five-year-old patient had a genetic disease that resulted in widely metastasized cancer, especially in his brain, and had undergone numerous brain surgeries. As the patient's wife was preparing for hospice, the neurosurgeon proposed another surgery. Previous surgeries and therapies had left the patient somewhat confused, but he could understand simple concepts. His wife didn't want to decide on the surgery without conferring with her husband.

WIFE: This is your decision.

PATIENT: I have lost a lot of brain cells in recent years.

WIFE: You started out with a lot. You are still smarter than a lot of people I know.

SISTER: The other surgeries have been in the back of your head, but this one will be in the front and might be noticeable.

PATIENT: I don't care. I have a little bald spot. I can get a hairpiece. I'd like to live a little longer, if you still want me around.

WIFE: We want you around if you are not in pain and suffering. I don't want to watch you in pain. You know that you won't be able to drive a car and you won't be able to work in the business. You'll have to let [names a man] run the business. But you can spend time with us. I would like the two doctors, the neurosurgeon and the oncologist, to get together and talk this through before we make the decision.

The next day, a nurse reported that the patient had been crying in bed. "Do whatever you can to buy me some extra time. I don't care if it's another week, month, or year." Four days later the patient had the surgical intervention. For some patients, physicians first ordered a psychiatric consult to determine whether they had capacity for some decisions but not others, or whether their refusal of a particular treatment or decision to "fire" their power of attorney should be honored.

The decision-making capacity of most ICU patients was compromised not by dementia but rather by loss of consciousness, sedation, or inability to speak because of neurological impairments or because they were on a ventilator. For some of these patients, physicians and families endeavored to facilitate communication, sometimes briefly arousing them from heavy sedation. They tried to elicit written responses (rarely successful), hand squeezing in response to questions, or eye blinking as health care staff pointed to letters on an alphabet board or in response to yes-or-no questions. A lip-reader was summoned for one patient desperately mouthing words over the ventilator; unfortunately, the patient kept falling asleep during the sessions and never did get her message out. These improvised facilitated conversations, though perhaps better than nothing, fell far short of informed consent. Two examples, one from each ICU, are especially troubling and poignant.

A seventy-six-year-old patient in the neurological ICU was "locked in" from a devastating stroke. She retained her full cognitive capacity but was completely paralyzed, capable only of blinking her eyes. The patient was heavily sedated because her attending physician felt it was the only humane thing to do (given how terrified he assumed she must be). Physicians questioned her family about whether the patient would want to remain locked in, kept alive by a ventilator and feeding tube indefinitely, or would want the ventilator removed and comfort care administered, whereupon she would die. Everyone (except for her husband, who said he didn't want to lose his wife) felt that the patient would opt for the latter. However, physicians wanted to hear from the patient. Her sedation was stopped and, over the course of three hours, the patient had several "conversations" with neurologists, critical care, and palliative care physicians who explained her prognosis and peppered her with questions to which she was told to blink once for yes and twice for no. They determined that the patient had decision-making capacity and understood her prognosis and treatment options.

Although the patient consistently responded that she wanted to die, I was struck by the questions she was not asked, but might well have wanted to opine on, had she the ability to speak on her own: Do you want more time to think about this? Do you want us to give you more information about the experience of other patients who were locked in? Would you like a brief trial of what it's like to be locked in before you decide? Do you want to spend some time with your family before you die or before you make this decision? Would you like a therapist to help you to communicate some final words with your family or a chaplain to pray with you? A few hours after their last conversation with the patient, physicians removed the patient's ventilator and withdrew life support. She died three days later.

The second example was described earlier in the discussion of informed consent in chapter 4. Recall the case of a twenty-one-year-old woman in the medical ICU with end-stage cancer. Sedated and on a ventilator, physicians turned to her family to advise about whether the patient would want a tracheostomy and discharge to a long-term acute care facility, where she would be housed until she died relatively soon or would want to remove the ventilator and die at the hospital with her family by her side. Over the course of several long meetings, every family member tearfully and unequivocally responded that the patient would not want a trach. But physicians wanted to hear from the patient. They lowered her sedation, and the physicians and family encircled her bed to question whether she wanted the tube down her throat replaced by a tube in her neck. Like the previous example from the neurological ICU, what was striking was what was not addressed. The questioning did not discuss an alternative to the trach, did not let on that this was really a question about goals of care, and did not provide any prognostic information, including the fact that the patient would die soon in either case. Woozy from the sedation and unable to speak, the patient assented to the trach with a slight nod of her head, stunning everyone in the room (who had opined earlier that she would make an entirely different choice). Nonetheless, the patient's mother subsequently announced in Spanish that they "will do what she wants" and the patient received a trach. She died a week later.

In both of these cases, as well as many others, physicians were unsure over the course of treatment whether or not the patient had some capacity for decision making or eventually would. So they hedged their bets, questioning family members as well as patients and sometimes asking loved ones whether the patient's response rang true. As in the second example, sometimes their answers did not correspond. Although physicians and family followed the direction of the young cancer patient in the last example, in other cases loved ones refused to allow them to do so. Recall the scenario that opened the book in which a patient who was experiencing difficulty breathing in the middle of the night agreed to be intubated. The next morning his family was livid, his wife ordering physicians to "just pull the damn plug!" In another case, a manipulative and domineering son, learning that his mother had requested a trach, insisted that she be questioned again in his presence.

CRITICAL CARE RESIDENT: We are trying to extubate her and we may succeed in a few days. We have been giving her breathing trials, but she tires out. But even if she passes her breathing trial, we are concerned that she will eventually not be able to continue breathing on her own and once again she will need to be reintubated. As her medical team, it is in our best interest that we consider what is the best interest for the patient. That's why we have recommended that she get a trach. We talked to your mother about a trach and she said that she wanted one. But she cares a lot about what her children think and so we wanted to have this conversation with you as well.
CRITICAL CARE RESIDENT: [*To Patient*] We want to know whether you still want a trach. It is okay to say "yes" or "no" or even "in between." Here is the letter board. Point to what you want.
PATIENT: [*Clearly intimidated by her son, points to "in between."*]

The patient's son then argued against the trach that his mother had previously authorized.

On many other occasions, physicians insisted that information the surrogate had elicited from the patient at the bedside was not reliable and that the surrogate had the responsibility to decide independently.

CRITICAL CARE ATTENDING: Do you think he wants a trach?
WIFE: He was more alert this morning. He opened his eyes. I asked him if he was in pain and he said yes. I asked him if he wanted a trach and he said he would think about it.
CRITICAL CARE ATTENDING: Unfortunately, I think this is a decision you have to make. We can't assess his mental status. But he can't handle complex

information. I can barely explain all the medical information to you. Asking him does not meet the requirements of informed consent.

Other family members asserted that the unresponsive patient's body would send them a signal or was telling them or would tell them what to do. Reflexes or random movements were deemed purposeful. Body language indicated that the patient's spirit had departed. Recall from chapter 5 the brother's insistence that rapid eye movements meant that his sister wanted to keep fighting.

DAUGHTER: What my father enjoys is fighting adversity.
SON: If he didn't want to fight this, it would be over. He will show us what we should do. We are not going to do this forever. But we want to give it more time. Give it time for him to show us.

SON: She has stopped eating. Maybe she is telling me something. The first time she got a G-tube [feeding tube], she was at a different nursing home. She wasn't eating enough, so they put in the tube. A little later she started eating like a horse. She ate everything they gave her. I even brought food into the nursing home and she ate all of that. Then, about a year ago, she stopped eating again and they put in another G-tube. I was hoping that she would start eating again like last time. But she hasn't. She hasn't been able to do much. She couldn't talk, but she used to understand. She used to laugh at funny things on TV and she would laugh at my jokes. She doesn't laugh any more.

WIFE: When he seems combative, I wonder whether perhaps he is angry at me for bringing him here.

Finally, some decision makers assumed that the nonresponsive patient would nonetheless make the decision.

NIECE: My uncle has a strong will. I really believe that this will be his choice. He will make the choice whether he breathes over the ventilator or not.

CRITICAL CARE ATTENDING: We are currently giving him the most aggressive treatment, not only what is available, but even things that are still only in clinical trials and published in medical journals. We do this and can do this and are happy to continue the aggressive care. We just want to make sure that we are all on the same page. That's why we wanted this meeting.

MOTHER: Unless there is something you are not telling us, I think ten days is too soon. He has a very strong spirit, even if he can't use it now because of the medications. He will show us what he wants.

In this rationale, surrogates request full aggressive treatment and the patient will then "decide" whether or not to survive. Physicians sometimes make similar arguments.

CRITICAL CARE RESIDENT: Well, if she continues to worsen, I think that's her body telling us she's had enough.

CRITICAL CARE FELLOW: Maybe he senses how hard this is on you and his body is letting go.

2. Reprising Patient Instructions

When the patient cannot decide, physicians and family members often try to determine how the patient would likely decide. As noted in the last chapter, the express directions of the patient—written or verbal—top the hierarchy of surrogate decision-making standards privileged by the law in most states. Though usually unaware of the legal standards, some surrogates and health care providers often begin along this trajectory, reprising the patient's instructions, sometimes made decades earlier.

Written Instructions

A minority of patients had prepared written instructions, either in advance directives—living wills and durable powers of attorney for health care[2]—or on their driver's license (regarding organ donation). Advance-directive documents will look somewhat different in each state; those in Illinois are fairly typical. Illinois boilerplate living wills state:

> If at any time I should have an incurable and irreversible injury, disease, or illness judged to be a terminal condition by my attending physician who has personally examined me and has determined that my death is imminent except for death delaying procedures, I direct that such procedures which would only prolong the dying process be withheld or withdrawn, and that I be permitted to die naturally with only the administration of medication, sustenance, or the performance of any medical procedure deemed necessary by my attending physician to provide me with comfort care.

Five percent of patients in the study had such a living will in their hospital record. Boilerplate Illinois power-of-attorney forms, which name the patient's legal decision maker, include three optional checkboxes. They include:[3]

> I do not want my life to be prolonged nor do I want life-sustaining treatment to be provided or continued if my agent believes the burdens of the treatment outweigh the expected benefits. I want my agent to consider the relief of suffering, the expense involved and the quality as well as the possible extension of my life in making decisions concerning life-sustaining treatment.

> I want my life to be prolonged and I want life-sustaining treatment to be provided or continued unless I am in a coma which my attending physician believes to be irreversible, in accordance with reasonable medical standards at the time of reference. If and when I have suffered irreversible coma, I want life-sustaining treatment to be withheld or discontinued.

> I want my life to be prolonged to the greatest extent possible without regard to my condition, the chances I have for recovery or the cost of the procedures.

Thirteen percent of patients in the study checked the first box, 2 percent the second, 1 percent the third, and 3 percent named a power of attorney but checked none of the optional boxes about their treatment preferences.[4] Another quarter of patients or their families claimed to have an advance directive but never provided a copy of it. As noted earlier, other research finds that many of these reported directives do not exist.[5] In any case, there is no way to determine what instructions, if any, these alleged documents provided.

About half of the patients whose directives were available for examination supplemented boilerplate language in their advance directives with additional instructions. Most often, they stated that they did (5 percent of all patients) or did not (2 percent) want to donate organs or addressed nutrition and hydration (3 percent) or functional or mental capacity (2 percent). Even fewer wrote about quality of life or eschewed specific procedures or heroic measures. Over the course of observation of conversations about organ donation, I learned that another six patients (3 percent) without advance directives had registered with the state as organ donors. Undoubtedly other ICU patients had as well, but because they were not facing death or were not candidates for organ donation, no one checked on or disclosed their documented donor status.

In short, only about one in four ICU patients left any sort of written instructions to which their surrogates had access regarding medical decision making. But even those few surrogates fortunate enough to have written instructions often found that they offered little guidance. Most instructions gave them considerable discretion with little direction about how to exercise it (first optional checkbox on the power-of-attorney form) or referred to situations (imminent death, irreversible coma) that didn't apply.

NEUROLOGY FELLOW: She is having another episode requiring chest compressions. There's blood coming out of her trach. The chest compressions are very aggressive. It's up to you as her family, but my recommendation would be to just have them stop doing the compressions and stop trying to resuscitate her. It's a very painful process, and the chances that she would have any neurological functioning after a third cardiac arrest and resuscitation are very low.

SISTER-IN-LAW: [*In tears*] Just let her go!

HUSBAND: It's all on the paper. It's out of my control. Look, I don't want her to suffer any more than anyone in this room. [*He shoves the advance-directive form in front of the neurology fellow.*] You're the doctor. Just read it. You're the doctor, you figure it out. Is she gonna be brain-dead?

NEUROLOGY FELLOW: I can't tell you—

HUSBAND: Read it!!

NEUROLOGY FELLOW: [*Glances at the form and then puts his hand on the husband's arm.*] I read it, and I'm very familiar with these forms. Unfortunately they're very obscure in practice. They rarely translate well to actual situations. I can't definitively say whether she will be in a coma. She has brain-stem functioning, so she's not brain-dead. Brain death only occurs when there is no brain-stem functioning even. She could have brain functioning but be in a persistent vegetative state. I can't give you any numbers, but I would say that if her heart stops again, the chance of her having any neurological functioning would be next to zero. I think the important thing to think about is this: If she were able to sit here with us and understand what was happening to her, do you think that she would want this?

[*Husband doesn't answer.*]

Despite the neurology fellow's disdain for these written directives, compounded by the fact that few physicians bother to look for or read them, physicians occasionally summarize or even read from the patient's written directives, sometimes advising on the treatment that followed from their instructions.

NEUROLOGY ATTENDING: The stroke has now developed what we call hemorrhagic conversion. There is more bleeding in the brain. It is swelling in the brain and putting pressure on the brain. As I described yesterday, there is a surgical option. They can remove the skull and put a drain in his brain to relieve the pressure.

[Daughters and son-in-law are gritting their teeth or subtly shaking their heads "no."]

NEUROLOGY ATTENDING: We read his living will yesterday. This is exactly what he said he didn't want.

CRITICAL CARE FELLOW: Whenever possible, we like to discuss goals of care with patients themselves. But unfortunately your loved one is not in a position to discuss that with us. I was looking over her chart, though, and I found her living will. We were reviewing it earlier as a team. As her family, you make the decisions on her behalf. But this document is a way for her to express herself, since she is not able to right now. It says:

"My dying shall not be artificially prolonged under the circumstances set forth below, and I declare: If at any time my attending physician certifies in writing that: (1) I have an incurable injury, disease, or illness; (2) my death will occur within a short time; and (3) the use of life-prolonging procedures would serve only to artificially prolong the dying process, I direct that such procedures be withheld or withdrawn, and that I be permitted to die naturally with only the performance or provision of any medical procedure or medication necessary to provide me with comfort care or to alleviate pain, and if I have so indicated below, the provision of artificially supplied nutrition and hydration."

Now, sometimes these documents can be pretty obscure. But I think this one is actually pretty clear.

HUSBAND: We have a lawyer friend who came over and went through this with her. It's what her wishes were. I think it's very clear.

CRITICAL CARE FELLOW: Yes. So as for the three criteria, her cancer is not curable. I don't know when she would otherwise die from it, but the oncologists have determined that it is not treatable. And now with the septic shock on top of that, the chances are very low that she would survive. I believe she would die very quickly if we were to withdraw support. And she is on artificial life support—the ventilator and the blood-pressure medications.

And, on at least one occasion, a physician misinterpreted the instructions as he pressed family members to follow them.

CRITICAL CARE RESIDENT: Is your mother going to be in today?

DAUGHTER: No, she's not. She's eighty-nine years old, so it's really hard for her to get around.

CRITICAL CARE RESIDENT: I understand. I wanted to talk to her about his code status. When he was admitted, she'd said that he has a living will. I've seen it in the computer and it says he doesn't want to be intubated, so basically no resuscitation. She said she wanted to honor his wishes. But then apparently yesterday she said she wanted him to be full code.

. . .

DAUGHTER: . . . I know she wants him to be full code.

CRITICAL CARE RESIDENT: Well, it's not about what she wants. She is his power of attorney, so she makes the decision. But the decision is supposed to be made based on what her perception is of what *he* would want.

DAUGHTER: I think that's what he would want too.

CRITICAL CARE RESIDENT: Well, here's where it gets tricky. He has this living will that says he would not want to be intubated.

DAUGHTER: Well, when is that from?

CRITICAL CARE RESIDENT: I don't know; I'd have to look it up.

DAUGHTER: Because if it's from before that last time when he was intubated three or four years ago, then maybe he didn't realize that it could be something that he could recover from. Maybe he feels differently about it, but just never changed it.

CRITICAL CARE RESIDENT: Here, I'll look it up. But the reason we have these documents is so that, if we're ever in a situation where we can't speak for ourselves, it's straightforward and you can just look to the document. That's why it's really important to update it.

DAUGHTER: Well, maybe he meant that if he were intubated but it was hopeless, then he would want to be taken off the machine.

CRITICAL CARE RESIDENT: That's not what he said in the living will, though.

DAUGHTER: It seems like it would be vague.

CRITICAL CARE RESIDENT: It's actually very clear-cut. I'll show you. But I don't think, based on the box he checked, that there's room for interpretation. . . . Okay, I have the living will here. It's dated October 9, 1999. I'll read you what he wrote: "No limitations. I do not want my life to be prolonged nor do I want life-sustaining treatment to be provided or continued if my agent believes the burdens of the treatment outweigh the expected benefits. I want my agent to consider the relief of suffering, the expense involved, and the quality as well as possible extension of my life in making decisions concerning life-sustaining treatment." The other options are: "I want my life to be prolonged and I want life-sustaining treatment to be provided or continued unless I am in a coma which my attending physician believes to be irreversible in accordance with reasonable medical standards at the time of reference. If and when I have suffered irreversible coma, I want life-sustaining treatment to be withheld or discontinued."

DAUGHTER: Yeah, that's definitely what he would have wanted.

CRITICAL CARE RESIDENT: But that's not the box he checked. He checked the one saying he doesn't want any lifesaving measures.

Disturbingly, the critical care resident in this example apparently considered only the first few words of the directive, unaware that treatment should be withheld or discontinued *only* if the surrogate deemed the burdens of treatment outweighed the benefits—a subjective judgment the resident was not qualified to make.

Family members occasionally described the patient's written directives as well.

HUSBAND: I don't want to think about withdrawing care or any of that until I have to.

PALLIATIVE CARE FELLOW: We're not there yet.

HUSBAND: Well, that's good.

PALLIATIVE CARE FELLOW: And hopefully we won't get there.

HUSBAND: That would be even better. Her mother had a special paragraph added to her living will saying that she did not want to be on a ventilator or any machines. My wife had that same paragraph added to her living will.

PALLIATIVE CARE FELLOW: So she would not want to be on machines if there was no hope for recovery?

HUSBAND: Right.

PALLIATIVE CARE FELLOW: Well, I think we're not at that point yet.

Roughly equal proportions of physicians and family members initiated discussions of treatment preferences specified in written directives. But it is striking how rarely they did so. For only a third of patients with written directives in the hospital chart did anyone—health care provider or family member—mention, describe, or even ask about the patient's written wishes or instructions; this was true of only 11 percent of those claiming to have a written directive elsewhere. Moreover, when written directives were mentioned, they came up only after discussion of the patient's expressed verbal wishes or inferences of what they would likely be; this was true of all but one patient. The directive was more a coda than a leading melody. And of course, reprising a directive is not the same thing as honoring it or using it to formulate a treatment decision. In short, evidence of the significance of written instructions in the formulation of surrogate decisions is surprisingly limited.

This is less true of decisions—however infrequent—around organ donation.

MOTHER: He would want this. His driver's license was just renewed last fall, so this is recent. We know that this is what he would have wanted.

Surrogates invoked the patient's driver's license in considering organ donation more often than they consulted written directives when deliberating on other medical interventions. Of course, it is often easier to retrieve driver's licenses than advance directives. And, perhaps because the instructions on a donor card are so straightforward, surrogates honored them more often than they did the abstract, inapplicable, or equivocal instructions in advance directives.

Although written directives were decisive on rare occasions, surrogates usually disregarded them for a number of reasons. Many had never read them; others had forgotten exactly what they said; and many documents were unavailable (or nonexistent) for a quick review. Moreover, as noted earlier, most boilerplate documents provide little guidance about the patients' wishes or how to interpret their preferred decision-making criteria under the circumstances at hand.

Verbal Instructions

Initiated by physicians and family members in roughly equal proportions, the patient's verbal instructions were more likely to be reprised than their written ones. Most often physicians initiated discussion of patient instructions by asking family members about them. But on occasion, when physicians had preexisting relationships with patients or had spoken with them before they lost capacity, they reprised the patient's wishes themselves.

ONCOLOGY ATTENDING: For what it's worth, I spoke to him in Greek about what his wishes were. He was giving mixed signals in English to the house staff, but he told me he wanted everything done.

CRITICAL CARE ATTENDING: If he didn't want to be on machines or anything, I would say it's time to quit. But that's not what he said; he told us to go ahead and try to make him better. He definitely has a good chance of getting better.

Then again, if I said you have a 30 percent chance of dying, it's not a position you want to be in.

DAUGHTER: I just hope I'm making the right choice.
PRIMARY CARE PHYSICIAN: You absolutely are. There's no doubt in my mind.
DAUGHTER: Thanks, I really needed to hear that.
PRIMARY CARE PHYSICIAN: And she made it very clear to me, many times. Believe me. [*Laughs.*]
DAUGHTER: I'm glad she told you, because she didn't tell me.

Far more often, family members weighed in with their loved one's wishes, reporting preferences or instructions that the patient had previously expressed to them, some in recent weeks and others decades earlier:

He said that he did not want to be intubated and on a ventilator; he did not want a feeding tube; he did not want any surgical interventions; he did not want CPR.

Well, he told me, "Do everything you can to keep me alive."

She said, "Don't do to me what you did to your mother."

She told me that as long as she's a viable person, she will keep fighting, but once she's not a viable person, she doesn't want any extreme measures taken. . . . But what does that mean? I don't know.

She felt that if she were unresponsive or in a persistent vegetative state or any other state, she did not want to be kept alive by artificial means.

My husband told me often and very seriously that he would not want his death prolonged if he couldn't function.

As in the first example, some left instructions about specific medical procedures (usually eschewing them). As in the second and third examples, others expressed unconditional preferences about goals of care. The remaining quotes reprise instructions that goals of care be conditional, usually on prognosis, functional status, or quality of life. And a few surrogates reprised specific promises that they had made with the patients.

DAUGHTER: We made promises to her too—about quality of life, about life support.

WIFE: He never wanted to be on a respirator. We made that agreement years ago.

HUSBAND: [Patient's] mother had a stroke that really wiped her out. Then she had another one. She had a living will that said that she did not want to be on artificial life support. So [Patient] took her off the machines and she died. [*Husband gets choked up.*] [Patient] made me promise to do the same for her. So I need to know if this is something she can come out of. Because if it's not, I need to take her off all the machines.

As these examples demonstrate, some expressed instructions are considerably more specific or amenable to operationalization than others. What does it mean to be "viable" (the patient's mother didn't know)?[6] Does "functioning" mean the ability to work full-time, to prepare one's taxes, to drive, to dress oneself, to have a meaningful conversation, to watch TV? Should the surrogate who recounted his wife's reaction to his decision making on behalf of his mother refuse the treatments he authorized for his mother for every medical problem his wife now faces, even for a minor or reversible one? What about heroic treatments that were not offered to his mother but recommended for his wife?

Moreover, medical jargon and technological options rarely correspond with the understandings of laypersons.

ETHICS ATTENDING: You see here, your mother checked this box that says that she wants to have aggressive care unless she is in an irreversible coma.
SON: Yes. I never really read the form. That's what she is now.
ETHICS ATTENDING: Unfortunately, a coma is a medical term with a very precise meaning. . . . Your mother is not in a coma. She may experience some cognitive limitations—severe cognitive limitations—but they are not a coma, and not an irreversible coma. This hospital has a strict policy that if this box is checked, we have to provide aggressive care, even if that's not what the patient would have wanted or even told their family.

As a result, a patient's seemingly specific instructions often turn out to be imprecise. One example comes from the daughter and her two brothers whose conflict was recounted in chapter 4.

CRITICAL CARE RESIDENT: So, the issue right now is whether to give her a feeding tube.

SON NO. 1: We know that she did not want a feeding tube. She said that and there were witnesses.

DAUGHTER: Where would the feeding tube go? I was told that there's a risk of aspiration with the feeding tube.

CRITICAL CARE RESIDENT: Yes, there is. And so instead of that kind, we would give her what we call a Dobhoff tube, which goes past the stomach, through the sphincter and into the intestine. That way there's less of a risk for aspiration.

DAUGHTER: Does that go through the nose also?

CRITICAL CARE RESIDENT: Yes.

SON NO. 1: But we know that she didn't want a feeding tube.

DAUGHTER: But we don't know what she meant by that.

SON NO. 1: Right, we don't know if she meant here [*points to his nose*] or just here [*points to his stomach*].

DAUGHTER: [Primary Care Physician] said that the kind through the nose isn't real invasive.

SON NO. 1: He said he didn't think that she wanted any feeding tube.

DAUGHTER: Are you sure? That's not what [Son No. 2] thought she meant. I'll have to check with him; maybe he didn't understand the difference.

Or the instructions do not apply.

FRIEND: He told me that he didn't want to be in a vegetative state.

NEUROLOGY ATTENDING: He probably won't be in a vegetative state. He may even be awake. But he won't be independent. He may not speak. He may not understand.

Or family members may believe that circumstances are now so different that the patient's original instructions may no longer be appropriate.

CRITICAL CARE RESIDENT: Have you discussed advance directives with your father?

DAUGHTER: Yes, we have. My sister and I are both his powers of attorney.

CRITICAL CARE RESIDENT: . . . If his heart were to stop, we would do chest compressions and might have to shock his heart—so CPR basically—to try to bring him back. I'm not sure that we'd be able to bring him back. And if we could, there might be significant damage to his heart and brain.

DAUGHTER: Do you know he has a defibrillator?

CRITICAL CARE RESIDENT: Yes, I'm aware. If you were to choose not to have us resuscitate him, then we would go ahead and turn off the defibrillator. Do you know what he would have wanted in this situation?

DAUGHTER: Well, when we talked about it, I think he couldn't have imagined being this sick. He wanted to live before. But he's so sick now. I just don't know if there would be any quality of life for him. I'll talk to my sister; we'll have to discuss it.

And a few surrogates were dismissive of patient instructions, especially those expressed before they lost capacity, claiming that the patient was depressed, fearful, confused, or manipulated by physicians. (Undoubtedly, some felt this way because the patient's instructions didn't square with the surrogates' own hopes for the patient.)

But even when the recollection and retelling of the patient's instructions is powerful and unequivocal, fidelity to the patient's wishes may still be problematic. Take the following conversation, which brought a physician to tears.

MOTHER: I don't have a choice. This is what [Patient] wanted. [Patient] told his doctor, [Oncology Attending], he said, "Mama, I do not want DNR."

CRITICAL CARE FELLOW: I do not want to what?

MOTHER: Do Not Resuscitate, or whatever. Do not Do Not Resuscitate. Well, he didn't say it that way, but he said he wanted to be resuscitated. I wish that I could do it differently, but that's what [Patient] wanted.

FATHER: I know you probably think we don't care about him.

CRITICAL CARE FELLOW: No, I absolutely think you do.

CRITICAL CARE RESIDENT: Of course.

FATHER: I've heard the comment, "How could you?" And that hurts so much. This is what [Patient] wanted. He was insistent. He said it in front of [Oncology Attending] and his mother. [Patient] is very strong-willed.

CRITICAL CARE RESIDENT: Absolutely. Most people would not be able to survive this.

FATHER: He decided exactly what he wanted, where he wanted his funeral and everything. We have to do everything we can to honor his wishes, as hard as that may be. So the question is not, how could we? The question is, how could we not? I can't be in the room; I have to walk out every time I hear the machine beeping when his blood pressure drops. I can't watch it happen. It's so hard. When I see him— [gets choked up and begins sobbing]

MOTHER: We were talking to [Oncology Attending], and he was telling [Patient] that it's so painful to go through, and he should just be DNR. [Patient] said, "Mama, we talked about this. I want everything done." I wish that at this point we could just take him off the machines. But I would feel guilty for the rest of my life if I didn't carry out his wishes. I don't have a choice. I need to follow his wishes to let him keep his dignity. We understand. We really do. We know what's happening. And you know that. But this is what he wanted, and so I will fight tooth and nail to do everything I can for him, because that is what he wanted. I don't want to talk about any of this again. I just want to go back and be with [Patient].

CRITICAL CARE FELLOW: I'm so glad you had those conversations with him. That's so important. We will do everything we can for [Patient]. I totally understand where you're coming from now; that's why these conversations are so important. You are some of the most caring, most loving parents I have seen in my whole life. It really pains my heart [*starts to cry a little*].

CRITICAL CARE RESIDENT: We will give [Patient] the most aggressive care we can. We will do everything.

The patient died the next day after four unsuccessful rounds of resuscitation, as fiercely demanded by his parents. However, medical records written before the patient lost capacity and was transferred to the ICU suggest that he may only have wanted aggressive treatment if his cancer prognosis was good. They also indicate that the patient had multiple conversations with the oncology chaplain about pressure he was feeling from his mother to keep pursuing aggressive treatment. Although he undoubtedly expressed the wish to be resuscitated, one wonders whether he had succumbed to his mother's pressure. Perhaps some of the instructions that patients express are not authentic, but rather result from familial pressure or a desire to please or protect loved ones whom patients feel they have caused so much pain. The case also reminds us that instructions are often conditional on good prognoses and require reassessment when things go south.

Many patients left no instructions—general or specific—or refused to talk with their loved ones about their end-of-life wishes. Where expressed statements were never made or provide insufficient or inappropriate guidance, as they often do, some participants turned to other ways of bringing the patient's wishes into the conversation. And others, as we will see, jumped right over the third trajectory to pursue alternative decision-making criteria.

3. Standing in the Patient's Shoes

As described in chapter 6, when patients leave no written or verbal instructions about their medical treatment preferences, legal rules in most states dictate that surrogates should exercise substituted judgment, standing in the patient's shoes and deciding as the patient would decide if he or she were aware of all of the relevant facts and circumstances. Although, as noted earlier, the words "substituted judgment" were never uttered during the two-plus years we observed in the two ICUs, a least a superficial version of substituted judgment was common, offered for many of the same patients for whom written or verbal expressed instructions were also reprised, though often without offering sufficient guidance.

About half the time, these inferences about the patient's likely wishes were elicited by physicians.

NEUROSURGERY RESIDENT: The patient had a very large hematoma [mass of blood] in the dominant side of his brain. We opted for maximum therapy. We surgically removed most of the hematoma, removed the skull so that his brain would have room to expand, and put in a drain to monitor his brain and to remove fluid if that became necessary. When the patient came into the hospital, there was some evidence of slight herniation—in other words, the brain tissue was pressing on his brain stem. There has been slight damage to his brain stem, but it is basically intact. But he has no cognitive functions above the brain stem. He has no executive functions, for example, to understand language—

SON: To communicate?

NEUROSURGERY RESIDENT: To communicate. This is especially difficult in a high-functioning person like him. Normally, within a week's time, you will see some improvement at this point. For example, patients will try to push away a noxious stimulus—what we call localizing to pain—but he is only withdrawing to pain. He is showing very primitive responses. But after a week, he is virtually unchanged. Unfortunately, we see this often. This is the worst part of this kind of medicine.

WIFE: So what comes next?

NEUROSURGERY RESIDENT: From our perspective, the next step is to determine what the patient's wishes would be under these circumstances. That is step 1, step 2, step 3, step 5, step 20.

NEUROLOGY ATTENDING: I think the important thing to consider is his quality of life. He will never walk, never talk, won't watch TV, won't go to a football game. He will have no quality of life. It's not what you want. It's not what I want. It's not what someone else wants. We have to do what he would want. It's as if we woke him up, he sat up in bed, and we asked him, [Patient], what quality of life do you want?

PALLIATIVE CARE ATTENDING: The most important thing is what she would want, not what you would do for yourselves. This would be based on her past decisions that she's made in her life, or perhaps on comments she's made about others who may have been in a similar situation. Maybe she said, I would definitely not want that, or, if that happens to me, then go for it. These kinds of conversations are very important in helping you determine what it is she would want.

SOCIAL WORKER: Being a power of attorney is a heavy responsibility. You are speaking for him. You need to determine what he would want. Remember, you told me about the kind of person that he was—that he was very stubborn. Think about what he would want.

Families responded to these questions and, just as often, stepped into the patient's shoes on their own initiative without prodding by health care staff. Drawing on more general or related statements the patient made in the past, prior experiences, or the patient's values, they described the criteria they used to make inferences about what they imagined the patient would want under the circumstances. Some family members explained why they thought that the patient would want to continue aggressive treatment.

BROTHER: She has always been really independent, and she is definitely a fighter. Everyone who knows her agrees. . . . Here, this is the best way I can explain it. Who do you look up to in your life? Who do you really admire? . . . Well, let me tell you who she most admired: Christopher Reeve [actor who played Superman and was subsequently paralyzed after being thrown from a horse]. . . . She admired Christopher Reeve because he went from having fame, wealth, everything, to nothing. And he continued despite losing his functioning. I hope that helps you understand. That's what really reassured me that this is what she would want.

DAUGHTER: I mean, yesterday I guess someone had told him he'd had a heart attack, and he said to me, "Well can't they just put a stent in, like they did to John?" So to me, I think that would mean he wants to be saved.
WIFE: . . . Yeah, I agree. He said something to me about getting a stent too. So I think he wants us to do everything we can for him.

BROTHER-IN-LAW: He's got a fifteen-year-old son, too.
SISTER: That's why he would want all this.
BROTHER: He lives for his son.

Others described why they thought that the patient would want to change goals of care from aggressive interventions to comfort care.

BROTHER: She is a very active person. She is always doing something. She takes care of her appearance. Always wears makeup. Always fixes her hair. She wouldn't want this.

DAUGHTER: My mother is very vain about her intellect and very upset about the losses she has experienced. She won't accept this.

DAUGHTER: I know he wouldn't want this. He doesn't even like being in bed.

Inferences sometimes drew on features of the patient's personality or other values.

DAUGHTER: I think you ought to know that he is a fighter. His town was taken over by the Nazis. Then he served in the American army during the war. . . . What my father enjoys is fighting adversity.

DAUGHTER: She wasn't a fighter. She was agoraphobic and didn't want to go outside. She was very depressed.

SISTER: I know my brother. My brother was terrified of pain, of suffering, of death.

WIFE: I understand that he is a quadriplegic, that he has severe brain damage. Basically, he is just a body lying there in the bed. He is not the man who I fell in love with. He is not a man who would tolerate these injuries. He would hate me. He would hate me.

DAUGHTER: She's a brave woman. If there's hope, then I think she'd want to fight for her life.

Sometimes family members drew inferences from the patient's views about an acceptable quality of life.

DAUGHTER: This is all about quality of life. She would not want to be DNR if some of this could be reversed and she could return to a good quality of life. Maybe not being able to walk, but able to use a walker. Able to watch TV and the Chicago Cubs and the things she really loved.

HUSBAND: I know that she wanted to watch her children grow up. But she wanted to interact with them, watch it happen. Not just be alive for it.

DAUGHTER: . . . the dramatic changes that would be required after she left the hospital would be intolerable to her. She would absolutely hate being in a nursing home. I'm sure I would hate being in a nursing home. But she would hate it much, much more. I've really been fearful that she would get better enough to live just as she has said she doesn't want to.

And at least one surrogate drew on her father's approach to decision making rather than just his values themselves.

DAUGHTER: My father has very strong opinions. He told us what he wanted. But he also led us by example. We are responding in the way he would have wanted us to manage this situation. . . . My father always taught us since we were children to collect all the information and then make a decision. Don't rush. Sleep on it if you are upset. That is what we are doing.

For a handful of surrogates, standing in another's shoes began first in their own shoes, imagining what they we would want for themselves and then drawing inferences about the patient.

FATHER: I know what I want. I have no need for this [*gesturing to his body*]. [Patient] is the same way.

But this exercise is surprisingly rare. Far more often, when surrogates or other family members spoke about what they would want for themselves under the circumstances, they did so to highlight their belief that the patient's wishes were different.

DAUGHTER: We want to do what she wants. I wouldn't want this for myself. But it's not me.

BROTHER: If it was me, I'd have given up when I got the diagnosis. But that's me. We're very different.

On rare occasions, substituted judgments were offered by health care providers who drew on their knowledge of the patient or on comments they heard throughout the ICU admission.

SON: My mother told me that she never wanted to be kept alive if she was like that. I know that I asked you to do everything. But if she isn't going to get better, I can't ask you to continue aggressive treatment. I don't want her to suffer; I don't want her to feel pain.

NEUROSURGERY ATTENDING: I expect that she would leave the hospital and go into a nursing home. That's not what she would want.

DAUGHTER: If you think something different, if you were to tell me there's a 20 or 40 percent chance that he'd be okay— He just has no quality of life right now. He would not have wanted that.

ONCOLOGY ATTENDING: Yes, I don't think he would want this either. I really underestimated the state of his cancer. It didn't appear to be nearly as advanced or extensive.

PALLIATIVE CARE RESIDENT: It sounds like your mother's wishes, based on what you told me about how she had attempted to commit suicide, were to not live like this.

NEUROLOGY ATTENDING: It's not what you want, but what he wants. It doesn't look like that is what he would want. I've been talking to your sister and that's what she has been saying.

You may recall from chapter 6 that courts and legal commentators have described the quality of evidence that make such substituted judgments persuasive—for example, how specific, deliberate, recent, consistent, or multisourced it is. Rarely would the inferential exercises surrogates undertook in the two ICUs to fit in the patient's shoes meet this high bar. Nor were many family members as reflective as the daughter quoted earlier, who observed, "Well, when we talked about it, I think he couldn't have imagined being this sick." Rarely did surrogates consider the possibility that the patient's preferences that they were trying to reprise or recreate might have changed. But many speakers did reinforce their accounts, memories, or inferences with evidentiary authority. Some shared stories about the patient or cited specific conversations.

BROTHER: Over Christmas, she told me that she never would want this. She told others too.

BROTHER: Some time ago I spoke with him because I was asking him to serve as a backup on my estate. We had a long conversation about these issues, and he expressed the same thing to me.

SON: We really only had one conversation. It was about seven or eight years ago. It was when her sister was very sick. She was in dialysis and was in a lot of pain. My mother told me that she never wanted to be in that kind of pain. . . . That was our only conversation. Later she developed dementia and she didn't talk much.

DAUGHTER: My mother is not an effusive woman. She is like E. F. Hutton; when she speaks, you listen [from a vintage commercial for a stock brokerage firm]. A few months ago after her heart attack, I was lying in bed with her before she went to an angio [angiogram—an X-ray of blood flow in an artery or vein] and she said: "When will this end? I don't want to spend my life lying in a bed and looking at the wall." This was just an angio! I said, "Mom, don't be silly. This is just an angio. It will get better."

Some, like the patient's son in the quote above whose aunt was on dialysis, cited the patient's reaction to the misfortune of others.

HUSBAND: Absolutely. I mean, her father was on home oxygen and we talked about that—she never even wanted that.

Some drew on prior decisions patients made on their own behalf or that of others.

SON: We were torn about even bringing him here. But he chose to do the chemo, and so we felt that we should keep doing everything to see that through. He's been fighting, and he's so strong. But you can't expect someone to get through all this. The dialysis is definitely not something we would be comfortable with.

DAUGHTER: He didn't want an autopsy for [his mother], so that's why we know he wouldn't have wanted one.

Some described how well they knew the patient's wishes and values.

DAUGHTER: I've really spent a lot of time with her in the last eighteen months. I sold my house and moved in with them.

DAUGHTER: My mother's wishes were very clear and I know her very well. She would not want to live if she couldn't fully recover from this. She would hate it. She would hate it. She would hate it. I'm sitting here doing crossword puzzles. Maybe she wouldn't do the Sunday crossword, but she would want to be able to do an easy crossword. She is very independent. Even when she went on this outing to the museum [where the patient fell and hit her head], I asked her to bring someone along to help or to take her walker and she refused. I live a few blocks from my mother and I see her often, especially since my father died a year and a half ago. I know her very well.

Others emphasized the consistency and frequency of the patient's statements.

DAUGHTER: We lived with her. You didn't. She told all of us what she wanted. I asked her many times what she wanted.

Like the son quoted earlier who argued with his sister about a feeding tube for their mother, some surrogates invoked witnesses. Others cited consensus among friends and family.

BROTHER: I've asked a lot of other people for advice on this so that it's not a biased opinion: her friend of thirty-five years and more current people, too. They all agree that this is what she would want.

SON: As we were encouraged to do, the family met on Saturday. We are fortunate because our mother has a recent living will; she updated it in May. We spoke about what would be our mother's wishes and what would be our wishes. We are concerned about her quality of life. We felt that a best-case scenario, if she was in a wheelchair, unable to walk but could think clearly, and she could be with her family and watch her grandchildren grow up, that would be an acceptable outcome. She would not want that; she would tell us to stop. But that is something that we think would be acceptable to us, in light of her wishes.

And other surrogates just knew what the patient would want, without offering any basis for their conclusion or any evidentiary support:

I know/think that he/she would want _____.
- everything you can do
- to fight for his/her life
- us to make him/her comfortable
- to pull the plug
- to donate his/her organs

I know/think that he/she would not want _____.
- . "this"
- . to live this way
- . any heroic measures, aggressive care, machines, tubes, chest compressions or shocks to restart the heart, a trach, dialysis, nutrition, medications, and so on

And some added a conditional element:
- . if he/she wouldn't improve
- . if he/she was in a vegetative state
- . if there's a chance he/she could come out of this, become a normal person again
- . if there is hope

You may notice from these examples of substituted judgment the preponderance of inferences offered by the patients' adult children. This is borne out statistically as well. Although children contribute about a third of all family discourse in the two ICUs, they initiate half of all discussions about the patient's wishes or likely treatment preferences. One daughter's reflection is telling.

> Our father has always told us that he wants to die in his sleep. He doesn't want any tubes. . . . He doesn't want any pain. He doesn't want to suffer. He wants a quality of life. When he was fifty years old, he thought he was going to die. Every year since then he thought he was going to die. We have thirty-six years of practice. He has groomed us. He has told us what he wants and we know what he wants.

Children, perhaps more than anyone in their parents' lives, have been groomed over a lifetime and inculcated with their parents' priorities and values. Perhaps that is why they are unusually ready to champion these values and instructions at the bedside.

Chapter 6 reviewed evidence from numerous empirical studies, relying on hypothetical scenarios, that the substituted judgments of would-be surrogates frequently do not match the treatment preferences of would-be patients. Is this true of the substituted judgments formulated in real-world intensive care units? There is no way to know, of course, since the patients in the study had no capacity to express their treatment preferences. But real-world ICUs are also different from *Newlywed Game*–type hypothetical studies in that substituted judgments at the bedside often emerge over many conversations by multiple significant others deliberating together—spouses, children, parents, siblings, grandchildren, in-laws, sometimes even ex-spouses and friends—as well as health care providers, and not by a single research subject staring at a piece of paper for a minute or two.

It is surprising how rarely the significant others who surrounded the patient disagreed or even differed about the patient's expressed treatment preferences or their inferences about what they would likely be. This finding is especially striking given that patients often confide different things in different people at different stages of life, and that experiences shared with some but not others give rise to different memories that significant others reprise at the bedside. Although it was not unusual to see participants bristle at, quarrel about, or clash over how to implement or act on a patient's wishes—for example, whether it is appropriate to continue or to stop aggressive treatments—for only a couple of patients did even minor disagreement about the expressed wishes or substituted judgments themselves develop.

Although many friends and family reprised patient instructions or stood in their shoes in order to formulate substituted judgments of their likely preferences, that does not mean that this exercise determined the surrogate's decisions. Surrogates may well have known or suspected what decisions their loved one would choose and still disregarded them in favor of other decision-making criteria. Though flirting with the "shoes" trajectory, they ultimately opted for another. More on this in chapter 8.

Some surrogates in the study, clearly mindful of the patient's instructions, were nonetheless unable to resist the desperate efforts of physicians or other family members to keep fighting. One patient, a forty-two-year-old professional woman, had been diagnosed with a brain tumor nine years earlier and had since had six brain surgeries. She was admitted to the hospital for a seventh surgery, developed a brain hemorrhage, and returned to the operating room for an eighth surgery, after which the patient's neurosurgeon met with the family. Her best friend served as her power of attorney.

MOTHER: So what will she be like?

NEUROSURGERY ATTENDING: It is very hard to know. Probably the best we can expect is for her to be slightly worse than she was before she arrived.

SISTER: [Crying] We just want to respect her wishes. She was very clear about what was acceptable to her.

BEST FRIEND: [*Firmly*] She told us that she didn't want to continue to live the way she *was* living.

FATHER: Her wishes were very clearly stated, even in writing.

Despite these protests from the friend and sister, the patient remained in the hospital for two more months, during which she had several additional surgeries, underwent more procedures, had feeding and tracheostomy tubes placed, and developed infections, rashes, kidney failure, spasms, and fevers. Her mental status did not improve. She was transferred to a long-term acute care facility—in hopes that she would recover—with a helmet in place of the skull that had been removed. After two months in the facility, the patient was no better.

And some family members remained clueless about their loved one's wishes.

DAUGHTER: I just wish he could say what he wanted. It's like having a baby again; you wish you could know what they're thinking. It's so hard.

PALLIATIVE CARE ATTENDING: What do you think her wishes would be in this situation?

DAUGHTER: I don't know. I didn't even know that she had cancer until two weeks ago.

DAUGHTER: We never discussed it, and I feel an obligation to my mother to do everything.

WIFE: [Son], I don't know that that's what he would say. I just don't know. We never talked about it.

These surrogates moved on to another trajectory.

4. Beneficence

The previous trajectories seek to give voice to the patient's autonomy. On beneficence trajectories, decision makers maximize the patient's welfare. As recounted in chapter 6, when a patient's wishes are unknown or contradictory, or cannot be inferred, legal rules call for a "best interest" standard—to advance the patients' interests, promote their well-being, and choose, after weighing the benefits and burdens, a course of action with the greatest net benefit. Surrogates may pursue a best-interest strategy when they want to honor the patient's wishes but don't know what these wishes, values, or treatment preferences might be in this situation or don't trust their judgment or know what to do. Like the previous trajectories, health care providers sometimes help surrogates find and navigate this path.

Recall that patients who leave written instructions are most likely to request that their surrogate focus on beneficence, weighing the benefits and burdens of treatment (the first optional checkbox on the power-of-attorney form). So, even when they have the opportunity to be specific, many recognize the difficulty of anticipating the exact circumstances, risks, decisions, and trade-offs their loved ones might someday face. Just as surrogates gravitate to best interests when they are unsure what the patient wanted, so do patients themselves.

Of course, these patients hope that their decision maker will take into consideration what the patients *personally* would find beneficial or burdensome. Numerous examples in the previous section illustrated how families reflected on how the patient would regard the outcomes of a particular treatment or possible prognosis (e.g., "She would hate it. She would hate it. She would hate it"). Unlike decision-making criteria that seek to solicit, reprise, or reproduce the patient's preferences, the beneficence trajectory is generic and depersonalized—what the bioethics literature labels "objective." On this trajectory, surrogates do not know what the specific patient would deem to be in his or her best interest or would find beneficial or burdensome—considerations that are important when surrogates stand in the patient's shoes—but rather consider what a typical patient or reasonable person would find beneficial or burdensome.

Chapter 4 revealed how conversations about particular medical treatments often involve routine considerations of benefit and burden. What are the risks? What are the side effects? Will anesthesia be used? How painful is it? Will it require subsequent physical therapy or rehabilitation? Is it reversible? How long will it continue (for ongoing therapies such as dialysis)? Are there more benign alternatives? What would happen if you did nothing at all? Is it worth the risk if the patient is dying of something else? What is the best that might be expected? What is the worst? Will the intervention allow the patient to go home, or will he or she require institutional care? What impact will it have on the patient's quality of life? And so on. However, when these decisions are framed as goals of care and a choice between cure and comfort, most surrogates turn away from this objective, impersonal balancing act to reflect on the patient's wishes or values—if they can be determined—or on other considerations.

Chapter 6 noted that some bioethicists frame "best interest" as what typical or reasonable people would choose for themselves. The ICU variant of a reasonable-person standard is to ask (or offer) what health care providers would do if this was their loved one, and occasionally what other families do. Physicians were almost twice as likely as family members to initiate such conversations.

NEUROSURGERY ATTENDING: So if it were my family member in [room number] or I was the patient and my family was in your position, I would want them to make me comfortable and stop interventions.

NEUROLOGY ATTENDING: If it's any consolation, I have asked this very question of my parents, and they said that they would not want to continue care in this circumstance.

CRITICAL CARE ATTENDING: I really want to make sure that we are on the same page. There is a possibility that your wife's heart may stop and it would be necessary to put pressure or do compressions on her chest to get it going. If that were to happen, it would be very unlikely that it would result in a good outcome. I don't think it is in her best interest for us to do this. If this were my mother or another relative, I would not want them to do it. It is not in their best interests.

When family members asked what the physicians would do if the shoe were on their foot, a few physicians responded directly.

ONCOLOGY ATTENDING: So what they would do is put in a trach. It's a hole right here in the neck instead of having the tube down her throat.
DAUGHTER: What would you do?
ONCOLOGY ATTENDING: If was me, I wouldn't do it. But it's not me. It's her. [*Hesitates*] I think we shouldn't do it to her. But I want to hear what the MICU [medical ICU] team has to say about it.

DAUGHTER: What if it was your mother and she told you that she never wanted to be in this condition, didn't want to suffer, what would you do?
NEUROSURGERY ATTENDING: Actually, she did tell me that, and I'll tell you what I would do. I don't want to make this too personal, but if she told me that

she didn't want to be in a vegetative state, I would give it enough time to make sure that she had a chance to recover.

Physicians were more likely to turn the conversation back to the patient's own preferences than to answer directly.

WIFE: This is an unfair question, but what would you do if it was your parent?

NEUROLOGY FELLOW: Well, that's a really tricky question. I know what my parents want. Everyone is different, though, so it really doesn't matter what I would do for them.

WIFE: What do they want?

NEUROLOGY FELLOW: I would say that's too personal to share. The issue is what you think [Patient] would want. Different people would want different things. The other thing I will point out is that I'm also not in your shoes right now. I can answer the question hypothetically, but I can't know what I would do unless I was actually in that situation and understood how it felt.

PARTNER: I don't mean to be dramatic, but if you were his brother or father [gets really choked up; whispers the rest of the sentence], what would you do?

INFECTIOUS DISEASES ATTENDING: I think it would really depend on what his wishes were. I know you've had conversations about that with him before. What would he want?

Even less frequently, surrogates asked health care providers what treatment they would want if they were the patient.

FAMILY FRIEND: [To two residents and medical social worker] What about you three? You're pretty, young girls. But if you were in her situation, with widely metastatic cancer, what would you do?

FIRST CRITICAL CARE RESIDENT: Well, for me, I wouldn't want this. I would just want to be made comfortable, because even if I could get through the acute phase, what do I have to come back to? A lot of pain and an untreatable cancer.

FAMILY FRIEND: [To second critical care resident] What about you?

SECOND CRITICAL CARE RESIDENT: Me too.

FAMILY FRIEND: You too what?

SECOND CRITICAL CARE RESIDENT: I would want to be made comfortable also. I've been through this with my own family members, though, and it's very difficult. [Resident starts to cry.]

The beneficence trajectory includes more than best-interest calculations or the likely preferences of a typical or reasonable person. "Beneficence" embraces concerns for patient welfare and is sometimes honored even when surrogates are well aware of the patient's treatment preferences. Surrogates are sometimes propelled onto the beneficence trajectory when the patient's present or future condition has become so precarious or abhorrent that surrogates no longer stick to their original path. Some surrogates shift to the beneficence trajectory later in the ICU admission because they are overcome by the patients' pain and suffering or hopeless about their quality of life should they ever be discharged from the ICU. They attend not to recollections or surmises about the patient's tolerance for pain or suffering or what the patient would consider an acceptable quality of life—judgments along the "Patients' Shoes" trajectory—but rather to their objective sense that the patient had reached what would be an unacceptable threshold for anyone. In the face of these objective circumstances, they could no longer continue to follow their initial decision-making strategy, whether it was to wait for the patient's or God's decision, reproduce the patient's wishes, pursue their own self-interest, or even avoid making any decision at all.

Discussions of pain and/or suffering and about quality of life are very common in the ICU. Participants addressed pain or suffering in 32 percent of the observed meetings (and at least once for 69 percent of patients) and quality of life in 6 percent and 23 percent, respectively. As explained in earlier chapters, loved ones inquire and physicians prognosticate about the patient's likely quality of life after discharge from the hospital. Family members also ask about, and health care providers describe, how painful a prospective treatment is likely to be, and they share with one another their concern that the patient is in pain or is suffering. However, the beneficence trajectory only includes patients for whom these considerations were central in surrogate decision making, usually as reasons or justifications to stop, limit, or withdraw treatment.

Usually loved ones shifted the trajectory to concern over pain and suffering.

DAUGHTER: I just want her to be as comfortable as possible. I don't see any hope here. I don't want her to struggle at the end. She's not enjoying this.

SON: I understand it [the disease] is very aggressive. She is sick. She is old. This happens. This is life. I just don't want her in no pain. So if we think that she won't get better, then— How do we do this?

Sometimes physicians tried to do so as well. As I followed the critical care team along on rounds each morning, conversations between physicians and nurses—out of earshot of the patients' families—often gravitated to the patients' pain and suffering, their obligations to do no harm and protect the patient, and what for some of them sometimes became overwhelming anguish about their complicity in extending or exacerbating the patient's needless suffering when the family insisted on futile interventions. Health care providers sometimes struggled to convince surrogates to consider or embark on the beneficence trajectory.

CRITICAL CARE ATTENDING: What we are doing to her is painful, in my opinion—much worse than dialysis. Many of the procedures in an ICU are painful. The ventilator is uncomfortable. The tracheostomy will be uncomfortable. She came to the hospital from the nursing home with a decubitus ulcer—a bedsore; treating that will be painful. We have tubes feeding her. We have invasive tubes into her bladder. These things are painful. Many procedures in a hospital are painful—fixing a broken hip, removing an appendix, chemotherapy. But we do these things because the benefits outweigh the pain. We do these things because we expect the patient to get better. But in your mother's case, it seems that the pain outweighs the benefit. She isn't likely to get much better.

CRITICAL CARE FELLOW: We really don't mean to badger you. But the most important thing to keep in mind when you're making these decisions is what the patient would want. I know it's hard, and a lot of times people aren't ready to let go, and so they make decisions based on their own needs, because they're not ready to lose the person. But you need to put yourself in her shoes and think about what it is you would want if you were in her situation, hooked up to a ventilator for the rest of your life, with metastatic breast cancer and in a lot of pain. She is suffering.

Some concerns about suffering overlap with those about quality of life.

WIFE: I think we should just make him comfortable. I don't want him to suffer. He had trouble walking. When he would get up to go to the bathroom, he would have to lie down. He'd get up to eat and have to lie down. He couldn't really do anything without lying down. Then he started making mistakes with the finances. He's just had a really difficult time. He never complained. But he's been miserable.

But what constitutes an acceptable quality of life varies across decision makers.

HUSBAND: I just spent some time with her, gave her kisses and talked to her. I told her to blink and she gave me a weak blink. Before I could tolerate her even when she couldn't walk or anything because we could still have great conversations. But this is no quality of life. After I talked to you yesterday, I had some quiet time to think about everything. You know, you make a snap decision but then you get some alone time and you really think about everything and it sinks in.

DAUGHTER: This just isn't her. She can't play bridge anymore. She loved bridge.
PRIMARY CARE PHYSICIAN: [*To the critical care attending*] She was a bridge champion.
CRITICAL CARE ATTENDING: Oh wow.
DAUGHTER: She can't even read fast enough now. That's all she does, read and watch *Jeopardy*. So if she doesn't have that, then what's left? I call her every day and ask how she's doing. She says, "I'm ninety. What do you want from me?"

BROTHER-IN-LAW: With all of these problems, I wonder how he will recover. What will be his quality of life? It seems like he will require some institutional care.
CRITICAL CARE ATTENDING: Yes, that is likely.
. . .
BROTHER-IN-LAW: Let's get to the bottom line. What is the very best that his quality of life will be?
NEUROSURGERY RESIDENT: [*Without skipping a beat*] That he will be alive.
SISTER: That is not acceptable.

SISTER: How long will she stay in the ICU?
CRITICAL CARE ATTENDING: Right now she must remain in the ICU because of her ventilator and her other needs. Eventually she would go to a long-term facility.
SISTER: What do you mean by a long-term facility?
CRITICAL CARE ATTENDING: A place that would care for her.
DAUGHTER: That's no quality of life!!!!
CRITICAL CARE ATTENDING: Remember what we said before about quality of life? Quality of life is in the eye of the beholder. What is a decent quality of

life for me may not be acceptable to you. If this were me or a member of my family, a long-term facility would not be a quality of life. In fact it would be negative. But it's not what I want.

These examples suggest that although beneficence may be generic and objective, where surrogates read the needle on the scale as acceptable or intolerable is quite subjective. A couple of families inquired about performing brain transplants, a state of affairs that most of their counterparts would consider abhorrent even if such interventions were medically possible. And more often, physicians colorfully described the inordinate pain and suffering a proposed treatment would inflict on the patient, only to be met with indifference, silence, or even acceptance.

PALLIATIVE CARE ATTENDING: I think the question at this point is how long are we going to allow her to suffer?
GRANDDAUGHTER-IN-LAW: That don't matter to us, we just want her alive.

CRITICAL CARE FELLOW: Another issue I want to address with you is what you would want done if something very acute were to happen and her heart were to stop. Would you want us to do heroic measures to restart her heart if it were to stop? That would mean doing shocks and chest compressions and probably breaking ribs. Also because of her bleeding, she would probably bleed out into her chest. I think that based on her condition, the chances of her being able to be resuscitated are next to zero. It's certainly up to you and it's a matter of what you think she would want. But my recommendation to you would be that you not have us do those things.
SISTER: But even if you don't do it, she's gonna die?
CRITICAL CARE FELLOW: Right.
SISTER: Then I say do the shocks, break the ribs. She's gonna die either way.

Because impersonal, objective beneficence or best-interest considerations come up early in an ICU admission when specific interventions are being considered and much later when they have all failed, leaving only pain and suffering in their wake, the beneficence trajectory has multiple entry points. Some surrogates begin there and later move on to other trajectories as the stakes get higher. For these and other decision makers, beneficence also becomes a trajectory of last resort when other decision-making strategies have seemingly failed the patient.

5. It's God's Decision

It is not surprising that end-of-life conversations include references to God, religion, faith, miracles, and the like.[7] At least an offhand comment was expressed in a little more than one in ten observed meetings and for more than a third of the patients—by family, friends, and health care providers alike. If these numbers appear low, that might be because chaplains and occasionally outside clergy visit patients and families in the ICU, and some religious reflections, prayers, or entreaties may have been reserved for these unobserved visits.

For a handful of the encounters with physicians, God plays a very particular role in treatment decisions. These participants profess that God has the final word. But that belief leads to sometimes disparate approaches to decision making. Most often, these surrogates delay or refuse to consider any life-limiting decisions that might be seen as playing God.

NEUROSURGERY RESIDENT: The likelihood that she will recover is extremely low. So the question is how you want us to proceed. . . . I am not asking you to make a decision now, but perhaps you have already had discussions about what your mother would want and as a family know what you want us to do.

DAUGHTER: My mother loved life. She would want to live. We will leave this in God's hands.

SON: Our mother has recovered many times before. She's had three strokes and three heart attacks, two of them massive. And she's recovered. She couldn't run a race, but she is still able to live her life. . . . I understand that the odds are not very good and that this is the sort of situation in which the patient only recovers in rare and extraordinary circumstances. But we want to take that chance. We want to give it more time and see if she improves. This is God's will, and He will chart her course.

NEUROSURGERY RESIDENT: The damage to the brain was very great and she will never get better. Never open her eyes. Never respond to anything. She isn't technically brain-dead, but might become so in the next few days. In Illinois, when you are brain-dead, you are considered dead.

NIECE: Is she a vegetable?

NEUROSURGERY RESIDENT: She is actually worse than a vegetable. But she isn't experiencing any pain. We have a few options. One would be to continue to do what we are doing—keep her on a ventilator, treat her medically. She will not get better, and she will probably still die, probably relatively soon. Another would be to remove the ventilator and give her comfort care. Let me give you a range of the possibilities: at the worst, she will die soon, no matter what we do; at the best, she will live for some time, but on a ventilator and completely unresponsive.

. . .

FRIEND OF PATIENT: This is in God's hands. He knows more than we do. We leave this to the Almighty up there to make the decision. I know her; she is a very strong woman; she might make it.

ONCOLOGY ATTENDING: I understand that you want to wait to make these decisions. But I worry that he'll have a bump in the road. There will definitely be bumps in the road. Some will be hills and some will be mountains, and some will be insurmountable mountains. I worry that he'll have one of these bumps, either at the hospital or at home, and I worry. You know me, I worry. That's what I do.

WIFE: [*Interrupting*] But I don't worry. When I worry I can't make decisions, I make mistakes. Worry breeds fear. We don't talk about that stuff. Fear will not allow him to live his life. I believe you should live until you die. . . . So we don't talk about those things. It doesn't help anything. If he does go to be with the Lord, that's fine. We understand. It's all in God's hands.

ONCOLOGY ATTENDING: If his breathing were to become difficult again, would you want us to put [Patient] on a ventilator?

WIFE: Whether he's on a ventilator or not, it's all in the Lord's hands.

Of course, while the surrogates in these examples abjure one sort of decision, they implicitly authorize another—aggressive treatment, the default. A smaller number of surrogates see their role differently. They decide to limit treatment, asserting that God can nonetheless intervene and save the patient.

CRITICAL CARE RESIDENT: Did you talk about what we discussed before— whether you want us to resuscitate him if his heart stops?

WIFE: No compressions. We will leave it in God's hands.

SON: I think that given what we know about my mother, things have changed significantly enough that the best course of action would be to stop the treatment and focus on her comfort. Only a higher power can determine what happens from here. He/She/It/Whatever is the one who decides whether my mother will live or die. So if there is going to be divine intervention, then so be it. We'll allow that to happen, but either way, we should proceed with the comfort measures.

More unusual still, loved ones expressed a more direct relationship with the divine, knowing God's decision and trying not to stand in the way.

FATHER: I'm not happy with [Oncologist]. He thinks he knows everything. He's not open-minded. [Oncologist] is the best at what he does, but he can't know anything for sure. Nobody can. Telling someone there's no hope is taking away what's possible. I'm a Christian and I believe that only God determines what is possible. Everything is up to God. We don't know what God has in store for [Patient], only God knows. Nobody can know for sure, so taking away someone's hope, that's just not right in my opinion—

ONCOLOGY NURSE: Can I go out on a limb? . . . I think that the message was probably not delivered well, but I think his intentions were good. I think he was trying to prepare you for what he saw, from his mortal perspective, as inevitable.

FATHER: Oh, I understand that. And God takes everyone sometime. But my son is very powerful, and God has not decided it's his time yet.

Or they expect God to send them a sign.

DAUGHTER: The Lord has the last word. He decide everything. If He gonna take her away from us, then that's the Lord's decision. But maybe He wanna keep her here. It's up to Him to decide.

PALLIATIVE CARE ATTENDING: I think we are at a point where we are getting in the way of what the Lord is trying to do.

DAUGHTER: Now that's where you're wrong. The Lord is guiding your hand. He is behind everything you do.

PALLIATIVE CARE ATTENDING: I understand that. But there are some situations where we are preventing the Lord from doing His work. He has given her lungs to breathe with. They have stopped working, but we put this tube down her throat to make her lungs keep expanding.

DAUGHTER: The Lord always has the final word. That I know. Everything you do, that's the Lord's doing. I ain't always been a good Christian; I done bad things. But I believe in the Almighty. I know that He'll give me a sign. He gave me a sign before my father got killed. I couldn't sleep that night, I was walkin' up and down the hall. Then he was lying there. He got shot. The Lord gave me a sign then and He'll give me a sign this time too. So I'll just have to wait for it. I'm not gonna make a decision now.

As reflected in this last example, some physicians push back about God's role in decision making. But other physicians initiate this discussion themselves. The following two examples come from a critical care fellow who did not shy away from talk of God, faith, or heaven.

> Sometimes it's just in God's hands. We did everything we could. . . . Sometimes He makes the ultimate decision. Most of the time He does.

Or, awkwardly:

SON: Do you know how much time she has?
CRITICAL CARE FELLOW: That's very hard to say. You know, this isn't my decision. It's—
[*Simultaneously*]
SON: It's ours—
CRITICAL CARE FELLOW: God's decision.

The deeper philosophical or theological questions that undergird these diverse responses are rarely explored at the bedside. What is the division of labor at the end of life? If God has the final word, why go to an ICU at all? Why does one play God by refusing an intervention but not by authorizing it? (For example, why is one not playing God by ordering CPR to bring a dead patient back to life?) If God is guiding the hand of the physicians, at what point, if ever, are the latter "preventing the Lord from doing His work"? If you don't receive a divine sign, does that mean that God favors the default, or, rather, that God doesn't micromanage ICUs? What role do mortals play and what responsibility do they hold regarding the patients in their care, even if the final outcome is out of their control?

In the face of these difficult questions, the voice of an anguished sister provides a counterpoint to the sentiments expressed above: "I love my brother. I have to do what is best for him. God will have to understand." Travelers along this trajectory would presumably be appalled by her conclusion. God does not defer to their judgment. This small group of ICU decision makers choose silence and "let" God set the course. The patients for whom they speak often endure more heroic interventions and longer ICU stays while awaiting God's decision to manifest itself. These surrogates did not indicate whether their belief about divine intervention was personal or was also shared by the patient (which would move them to the reprising instructions or shoes trajectory).

6. What We Want

DAUGHTER: We want everything done.

CRITICAL CARE RESIDENT: Is that what the patient wants?

DAUGHTER: It doesn't matter. This is what we want.

Physicians frequently exhort surrogates, "It's not what you want, it's what the patient wants"—instructions often delivered prior to any inkling that decision makers are considering their own interests or desires. In time, though, dialogue at the bedside suggests that what the surrogate or other family members want may sometimes play a role in medical decision making.

This should come as no surprise. As explained in the discussion of conflict of interest in the previous chapter, surrogate decision makers, whether named prospectively in advance directives or identified retroactively by default rules, tend to have preexisting, ongoing, intimate relationships with those they serve. Intimates presumably know patients better and are more likely to be willing to take on the onerous responsibilities of navigating and sometimes choreographing the end of another's life. But the interests of patients and surrogates are profoundly entangled in end-of-life decision making.[8] Intimates have the most to gain or lose from the medical decisions they make on the patients' behalf.[9] As a result, the impact of medical decisions—economic, emotional, interpersonal—on surrogates and other loved ones percolate through conversations at the bedside. We heard significant others reflect on financial concerns and the cost of treatment, caregiving responsibilities, fear of loss, guilt, the emotional burden of decision making, personal values that conflicted with those of the patient, concern for impacts on others, and pressure from others. The more difficult questions, as we will see, are whether these worries or interests affect the decisions surrogates make and whether the patient actually wanted them to.

Surrogates and other family members face substantial financial costs and potential benefits related to the admission of a loved one to an intensive care unit. On the one hand, ICU care is extraordinarily expensive. Authorizing aggressive or experimental treatments increases both the cost of care and the length of hospitalization. Few ICU patients return home immediately without continuing health care expenses. Some end up in rehabilitation facilities, nursing homes, or long-term acute care hospitals. Even those who go home may incur expenses for visiting nurses or caregivers, outpatient therapies, medical equipment, or pharmaceutical or hospice costs. Eighty-six percent of the patients in the study had some form of health insurance or public aid. But even these more fortunate patients face coverage exclusions, deductibles and co-payments, and yearly or lifetime maximum coverage ceilings or limited numbers of days of hospitalization, rehabilitation, or long-term care. These uncovered expenditures diminish or deplete the patient's estate (if any), which some surrogates expect to inherit. Many other surrogates must cover these costs with their own financial resources or those of their parents, children, or others. And many will lose income from time off from work while tending to the patient in the ICU or elsewhere. For some surrogates, the timely death of the patient will stop the hemorrhaging of family financial assets; others may even enjoy a resulting life-insurance windfall. In short, the death of the patient might serve the financial interests of surrogates or of others who they also serve.

Less often, the death of the patient will threaten the financial interests of the surrogate or others. The patient may own a lucrative business that will not survive his or her death, or retirement benefits on which the surrogate relied may end upon the patient's death. Chillingly, in a famous bioethics case,[10] the mother of a severely burned patient was advised by her lawyer that the patient (who was pleading to be allowed to die) was worth much more alive than dead in an upcoming lawsuit against the company whose pipeline had exploded. (The mother ultimately ignored her son's pleas and ordered that the excruciating treatment be continued.) On occasion, then, surrogates face financial incentives to undertake aggressive medical interventions to keep patients alive, sometimes against their will. As these examples suggest, the financial consequences of a particular medical decision may affect the interests of various friends and family members differently, another reason significant others may disagree about goals of medical care.

From time to time, even health care providers have suspicions about the financial motivations of decision makers.

NEUROSURGERY ATTENDING: One of the things I need to talk about is all of the delays that have occurred when your family refused or questioned various interventions that our medical team felt was necessary to provide appropriate care.

DAUGHTER: What are you referring to? The delay in the EVD [a drain to remove fluid from the brain]? . . . We asked the resident if it could wait until the morning and he said that it could.

SON-IN-LAW: With some risk.

DAUGHTER: With some risk. The next morning, when you said it was necessary, we agreed to it right away.

NEUROSURGERY ATTENDING: With your delay on the decision regarding the EVD, we thought that maybe you were trying to decide whether to pursue the most aggressive care or whether to let him pass. But there have been many other delays or the refusal by your family to allow the doctors to perform what was in your father's best interest. I have had no problem with you. I have been able to work smoothly with you. But I have heard complaints among the staff that there was some motivation for your delay, that maybe you didn't have your father's best interests in mind. I am the physician of record in this case. . . . If anyone makes an allegation, I am responsible. I need to air it and get it out on the record. If there is an appearance of impropriety, I need to consider it. Someday, if there is a dispute about an inheritance, for example, I don't want to be responsible.

DAUGHTER: Who has made these allegations? What exactly did they say?

NEUROSURGERY ATTENDING: I don't think it would be appropriate for me to say more. I don't want to do anything that might undermine his care. . . . I am not making any accusations.

DAUGHTER: You said "appearance of impropriety"; that's a quote. . . . I could be a little offended by what you are saying. Actually, I could be extremely offended.

NEUROSURGERY ATTENDING: I'm sorry, but you are not my client. The patient is my client.

. . .

SON: I am a simple man. All last week, we were told that there is a fork in the road and we need to decide which fork to take. If we wanted to do my father harm, we could have easily taken the other fork. We wouldn't have needed to delay procedures to do this.

Nonetheless, as described in chapter 2, there is surprisingly little talk of money in an intensive care unit—by patients, families, or even physicians. Concern about the impact of the patient's hospitalization on familial economic well-being comes up occasionally. Loved ones worry about their farm or business going down the tubes in their absence or despair about the ability to pay rent without the patient's income. A mother explained that the family had run out of money to pay the patient's medical expenses and was seeking a legal mechanism to get access to the patient's 401K. A husband in chapter 5 explained the need to pick up some odd jobs in between hospital visits and to borrow money to pay for gas or parking at the hospital. Another spouse complained that he could not afford the cell phone charges from messages left by hospital personnel.

Comments that suggest that financial concerns may play a role in surrogate decision making are rare. For only 5 percent of patients did decision makers ask or express concern about the cost of a new treatment or inquire about whether it was covered by insurance. Two surrogates in the study were unusually blunt. One, a nurse and the wife of a patient with a life-threatening genetic condition that had already required scores of surgeries—quoted earlier in the chapter—was approaching the lifetime maximum on the patient's medical-insurance policy. She expressed her doubts about the point of continuing aggressive care in the face of the patient's impending suffering and death and commented: "The technicians thought I was nuts when I wouldn't let them do their tests because we couldn't afford them. They can practice medicine the old-fashioned way. They can start with a small amount of medicine and gradually increase it. They don't need to run tests to determine the dosage." (After the insurance company increased the lifetime maximum, the spouse authorized another surgery.) A spouse in the other ICU also expressed financial concerns (among others) in deciding whether to reintubate his wife.

CRITICAL CARE RESIDENT: So one option is to take the tube out and, if she needs it back in, we could do everything possible to treat her, including putting the tube back in.

SPOUSE: So she'd need to be in a nursing home, right?

CRITICAL CARE RESIDENT: If we were to continue treating her and doing everything, then, yes, she would ultimately need to be in a facility.

SPOUSE: I can't afford a nursing home. With the ventilator and the feeding tube and everything, that'd put me in the poorhouse. I just can't afford that. Neither of us can really. I don't want that tube back in; I'm set on that.

Loved ones were at least as likely to volunteer to pay extra out of pocket to secure experimental treatments or treatments physicians resisted as they were to refuse a proposed intervention because of its cost. Most often, discussion of resources pertained to patient discharge rather than treatment. Physicians or social workers would explain that a desired discharge facility was not covered by their insurance or was unavailable because of their lack of insurance.

Undoubtedly, other—perhaps many other—loved ones kept their financial incentives or concerns to themselves. Yet it is striking how few ask even circuitous questions or make indirect comments that would suggest that money or insurance coverage is on their minds. A number of patients and families appeared destitute; perhaps they didn't talk about money because they had none and knew that someone else would have to foot the medical bill.

Caregiving responsibilities represent a related source of potential self-interest. The trajectory of a decision to undertake more aggressive treatment usually requires more long-term familial involvement. Whether it is to quit one's job or take family leave to care for the patient, to provide a host of therapies to the patient at home, to move in with the patient or renovate the home to accommodate patient disabilities or medical equipment, or to commit time to visiting a patient who is institutionalized in a treatment facility, the long-term responsibilities typically exceed those of a decision to withhold or withdraw life-supporting therapies. Yet it was far more common to hear family members express willingness or even insistence to take on these responsibilities (many of them too busy to visit patients during their brief stint in the ICU) than to eschew them. On occasion, though, a surrogate would refuse a recommended intervention because it would require familial assistance after the patient was released from the hospital. Surrogates of several other patients requested that the patient be moved—to their homes or to facilities sometimes thousands of miles away, often at great peril to the patient—because it was easier on the surrogate or other family members.

WIFE: This is very difficult. I have no support here. I come here all day to be with him. In Paris we have some family, friends. This is not a good environment for me.

CRITICAL CARE ATTENDING: I want to make sure that we are on the same page, so tell me what your goals are for your son, your relative.

MALE COUSIN: We would like for him to come home, be able to talk and walk, and so on.

CRITICAL CARE ATTENDING: He won't be walking around.

MALE COUSIN: But we understand that that is not likely. So we want him to come home.

CRITICAL CARE ATTENDING: You cannot set up ventilators and service them in a home.

MALE COUSIN: We understand that.

CRITICAL CARE ATTENDING: I don't think he will survive at home.

MALE COUSIN: That's okay. We want him to come home, even if he will die at home.

NURSE: Normally, the way to do this would be to remove everything and see how it does for a couple of days. If he seems stable and able to make the trip home, then we would arrange for him to go home. Truthfully, he may not survive in the hospital long enough to go home.

CRITICAL CARE ATTENDING: He has pneumonia and very low blood pressure. All of this is the result of his liver. Unfortunately, there is nothing we can do to fix his liver, and he is not a candidate for a transplant.

[*At this, the patient's mother begins to cry inconsolably, putting her head in her lap.*]

MALE COUSIN: She doesn't want him to die in the hospital.

NURSE: Truthfully, his window is so narrow now, I don't think he realizes whether or not he is in the hospital. He can't see out the window. He is simply concentrating on taking a breath and staying alive. Perhaps he is aware that you are with him. But that is all.

FEMALE COUSIN: She wants him to come home so that his father can see him. His father had a stroke a year ago and cannot leave his bed.

MALE COUSIN: She is okay with him dying at home, if that is what happens.

CRITICAL CARE ATTENDING: I am not sure that he can even make it home. He may die in the ambulance.

MALE COUSIN: You mean he can't make even a twenty-mile ride home?

CRITICAL CARE ATTENDING: Yes.

MALE COUSIN: She is okay with that, as long as we try to bring him home.

CRITICAL CARE ATTENDING: I am his physician. My concern is his suffering. You may be okay with him dying in an ambulance. But I am not. I don't want him to die in pain or gasping for air. I want to ensure that he is as comfortable as possible when he dies. I don't want him to suffer.

Far more often than financial or other responsibilities that might color their decision-making process, surrogates expressed emotional concerns, especially fear of loss.

SON: I'd like my mother to live forever. But I'm wondering whether I am doing what she wants or what I'd like for myself. The doctors yesterday got me to think about that, that maybe I'm doing this for me. I don't want my mother to suffer.

CRITICAL CARE FELLOW: But before we get into all the details of the tracheostomy, I think it's important to look at where things are at with him. He's very critically ill. I don't know him as well as you folks do, and that's why it's important to look to you guys to ask what he would have wanted in this situation, and what his wishes were.

[*Patient's partner starts to cry.*]

CRITICAL CARE FELLOW: I'm sorry to upset you. It's just really important to stop and think about what it is that he would want in this situation, since he's so sick.

[*Partner totally breaks down.*]

PARTNER: I want *everything* done for him. So the trachea whatever, let's do it.

CRITICAL CARE FELLOW: Okay, and this is what [Patient] would have wanted?

PARTNER: [*Nods*] Please do everything you can for him. Be aggressive.

[*Seven days later*]

CRITICAL CARE ATTENDING: So the update for today is basically that he's doing worse now. . . . You know, the risk—I mean, the chances of him recovering at this point are in the miracle range.

PARTNER: I just, I'm having a really hard time giving up. [*Starts to cry*] I'm sorry.

CRITICAL CARE ATTENDING: I would like to point out that you're really not giving up. . . . We've really done everything possible to support him and, despite all those measures, his body is not able to fight all this. Have you two ever talked about what his wishes would be in this situation?

PARTNER: Oh yes. [*Laughs*] He would not be here. I know that for sure. I don't care, though. [*Laughing*] I just don't care. I know it's selfish, but I don't want to let go. I know I'm not being rational right now. I just can't imagine not having him. [*Starts to cry more.*]

CRITICAL CARE ATTENDING: I just think it's important to think about what he would want.

Few surrogates were as open as this partner about their fear of loss or their unwillingness to put their selfish interests aside to honor patient wishes, even if it meant misrepresenting those wishes. But fear of loss, of letting go of a life partner they cannot bear to live without, of being alone, comes up pretty frequently in discussions about goals of care. And several surrogates admitted regretfully after the patient's death or after months of torturous, futile treatment that they had been selfish and should have decided to stop aggressive care much earlier. As the mother of the forty-two-year-old described earlier who had suffered multiple surgeries and interventions for a devastating brain tumor confessed many months into her child's hospitalization, "We have been flouting her living will [which indicated that the patient didn't want to continue to live the way she had been living] and perhaps it is time to honor it."

Surrogates expressed other emotional needs as well. They included anger (e.g., at the doctors, which was expressed in refusal to accede to their recommendations, thereby causing sometimes needless suffering for the patient), the emotional stress of decision making (which resulted in avoidance or delay, again increasing patient suffering and sometimes undermining care), or suffering from watching the patient suffer (which might be alleviated by the patient's death). Most often they expressed guilt or fear of being responsible or blamed for the patient's death (which was typically manifested in demands for continued, usually futile, treatment and interventions long beyond what was in the patient's best interest).

HUSBAND: We've decided to keep giving her nutrition.

PALLIATIVE CARE FELLOW: Usually when we withdraw care we stop giving nutrition.

HUSBAND: That decision is universal; the whole family agrees.

PALLIATIVE CARE FELLOW: Can I ask why you've decided to continue the nutrition?

HUSBAND: I'd feel like I was starving her to death.

BROTHER: Our family had an experience with a relative who was very sick and we went through all this, and well, it's a big family story, but basically we decided to discontinue nutrition. And then when the death certificate came out, it said the cause of death was malnutrition. It was horrible.

PALLIATIVE CARE FELLOW: Actually the nutrition support can eventually cause the patient to be uncomfortable because there's no way for them to get rid of the input. So they become fluid overloaded and become uncomfortable. Also, the nutrition can lead to further infection.

. . .

HUSBAND: I understand that. And if it was up to [Patient], she probably wouldn't have had the paramedics resuscitate her in the first place. But we're so fortunate that we've had this limbo time to adjust. Not everyone gets that. I think that she wouldn't want the nutrition, but selfishly, for me, it would be easier to give her that. I would just feel like I was killing her.

BROTHER: So are we making a decision today?

HUSBAND: [Pointing at the patient's brother and shaking his finger at him] No, [Brother]. I'm not making any decisions. It's all in the living will, so don't even go there. *Don't put this on me!*

The wife of one patient described overwhelming guilt that she hadn't sought medical attention for her husband sooner. Because of her guilt, she said that her husband *had* to recover.

On rare occasions, the values or religious beliefs of the surrogate and patient conflicted. One of the most ethically mindful of surrogates in the study acknowledged as much and asked to meet with the hospital ethics committee and a priest. The spouse explained that, although the patient was an agnostic and had expressed in a lifetime of conversations that he would not want to be kept alive under existing circumstances, she was a practicing Catholic and concerned about the moral claims of the Church. Whether she put her beliefs aside or was counseled how to reconcile the conflict, ultimately the spouse forcefully and lovingly reprised and advocated for her husband's wishes, despite her own religious beliefs. Whether surrogates on the "God" trajectory were expressing the religious beliefs of the patient or merely their own was never shared in bedside conversations. As described in the next chapter, some of them straddled both the "God" and "What We Want" trajectories simultaneously.

As noted earlier, a minority of patients bothered to name their own surrogate decision makers; the rest were chosen according to legal default rules, which do not always identify the most appropriate default surrogate for a particular patient. It was not uncommon for the prior relationship between patients and family members to be fractious or dysfunctional. Some patients were estranged from their default decision maker, sometimes even in the process of divorcing them. A few surrogates learned at the bedside that the patient had been cheating on them. In a couple of instances, health care staff or family members alleged or suspected that the default surrogate was responsible for the injuries (physical or substance abuse) that landed the patient in the hospital. Needless to say, compromised surrogates may experience greater difficulty silencing their own interests. Some of these would-be surrogates sensibly delegated their decision-making responsibility to another. Others perhaps rose above their own interests, despite the obvious challenges. And others probably did not. In one troubling case reported in chapter 4, a patient's extended family believed that her husband/surrogate was responsible for a fall that caused life-threatening brain injuries. The husband believed that his wife would want to donate her organs. But the family threatened that, if he decided to do that, they would file criminal charges against him. So, tearfully, he decided against organ donation.

Like this last spouse, some surrogates were pressured by others or by responsibilities toward others—typically their children—that conflicted with their obligations to the patient. They were torn about the impact of financial pressures occasioned by the extended treatment of the patient on their obligations to provide for their children, about caregiving responsibilities to the patient that would steal time away from their children or other vulnerable family members, or about the emotional consequences of the patient's death or disability for the children or others. One extremely distraught and tearful sister insisted that her brother remain on life support until his financial estate was legally processed because she felt an obligation to her brother's employees, to whom he had left his business, and who might not receive it if the patient died before the paperwork was completed. And some surrogates were pressured by family members to take a different medical course from the one they had chosen; this was especially common when the surrogate was a recent spouse, significant other, friend, or more distant relative.

CRITICAL CARE FELLOW: He is very critically ill. And even if we could fix his liver, kidney, brain, lungs—my biggest concern is the underlying leukemia. He's got blasts [abnormal, immature white blood cells] circulating in his blood. I talked to [Oncologist], and she said that, just in terms of the leukemia, he only has weeks to live—and that's if he wasn't critically ill in the ICU. He's dying. I hate to tell you that. But he is.

NIECE: [Critical Care Attending] told me that very bluntly the other day. I appreciated that. I needed to know that.

CRITICAL CARE FELLOW: I'm not as straight up as him, but even I think that he's actively dying right now. It's just a matter of how it happens at this point.

NIECE: I know. I've heard this from a lot of doctors.

CRITICAL CARE FELLOW: I hate having these meetings because, by being honest, I feel like I'm hurting you, the family. And I really hate to do that. But right now I feel like he's supposed to go somewhere [*looks upward*] and I'm keeping him from going. I'm fighting it.

NIECE: The thing is, I understand all that, but his family doesn't. They're in another country, thousands of miles away, and they call all the time asking what's going on, but they don't see what's going on.

CRITICAL CARE FELLOW: What do they want?

NIECE: For me to keep him alive as long as possible. But I have the POA [power of attorney] and I know that he never wanted this. So this is a really difficult situation.

CRITICAL CARE FELLOW: I understand—it's very difficult.

NIECE: They call all the time. Every day I get calls galore asking for updates.

CRITICAL CARE FELLOW: I like to talk to families about quality of life.

NIECE: He's got none like this.

CRITICAL CARE FELLOW: Exactly. We are darn good at keeping people alive. All we need is a beating heart. We don't need the liver, kidneys, brain, lungs, any of that. We have machines for those things. So all we need is to keep his heart beating. But for what?

NIECE: Let's just say he could come off [the] breathing tube—and you don't think he can, right?

CRITICAL CARE FELLOW: [*Nods.*]

NIECE: Do you think he could breathe on his own?

CRITICAL CARE FELLOW: At this point, no. He has leukemic infiltrates in his lungs. And we can't keep the breathing tube in forever.

NIECE: How long can it stay in?

CRITICAL CARE FELLOW: Two weeks, and then we need to consider a tracheostomy. But I doubt he could even survive the surgery because his platelets are so low and he's so unstable.

NIECE: Okay, so two weeks. It's already been a week.

NIECE'S DAUGHTER: So we have a week left.

NIECE: And after that week, then that's it. No more. They'll just have to understand.

NIECE'S DAUGHTER: If his sister wants to visit, she's got a week to get here.

NIECE: She thinks she's going to come and he'll wake up.

CRITICAL CARE FELLOW: So what did his power-of-attorney document say?

NIECE: That he never wanted to be on a ventilator. But they really just want me to keep him alive.

NURSE: That's easier said than done.

NIECE: Right. Even though I have the POA, it's his sister, so I have to respect what they want too.

CRITICAL CARE FELLOW: There's really an ethical dilemma here. It's a matter of doing the right thing versus doing the wrong thing. I mean, if he didn't want this and we're doing it to him anyway, it's bordering on harassment.

NIECE: Yeah, his family is thousands of miles away. I understand—it's his sister, but still.

CRITICAL CARE FELLOW: We have ethics consults to discuss issues like these.

NIECE'S DAUGHTER: It's also a matter of religious ethics. They think that if he moves an arm, he's still alive, so if you stop the machines, then you're killing him.

NURSE: But we have a POA saying he didn't want this.

NIECE: Yes, but they're going to say I killed him. They're going to blame it all on me.

CRITICAL CARE FELLOW: You're really stuck in the middle here.

NIECE: Yes, I absolutely am. I never thought it would be this difficult. I never wanted to be in this position. They don't see how he is.

And, like the niece, numerous other decision makers delayed medical decisions or interventions until family could travel to the ICU to say goodbye.

As described in the previous chapter, these examples of self- or other-regarding behavior are more complicated than they appear because they sometimes comply with patient instructions to give priority to the needs or interests of others (including the surrogate) over their own. The distraught sister's sense of obligation to her brother's employees described above was inflamed by the patient himself, who on his deathbed had prepared his financial will in order to ensure that his employees would inherit the business. Patients frequently express that they do not want to be a burden to their family, and empirical research described in the last chapter suggests that many give surrogates leeway to disregard their stated treatment preferences if they undermine the interests of their loved ones. Such priorities are occasionally shared at the bedside.

SON: I have been here for three weeks, almost a month, first with my father, and now with her. It's taken a great toll on me, and I haven't even really had time to grieve for my father. I don't know if I can handle prolonging this if there's no real hope of her improving. I think that if she were here, my mother would say she wouldn't want me to suffer, or the rest of my family.

HUSBAND: I still want to save her.
SON: You know that Mom doesn't want to put you through this.

ONCOLOGY ATTENDING: I strongly believe that you're following his wishes. He never wanted to be a burden.
DAUGHTER: He wasn't a burden.
ONCOLOGY ATTENDING: I understand, but he said that to me and I really don't think that he would've wanted to live like this.

So some surrogates who appear to be choosing the treatment that "they want" or that is best for them are actually following the patients' instructions to put the interests of the family over their own. But how do we know if this is the case, especially when these unwritten instructions are often reprised by the seemingly self-interested surrogate?

Finally, like the daughter at the beginning of this section, some surrogates simply expressed the view that this was their decision—including whether or not to honor the patient's wishes—and they would do what they wanted.

BROTHER: If [Patient] was interested in organ donation, how would that work?
NEUROLOGY ATTENDING: We would have to wait until she became brain-dead

or her heart stopped beating—until she's passed—and then we could harvest her organs.

CRITICAL CARE FELLOW: Is that what she wanted?

HUSBAND: Yes. But that's my decision too.

In short, surrogates and significant others had many reasons to reflect on what treatment decisions "they want" or what would be best or least burdensome or least expensive for themselves or other loved ones. One or more of these concerns weighed heavily on some surrogates as they deliberated about treatment. The loved ones of other patients undoubtedly engaged in self-censorship, maintaining silence in meetings with physicians about their interests, worries, motivations, and pressures from others, especially when staff lectured them that they should only consider what the patient would want. And still others were probably unaware that their interests or preferences conflicted with those of the patient.[11]

Although surrogates may not intentionally lie about the patient's preferences so that they appear consistent with their own, many may not be aware of the divergences.

CRITICAL CARE ATTENDING: He's on a ventilator and will likely remain on a ventilator for the rest of his life. He's not interactive, he can't talk or eat. It's important to do everything that he would want done to him, and not do everything he wouldn't want done to him. Did you ever talk to him about what he would want?

SON: We want to fight the fight as long as we can. We're going to give him every possible opportunity, do everything we possibly can.

WIFE: Yes, of course we want to do everything for him.

CRITICAL CARE ATTENDING: Sometimes the focus is lost on what the patient would want and instead it becomes what other family members would want. Before the surgery, did he tell you what his medical wishes are, what he would and would not want? Did you talk about any of that?

WIFE: To be honest, we didn't. [Thoracic Surgery Attending] was very positive about this surgery. We thought it would go fine.

. . .

CRITICAL CARE ATTENDING: Knowing him as you do, do you think that this is what he would want? Some people would say, if I can't be independent and do things for myself, or if I am on a ventilator permanently, then that is not an acceptable lifestyle for me. Other people think that life is just so precious that one more day, regardless of the condition, is worth it.

SON: The second one.

CRITICAL CARE ATTENDING: I understand where you stand on it. I'm wondering where he would stand. You know him far better than I do. What do you think he would want?

SON: Everything. If there's a fight to be fought, then we need to do everything we can to fight. If there's even a 1 percent chance, then we need to try.

WIFE: [Son], I don't know that that's what he would say. I just don't know. We never talked about it.

As elaborated in the last chapter, scholars have observed that our preferences are first formed in the cauldron of family values; surrogates may therefore erroneously assume that what they want for themselves resembles what patients also want.[12] Social psychologists label this heuristic bias "projection" or the "false consensus effect," in which individuals— even strangers—tend to overestimate how much others agree with their judgments, values, positions, choices, or behaviors.[13] In short, some surrogates may confuse what they want with what the patient wants and thereby fail to acknowledge (to observers as well as to themselves) that they are actually acting on their own wishes and not those of the patient.

Family members reflected publicly and privately on the impact of a treatment decision on themselves and others. But thinking is not doing. For a handful of patients, these interests clearly defined the decision-making process, propelling them onto the "What We Want" trajectory. Others considered, flirted, addressed, or struggled with these interests, eventually to resist the magnetic pull of this path. And still others began their journey on this trajectory—for example, authorizing aggressive care because they selfishly could not envision life without the patient or bear the guilt of responsibility for the patient's death—but eventually changed their path, whether because the prognosis seemed hopeless, because of the patient's suffering, or because a physician or significant other goaded them to think about what the patient would want.

7. Denial, Opting Out

The patient is an active eighty-four-year-old woman. Her family is sitting in a conference room with the palliative care team. The fellow has just explained that the patient's infection is widespread—in her brain, her spine, and her organs.

GRANDDAUGHTER-IN-LAW: Well why can't they do a transplant? Can't one of us give her a kidney or somethin'?

PALLIATIVE CARE ATTENDING: The infection is affecting all of her organs. She is also very sick, too sick for a transplant.

DAUGHTER: Her [the granddaughter-in-law's] mother was real sick and she got the transplant.

GRANDDAUGHTER-IN-LAW: Yeah, my mom was so sick, she was about to die too, and they were having the same conversation you guys are havin' with us. Her organs was failing, the liver, the kidneys. Then she got a transplant and she's fine.

PALLIATIVE CARE ATTENDING: I understand that you have had this experience. And I am very glad that the outcome was positive for your mother. It's a very different situation here though. [Patient's] entire body is infected. There is no way for us to transplant the entire inside of someone's body. Based on what everyone has told you, what all the doctors think of her prognosis, what do you think will happen to her?

DAUGHTER: Well, I'm hopin' that she gonna get better and come home.

GRANDDAUGHTER-IN-LAW: We don't wanna give up.

PALLIATIVE CARE ATTENDING: I can tell you that you have done everything you can for her. I think instead of thinking of it as giving up, you should think of it as letting go.

GRANDDAUGHTER-IN-LAW: No, we don't wanna let go.

PALLIATIVE CARE ATTENDING: Of course you do not. But there are a lot of things that we must do in life even though we don't want to. Perhaps you can think of this as the time to say good-bye.

GRANDDAUGHTER-IN-LAW: No, we don't want to say good-bye. We don't want her to die.

PALLIATIVE CARE ATTENDING: Yes, but everyone dies at some point. Nobody lives forever. And I believe that this is [Patient's] time.

GREAT-GRANDSON: We thought you wasn't gonna convince us or anything, but it seems like that's what you're tryin' to do. [*Up until this point, he has mostly been looking down with a stunned look on his face. Now he seems upset and suspicious.*]

PALLIATIVE CARE ATTENDING: I apologize that it's coming across that way. I am trying to be honest with you. I assume you want honesty from your doctors?

DAUGHTER: Yeah, we do.

PALLIATIVE CARE ATTENDING: I wouldn't want to lie to you. I am giving you our honest recommendations based on what we believe her chances of recovery are.

GRANDDAUGHTER-IN-LAW: We thought you guys was callin' us in here because you had some good news for us, you were gonna give us some hope.

PALLIATIVE CARE ATTENDING: I'm sorry. I know this is so difficult for you all. Why don't you tell me what your hopes are for her?

DAUGHTER: I don't want her to die.

PALLIATIVE CARE ATTENDING: I know that. Nobody wants anyone they love to die. But we're all adults here. We understand that there are things in life that you have to accept even when you don't want to. What are your hopes for her if you continue treating her?

DAUGHTER: I want her to come back home and be like she was.

PALLIATIVE CARE ATTENDING: It sounds to me like you want her to come home and be the same person she was before.

DAUGHTER: It would be okay if she was only partial what she was before. If she could just be talkin', walkin', something.

PALLIATIVE CARE FELLOW: I don't think that's going to happen.

PALLIATIVE CARE ATTENDING: Do you think that's realistic?

DAUGHTER: I don't know. Every time I see her move, I get excited and think she gonna be able to get up and come home with us.

Many loved ones probably have difficulty initially taking in a horrific diagnosis or prognosis. But, like the members of this family, a handful of other ICU families experienced continued disbelief or denial about the dismal prognosis of their loved one. As described in more detail in chapter 5, some disagreed with specialists about the ability of the patient to understand what was happening, the severity of the illness, the likelihood of recovery, or the possibility of a miracle. Like the family whose story opened chapter 1, a few families even refused to believe that the patient was brain-dead.

These debates played out on various stages. A few desperate surrogates scoured the Internet for experimental treatments or more talented physicians at other hospitals and pleaded that the team undertake the former and consult with the latter. Others refused to speak with physicians who they believed had given up hope. Recall the sister in chapter 5 who asked when the critical care attending's rotation would end because all he does "is talk about funeral services" and that her sister is going to die. She didn't want to see him any more unless he could "tell me reasons to have hope."

Like the granddaughter-in-law in the last example, several pointed to other family members, acquaintances, or even the patients themselves who had previously recovered from a similarly desperate prognosis.

MOTHER-IN-LAW: The thing is, we've had so many different opinions. When she was first at [Outside Hospital], they said there was no chance. But then she went to rehab and she was moving her arm and improving. So it's hard to trust what the doctors are saying because it's changed so much. It's real fickle, ya know?

Others relied on their understandings or beliefs about medical science. One patient in the study had been shot in the head, the bullet ricocheting throughout the brain before coming to rest in an inoperable location. Despite receiving dismal prognostic reports from the neurosurgeons and neurologists, the patient's family members spoke repeatedly about hearing that people only use 2 percent of their brains. They therefore expressed confidence that the patient would be okay and resisted entreaties by physicians to reconsider goals of care.

Some surrogates felt that their bedside observations of a seemingly responsive patient did not square with the diagnoses professionals insisted upon.

ETHICS ATTENDING: I just don't know if she's past the point where she can communicate.

DAUGHTER: She's been nodding to me today and she squeezes my hand. I know you disagree with me, but I think that she's with it and communicating fine.

ETHICS ATTENDING: When I saw her last night—

DAUGHTER: I know, she was agitated.

ETHICS ATTENDING: She was looking frantically around. She really seemed delirious to me.

DAUGHTER: I don't agree with that. There is absolutely no evidence to support that.

ETHICS ATTENDING: Maybe I should explain what that means medically, the way I'm using it. It means that there are problems with her brain functioning.

DAUGHTER: No, if that were the case, it would be occurring today also and it's not.

ETHICS ATTENDING: No, that's not necessarily true.

DAUGHTER: She's with it; I know she is.

ETHICS ATTENDING: Ethically, clinically, and legally, in order for a patient to give consent, they need to demonstrate that they have an understanding of what the options are and what's going on—

DAUGHTER: She knows.

ETHICS ATTENDING: Ethically, she needs to be able to repeat back to us her understanding of her options.

CAREGIVER: How can she do that if she can't talk?

ETHICS ATTENDING: We may be past the point where she can communicate that to us.

DAUGHTER: I am a [profession]. I specialize in communication. She squeezes my hand to communicate with me.

ETHICS ATTENDING: Patients cannot demonstrate an understanding of all the issues involved just by yes or no.

DAUGHTER: I know you disagree with my decision, but we're not changing our minds.

ETHICS ATTENDING: I don't agree or disagree. I just—

DAUGHTER: Basically you're saying that regardless of what our decision is and what her wishes are, you're going to do what you want instead.

ETHICS ATTENDING: [*Throws head back at this comment and looks shocked.*] Did you get that from what I said?

DAUGHTER: Yeah, that's what it sounds like to me.

Recall as well the brother in chapter 5 who observed his sister blinking at three in the morning and argued that this was a sign that she will "rebound."

Like the daughter in the previous example, others simply distrusted the medical team and did not believe that it had the best interest of the patient at heart.

MEDICAL STUDENT: That's why we're going to do the apnea test [a test for brain death in which the patient is temporarily removed from the ventilator and, under controlled conditions, neurologists determine whether the patient tries to breathe]. If she doesn't pass [the test], it means she's no longer with us. But we're hoping that won't be the case.

MOTHER-IN-LAW: If she passed the test, would you tell us the truth?

MEDICAL STUDENT: No, no, of course we would. That's what we're hoping for, because that's what you want. We would absolutely not lie to you. There will be a lot of people in the room to witness it, so a lot of people will see it happen and we will be 100 percent honest with you.

Recall from chapter 4 the daughter who accused the doctors of declaring her mother brain-dead so that they could steal her organs.

Because surrogates traversing this last trajectory were distrustful of the medical team or considerably more hopeful about the outcome for their loved ones, their encounters with the team tended to be more argumentative, hostile, or adversarial. Family members focused on or questioned small details—test results, dosages, settings or numbers on the monitors—unwilling or unable to see the forest for the trees. Recall from chapter 5 an impassioned plea by a critical care attending about a young patient tragically dying of metastatic breast cancer. After expressing his certainty that she would die, he shared his fear that she may be suffering.

CRITICAL CARE ATTENDING: I can't say for sure whether she is in any pain or not, because the only person who knows is [Patient] and she can't tell us. But in situations like this, the family needs to decide whether this is what the patient would have wanted. Some people think that life is just so precious that any extra moment, minute, day, regardless of the quality or whether the person even has any awareness, is worth living. Other people put limits on what is acceptable. It can have to do with religious reasons, cultural reasons, experiences, whatever. But as her family, we need you to make the decision that she would have wanted under these circumstances. We have been treating her very aggressively. I don't make judgments on what patients choose for themselves, or what families choose for patients, assuming it's what they believe in their hearts the patient would want.

MOTHER: Can you explain to me why we just turned the fentanyl [pain medication] off entirely?

CRITICAL CARE ATTENDING: Hang on. We can talk about that. But first can you respond to the first part, everything I just said a moment ago?

In another example from chapter 5, a neurosurgery attending updated a patient's daughter on her mother's poor prognosis. He then explained that if the family wanted to "continue to do everything, she will need a shunt and a few other medical things." But then the critical care attending weighed in.

CRITICAL CARE ATTENDING: I want to be clear. Even in a best-case scenario, she will probably need twenty-four-hour care and lots of help. And she won't ever get back to where she was before this happened.

DAUGHTER: How's her CT?

NEUROSURGERY ATTENDING: The ventricles are a little smaller.

DAUGHTER: How's her X-ray?

CRITICAL CARE ATTENDING: Her lungs look better. There is a little more fluid, but that's to be expected since we clamped the drains. The issue is really her brain.

Like the mother and daughter in these two examples and others throughout the book, it is not uncommon for loved ones to respond to difficult prognostic news by changing the subject or focusing on small details.

Some surrogates simply avoided the encounters altogether, staying away from the hospital, refusing to take or return phone calls from the hospital, being unavailable when staff wanted to schedule a family meeting, and refusing to reconsider goals of care.[14] These surrogates readily authorized more interventions but avoided decisions or even conversations to back off of treatment. Because aggressive treatment is the legal default, these avoidance techniques ensured that patients received the care that their families believed would cure them. They secured treatment without having to make decisions.

Patients whose surrogates took the opt out or denial trajectory often languished in the ICU longer than most other patients. Their suffering and distress was especially difficult on the health care staff who cared for them. A critical care resident treating the young woman with metastatic breast cancer (the subject of the conversation between the attending and her mother above) confessed, "A little piece of my soul dies every time I walk into her room. I know it sounds cheesy, but it's true." A second critical care resident and a fellow responded that they were very torn up over this and reported that nurses in the ICU were complaining that they were being ordered to torture the patient.

Conclusion

Some existing studies of the surrogate decision-making process ask surrogates or other family members—usually weeks or months after the patient died—how they made their treatment decisions. Overall, these studies suggest that the decision-making process has cognitive, emotional, and interpersonal elements.[15] The studies find that, over time, surrogates come to understand and reframe the situation and make an internal judgment before expressing a decision to health care providers. They draw on and are influenced by cues discerned from the patient; impressions; moral intuitions; distressing emotions; review and rewriting of the patient's life story; the surrogate's own beliefs, values, needs, and interests; family needs, relationships, well-being, and consensus; and relationships with health care providers. Within this general framework, the studies find that surrogates vary in whether they understand the severity of the patient's illness or are still quite hopeful, make decisions based more on facts or emotions, have difficulty processing information, communicate well or poorly, or experience substantial conflict with their extended family.[16]

Many of these findings complement what the medical social worker and I observed in the two intensive care units. In appendix A, I elaborate on the substantial biases inherent in the retrospective interviewing employed in these studies, which persuaded me to find an alternative strategy to understand surrogate decision making. The decision-making trajectories described in this chapter come from observing, day after day, what participants do, ask, answer, say (or do not say)—both in words and in body language. Observers certainly cannot see into the participants' heads, exposing their otherwise invisible cognitive and emotional experience throughout the course of the patient's critical illness. Some would say retrospective interviews cannot do so either. There is no doubt that we observed occasional self-censorship and that what is said at the bedside may not always correspond with what is felt or thought—or even what is said away from the ICU. But with numerous opportunities to observe, the continual questioning and jousting between family members and physicians alike, and the fact that because stakes are high, time is short, and nerves are frayed, statements are more raw and less embroidered, we usually got a reasonably good sense—if perhaps sometimes only a partial one—of how decisions were made.

Observations of decision making do not reveal how patients might have felt about the decision criteria, judgments, and inferences their surrogates formulated. What were the real-world results of the *Newlywed Game* scenarios played out in the ICUs? Even among the patients who survived their ICU admission, most rarely regained competence while still in the unit and able to weigh in on their surrogate's medical decisions or the criteria they employed to make them. And even when they did regain capacity, the fact that they could not witness in real time the excruciating choices— nested often in equivocal information—their surrogates faced day after day renders their judgments profoundly tainted by hindsight bias.

Still, the words of one such patient, the seventy-six-year-old wife of a farmer whose fear of losing her impelled him to seek aggressive treatment despite what he described as his wife's wishes, continue to haunt me. After she regained consciousness in the ICU, she bit through three breathing tubes in an effort to kill herself. Each day she pleaded with the nurses: "Please kill me. Please help me die. Make it quick." They did not, and the patient was transferred to a long-term acute care facility, where she died about six months later.

Though observations at the bedside do not witness how other ICU patients felt about the decision criteria employed or choices made by their surrogates, they do show what happened to patients whose surrogates traversed the varied trajectories. The next chapter examines which surrogates opted for one trajectory over another and describes what impact physicians, trajectory choice, and advance directives had on the ultimate treatment decisions that surrogates made on behalf of patients and the outcome of their stay in the ICU.

EIGHT

Making a Difference?

The last chapter mapped out the varied decision-making trajectories that surrogates constructed and followed as they made medical decisions on behalf of loved ones. Some trajectories were heavily traveled, others less so. This chapter explores the traffic patterns and the role of physicians in directing the traffic, examines which surrogates opted for one trajectory over another, and asks what difference, if any, the choice of trajectory or advance directives made in the process, outcome, or impact of decision making on patients and families.

When numbers were presented throughout the last chapter, they represented the frequency with which particular themes came up at the bedside—whether initiated by friends, family, surrogates, or health care providers—even if they did not ultimately influence the treatment decisions that surrogates made. Now only the decision criteria that were instrumental in surrogate deliberations are considered.

As noted at the end of the last chapter, because surrogates were not interviewed, it is impossible to know what was in their heads or hearts, or even what they claimed was in their heads or hearts. But observations do record what they said and how they said it, how they responded to the queries or advice or accusations of others, what they ignored or refused to acknowledge, what they protested or argued or pleaded about, what their bodies and emotions expressed, and how all of this evolved over time.

When their verbal expressions were limited or equivocal, I do not venture to guess the criteria surrogates employed. This was the case for 5 percent of the patients, usually because a crucial decision could not be observed or surrogates offered no clue to their reasoning. For another 30 percent, interactions between health care providers and patients' families were limited to medical updates, and deliberations about interventions or goals of care were never broached; these patients typically were less critically ill and spent less time in the ICUs. For the remaining patients, observations tracked which decision criteria were significant in deliberations throughout the ICU admission. For 44 percent of the remaining patients, only a single trajectory was followed; about half of their surrogates traversed two or three trajectories simultaneously or serially, the remainder as many as five. One in ten surrogates switched trajectories along the way.

The bars in figure 8.1 show how many surrogates ever followed a particular trajectory. Clearly some paths are far more crowded than others. For almost two-thirds of the patients, surrogates and other family members tried to replicate the patients' treatment preferences by reprising wishes that they expressed in the past (41 percent), standing in their shoes and exercising substituted judgment (53 percent), or both. A little more than a quarter of surrogates made decisions that favored the interests of self and others ("what we want"). And about one in five considered beneficence—either the patient's suffering or best interest or both. The other trajectories were far less busy, all but denial at or below 10 percent of surrogates.

Among the relatively small number of surrogates who switched trajectories over time, the biggest change is seen among those who initially prioritized their own needs over those of the patient. The number at admission's

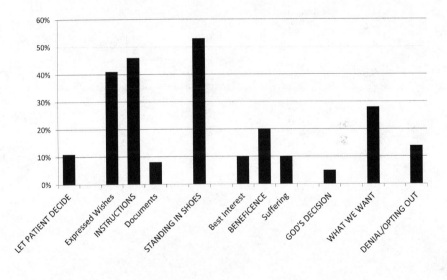

"INSTRUCTIONS" includes surrogates who relied on the patient's expressed wishes and/or documents. "BENEFICENCE" includes surrogates who cited best interest and/or suffering.

Figure 8.1. Decision Trajectories Followed

end is substantially lower than it was initially. Sizable changes can also be found among surrogates who initially felt that the patient should decide and those along the beneficence trajectory. The former numbers dropped, presumably when it became apparent that the patient would not regain decision-making capacity, and the latter numbers increased, perhaps as the patient's suffering intensified or became difficult to ignore or justify in light of increasingly futile interventions.

As noted above, more than half of the surrogates traversed several trajectories simultaneously or over the course of the ICU admission. For example, all of the surrogates who felt that the decision was up to God also followed additional trajectories in their treatment decisions. When families consider multiple decision-making criteria, the trajectories they travel show some distinctive patterns. Appendix C presents the percentage of each trajectory that was traversed alone or with one of the other trajectories.

Statistical techniques present these patterns visually and show the similarity or distance between the trajectories. Figure 8.2 provides a three-dimensional display of the statistical results.[1] The x-axis differentiates decisions that seek to fulfill the wishes of the patient (left) versus those of the

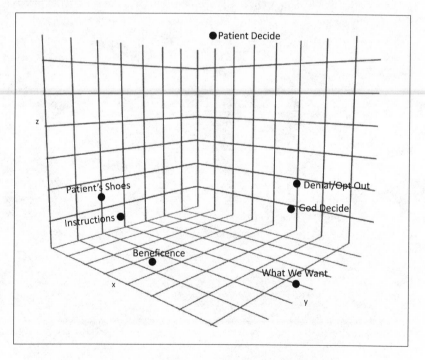

Figure 8.2. Relationships between Trajectories

surrogate or family (right). The y-axis differentiates those who won't decide or leave the decision to God (back) versus those who seek to do what's best for the patient (front). And the z-axis differentiates between those who want the patient to decide (top) and everyone else (at or near the bottom).

When surrogates travel more than one trajectory, they most likely follow one plotted close to the first. Surrogates on the "It's God's Decision" trajectory are often also traversing the "Denial, Opting Out" trajectory, perhaps in part because waiting for miracles or God's intervention may come across as denial or opting out of decision making. These surrogates in the back of the figure, embracing God or opting out, might also prioritize "What They Want" but are unlikely to consider "Beneficence," "Reprising Patient's Instructions," or "Standing in the Patient's Shoes," located in the front and left.

Surrogates following the patient's instructions often also stand in their shoes, especially perhaps where the instructions prove deficient. The "Patient Should Decide" trajectory perches high above the figure on the left. Though this trajectory stands alone on the figure, surrogates along this trajectory are more likely to consider the patients' instructions or stand in their shoes, especially as it becomes apparent that the patient won't decide. Horizontal distances on the figure differentiate trajectories on the left that seek to bring the patient's voice into the conversation and those on the right that are indifferent to the patient's actual or likely wishes.

Figure 8.2 displays very distinctive decision-making strategies that surrogates invent or adopt. A majority of surrogates gravitate to the bottom left-hand side of the figure—privileging beneficence or the patient's actual or likely wishes—as lawmakers and ethicists would hope. But many do not, giving voice to different values, beliefs, or interests.

The Role of Physicians

Numerous examples presented in the last chapter showed physicians trying to frame the decision-making process or to encourage surrogates to broaden or reconsider their decision-making criteria. Physicians played an active role in shaping the decision-making process for two-fifths of the surrogates. Some opined about process; others stated the patient's wishes or helped surrogates make the decision. On a few occasions, a physician who was displeased with the surrogate's preferences (usually to limit care) offloaded the surrogate onto a different physician. And, on occasion, physicians told surrogates what the treatment decisions would be. Here are two examples from each ICU, one to continue aggressive interventions, the other to limit them.

NEUROSURGERY ATTENDING: There is about a 20–30 percent chance of a good recovery. Some patients will come dancing back into my office. About 70 percent of all patients with this sort of injury have a poor recovery—they may need a nursing home or do not make it. We won't know much for a month, because we have to wait for the swelling of the brain to go down.

DAUGHTER NO. 2: She will be like this for a month? [*Some upset in her voice*]

NEUROSURGERY ATTENDING: What do you mean?

DAUGHTER NO. 2: Lying here on these machines?

DAUGHTER NO. 1: We just went through this two years ago with my father.

NEUROSURGERY ATTENDING: He had an aneurysm?

DAUGHTER NO. 2: No, a hemorrhagic stroke.

NEUROSURGERY ATTENDING: That's a completely different disease. It just looks the same.

DAUGHTER NO. 1: It's just that she was so clear—

[*The neurosurgery attending interrupts the daughter. I suspect that she was about to say that her mother was very clear that she didn't want this kind of treatment.*]

NEUROSURGERY ATTENDING: You will see lots of patients on this floor that look exactly the same, but the disease is very different.

DAUGHTER NO. 1: I just don't want her to suffer.

NEUROSURGERY ATTENDING: Most patients will not remember any of this.

DAUGHTER NO. 1: [*Mutters quietly*] Only we will.

NEUROSURGERY ATTENDING: Every once in a while, I will get a patient who will remember a little incident, but most don't. Early next week we will replace the breathing tube with something more permanent and will put a tube in her stomach for feeding. That will make her much more comfortable. We will do an MRA [scan of blood vessels] tomorrow. That only checks on the vessels. We will probably do an angio [another type of scan] next week. Perhaps we will do an MRI in about two weeks. That might tell us what areas of the brain were affected, which might help in the prognosis. The biggest risk is in the first two weeks after the rupture. There is a risk of vasospasm [sudden narrowing of the blood vessels, which can lead to stroke]. We check for that with Dopplers [type of ultrasound], like what they just did. Our goal is to give the very best care possible so that the patient makes it into the 30 percent. Some patients will take a year or two to get back to where they were. Others will come back 90 percent; they will be 90 percent themselves.

ONCOLOGY ATTENDING: So over the weekend, her blood pressure dropped very low. When the blood pressure drops like that, it is a sign that the patient is very, very, very sick. They gave her some medicine to raise her blood pressure. She doesn't need it now and isn't taking it now. This is my opinion. It may not be your opinion. But in my opinion, giving this medicine is really the same thing as resuscitation—giving shocks or chest compressions. If something should happen—if her heart should stop or her blood pressure drops again—I don't think we should do anything.

[*There is a long silence. Daughter starts crying.*]

ONCOLOGY ATTENDING: Talk to me, guys.

[*There is no response.*]

ONCOLOGY ATTENDING: They gave her sleeping medication. You remember before, it takes her about three days to wake up from the sleeping medication. [*Counts on her fingers.*] So it has already been two days without the medicine. Tomorrow will be three days. We don't want to remove the tube while she is sleepy. We want her to be as awake as possible before we do this. Then we will remove the tube and see if she can breathe on her own. If she can't, then we will give her morphine that will help her breathe, but the main reason is so she is comfortable and doesn't feel like she is choking to death.

. . .

CRITICAL CARE FELLOW: We want her to be the very best before we try this. If it doesn't look like she will be able to breathe on her own, we will talk to you before we remove the tube. Maybe we will give her a little more time and try again.

ONCOLOGY ATTENDING: That's right. Nothing is written in stone. [*Mutters to daughter under her breath.*] You can't live without your lungs.

[*Daughter begins to cry uncontrollably. Oncology attending puts her arms around her and strokes her hair.*]

ONCOLOGY ATTENDING: Oh, baby! We will do everything we can for her. But either we are helping her or we are torturing her. I don't want to make her suffer. This is what she would want.

Figure 8.3 displays the differences in physician engagement across trajectories. The figure shows that physicians tend to play a more active role in the adoption of trajectories that embrace legal and ethical standards—types of beneficence (especially patient suffering [93 percent], which sometimes caused deep distress for health care providers) as well as consideration of advance directives and standing in the patient's shoes. It is notable that physicians rarely play an active role in decisions in which the patient's wishes, values, personality, and the like are not mentioned (bar with horizontal dashes on far right of figure 8.3). When ethical standards are not being entertained, physicians often try to convince surrogates to consider a different path. This is reflected in the bar with the horizontal dashes on the near right-hand side of the figure, which indicates that, for

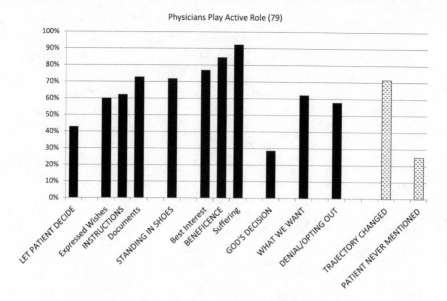

Figure 8.3. Physicians Play an Active Role in Decision Making

more than 70 percent of surrogate decisions to change course, physicians play a significant role in decision making. Physicians were more successful in persuading a course correction for some trajectories (suffering, self-interest) than for others (denial).

Opting for a Trajectory

Just as there are patterns in which decision-making trajectories tend to cluster together, there are patterns in the characteristics of patients or surrogates who adopt a particular trajectory. Several patient characteristics help predict their surrogate's location in the three-dimensional space represented in figure 8.2. The surrogates of black patients are more likely to be found in the back and right-hand side of the figure ("It's God's Decision," "Denial, Opting Out," "What We Want"); white, Hispanic, and patients of other ethnicities closer to the front and left ("Beneficence," "Reprising Patient Instructions," "Standing in the Patient's Shoes"). Surrogates of patients who are younger tend to opt for trajectories on the right-hand side of the figure ("What We Want"), those of older patients on the left ("Reprising Patient Instructions," "Standing in the Patient's Shoes"). And the surrogates who wait for the patient to decide (high above the figure) act on behalf of patients who are less critically ill. Presumably that is why they think that they can wait.

Although the severity of patients' illness,[2] their age, and to a lesser extent their race best predict the trajectories followed by surrogates, there are some more nuanced patterns as well. Bar charts (like those in figures 8.1 and 8.3) provide more detailed breakdowns on a variety of patient and surrogate characteristics across all of the decision trajectories. They are collected in appendix D. Because some of the categories presented in the figures are relatively small, some of the differences in these figures are not especially reliable or statistically significant. Nonetheless, several patterns are quite apparent.

For a number of characteristics, one finds sharp differences between trajectories on the left side of these bar charts ("The Patient Should Decide," "Beneficence," and especially "Reprising Patient Instructions" and "Standing in the Patient's Shoes") and those on the right ("It's God's Decision," "What We Want," and "Denial, Opting Out"). White patients are much more likely to be on the left and black patients on the right (with the few Hispanic patients in the study generally in between black and white patients). This pattern is replicated between older (left) and younger (right) patients, sickest (left, except as noted before, those who want the patient to decide) and least critically ill (right); patients with preexisting medical problems (left) and those whose problems came out of the blue (right);[3] Catholics and Jews (left) and Protestants (black, white, and other—right); and parents as surrogates (right) and everyone else (left). The figures show few gender differences, though there is a tendency, when patients are female, for surrogates to be both more concerned about patient documents and suffering and less deferential to God's decision. Male surrogates are more likely to follow documents, female surrogates God.

Of course, patients and surrogates possess bundles of characteristics, simultaneously affecting the choices made. The patient's age may propel surrogates in one direction, their race in another, and the severity of their illness in another. For example, parents who serve as surrogates are also more likely to speak on behalf of younger as well as black patients.[4] Several possible explanations may account for the distinctive decision criteria that parents adopt. First, younger patients are less likely to have preexisting medical problems. Second, these patients undoubtedly provide less guidance to their surrogates about medical decision making, making it difficult to reprise their instructions or stand in their shoes. Third, perhaps parents don't accord their children much autonomy over their own self-interests or—reflecting projection or false-consensus bias—assume that the values and preferences of their children are identical to their own. Fourth, African American patients and families may bring different religious beliefs, cultural expectations, values, and histories with the health care system to the bedside, which would affect their priorities. Finally, surrogates and physicians alike tend to push ahead aggressively when patients are younger because their chance of recovery is greater (even when desperately ill) and because many find it especially tragic to give up on younger patients with a promising life ahead of them. Unfortunately, these and more nuanced explanations are not easily disentangled with these data.

Whatever the reasons, 36 percent of the surrogates of young black patients, for example, felt that God should decide compared to 0 percent of those of elderly white patients. Nine percent of the former stand in the patient's shoes, compared to 59 percent of the latter; and 55 percent of the former consider their own self-interest, versus 24 percent of the latter. Surrogates of older black patients and younger white patients generally fall between the first two groups. To take another example, among patients whose religious preference is known, 70 percent of surrogates representing older white Catholics share the patients' expressed instructions, compared to 29 percent of those for older white Protestants; 10 percent of the former decide based on self-interest, compared to 24 percent of the latter. And so on. The decision criteria that surrogates adopt are often a reflection of those for whom they decide—so much so that on several occasions I would be startled when a surrogate in an especially predictable demographic category would go way "off script." (However, sometimes they did so in only a single encounter, switching back to a more predictable trajectory in subsequent encounters.)

However intriguing these apparent differences, techniques that disentangle the simultaneous effect of multiple characteristics find that only a few predict the decision-making criteria adopted:[5] surrogates of patients with more severe illness are more likely to traverse the "Standing in the Patient's Shoes" and "Suffering" trajectories. As noted earlier, those with less severe illness follow the "Patient Should Decide" trajectory. Surrogates of older patients reprised their expressed wishes. Surrogates of black patients felt that God should decide. None of the other matchups of characteristics (net of the others) and trajectories are statistically significant, although this may reflect the relatively small number of patients in the study in certain demographic categories.

Outcomes

It should come as no surprise that the criteria that surrogates embrace lead to different decisions and ultimately different outcomes for patients as well as surrogates. Figure 8.4 provides one perspective on decisions made for the *most* critically ill patients. It displays the goals of care that surrogates embraced at the conclusion of the patients' ICU admission. The black bars indicate the percentage of surrogates who authorized continued aggressive interventions intended to keep the patient alive—surgeries, cardiac resuscitation (CPR), medications to raise the patient's blood pressure (pressors) and other lifesaving medications, ventilators, dialysis, tracheostomies, feeding tubes, blood transfusions, and the like. The bars with horizontal dashes show the percentage of surrogates who did not authorize these interventions or requested that they be removed or that there be no escalation of care.

Although most surrogates—even of the most critically ill patients—authorized at least some aggressive interventions at the beginning of the ICU admission, they were almost four times more likely at the very end to limit interventions than to continue or escalate them. Figure 8.4 shows considerable variation in this ratio across the decision trajectories, however. At one extreme, 100 percent of the surrogates who cited the patient's

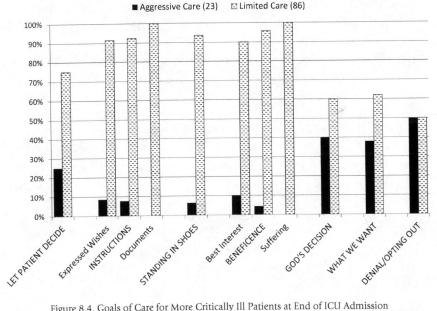

Figure 8.4. Goals of Care for More Critically Ill Patients at End of ICU Admission

documents or were worried about their suffering chose to limit care. At the other extreme, surrogates in denial or who opted out were no more likely to limit aggressive care than to authorize it. Although the remaining trajectories led to decisions more likely to limit than continue aggressive care, the "It's God's Decision," "What We Want," and (to a lesser extent) "The Patient Should Decide" trajectories authorized aggressive care considerably more often than the others.

These differences in the embrace of aggressive versus limited care are reflected in the length of ICU admissions. While half of the patients whose surrogates followed most of the trajectories spent eight or nine days in the ICU, those on the "The Patient Should Decide" trajectory spent twelve days on average, "What We Want" thirteen days, and those in denial or who chose to opt out a stunning twenty-four days—three times longer on average than patients whose surrogates reprised their expressed wishes or stood in their shoes.

For these most critically ill patients, their ultimate fate mirrored their surrogates' decisions to authorize or limit aggressive care. Where care was limited, patients died. Where surrogates sought aggressive interventions right up to the end, 39 percent of the patients died in the hospital despite heroic efforts and lengthy hospitalization, slightly more than half were discharged to a long-term acute care facility (which takes patients on ventilators and where about half died within the first six months), and only 9 percent were discharged to a nursing home, a rehabilitation facility, or the patient's residence (the outcome for almost two-thirds of the least critically ill patients).

Figure 8.5, which breaks down the final outcome by trajectory for the more critically ill patients in the ICU, follows directly from figure 8.4. The bars with horizontal dashes reflect the percentage of critically ill patients who died; the black bars, those sent on ventilators to a long-term acute care facility; and the white bars, those who were discharged home or to a nursing home or rehabilitation facility. Because patients do not always survive aggressive interventions, the black bars (aggressive care) in figure 8.4 are a bit taller than the sum of the black and white bars (anything but death) in figure 8.5. Strikingly, while 40 percent of patients on the "It's God's Decision" trajectory were recipients of aggressive care, they nonetheless all died in the ICU. Still, a not-insignificant number of patients whose surrogates followed their own interests, opted out of decision making, or waited for the patient to decide survived their unusually long ICU admissions, albeit for a relatively short time or with permanent disabilities.

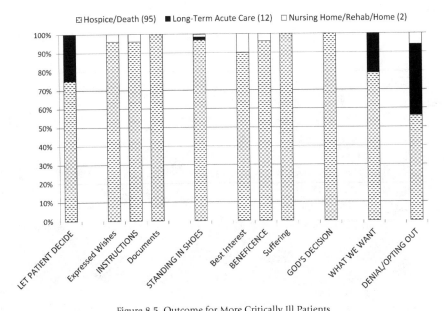

Figure 8.5. Outcome for More Critically Ill Patients

These figures suggest that the decision-making trajectory chosen leads to the final outcome. For example, distress about the patient's suffering causes surrogates to limit the source of suffering, which thereby results in the patient's death. Or denial that the patient is gravely ill causes surrogates to insist on continued aggressive interventions over many weeks, which ultimately stabilizes some patients enough to be transferred to another facility. But an alternative interpretation is certainly worth considering: that the surrogate decides on the outcome first and then finds a rationalization that supports it. For example, surrogates decide to discontinue treatment and then explain that the patient has suffered enough or that the patient would have wanted this (the "Standing in the Patient's Shoes" trajectory). Or they want to keep the patient alive at all costs and invoke God as the reason that treatment must continue, a perhaps somewhat cynical perspective on the surrogates' struggles.

Although such post hoc rationalizations or justifications may play a role in the decision-making process for some surrogates, they are not supported by much of the data. If data were only available on the last encounter over the final treatment decision, it would be more difficult to disentangle the causal order of whether rationale came first or second. But observers witnessed encounters over many days or weeks surrounding varied treatment decisions or none at all. Decision makers gave voice to fears, beliefs, memories, instructions, values, priorities, promises, distrust, disbelief, and personal experience often before any treatment decision was entertained and certainly before life-or-death decisions were considered. In short, surrogates had started down the trajectories even before they encountered a decision point, especially the final one. Less often surrogates reflected in hindsight about the decision-making process, confessing, for example, that they had flouted the patient's wishes, been selfish, or acted out of guilt. Perhaps a handful of surrogates who wanted to keep the patient alive at all costs ignored their directives or discounted their apparent suffering. But for so many of the others, decision-making priorities preceded the decisions themselves and undoubtedly helped surrogates to formulate them.

The decision-making trajectory chosen appeared to have an impact on family members as well as patients. Throughout the ICU admission, surrogates and family members commented on the emotional burden of decision making. The first example comes from a father who reprised his son's instructions in chapter 7.

FATHER: This is my son. This is the hardest thing I've ever been through, and I've been through some really hard stuff.

ONCOLOGY NURSE: Of course—it's the hardest thing in the world.

FATHER: When I first got here, I thought we were losing him. His hemoglobin was 7, and I thought he was going to die that day. I lost my mother a few years ago. She told me she was ready to go. It was the hardest thing for me to do, saying okay and letting her go. But I asked [Patient] what he wants when it's time to pull the plug. His mother asked him and he said, "Fight for me, Mom." So that's what we're doing. We're not hanging on to him, we're hanging on to what he asked of us and we're doing everything we can to fight for him. I'm sitting here, at his bedside, right now—you can see—looking up everything I can to see what's out there for him. This is my son, and he said, "Fight for me, Dad." So I'm going to fight for him. These doctors don't understand that. I'm not going to give up on my son because he asked me to fight for him. . . . I can't be in the room. I have to walk out every time I hear the machine beeping when his blood pressure drops. I can't watch it happen. It's so hard. When I see him—[gets choked up and begins sobbing].

DAUGHTER: He's just such a proud man. I don't know if he would want this. I just wish he would've figured this all out for himself. Even when he can talk, he doesn't. So it's hard to know if he's with it or not. I have a twenty-five-year-old cat at home. He's blind and he runs into the walls but I can't bear to put him down. So this decision is like—

DAUGHTER: This is so difficult. I tell people to do powers of attorney all the time. I didn't know how difficult this is. I don't want to kill her, but— I am flummoxed. What keeps me up at night— We have been talking about this pretty much nonstop since this happened. That is pretty much all we talk about. . . . I never realized what a burden it is to be a power of attorney.

SISTER: This is a nightmare. . . . This is like a mountain and we are at the bottom of the mountain. I live in terror that I am sentencing him to this [*points to her brother on all the machines*].

CRITICAL CARE ATTENDING [*Writing about the patient's wife*]: She tearfully told me that she felt "heartbroken" and "sick with worry" for the patient; she is unable to imagine a point in the future when she would feel good about transitioning the patient out of the ICU to another facility; she admits to overwhelming fears that he may worsen in the future, particularly at a long-term acute-care facility, and she "could not handle him getting sicker"; she acknowledges that we are providing good medical care for the patient and that she understands our recommendations. However, she cries daily and feels unable to handle the stress of the current situation.

This was a common lament; members of more than half of the families shared their distress at least once. Recall that the medical social worker and I did not speak with or interview surrogates or family members, so these complaints were spontaneously expressed during encounters with physicians. Undoubtedly others bore their anguish silently. Expressions of emotional burden were observed regardless of outcome; families who ultimately chose to limit care expressed only slightly more distress than those who did not. Still, as displayed in figure 8.6, the frequency of such expressions varied across the trajectories.

Generally, the bars and distress in figure 8.6 are lowest for trajectories in which surrogates avoid trying to determine the patient's wishes, as laws and bioethics rules require that surrogates try to do first. The trajectories on which families experience the least emotional burden include honoring the interests of the surrogate or family, determining what objectively is in the patient's best interest, and waiting for the patient to decide. In contrast, the emotional burden is highest when surrogates try to honor the

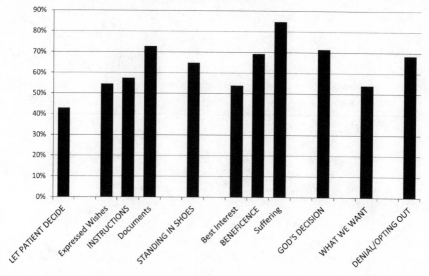

Figure 8.6. Emotional Burden of Decision Making

patients' expressed or documented wishes or their substituted judgments of the patients' likely wishes, or when they struggle with the patient's suffering.[6] Clearly, leaving instructions verbally or in writing does not help ameliorate the anguish suffered by loved ones. Interestingly, though, leaving the decision to God does not seem to relieve family members' distress nor does burying their heads in the sand, though perhaps these expressions of distress arise when physicians pressure them to consider or switch to another trajectory (i.e., the burden comes from the physicians and not the decision).

I Thought the Law Would Take Care of This

Since the living will was first conceived in the late 1960s, Americans have been encouraged—indeed, implored—by lawyers, physicians, health care institutions, journalists, celebrities, advocacy and community organizations, legislators, even an annual National Healthcare Decisions Day—to prepare advance directives. As elaborated in chapter 6, these legal documents specify the person to make health care decisions should one lose capacity in the future (proxy directives or health care powers of attorney) and/or state the type or amount of treatment desired (instructional directives or living wills). Although few of these advocates have declared the advance directive a panacea, most assert that it is essential and will help protect patients and their loved ones when the former can no longer speak for themselves. As the journalist Paula Span observed, "Nothing on paper can make such a moment less than wrenching, but the lack of something in writing can make it much, much worse."[7] Despite the encouragement and substantial resources devoted over half a century to assist Americans in preparing these documents, only a minority have followed through. Those who have probably assume that their directives will be at least as effective as Span promised. But are they?

The balance of empirical evidence on this question to date suggests otherwise.[8] But, although the studies are plentiful, many are plagued by a host of methodological compromises (described in appendix A) that yield equivocal answers at best. The observational ICU data provide a unique window on the process during which advance directives are invoked, ignored, interpreted, reinterpreted, or disputed, day after day, as a medical crisis plays out and decisions are made and remade. Unfortunately, the ICU data do not provide any more reassurance about the efficacy of advance directives.

Recall from the discussion of written instructions in chapter 7 that 23 percent of patients or their families produced copies of their advance directives and another 26 percent claimed—some erroneously—to have the documents elsewhere. The numbers for the two thousand–plus patients who passed through the two ICUs who did not qualify for the study were even worse: 8 percent and 26 percent, respectively. This latter group was a little younger and less severely ill than patients in the observational study, which may explain their lack of interest in advance directives. Still, among American adults sick enough to be admitted to an intensive care unit—if all claims are accurate—at best slightly more than a third prepared an advance directive. Even if the ICU data were to affirm that "the law does take care of it," policy makers would still face an enormous challenge getting substantial majorities of Americans to prepare these legal documents. But the ICU data do not find that advance directives make much difference.

The role and efficacy of advance directives in the ICU can be evaluated in a number of ways. First, was the document consulted or invoked in any of the conversations at the bedside? Some logistical discussions, often for patients without directives, were observed, for example: "Does the patient have a living will or power of attorney?" "Which of you guys is the power of attorney?" "It is important that you bring in a copy." "We brought it in yesterday; did you see it?" However, there was far less substantive discussion of the content of the directives. As presented in chapter 7, for only a third of patients with written directives in the hospital chart did anyone—health care provider or family member—mention, describe, or even ask about the patient's written wishes or instructions. One would expect even more discussion of these documented preferences when the alleged documents were off-site and unavailable for examination. Yet descriptions or even questions arose for only 11 percent of those claiming to have a written directive elsewhere. Moreover, in only 9 percent of the meetings in which goals of care were addressed—arguably where the patient's wishes are most relevant—did anyone ask about or describe treatment preferences specified in the advance directive.

Of course, the fact that the document is never mentioned does not mean that advance directives are not exerting an influence on how information is processed, how decisions are made, or who is making them. So, for those patients with copies of their directives in the hospital record, whose treatment preferences are therefore known, a second analysis examined the evidence of the directives' role in helping to honor patient wishes.[9] Tracking fine-grained observations of decision-making encounters, day after day, I found that for 45 percent of patients with in-hospital documents, directives made no discernible difference in the process or outcomes of decision making. There was no mention of directives in any of the conversations. Or family members were adamant about knowing and honoring the patient's wishes, and any reference to directives fell on deaf ears. Or the directives provided no guidance; they were either too general or addressed issues that did not apply.

Moreover, for every advance directive that seemingly helped honor patient wishes (26 percent of in-hospital directives)—by providing guidance, clarification, corroboration, or closure; fostering consensus; or assuaging guilt—another seemingly failed to do so or even undermined the patient's wishes (29 percent of directives). Most often, directives failed because their instructions were flouted, ignored, or misunderstood, or because surrogates insisted on following their own wishes or stated that it was their decision whether or not to honor the patient's wishes. Sometimes the directives did not represent the patient's preferences, either because the form had been filled out by someone else, used medical terms that the patient misunderstood, used jargon that meant something different to the family than to physicians, had been completed by the patient under pressure from a family member, or because the document was out-of-date and patient preferences, as expressed to hospital staff before the patient lost the capacity to make decisions, had changed. And occasionally the directive itself stood in the way of making the right decision because it was misinterpreted by a physician or family member or because the surrogate hid behind the document and refused to make any decision at all when the directive provided insufficient guidance.

This second analysis only pertains to the minority of patients who had a directive in the hospital record and whose wishes were known. An appreciation of the role of advance directives is profoundly incomplete without taking into account the vast majority of patients who do not have them at all. Do patients with no directives at all fare differently or perhaps even better than those with them? That is the true test of the efficacy of advance directives. Unfortunately, one cannot know the wishes of patients who never bothered to document them. So it is impossible to assess whether the treatment preferences of these patients were honored or abrogated by their surrogates. But if advance directives, or the conversations their completion occasions, provide authority, information, guidance, reassurance, or even absolution for family members or health care providers, or help foster consensus, one would expect to see their footprints somewhere in the decisions made or how they were reached.

A third analysis draws on data from the thousand-plus observed encounters to see whether there are any differences between decision makers armed with advance directives and those without them.[10] Statistical analyses control for patient characteristics and severity and suddenness of illness,[11] which are related to the likelihood of having or reporting an advance directive as well as prognosis, treatments considered, and how decision makers think about them. Across almost three dozen aspects of the decision-making process, outcomes, or impact—listed in appendix E, along with the statistical results—from whether and how participants described patient wishes to the decision criteria considered, how quickly decisions were reached, conflict, the emotional burden on family members, responses of health care providers, even the decisions themselves (from refusing an intervention to withdrawing life support), only one significant difference could be found. Although family members of patients with and without advance directives were equally likely to discuss goals of care, those of patients with directives more often initiated these discussions. Aside from that one exception, treatment decisions for patients with and without directives were not different, were made no faster, weighed similar criteria, and appeared to be no less burdensome for families.

Even if it were not surprising that there are no differences between families with and without directives in how they talk about decision making, the criteria they consider, or even the decisions they make, it would still be surprising that decisions were made at the same speed and with no difference in the extent of conflict among or emotional distress experienced by family members. One reason advocates tout advance directives is to protect family members from struggling to discern and take responsibility for difficult decisions on the patient's behalf. Physicians try to convey this comforting message when they explain to surrogates: "You are not making the decision. The patient made the decision; you are simply honoring her wishes." Advocates also promise that directives help foster consensus, since family members are simply following the instructions of the patient. And with greater ease in reaching consensus comes less protracted decisions and less conflict. Yet none of this was true in the two ICUs we observed.

Perhaps advance-directive documents outside of ICUs or in another jurisdiction are more directive than are those in this study. Perhaps they even help keep patients out of hospitals or intensive care units altogether—something that ICU data cannot address. But, at least in this ICU setting, there is very little support for the notion that directives are "taking care of this." One important implication of this study is that assuming that the extraordinary challenges of speaking for another near his or her life's end can be overcome or even mitigated with legal documents drafted in advance of incapacity is simply unsupported by the evidence.

Does Any of This Matter?

Findings about the efficacy of advance directives, coupled with those portrayed in figures 8.5 and 8.6 provide a very dispiriting conclusion to this chapter. On the one hand, most of the trajectories ultimately lead to the same destination—almost everyone who is more critically ill dies in the ICU or shortly thereafter. On the other hand, surrogates who strive for fidelity to patient wishes and who follow legal and ethical decision-making standards—whether intentionally or unknowingly—tend to experience the greatest emotional distress. And that is even before the patient dies. It looks like a lose-lose proposition. What should one make of this? And then it turns out that advance directives, touted to help ameliorate these challenges, make little difference. If the process is inevitably wrenching, as Span promised, and if she was wrong about advance directives making things "less worse," is there nothing to do? The concluding chapter weighs in on these and other questions.

NINE

The End

The end of the ICU visit—even in a first-rate teaching hospital—is rarely a happy occasion. The last chapter showed that the majority of the most severely ill ICU patients did not survive their hospitalization, either because surrogates decided to stop aggressive interventions or because the interventions failed. Table 9.1 shows that more than half of *all* patients in the ICU study died during their admission or in hospice thereafter, though the likelihood varied from 15 percent to 93 percent depending on the severity of their illness and the actions of their surrogate.[1] Still, overall, not even one in ten patients in the study went home, and not even one in three was discharged home or to a nursing or rehabilitation facility. And after six months, almost three-quarters of the patients in the study had died, even a substantial number who had been less critically ill.

Of course, as noted earlier, patients in the observational study were more critically ill than their counterparts who did not qualify for the study and who passed through the two ICUs, often for shorter periods and with decision-making capacity intact. And do not forget the handful of desperately ill patients in the observational study, described in chapter 5, whose recovery physicians reacted to as miraculous. So, for many patients, intensive care is lifesaving; indeed, for a very small minority, it is miraculous. The moral of this story is not to eschew intensive care. Rather, it is to be realistic about its promise.

Data are not available on the long-term quality of life of those who survived. Given the nature of their injuries, some were no doubt severely disabled. Surrogates who agonized about fates worse than death or making patients "better enough to be where they won't want" remind us that survival is not the only relevant measure of the efficacy of an ICU admission.

Table 9.1 Outcome of ICU Admission

	Critically ill			
	Least	Medium	Most	Total
Home	21%	2%	0%	7%
Rehab/nursing home	57%	14%	0%	23%
Long-term acute care*	7%	27%	7%	13%
Died despite full support	2%	2%	13%	6%
Died—limited care	13%	55%	80%	51%
Total	67	63	75	205
Dead within 6 months	39%	77%	97%	72%

*Long-term acute care (LTAC) hospitals take patients on ventilators. Patients who have been stabilized in the ICU but are unable to breathe on their own are typically discharged to an LTAC, where some are weaned off the ventilator and transferred elsewhere and where others live out the rest of their lives.

For some, remorse at ICU discharge may reflect the realization that survival and recovery are quite different outcomes.

The question is not simply whether, in hindsight, patients or their surrogates should have elected to visit an intensive care unit at all, but rather what specific interventions and overall goals of care should have been pursued, and for how long. Recall from the last chapter that there is substantial variability in the length of stay in the ICU depending on the decision-making trajectory that the surrogate followed. For example, the chapter demonstrated that the most critically ill patients whose surrogates were in denial or who chose to opt out of decision making were admitted to the ICU for twenty-four days on average—three times longer than those whose surrogates reprised their expressed wishes or stood in their shoes.

This is not to suggest that patients whose surrogates followed the patient's expressed or likely wishes had a better outcome than those whose surrogates were in denial. Overall, patients with less severe illness and better outcomes spent the longest time in the ICU. The most critically ill patients were admitted for a median of nine days; those moderately ill, eleven days; and those least critically ill, thirteen days. Similarly, patients whose surrogates chose to limit care spent a median of eight days in the ICU before they died; those who died despite aggressive interventions spent ten and a half days; and those who survived their ICU admission, fifteen days. But length of stay is relevant, of course, because it affects not only the cost of hospitalization and other policy considerations, but also the length of patient and family suffering. Patients who died after their surrogates reprised their instructions or stood in their shoes perhaps experienced less suffering than those who died weeks later whose surrogates were in denial or opted out of decision making. But they also lost the chance of that rare miracle that might have materialized in the two-plus weeks after their surrogates chose to remove their life support. Then again, the miracle may have saved the patient's life, but not saved him or her from a fate worse than death. There are no easy answers here.

Differences in length of hospitalization tied to family goals of care gives rise to concerns about medical futility—prolonging life with no hope of benefit. A study of over a thousand patients being treated in five intensive care units found that physicians felt that 11 percent were certainly receiving futile treatment and an additional 9 percent probably were. The former patients received anywhere from one to fifty-eight days of futile treatment, accounting for 7 percent of all patient days in the five ICUs. Moreover, researchers found that the

> outcomes of these patients were uniformly poor; two-thirds died during the hospitalization and 85% died within 6 months. "Survivors" of treatment perceived to be futile were often discharged in severely compromised health states that some might perceive to be worse than death, such as being permanently severely neurologically compromised and dependent on life-sustaining machines.[2]

Contrary to some expectations, the researchers also found that the "cost of perceived futile treatment, although sizable, accounted for only a small percentage [3.5 percent] of critical care expenditures at the health system during the study period."

The theme of futile treatment comes up more frequently in medical journals than it did at the ICU bedside. As one critical care attending I observed explained to his residents, "Our role is to do the impossible." So some physicians experience ambivalence about admitting there is nothing more to do. Although hospital staff did occasionally commiserate privately among themselves about the futility of continued treatment of particular patients, they were more reticent to address it with patients' families. Futility was raised more frequently by the patients' significant others than by their physicians. Like the critical care fellow in chapter 7 who reprised the patient's living will, some physicians danced around a prognostication of futility.

CRITICAL CARE FELLOW: . . . her cancer is not curable. I don't know when she would otherwise die from it, but the oncologists have determined that it is not treatable. And now, with the septic shock on top of that, the chances are very low that she would survive. I believe she would die very quickly if we were to withdraw support. And she is on artificial life support, the ventilator and the blood pressure medications. In terms of futility, is it 100 percent? No. I can never make that judgment. . . . But what I can say is that the chances of her surviving this hospitalization and going home and resuming any of her normal activities are pretty much zero.

Others spoke in hypotheticals.

CRITICAL CARE RESIDENT: It is our practice to do what the patient or the family tells us to do. We may give the family options, but it is their decision. But if it turns out that he does have an irreversible stroke that would indicate medical futility, we might be more emphatic about our recommendation that doing everything is actually doing more harm than good.

For only four patients (2 percent) did physicians directly tell families that further treatment would be futile.

CRITICAL CARE ATTENDING: The CT scan from this morning shows that he had a big stroke that covers the entire right side of his brain. All of the tissue on that side of his brain has died. His ICPs [intracranial pressure readings] are getting higher and the oxygen in his brain is getting lower. There is a great deal of pressure in his brain, which is pushing the tissue over to the other side of his brain. There is no place for the tissue to go. Under some circumstances, we would remove part of the skull to give the brain more room to swell. But he wouldn't tolerate the procedure. We have given him the maximum therapy available. There is nowhere for us to go. We have reached the point where any further treatment is futile. The chance of any reasonable neurological recovery is now gone.

Implications

Even with hindsight, surrogates can never know what the outcome would have been had they taken a different course or done so more quickly or judiciously or used different criteria to set their course. That is why so many surrogates are haunted by their decisions months or even years later.[3] But their collective experience yields a few lessons for the rest of us. In the beginning of this book, I suggested that the stories that are written at ICU bedsides and in waiting rooms, hallways, and conference rooms may someday be our stories. What do they teach us? This chapter concludes with lessons for future patients, surrogates, and loved ones; health care institutions and providers; lawyers; and policy makers. Like any study, this one has limitations (described in appendix A). But the lessons with which the book concludes draw not only on the evidence unearthed in the two ICUs, but from other studies as well.

This Is So Difficult. I Tell People to Do Powers of Attorney All the Time. I Didn't Know How Difficult This Is.

These words, reprised from chapter 8, of one of the surrogates in the ICU—a lawyer—express her surprise and dismay that her mother's legal documents did not ease the excruciating choices she faced. This book has repeatedly shown the many reasons that treatment decisions in the ICU are so difficult.

As explained in chapter 5, many challenges arise because prognostic information is elusive and often equivocal, compounded sometimes by mixed messages delivered by different specialists or teams of physicians. Prognostic information comes in fits and starts; some will only be available weeks or even months after a treatment decision must be made or a window of opportunity closes. Predictions about functional abilities or quality of life are even harder to come by than those about the likelihood of survival.

But these challenges are not solely the result of deficiencies of information. Physicians and laypersons alike have difficulty processing probabilities and relative risk. And both experience heuristic and cognitive biases that distort the information they attend to and interpret that variably give rise to excessive optimism, overestimation of the probability of rare events, risk seeking to avoid loss, projection, preference for inaction, and much more. Surrogates also struggle with uncertainty about the patient's preferences, obligations to others, overwhelming emotions, and managing communication and consensus building across diverse health care providers and distant branches on the family tree.

Moreover, the patient's instructions, whether made verbally, in writing, or in offhand comments over the years, rarely help. It is no wonder that some instructions are so vague or do not apply. Healthy individuals cannot anticipate the combination of medical crises or interventions they may face in the distant future, how medical science may make some of them more treatable or tolerable, or how they will feel about them down the road in light of the infirmities and limitations of sickness or old age. And even when they apply, instructions tend to be black-and-white, with no room for a short trial or a limited intervention to address a small bump in the road or temporary side effect of a particular treatment. Recall from chapter 7 some of the difficulties surrogates faced when explicit instructions locked them into decisions that were inconsistent with the patient's actual wishes, whether because patients used incorrect jargon or because they didn't specify that their instructions were not absolute, but rather contingent, for example, on a good prognosis.

Patient instructions typically address outcome rather than the decision-making process. But surrogates often already know the desired outcome; it's the process with which they struggle: What decision criteria are most important? When criteria conflict, how should they be weighed and trade-offs balanced? How should surrogates think about probability, risk, and prognostic uncertainty? How confident must they be? How long should they authorize a trial intervention or continue heroic measures before shifting from cure to comfort? How much suffering is acceptable? What kinds of disability are tolerable? What constitutes an acceptable quality of life? What fates are worse than death? What if significant others disagree? Should they consider the needs of the family?

Below I consider some preemptive actions that we should all take when our faculties or those of our loved ones are still intact and some possible responses when it's too late.

Before It's Too Late

"A Good Surrogate Is Hard to Find"

Although the ICU data presented in chapter 8 revealed few footprints of advance directives in the process, outcomes, or impact of surrogate decision making, they did provide somewhat better news about the role of proxy directives that name the patient's legal decision maker. For 70 percent of patients with copies of a power of attorney or proxy directive in their hospital chart—and, therefore, for whom their legally designated decision maker is known—the chosen surrogate made all medical decisions throughout their ICU stay; for 12 percent, the surrogate made some decisions; for 3 percent, the surrogate made no decisions; and for 15 percent, it was unclear who was making some of the decisions. So most ICU patients whose directive was in the hospital got the decision maker they named most of the time.

But the good news goes only so far. The majority of ICU patients—or American adults in general—never designated a legal proxy. And some of those who did probably selected the wrong person in their social network to speak on their behalf. Similarly, those who didn't bother to name a surrogate would have been better served if they had ensured that someone other than the default surrogate specified by legal statute was their spokesperson. Or so it appeared to observers who scrutinized how legally designated or default surrogates behaved compared to other friends and loved ones around the bedside.

The last chapter showed that, on the one hand, the decision criteria surrogates adopt have considerable impact on the patient's fate and on their own emotional distress. On the other hand, it showed that instructional directives that state the patient's wishes and treatment preferences make little difference. Surrogates play an enormous role in setting the course of what may be the end of another's life, even if the patient's treatment preferences were expressed or documented. Therefore choice of surrogate is very consequential.

Unfortunately, as the humorist and columnist Art Buchwald—writing from his hospice bed—warned, "a good surrogate is hard to find."[4] It takes an unusual combination of talents and resources to be an effective surrogate. Being the closest to the patient on the family tree or the person most likely to be offended if not chosen does not necessarily make one most qualified to take on this onerous responsibility.[5]

The most effective surrogates observed knew the patients really well, had communicated frequently with them in recent years, and understood their values, preferences, and fears. But, as elaborated in chapter 6, because healthy would-be patients rarely know or communicate what they want regarding the torrent of complex decisions, nested in often uncertain, equivocal information, that their surrogates might face about some unanticipated medical problem, knowing the patient's wishes is far from enough. Effective surrogates were also good listeners and communicators, were intelligent, had an open mind, were decisive, could process complex, incomplete, sometimes conflicting information, and were able to see the forest as well as the trees. They were effective advocates and took the initiative to engage health care providers, gather information, and ask difficult questions. They were not easily intimidated or distracted; they stood up to doctors and even family members, when necessary, but were also consensus builders. They were sensitive about separating their interests from those of the patient. They were willing to take on these responsibilities and able to devote considerable time to visit the hospital repeatedly, observe the patient, and meet with varied teams of physicians, often waiting long stretches for the latter to show up. And they inspired trust among the patient's significant others. Surrogates who lacked some of these attributes risked relying on insufficient data or misunderstanding it, making the wrong decisions, exacerbating the patient's suffering, or creating havoc or conflict among loved ones. The previous chapters provided plenty of examples of seemingly poor choices of surrogate.

Not all of us know someone with that mix of personal knowledge, talents, and resources who would also be willing to serve as our advocate. But the job description demonstrates that the selection of a surrogate to speak on our behalf should not be taken lightly. It also shows why burying our heads in the sand and relying on a legal default surrogate is unlikely to do us justice or to be fair to the person legal rules select for us. We are expecting of surrogates what many consider the most wrenching decisions of their lives; the least we can do is to ask for their permission up front. And in jurisdictions, such as Illinois, where default surrogates are not permitted to weigh in on certain end-of-life decisions, legally formalizing our choice may literally be a matter of life, death, or a fate worse than death.

The most important preemptive action one can take is to weigh the qualifications and trade-offs in the job description of an effective surrogate, find a trusted associate that best fits the bill, ensure that he or she is willing and up to the task, and document the choice in an advance directive. To ensure that documents are available, cell phone apps that record one's own directives and those of other family members provide access 24/7, and some states and private companies offer advance-directive registries as well. Once the choice of a surrogate has been made, it is essential to inform health care providers and significant others of the decision, comfort those whose feelings were hurt, and insist that everyone work with and support the chosen advocate. This task is especially important if one bypasses persons closer on the family tree and opts for a friend, colleague, or more distant relative who may be resented by family members or ignored by health care providers. And as the years go by and needs and priorities change along with the composition and abilities of the members of one's social networks, one should reassess the choice of surrogate and perhaps begin again.

In most jurisdictions, completing a proxy directive is relatively easy, requiring neither lawyers nor notaries, and forms are available free in hospitals and online. Policy makers could facilitate this process by making legal documents even more accessible. For example, what if, just as one can indicate willingness to donate organs on a driver's license, one could name a legal surrogate there as well, the very place health care providers look first to identify a patient after an emergency? Driver's licenses would not replace existing proxy directive documents. But they have the virtue of being very common, and renewals give licensees the opportunity to rethink their legal surrogate every few years. Of course, even if driver's license applications include literature about how to select and prepare a surrogate, the selection process will rarely meet the expectations set out above. But it might be better than the current situation, in which very few adults have legally designated decision makers at all.

Advance-Care Planning

Because so much of surrogacy is not about following instructions but about asking questions, analyzing complex equivocal information, drawing inferences, exercising judgment, improvising, forging consensus, and simply being there, the importance of choosing an effective surrogate cannot be overstated. But picking a surrogate is just the beginning. Most of the surrogates in the study could have been better prepared for the onerous responsibilities they bore.

Fortunately, there are many resources already available to prepare would-be patients, surrogates, and other loved ones, although there is no evidence that any of the nine hundred–plus patients or significant others in the study ever made use of them. In different forums—from doctors' or lawyers' offices to senior or community centers to houses of worship to private homes—and by offering varied stimulus materials—questionnaires, videos, online exercises, workshops, facilitated dinner conversations, letter-writing projects, even card games—advance-care planning programs assist in thinking and talking with loved ones about expectations, goals, values, trade-offs, priorities, and fears.[6] To a far lesser extent, these programs also provide guidance in selecting appropriate surrogates and preparing them for their role.[7] Medicare has begun paying for such conversations facilitated by health care practitioners, and some insurance companies are doing so as well for their clients facing life-threatening illness (with some reporting that such counseling results in reduced health care spending).[8] And, as described in chapter 6, in a number of states, the most vulnerable patients can request that their physicians complete a portable medical order that specifies the treatments that they do or do not want.[9]

Because the materials and programs keep growing and becoming ever more compelling and creative, I will not try to document a moving target. But findings from the ICU study do offer some lessons for their developers and for those who choose to undertake some advance-care planning. First, as described earlier, conversations about process or decision-making criteria are at least as helpful to surrogates as are those about specific desired outcomes (which are likely to change with experience, infirmity, or the passage of time). How do would-be patients and their significant others feel about the decision-making trajectories that surrogates fashioned and followed in the ICUs? How might they have done it differently? What information would they have sought? How long would they have waited before changing course, or would they?

The goal of advance-care planning should not be to document instructions or draft better scripts for surrogates to follow, but to brainstorm together how to improvise when much is changing, unexpected, equivocal, or uncertain. Indeed, memorializing these conversations in written documents may well backfire if they discourage continuing dialogue with all stakeholders, undermine flexibility and improvisation in response to unforeseen contingencies, and generate paperwork that will confuse health care providers, who are accustomed to boilerplate legal checklists and will understand and enforce written documentation as regulatory formulae rather than aspirational guides. The end point of these conversations should not be to put instructions in writing, but rather to inspire more conversation.

Second, facilitating conversation between prospective patients and their loved ones is only as valuable as the quality of information shared. When understandings, terminology, expectations, wishes, and fears reflect misinformation derived from heroic television fare, gossip about the medical misfortunes or miracles of others, Internet blogs, or stereotypes about the experience of disability—all of which were uttered by laypersons in the ICUs—surrogates may take away misguided directions from those they may someday represent. Advance-care planning would benefit from better stimulus materials for prospective patients and surrogates alike that correct for misinformation and convey what various procedures, medical conditions, and outcomes actually look like; what to expect from hospital routines and personnel; what sorts of information to demand from health care providers; how much inconclusive or inconsistent information to expect; how to negotiate the decision-making process; and where to turn when physicians and others are not responsive. Again, much of this is about process.

Third, even for older and sicker patients, for whom discussion of specific medical conditions and related treatment preferences may be more appropriate, advance-care planning ought to devote as much attention to surrogates as it does to process or wishes. Advance-care planning should help patients identify who in their circle would be the most faithful and effective advocate and assist them in how to make the best choice without offending others on the family tree while enlisting their cooperation. Moreover, because many face challenges finding or enlisting effective advocates, advance-care planning efforts should help surrogates step up to a task for which they may not be well suited.

Finally, one of the many obstacles to naming a surrogate or advance-care planning is the assumption by many younger or healthier adults that these issues do not apply to them. Data from the ICU indicate otherwise. Almost two-thirds of ICU patients in the study were under sixty and/or with no preexisting medical problems. Their surrogates, on average, were about a decade younger; and other loved ones at the bedside, two decades younger. Chances are that many of these patients had no idea what would cause them to end up in an ICU the next day. Given these demographics, guidance on how to select and prepare the most effective surrogate is far more appropriate than guidance on how to express and document wishes about a host of abstract medical problems and treatments that may or may not arise down the road. And programs must develop more effective strategies to reach younger and healthier adults who are at risk of ending up in an ICU bed or waiting room and motivating them to participate. Perhaps if the goal is not to memorialize a complicated document, or to be quizzed on right and wrong answers, but just to have ongoing, open-ended conversations, people may be less reluctant to participate.

Advance-care planning is necessary for everyone at the bedside, not just the patient and surrogate. Because many potential patients and surrogates are in denial about medical challenges down the road or procrastinate about addressing them, it may be necessary for other loved ones to initiate and sustain the advance-care planning process. Indeed, those who are unlikely to be either the patient or the surrogate—the patient's children, siblings, or best friend, for example—and therefore who have the least control over the decision-making process may be the most concerned about whether the surrogate is sufficiently prepared to take on this difficult role. As long as the ball gets rolling, it doesn't matter who starts it.

When It's Too Late

Of course, many will not get around to selecting a surrogate decision maker, making it legal, or participating in advance-care planning, however rudimentary. And the surrogates of some who did everything right will nonetheless find that the guidance they received was insufficient. But, whatever the preparation, many will eventually end up tethered to machines in an ICU bed. As noted in chapter 1, almost 40 percent of Medicare enrollees visit an ICU in the last six months of life (29 percent in the last month of life).[10] And these numbers do not include those victims of accidents, violence, substance abuse, or deadly disease who are too young to qualify for Medicare, nor do they include older patients who survive their ICU admission. Nor do they include countless others who face end-of-life decisions at home, in nursing homes, in regular hospital beds, or elsewhere. Yet 70 percent of older Americans who require treatment decisions in the final days of life, whether in an ICU or elsewhere, lack the capacity to make these decisions.[11]

In short, many will need a surrogate decision maker at some point in their lives. And some surrogates will get tapped for this terrible assignment after it is too late for them to confer with the patient about their responsibilities. As described in chapter 7, some surrogates in the study tried to postpone decisions in the hope that patients would regain capacity and take back the baton, but most were disappointed. The ICU study, perhaps more than any other, bears witness to the struggles surrogates face when it is too late.

This book has documented many struggles that arose after the patient lost capacity, from doubt about how to achieve fidelity to the patient to a dearth of relevant information, disentangling mixed messages, striving for certainty, interpersonal challenges within families and between families and physicians, communication problems, inattention, unbearable emotions, crises of faith, power plays, conflicts of interest, denial and other psychological blinders, cognitive and other biases, inexperience, disappearing options, or just exquisitely bad luck. Even families stocked with health care providers were sometimes as beset by these challenges as many of the others. Here are a few possible responses.

Actuarial Predictions

Researchers and policy makers are certainly mindful of the challenges in formulating substituted judgments or other treatment decisions when it is too late to confer with the patient. Because many patients leave few instructions or even hints about their end-of-life treatment preferences and surrogates (often under great emotional stress) have proven relatively ineffective in constructing accurate substituted judgments of these preferences (at least, according to some of the *Newlywed Game*–type studies described in chapter 6), some scholars have explored alternatives.

Variations on what some call a "patient preference predictor" propose large-scale surveys of diverse populations (that vary demographically, medically, and attitudinally) about their preferences about life-sustaining treatment across a series of hypothetical medical scenarios.[12] Statistical analysis of these survey data would generate actuarial models that would predict a patient's likely treatment preferences—based on age, gender, social class, ethnic or cultural background, education, place of residence, religion, other values, health status, quality of life, and the like. Stymied surrogates would fill in the demographic and other blanks and a computer program would spit out the decision the patient would likely make. Preliminary studies of small populations and that employ just a few demographic characteristics already find that these actuarial models predict patient preferences (in *Newlywed Game* studies) as well as or somewhat better than their loved ones do.[13]

Some proposals recommend that such actuarial predictions be provided to assist surrogates in decision making (or to lessen their stress); others, that they serve as a default decision, to be followed unless the surrogate objects or demonstrates that the prediction is not consistent with the patient's wishes. Some proposals also assume that patients' advance directives would dictate whether and how a patient preference predictor could be used by their surrogate, should they lose decision-making capacity.[14] Though, of course, few patients have advance directives, especially those who have left little guidance and whose surrogates often need the most help from these predictive models.

To its credit, this developing actuarial project is exploring the feasibility as well as the ethical, legal, logistical, methodological, and financial implications of the undertaking,[15] of which there are many. The PPP, as it is called, replicates the problems of the *Newlywed Game* studies of the concordance of preferences of would-be patients and predictions of would-be surrogates to hypothetical scenarios. As explained in chapter 6, would-be patients' preferences change as they experience illness and incapacity (and therefore the predictions derived from the preferences of healthy respondents would not apply to them); some respondents have no preferences at all; and respondents' reflections are likely more superficial in pen-and-paper tests than in real life. Heuristic biases and those about disability play a role in population surveys, just as they do for individual decision makers, and algorithms will likely reproduce these biases. Moreover, the most sophisticated actuarial models require information about the patient's values, attitudes about death and dying, views about quality of life, and so forth that would be matched up with those of respondents in the population surveys. But this information requires substituted judgments that surrogates would need to construct and may be just as difficult for them to formulate as the treatment preferences with which they are already struggling, without great success.

It is not clear how drawing on the treatment preferences of anonymous others respects a patient's autonomy or self-determination, which is the legal justification for surrogate decision making in the first place. Despite these significant concerns, efforts of this sort to take the stress, guesswork, and inaccuracy out of surrogate decision making will undoubtedly proceed apace. Future surrogates may one day seek out or be offered algorithms or default treatment recommendations as they determine how to act on behalf of loved ones. Surrogates may thereby avoid the demanding and painful process of trying to stand in the patients' shoes and replicate their wishes. Patients and surrogates may be no worse off. Then again, they may be much more so.

ICU Improvements

There are a number of steps that hospitals and ICUs can take to improve the process by which surrogate decisions are made, increase fidelity to patient wishes, and ameliorate the emotional distress experienced by family members. Because the strengths and weaknesses of the two ICUs in this study may be idiosyncratic, I will consider only steps that are responsive to challenges they share with other ICUs described in the research literature.

COMMUNICATION SKILLS. In reading through the transcripts of encounters presented throughout the book, it is clear that some health care providers are better at communicating, facilitating decision making, and supporting families than others. Studies of ICU communication in other settings confirm that there is considerable room for improvement.[16] Several researchers have developed interventions incorporating instruction, simulation, and role-playing to instill better communication skills in health care providers, some of which seem to make a difference, while others do not.[17] But the work is promising and, with ongoing refinements, likely to improve surrogate decision making.

Enhancing communication also requires consideration of the content as well as of the timing or style of communication. Even the choice of words matters. For example, researchers found that asking what the patient would "want" in conversations about patient treatment preferences—used in 70 percent of the meetings they studied—led "to worse decision making and less information about the patient's values" than asking, for example, what the patient would "think" or "say."[18] Material on framing and heuristic biases presented in chapters 5 and 6 suggests that the ways in which physicians present information may profoundly affect how and what decisions are made. Work in behavioral economics on "choice architecture" also suggests that decisions can be influenced or even "nudged" by how choices and defaults are presented.[19] In short, surrogate decision making and its outcomes and impact will likely improve with additional training—stylistic and substantive—of physicians and other health care providers.

RESOURCES. Studies also find that providing family members with printed materials improves outcomes. But ICUs could do much more. Videos, simulations, interactive decision aids and checklists, and online virtual worlds could illustrate what typical interventions or outcomes look like and help prepare surrogates for upcoming decisions. A tablet, Wi-Fi, and headphones are all that are needed. And many surrogates have plenty of time to partake of these media as they sit with noncommunicative patients hour upon hour, languish in waiting rooms, or hang out at the bedside in the hope that a specialist might drop by.

There is also need for technological improvements. Chapter 6 described the challenges in the two ICUs, where alleged advance directives never materialized, physicians neglected to read those that made it to the ICU and didn't always know where to find them, and others erroneously assumed that default surrogates were legally designated powers of attorney. Some of these deficiencies require better training of health care staff regarding the legal requirements surrounding surrogate decision making. But some would be ameliorated with better electronic record systems. Researchers in various settings have found many deficiencies with and offered recommendations to improve the documentation of advance-care planning and directives in electronic health records.[20] Such improvements are likely to have some impact.

FACILITATORS. Excluding encounters between families and health care staff that occurred during critical care rounds, not even 3 percent of the observed meetings included a member of the ethics committee, only 7 percent included someone from palliative care, only 14 percent included a nurse,[21] and not even 2 percent included a social worker or chaplain—health care professionals who in many other studies have been found to make an invaluable contribution in facilitating surrogate decision making. There are many reasons for these small numbers. The participation of ethicists and palliative care physicians must be requested by the primary or critical care team. And some team members assert that these specialists are not needed or would make matters worse. It is instructive that more than once in the observed meetings, physicians brought in the ethics committee solely as an excuse to delay the decision-making process, not because they felt it provided added value. And, of course, all of these supportive professionals have very large caseloads undertaking their regular responsibilities. When nurses are enlisted to participate in a family meeting, for example, they must find someone willing and able to cover their vulnerable patients. Although it might be possible to find resources and to brainstorm organizational and logistical strategies to increase these participation numbers, an alternative is more compelling.

One of the striking lessons of the ICU observations is how much surrogates struggled alone. Except for those patients who passed quickly through the unit, my colleague and I were often the only ones who bore witness to these struggles from beginning to end, as significant others met with critical care physicians and other specialists, palliative care doctors, ethicists, and organ-donation facilitators while surrogates decided the fate of their loved ones. Surely a number of different health care specialists met with families; we observed almost three hundred of them. But their rotations did not extend for the duration of a given patient's ICU admission, or they worked in their silos, meeting individually with families about their own organ system or jurisdictional concerns but not about those of other practitioners. Surely some read the electronic notes of colleagues or other specialists and conferred with one another by page or text, and sometimes even in person, to coordinate treatment details. And on rare occasions specialists from different teams collaborated in multidisciplinary family meetings (6 percent of all meetings), usually when the end was near. But few health care providers knew the big, multifaceted picture that evolved day after day with which surrogates must contend. Although physicians should certainly receive better training in facilitating end-of-life conversations and decision making, these structural blinders limit their efficacy in this role.

Families sometimes need an interpreter of medical data and jargon, a facilitator, negotiator, dispute manager, secretary, philosopher or ethicist, enforcer, statistician, or counselor. This is not merely about emotional or spiritual support, though that is of course necessary. Families also need professionals to help them disentangle the mixed messages, make sense of equivocal prognostic information, disabuse them of inaccurate understandings, help them prepare for family meetings and ask the right questions of physicians (and make sure that they are answered), encourage reflection about the patient and his or her values, foster better communication, respond to questions about what other families do, point out or disable heuristic biases (of both surrogates and physicians), goad surrogates to think more about the decision-making criteria they have adopted and reconsider the decision trajectory they are following, help them resolve interpersonal conflicts among themselves and with health care providers, and provide perspective. And so much more. Hospitals are filled with professionals who do all these things, and some of them may even cross paths with a surrogate or extended family from time to time. But their responsibilities lie elsewhere, and none of them have the time or the multidisciplinary longitudinal perspective that my colleague and I enjoyed.

If there is one thing hospitals could do to respond "when it is too late," it would be to add a health care professional to the critical care team to serve as a surrogate facilitator or advocate. These advocates would not supplant the role of physicians in updating families about the patient's medical status, negotiating informed consent, or developing goals of care. But they would support surrogate decision makers in most other ways. Part nurse, part social worker, part ethicist, and part teacher, the advocate would provide continuity and take the long view, interacting with surrogates and family members throughout the hospitalization as teams and specialists come and go and sometimes disagree. Like my colleague and me, advocates would sit in on family meetings with medical specialists from various teams. But although we necessarily took in the interactions in silence, advocates would participate and engage with families in a kind of postmortem after the meetings ended. And, away from meetings, they would instruct surrogates in their new role, prepare families for the rhythms of critical illness, answer questions, help collect, synthesize, and translate complex medical information for decision makers, facilitate communication, bring new participants up to speed, provide counseling and dispute resolution, serve as a liaison with medical staff, break down logistical barriers, and assist and support surrogates and other family members in navigating the decision-making process.

Whether advocates would help maximize patient autonomy or minimize their suffering, lead to better or faster decision making, ameliorate conflict, or help free up resources, their primary goal would simply be to lessen the emotional burden of decision making and help ensure that surrogates are prepared for their responsibilities and have the richest and most accurate information about matters they consider important in formulating treatment decisions and selecting goals of care.

It turns out that I am not the only one with this idea, suggesting that this need exists elsewhere. Several independent feasibility studies conducted in other ICUs have explored introducing specially trained nurses and/or social workers into the critical care team to provide emotional, cognitive, communication, mediation, and/or organizational support to surrogates and have found that such a role has promise.[22] Other institutions have implemented volunteer programs, although the need for continuity and credibility suggests that using professional members of the critical care team for this surrogate advocacy role is of paramount importance.

COST CONSIDERATIONS. Many of these proposals, especially the addition of another health care professional to the critical care team, take resources, of course. Because various proposals may reduce the amount of time physicians spend with families, help ensure that patients get only the treatment they want, and help surrogates become more decisive or families reach consensus faster with better information and support, they may provide some cost savings. Several studies of innovations in communication-skills training and the expanded use of professionals or of specially designated facilitators have found substantial benefits not only in the emotional impact on family members, but on the use of ICU resources. Although the cost savings from some interventions have been negative or inconclusive,[23] others have resulted in significantly shorter ICU stays, a reduced intensity of treatment, and significantly lower aggregate and average daily ICU costs, even factoring in the cost of the interventions.[24] Of course, the devil is in the details. Hospitals, insurers, and regulators will have to decide whether the expenditures are justified.

The Role of Law

When all else fails, Americans tend to turn to law. The most vexing and contentious end-of-life questions and disputes sometimes end up in court. None of those surrounding the patients in the study did. (As noted earlier, over more than two years, a paid attorney only showed up once in the ICUs, for a thirty-five-minute meeting regarding the brain-dead patient introduced at the beginning of chapter 1, after which an understanding was reached and the lawyer's work was done.)

Over the lifetime of the ICU patients in the study, laws regarding end-of-life decision making have continually evolved. Judicial opinions have addressed the human tragedies and end-of-life disputes that have found their way onto court dockets. Federal and state statutes have been tweaked in fits and starts to catch up with changes in medical technologies, family structures and lifestyles, bioethical concerns, and ideologies that seek greater control for patients and loved ones over medical decision making.

New legal tools, forms, and regulations have been devised. And legal innovations have been revisited upon discovery of their failures, unintended consequences, and spaces where they do not apply.[25] Chapter 6 reviewed some of these legal developments, describing how state and federal law addresses surrogate decision making, articulates decision-making roles and standards, provides advance directives in which patients may name their legal representatives and treatment preferences, and offers criteria to sort out some of the evidentiary questions.

An archaeologist of our era would uncover a stratified patchwork of forms and regulations, different from state to state, stuffed in drawers and physical or virtual file cabinets, affixed by refrigerator magnets, or engraved on pieces of metal encircling arthritic wrist bones. Much of this stash of legal detritus will be found in the rubble of the two ICUs I observed, most of it signifying little.

In this book I have shown that law is at best irrelevant in the ICU. First, the findings presented in chapter 8 concluded that advance directives do not "take care of" the challenges surrogate decision makers face. Only a minority of patients prepare directives, documents that appear to make little or no difference in the process, outcomes, or impact of decision making. And when directives do play a role, they are at least as likely to undermine patient wishes as to help honor them. Second, surrogate default statutes are out of touch with the complex structures of modern American families and with how decision making actually works in the real world.[26] Moreover, the default surrogates defined in the law sometimes seem especially ill suited to speak on behalf of the patient compared to others on the family tree. Third, many physicians and loved ones at the bedside are unaware of the decision criteria that legal norms prescribe. Although many surrogates come up with a kind of substituted-judgment standard, others adopt decision trajectories unsanctioned by law. Fourth, it is exceedingly rare for physicians to enforce (or even know of) the legal rules that limit the ability of default surrogates to authorize the removal of life support, and many don't know whether they are dealing with a legally named proxy or a default decision maker. Fifth, standards of proof articulated in some courtrooms are unrealistic; listening to surrogates fashion substituted judgments shows that they would rarely meet these evidentiary standards. Indeed, studies show that patients themselves have less certainty about their wishes than many courtrooms demand of their surrogates.

It is not surprising that law provides a very crude tool with which to address surrogate decision making, especially in an ICU. Chapter 6 described the challenges of delegating law enforcement to busy physicians, though perhaps better training of health care staff and the addition of surrogate advocates, recommended earlier, will bring more legal awareness into the ICU. Moreover, the timelines and deliberative process of law and critical care rarely overlap; the former typically works in months to years, the latter in minutes to days. The legal decision on Nancy Cruzan came seven years after her accident, and that on Terri Schiavo, fifteen years after her injury. Perhaps the most delayed critical care decision is whether to insert a tracheostomy tube, which has a ten-day to two-week window. Often surrogates are given a couple of minutes to an hour to consent to a lifesaving intervention or to agree to stop resuscitation after a patient has not responded to multiple rounds of CPR.

Did I see legal rules protect the autonomy of patients in the ICUs? I did on a few occasions. Did I see instances in which legal rules made matters worse? Absolutely. Did I observe legal rules ignored or prove irrelevant? All the time. Because lawyers are almost never called to the ICU and day-to-day challenges regarding decision making rarely go to court, legal policy makers are largely in the dark about what really goes on at the bedside and whether legal norms help facilitate or complicate decision making at life's end. The findings of this study should be eye-opening.

Could law do more or address surrogate decision making differently? One impulse that I hear frequently from legal practitioners is a desire to fashion advance-directive documents that are more directive. I hope these pages have made abundantly clear why this is a fool's errand, except perhaps where patients are terminally ill and medical interventions on the horizon and their likely effect are clearly known. (These POLST—Physician Orders for Life-Sustaining Treatment—medical orders for the most vulnerable patients were described in chapter 6.)

Rather than devising "better" directives that cannot possibly anticipate the choices, contingencies, and uncertainties inherent in critical care, legal practitioners ought to put down their pens or laptops and switch their role from scrivener to counselor. First, they need to convince their clients to name a legal surrogate, advise them of the attributes most important in the role, help them find such a person in their social network, and help prepare their choice for this difficult responsibility. Second, they need to encourage their clients to begin advance-care planning conversations with their loved ones and to provide the stimulus materials that make such conversations productive. Third, they need to remind their clients that conversation is far more important than documentation, and that informed improvisation is preferable to following an arbitrary script when facing unforeseen end-of-life decisions. Physicians and other health care providers, some of whom can bill Medicare for such counseling, should also take the same approach with their patients.

The study suggests another area that legal policy makers ought to reconsider. Although the rules vary considerably from state to state, health care decision making and default surrogate consent statutes generally treat legally appointed and default decision makers quite differently. First, in a number of jurisdictions—such as Illinois—a default surrogate is not permitted to make the same range of decisions to withhold or withdraw life-sustaining treatment that is available to a legal proxy named in a power-of-attorney document. Presumably, the impulse of this default surrogate consent rule is to protect vulnerable patients who are unable to speak for themselves from individuals they never selected with the authority to end their lives. But this book has shown that this is not easy to do—not without harming the majority of patients, whose loved ones are responsible, earnest, faithful to their values, and striving to maximize their best interests. And, in any case, chapter 6 showed that this rule is rarely followed in the two ICUs. It is time to examine whether it is serving a useful purpose.

Second, default surrogate consent rules in most states specify a hierarchy of family members (and, in some states, friends or lovers) from which the default surrogate is to be chosen and decision rules when there is disagreement among those on a given rung of the hierarchy. Chapters 3 and 6 described all that goes wrong when diverse family structures and cultures are shoehorned into a single formulaic mold, not to mention the fact that the legal default chosen is not necessarily the best spokesperson for the patient. It appears that physicians do not always follow these rules either. A recent exploratory survey of critical care physicians and hospitalists across the United States found that many reject both the hierarchical formula and the rules for resolving disagreements, trying instead to foster consensus among friends and family who know the patient best.[27] This more flexible arrangement might empower an opportunist or more remote acquaintance to exert inappropriate influence. But again, protecting against the rare aberration disserves the majority of friends and families struggling to do right by the patient. Patients who do not want to entrust decision making to their entire social network or to whichever members show up at the bedside need only write a proxy directive specifying their choice of legal decision maker.

I would recommend that legal practitioners and policy makers be modest about the ability of law to regulate medical decision making at the end of life and to be mindful of its potential unforeseen consequences, especially in an ICU. And I would encourage them to think about whether relaxing standards, procedures, or hierarchies might better serve the autonomy and welfare of incapacitated patients than the current rules so often honored in the breach.

When "This" Happens to Me

Whether or not any of these ideas come to fruition, many of us will end up in an ICU in some capacity. In this book I have suggested that few of us will be prepared. But it is my hope that the stories you read, the dialogues you heard, and the excruciating decisions to which you bore witness will help you to think or say or do more before it is too late and to navigate around the shoals of intensive care more effectively if you find yourself there. As we can see, there are few right or wrong answers. What is a miracle to one is anathema to another. We each have to find our own trajectories. Let us hope that we do so with knowledge, clarity, and fidelity to those whose lives are in our hands.

The Research

Why Intensive Care Units?

Throughout my academic career I have been drawn to swindlers, stock-brokers, corporate executives, bankers, accountants, regulators, journalists, lawyers—agents who act on behalf of another (the so-called principal). What distinguishes these agents and makes them interesting to me is that they preside over asymmetric relationships—also called fiduciary or trust relationships—in which principals lack the expertise, access, or power to communicate with or monitor their agents, specify their obligations, or direct or control their actions. This asymmetry creates opportunities for trustees to exploit and deceive their principals and also challenges for trustees in construing their fiduciary duties and ensuring loyalty to principals with diverse and conflicting interests.[1]

But I've been especially intrigued about the extremes of asymmetry—the most asymmetric of the asymmetric—when trustees speak on behalf of those unable to speak for themselves, where traditional mechanisms for creating, structuring, regulating, and terminating trust relationships do not apply, and where principals are absolutely vulnerable and virtually powerless. Although such relationships afford easy opportunities to exploit the vulnerable, they also create greater challenges for trustees, who must determine how to act on behalf of those with whom they are unable to confer or take instruction.[2]

Intensive care units, perhaps more than any other site, collect these vulnerable principals, who lack the capacity to make life-and-death decisions, let alone to communicate their preferences or even choose (or fire) their agent. ICUs offer a rich setting in which to observe in real time how agents—"surrogates," in ICU lingo—determine how to act on their principals' behalf and how they manage the conflicting interests of patients, loved ones, and themselves. Although this book will provide a general guide to the intensive care unit and, for some, to life's end—what another author called a "handbook for mortals"[3]—its central question probes how trustees for such vulnerable patients create and construe the role, learn to act for another, formulate medical decisions on their behalf, the ethical challenges they face along the way, and the role of legal and regulatory strategies to protect the most vulnerable.

The Research Sites

The research began at a large urban teaching hospital in Illinois with an invitation to informally observe the stroke team and learn how surrogates make medical decisions for patients. For two months I observed the rotating team of attending physicians, nurses, residents, and medical students on morning rounds. When it became apparent that many hospitalized stroke patients have or quickly regain the capacity to make their own medical decisions, one of the attending physicians encouraged and helped arrange for me to observe the neurological intensive care unit, which housed patients who had experienced more severe strokes or who had other serious neurological problems (brain aneurysms, hemorrhages, traumas, cancers, and infections; seizures; spinal traumas and surgeries; etc.) that frequently robbed patients of the capacity to make medical decisions.

For eight months I informally observed critical care rounds each morning in the neurological ICU as well as interactions and family meetings throughout the day between hospital staff and representatives of patients without decision-making capacity. During this period, while I refined a research protocol and awaited approval from the hospital institutional review board (IRB), I collected no data. But this extended period of observation gave me an opportunity to learn about the rhythms, protocols, and record keeping of the ICU; to understand more about the diagnosis and treatment of neurological problems and their sequelae; to observe the diverse ways in which physicians and family members interact; and to develop familiarity with and earn the trust of physicians, nurses, chaplains, social workers, and pharmacists who work in the unit. After the research proposal had been vetted by the hospital and my own research institution and approved by the institutional review boards of both organizations, the research began. About a year and a half later, after observing interactions regarding almost a hundred patients, data collection ended in the neurological ICU.

Because I was concerned about the generalizability of the data and the possibility that they might be unique to the challenges of neurological illness and injury, the specialists that populate a neurological ICU (neurosurgeons, neurologists, anesthesiologists, and, to a lesser extent, oncologists and orthopedists), and the organizational structure and protocols of the neurological ICU, I sought a second research site. Wanting to control as much as possible—legal rules; patient and community characteristics; hospital culture, characteristics, and regulations; medical record-keeping systems, and so on—I decided to select another ICU in the same hospital.

The neurological ICU was an open unit; the primary specialists treating the patient (neurosurgeons, neurologists, and the like) were responsible for the patient and the ICU's critical care physicians served as consultants. In closed units, the critical care physicians have authority over and the ultimate responsibility for patient care, and specialists serve as consultants. As reported in chapter 2, the distinction between an open unit and a closed one is relevant in several respects: critical care physicians, who were always around the open neurological ICU and available to families, had less authority than specialists, who were usually off in other parts of the hospital (operating rooms, clinics, or offices). Moreover, significant conversations about the goals of care were often handled by the primary specialists rather than by the critical care consultants. I sought a closed unit for the second site. The hospital's medical ICU fit the bill.[4]

The medical ICU generally cares for patients whose problems do not involve their brains or hearts or the immediate aftermath of a surgical procedure. Patients in the medical ICU most frequently experienced respiratory problems, organ (liver, kidney, etc.) failure, cancer, sepsis and other serious infections, uncontrolled bleeding, and the like. The medical ICU had the same number of beds as the neurological ICU, but two different teams of physicians had responsibility for the patients. Because critical care rounds were held at the same time for both teams, only one team (covering roughly half the patients in the unit) was observed. After nine months, interactions regarding more than one hundred medical ICU patients had been observed. (Interestingly, even observing twice as many beds, it took twice as long to amass one hundred patients in the neurological as in the medical ICU—an indirect indicator that the two ICUs are quite different.)

Grants from the National Science Foundation and the M.D. Anderson Foundation enabled me to hire a medical social worker to do primary data collection in the medical ICU. I recruited a newly minted hospital social worker who had just completed an internship in the hospital in which the research was under way. To ensure that my new colleague replicated the methods employed in the neurological ICU, we began with several weeks of role-playing off-site. Then we began observations in the medical ICU to-gether, collecting duplicative data, then comparing our data each night and talking through the differences as well as ethical and other challenges that arose each day. After we had spent several weeks working together, my col-league took over. We talked about her cases and challenges each day, and I read and commented on her field notes and transcripts of the encounters she observed as she prepared them. I also covered for her on many occa-sions throughout the remainder of the study and got to know all of the physicians in the medical ICU, as well as many of the families. Because she was the age of the resident physicians and I was older than many of the attending physicians, we certainly were not indistinguishable as we tried to be flies on the ICU wall. But we tried as best as possible to mimic each other in other respects.

Data Collection

Data collection began early each morning by reviewing the overnight ad-missions to the ICUs and identifying from Glasgow Coma Scores and other information in the medical chart which new patients lacked decision-making capacity and whose surrogates would likely qualify for the study.[5] We would then join the critical care team as it began morning rounds. As described in chapter 2, critical care rounds collect a large number of white-coated participants, along with one or more "cows" (carts that carry laptop computers with secure Wi-Fi connections to the hospital electronic medical-record system), all snaking through the congested ICU hallway. A social science observer in a white coat quietly positioned along the outside perimeter attracts very little notice.[6]

Armed with a small tablet computer, my colleague or I would record basic demographic, admission, and medical information and advance-directive status on each ICU patient during lengthy team discussions of medical minutiae not relevant to the study (e.g., physiological measure-ments such as blood pressures, blood gases, ventilator settings and respi-ratory data, medication choices and doses, etc.).[7] When the team entered the patient's room, we would let the computer hang at our side and lis-ten attentively to conversations between members of the medical team and any visitors in the patient's room. After leaving the room, we would make entries in a database recording all encounters, write field notes, and reconstruct, from memory,[8] transcripts of any conversations regarding pa-tients in the study on the tablet computer, often while standing among the critical care team as they discussed the medical minutia regarding the next patient. On rare occasions when formal family meetings were initiated during rounds, we would peel off from the team and join the physicians meeting with the family, then rejoin rounds when the meeting was completed.

Depending on the ICU, the attending physician, and the complexity of medical problems or crises surrounding the roster of patients, rounds would last anywhere from one and a half to seven hours. When rounds ended, we would hang out in the hospital to observe spontaneous encounters and scheduled meetings between family members and health care providers. While waiting for observational opportunities, we worked on reconstructing transcripts of encounters, writing field notes, and updating databases. We both wore pagers and asked nurses or physicians to page us when meetings occurred or were scheduled when we were away from the hospital; this happened far less frequently than we had hoped.

Despite our best efforts, we missed some interactions between health care providers and patients' friends and family. Some occurred unexpectedly late at night or on weekends, some in the emergency room or away from the ICU. Some meetings took place at the same time as another meeting that we were observing. And other conversations were conducted over the telephone. Although we tried to anticipate these encounters and arrange to be there or listen in, we were not always successful, especially for spontaneous encounters that occurred during off-hours and about which we were unaware. The good news is that attending physicians are often away from the hospital the same times that we were, and many of the significant conversations are conducted by the most senior physicians on the case. So, except in emergencies (of which there are many in an ICU), many of the significant family meetings are conducted during business hours, when we were on-site.

Because we had access to physicians' notes, we knew of every missed meeting or conversation that physicians considered important enough to document—699 of them (compared to 1013 observed encounters). Although their notes were far less complete than our own records, they do provide some sense of what we missed, who participated, and what was discussed or decided. We also learned about missed meetings from reports to the rest of the team during subsequent rounds and by questioning residents or nurses. Data on missed encounters were entered into relevant databases and coded along with transcripts of observed meetings.

Physicians' notes rarely report on conversations held during critical care rounds. Although rounds represent almost half of all the observed meetings, they represent only 6 percent of physician-documented meetings that we did not observe. With that exception, comparisons between meetings that we observed and those that we missed but that were reported by health care providers show some logistical but few significant, substantive differences. Excluding critical care rounds, logistic regressions find significant differences between observed and unobserved meetings only in the day and time of the meeting, whether an attending physician is involved (all of which were expected) and patient race or ethnicity (which was not).[9] There are no significant differences in other demographic characteristics of patients, in the content of the conversations (e.g., discussions of the goals of care or resuscitation status [DNR]), in the proximity of the meeting to patient death or discharge (an indicator of urgency perhaps), or in outcomes.

None of the observed meetings were tape-recorded. Doing so would have required consent from all of the participants (some of whom show up mid-meeting), would have been logistically and technologically complicated, given the many sites in which encounters occur, and would have added another source of selection bias. We also refrained from taking any notes or even holding a pencil or computer during observations, lest we distract participants, somehow signal that some statements were more important than others, make participants uncomfortable or less spontaneous, or affect their conduct (for example, making physicians more patient or solicitous of family members). Observed meetings lasted from less than a minute to more than an hour and a half. On our busiest day, we observed fourteen meetings; on an average day, two meetings. Since we never knew what the next day would bring, we tried to complete transcripts and field notes before each night ended. There were many late nights over those two-plus years.

Readers may be dubious about the quality of transcripts prepared without notes. We discovered that it was far easier than we had expected, undoubtedly because of the power, poignancy, and emotional overlay of the interactions that riveted our attention. With more experience, we also realized that some meetings follow familiar scripts or sequences and that certain physicians rely on favorite expressions and routines that they repeat frequently. We each developed tricks to remember important details and sequences, the precise wording of important remarks, and mannerisms, as well as who said what. Reconstructing the emotional tone of their remarks was even easier. My colleague and I read each other's transcripts and flagged statements that didn't make sense or ring true and context or transitions that seemed missing in order to ensure that transcripts were as complete and unambiguous as possible. Unquestionably, we missed a lot, especially medical data and jargon that punctuate these conversations. Tape recordings would certainly have been more accurate and would have allowed refined linguistic coding and temporal sequencing. But tape recording would have been ethically, logistically, and methodologically problematic.

In addition to observation of critical care rounds and interactions with patients' families, I also observed family meetings conducted by representatives of the regional organ-transplant agency concerning patients who were approaching death and who might be appropriate candidates for organ donation; weekly rounds between ICU nurse managers, social workers, and chaplains; meetings of the hospital ethics committee; and monthly ethics programs for all hospital staff. We chose not to observe one-on-one encounters between families and clergy or chaplains that excluded medical staff; this struck us as a breach of privacy that seemed inappropriate, and in any case, surrogate decisions were not made during these encounters. Hospital chaplains tended to document these meetings in notes stored in the patients' electronic medical records (to which we had access), however, and we did review them.

The Strengths and Limitations of Observational Research

Clearly, the research question animating this inquiry could have been pursued in other ways. There is already a large body of research on surrogate decision making. A substantial literature relies on paper-and-pencil exercises among healthy individuals playing the role of patient or surrogate and responding to hypothetical scenarios.[10] Less frequently, researchers have surveyed or interviewed family members in the throes of a medical crisis or contacted them months later.[11] Others have surveyed physicians or other informants.[12] Some have abstracted information from medical records or Medicare claims data.[13] And others have observed ICUs or recorded selected in-hospital family meetings.[14]

Each of these methods has significant limitations and weaknesses that discouraged me from emulating their protocols. Dispassionate paper-and-pencil answers to hypothetical questions, without life-or-death consequences or any social context, reported over the course of a few minutes by relatively healthy respondents, about scenarios few of them have ever faced provide a limited understanding of how surrogate decision making actually occurs. Moreover, surrogates rarely make decisions alone, but rather arrive at them in consultation with health care providers and other friends and family. The hypothetical data, even if meaningful, at best tell us what decisions these would-be surrogates *might* make, not how and why they *did* make these decisions.

Retrospective interviews of surrogates or other family members typically question those who decided to remove or limit life support, but usually not those who refused or who were considering other medical interventions; nor do they examine the evolution of treatment decisions over time. Therefore, they consider patients who die, but rarely those who survive. One might assume that the decision-making process for the former would be quite different than that for the latter. Moreover, these retrospective interviews are conducted months after the death of the patient, after memories have faded. The interview studies have shown how surrogates "manipulate," "reconcile," "alter," "optimize," "sacrifice," and rationalize their memories, and how retrospective accounts of the decision-making process are "made," edited, and rewritten to make sense of the experience for the respondents themselves, to reconcile their grief, to regain control of their lives, to allay their guilt, to please or escape the accusations of family members, to impress or elicit the approval or sympathy of interviewers, or to tell them what respondents think the latter want to hear.[15] In short, these interviews are subject to recall, hindsight, social desirability, and selection biases.

The tape recording of family meetings has provided important new insights on surrogate decision making. But these studies suffer from significant selection biases as well. They record only meetings in which physicians anticipate discussing or delivering bad news and require consent in advance from all health care and family participants. In more than half of all targeted meetings, participants refuse to permit recording. The tape recordings provide snapshots of the dynamics of these encounters among a selective group of cooperative participants (who know that they are being recorded) but do not show the day-to-day process through which surrogates decide for another. And studies of medical records and insurance data may reveal what medical decisions are made, but not how they were made.

Many of these existing studies focus on an outcome or on a single static decision point rather than on the process or the evolution of decisions, study an individual decision maker (rather than entertaining the possibility that decisions may be a collective enterprise), assume that surrogates try to replicate patients' wishes rather than making this assumption problematic by investigating what it is surrogates actually do, neglect to ask decision makers how or why they made the reported decision, and are compromised by reactivity (the act of asking about or recording behavior risks changing it), limited samples (numerically or demographically), and even confusion of correlation and causation.

The strength of observational methods is that one doesn't have to rely on unrealistic simulations of the real world (through hypothetical scenarios) or on the recollections of participants, who may suffer from poor or self-serving memories, false consciousness, other recall bias, or secondhand information; nor does one intrude on the anxiety and grief of individuals in crisis by interviewing them. Observers witness conversations, reflection, and decision making as they unfold day after day.

Of course, there are weaknesses. The window of observation is circumscribed. Many critical interactions occur outside of the ICU—in the car, in the cafeteria, in the bedroom, over the phone—some of which, fortunately, are subsequently reprised in observed encounters with medical staff. Although participants may describe their thoughts, motivations, criteria or rationales, states of mind, fears, and the like during their interactions with doctors, many do not. Observations are limited to what they say (verbally or through body language) or fail to say. Other participants in the encounter may interrogate their statements or elicit a reaction, but rarely to the satisfaction of a social scientist. And we chose silence.

Moreover, observers pose a risk of reactivity, of changing the events, statements, outcomes, or even the feelings of those observed. I worried about having such an effect on families and medical staff alike. One of the reasons I didn't hurry to begin collecting data in the neurological ICU was that I wanted to allow enough time to elapse to become a fixture in the unit and a member of the team, and for hospital staff to become familiar and comfortable with me and with the project and to recognize that there was no hidden agenda. Undoubtedly, we weren't always successful in remaining a fly on the wall. Early on I was told that one of the resident physicians thought that I was a hand-washing spy.[16] A handful of times we wondered whether including our extra body in a meeting added gravitas or made families feel that they were respected by and important to hospital staff or that their concerns or grievances were being taken seriously. Occasionally family members or physicians would address my colleague and/or me or ask for our input (we both discovered an overactive blush response), though we were usually able to avoid responding.[17] In the early days in the medical ICU, we observed an attending physician seemingly overreact—perhaps for our benefit—to a fellow's description of trying unsuccessfully to persuade a family member to change the goals of care.

FELLOW: I did the best I could but—

ATTENDING: Hold on. Your job is not to push something on them. We don't have an agenda.

But dozens of hours each week over nine to eighteen months (depending on the ICU) is a long time to avoid certain topics or act out of character, especially when life-or-death encounters are at stake. We witnessed enough inappropriate or insensitive comments, obnoxious or arrogant behavior, corners cut, and mistakes made to feel confident that we were witnessing authentic behavior most of the time by physicians and families alike.

Although the institutional review board prohibited us from initiating interactions with research subjects, many knew who we were, either because we had been introduced by nurses or physicians,[18] because they read our badges, which indicated that we were "Research Coordinators," or because they asked us.[19] For patients who were in the ICU for a long period of time, we often provided the only familiar face and continuity for families, when residents and attending physicians rotated off the ICU service. On rare occasions, a family member, protesting the accuracy of a comment by a new physician, would turn in our direction and assert that we had been there and had witnessed the event in question. Often we were one of the few individuals in the room truly listening, not playing with or glancing furtively at a cell phone or pager or darting in and out of the room. Though we said nothing unless addressed (which happened rarely), we often bore silent witness to their experience.

Ethical Dilemmas

When one witnesses real life in real time, day after day, awkward moments and ethical dilemmas can be expected. They came in all shapes and sizes. Colleagues and acquaintances occasionally showed up as patients in the ICU. So did big celebrities, around whom hospital security was high. We witnessed mistakes made—a medication error that led to the death of a patient, and another in which a physician misinterpreted an advance directive and which might have led to the death of a patient had the family not ignored his instructions. We observed lesser mistakes as well—usually nonmedical ones (e.g., confusing a sister for a wife) of which we were seemingly the only ones cognizant. We witnessed situations in which physicians failed to comply with or tried to circumvent the law. We struggled through abusive or humiliating encounters (usually directed by families toward health care providers). We sat silently through introductions that mischaracterized our role. As outsiders, we were occasionally confided in or asked for advice or feedback. One of us was grabbed by a nurse who demanded assistance in a medical emergency. One of us had to deflect amorous advances by a member of the hospital staff and pleas for counseling by a distraught family member. And, like the medical staff, we sometimes had to fight back tears. We responded to these challenges mostly by lying low and remaining silent or saying as few words as possible. When important relationships or our integrity were in jeopardy, we responded or spoke up. But such occasions were fortunately rare.

The Sample

Potential research subjects included all friends, family, significant others, and other visitors of ICU patients who were deemed by their physicians to be unable to make medical decisions. To be included in the study, patients had to be under the care of the critical care team,[20] and we had to observe a discussion of goals of care or consent to a medical procedure, an ethics or palliative care consultation, a dispute, or at least three encounters of any kind between health care providers and patient friends or family. We included the latter (any three encounters in the absence of a more substantive conversation) because surrogates or physicians had an opportunity to raise goals of care and did not, therefore allowing assessment of potential selection bias. Many patients in the ICU (especially those admitted after an elective surgical procedure) do not lack or quickly regain decision-making capacity or are discharged from the ICU in a day or two before any treatment decisions are made; for others, family never visit and there are no encounters to observe. And some patients are not followed by the critical care team. That is why a relatively small proportion (205 out of 2595, or 8 percent) of all patients admitted to the two intensive care units is reflected in the observational study.[21]

ICU patients whose friends and family were included in the observational study were different in relatively predictable ways from those excluded. They tended to be sicker and to be subject to more surrogate medical decision making. Logistic regressions demonstrate that these patients were considerably more likely to lack decision-making capacity for most of their time in the ICU; they had longer ICU stays, and they were somewhat older. The two groups of patients were indistinguishable on other demographic characteristics. More refined treatment data available for the medical ICU also demonstrate that families who were part of the study were more likely to change code status from full code to do-not-resuscitate/do-not-intubate and more likely to opt for palliative care than those excluded (not surprising, since the patients were more critically ill).

Confidentiality and Consent

When data collection first began in the neurological ICU, surrogate decision makers were asked to consent to the observation of their interactions with physicians. The informed-consent form approved by the hospital IRB was six pages long (single-spaced) and included discussion of a "Certificate of Confidentiality" secured from the National Institutes of Health to help protect the privacy of research subjects.[22] For each patient who qualified for the study, I would seek out the individual named power of attorney for health care or, where there was none, the contact person noted in the hospital record and posted on the wall of the patient's ICU room. (The contact person was generally the person physicians would call when they needed consent to an emergency procedure, which they would secure over the phone with a second staff member serving as a witness.) Since consent to my study was a face-to-face process, I spent countless hours throughout the day and evening hoping to find the relevant person in the ICU or waiting room. When the person was eventually found, I would sometimes learn that they were actually not the legal decision maker at all,[23] that there was a dispute or ambiguity about the legitimate surrogate, or that they wanted me to approach other members of the family for consent in addition to their own consent. So the process would begin anew. In a handful of cases, the surrogate did not speak English. In others, events transpired too quickly to allow me to make contact. More often, I was unsuccessful in finding the surrogate decision maker on-site in the hospital. And some surrogates rarely visited the hospital until a major crisis, making it awkward or insensitive to pull them away from an emergency meeting to go through a long consent form before the meeting could start.

In the first six weeks of the study I sought consent from thirty-three surrogates. Seven agreed, and two others consented to the study contingent on the agreement of other family members, who could never be found. In another case, the third sibling of ten refused after the legal decision maker and a second sibling had previously consented. Because of the logistical challenges described above, I was unable to make contact with the remaining twenty-three surrogates (70 percent of those sought). An N of 33 is admittedly rather small, but, not unexpectedly, there were demographic differences between those from whom I secured consent and those from whom I failed to make contact. Patients associated with consenting surrogates were more likely to be older, white, with health insurance, and residing closer to the hospital. All of these characteristics are consistent with having greater ease and flexibility (from work or other commitments) to spend time at the hospital, where I would readily find them to discuss the project.

It quickly became apparent that requiring consent would create a serious selection bias in the sample. I was also beginning to learn that success in securing informed consent had a serious downside: it often created a bond between the surrogate and me. After sitting alone in an ICU room with a nonresponsive patient for hours on end, some surrogates found my visit a welcome distraction. Once we had discussed the study and signed the form, they would then engage me in long conversations—sharing their life story and that of the patient along with their fears and prior ICU experiences, complaining about the physicians and nurses, and seeking my advice and counsel. Having established a connection, some would then come over to talk with me whenever they saw me in the ICU. I worried that the unwanted relationship might also change their ICU experience or how they viewed or enacted their role.

In short, it was clear that seeking consent was bad for some surrogates and bad for the methodological rigor of the study as well. I went back to the IRB and secured a waiver of written informed consent. In exchange, I agreed that I would not approach the friends, family members, or significant others of patients, would maintain their privacy as well as that of the patient, and would not record identifying information. The waiver went into effect by the sixth week of the study, and the representatives of every patient who met inclusion criteria were subsequently included. One decision maker asked not to be part of the study (ironically, because she was angry that—on account of my promises to the IRB—I hadn't approached her and introduced myself); data already collected were destroyed, and we stayed away from all future interactions regarding the patient. Fortunately, this happened only once in more than two years of collecting data about more than seven hundred family members in the two ICUs.

The Data

The data collected from the two ICUs are rather complex, reflecting multiple sources, units of analysis, and temporal features. The data are variably recorded in Microsoft Access and Excel, SPSS, and Atlas.ti and include:

· limited demographic information, admission and discharge, diagnosis, patient decision-making capacity, insurance status, advance directives, characteristics of decision makers, and rudimentary treatment data on the roster of 2595 patients who passed through the two ICUs during the period of the study;

- more detailed information on social background, medical history, treatment decisions, bounce-back to the ICU, outcome, etc., on the 205 patients lacking decision-making capacity whose significant others are subjects of the observational study;

- data on the 1013 meetings observed regarding these 205 patients as well as more limited information abstracted from physicians' notes in electronic medical records or from subsequent accounts from participating doctors or nurses regarding the 699 encounters that were not observed. Data include the time, length, and location of the meeting, whether it was spontaneous or scheduled, characteristics of the participants, the physical configuration of the participants, social dynamics, and conflict; and

- data on the 20,396 statements made by participants in the observed encounters.[24] They include the demographic characteristics of the speakers, their relationship to the patient, and the text of the statement, as well as the statement's emotional tone.

Statement data (thematically coded in Atlas.ti) are also aggregated by meeting, by patient, and over time. Meeting data are aggregated by patient and over time. So, for example, we know for which patients a conversation about advance directives ever came up, when it came up and how often, who initiated the conversation each time it came up, in what context(s), and to what effect(s).

Generalizability of the Research

How well do the hospital and its patients in this one research site reflect their counterparts and the American public overall? The patients do remarkably well; the hospital, less so. We collected data on select demographic characteristics of all patients in the two ICUs during the period of the research. In the series of tables presented below, I contrast these demographic profiles of all ICU patients, those included in the observational study, and corresponding U.S. (and, where available, Standard Metropolitan Statistical Area) census data. The correspondence among the measures is not perfect; sources of data, time frames, units of analysis, operational definitions, and who gets counted may differ across databases. Still, it is clear that the research collects an unusually diverse sample that mirrors demographic trends nationwide. As documented on the next page, the ICU patients and the nation overall are identical on the distribution of gender as well as the proportion of whites and virtually the same on proportions of Asians. However, the study population has a higher representation of blacks and lower representation of Hispanics than the United States as a whole or even the region in which the hospital is located.[25] The disproportionate number of blacks in the sample affords an opportunity to examine more closely the decision-making process among members of this group; unfortunately, the smaller number of Hispanics limits analyses within this group.

As shown in table A.3 on the next page, ICU patients reside in zip codes that are somewhat more affluent in general than the nation as a whole, reflecting the greater affluence of the location of the hospital in a large metropolitan area. It is important to note, however, that even though median household income is somewhat higher in the places in which patients reside, their median poverty rates are at least as high as in the nation as a whole. Patients in the ICU are very diverse economically. They include more than a dozen homeless men, a few living in shelters, and others residing in neighborhoods whose median household income ranges from the first to the ninety-ninth percentile nationally.

Table A.1   Gender

Gender	United States (2006–10)	All ICU patients	ICU patients in study
Male	49%	50%	48%
Female	51%	50%	52%
Total	303,965,272	2595	205

Source: U.S. Census Bureau, ACS (American Community Survey) 2006–2010 (5-Year Estimates), Social Explorer Table T4. https://www.socialexplorer.com/tables/ACS2010_5yr.

Table A.2   Race/Ethnicity

Race/ethnicity	United States (2006–10)	SMSA*	All ICU patients	ICU patients in study
White	65%	54%	65%	65%
Black	12%	17%	23%	22%
Hispanic	16%	21%	7%	6%
Asian	5%	6%	3%	4%
Other	3%	2%	3%	3%
Total	303,965,272	8,516,535	2530	205

*Standard Metropolitan Statistical Area (e.g., region).
Source: U.S. Census Bureau, ACS (American Community Survey) 2006–2010 (5-Year Estimates), Social Explorer Tables T13, T14. https://www.socialexplorer.com/tables/ACS2010_5yr.

Table A.3   Income

Income indicators	United States (2006–10)	SMSA*	All ICU patients	ICU patients in study
Median household income	$51,914	$61,491	$62,475	$63,359
Per capita income	$27,334	$31,045	$29,029	$29,605
Household income below $25,000	24%	20%	20%	22%
Household income below $50,000	48%	41%	41%	39%
Household income above $100,000	21%	27%	24%	29%
Persons below poverty level	10%	9%	11%	12%
Total	114,235,996	3,099,874	2559	202

*Standard Metropolitan Statistical Area (e.g., region).
Sources: U.S. Census Bureau, ACS (American Community Survey) 2006–2010 (5-Year Estimates), Social Explorer Tables T56A. T56B. T57. T83. T113. https://www.socialexplorer.com/tables/ACS2010 _5yr. ICU income data reflect medians for the zip codes in which patients reside. Zip code data come from U.S. Census Bureau, ACS 2006–2010 (5-Year Estimates), using tract level data converted to zip codes, available from the Missouri Census Data Center, Dexter Data Extractor. http://mcdc2.missouri .edu/cgi-bin/broker?_PROGRAM=websas.uex2dex.sas&_SERVICE=appdev&path=/pub/data/ acs2010&dset=uszctas5yr&view=0.

Table A.4   Health Insurance

Health insurance	United States (2009)	All ICU patients	ICU patients in study
	Age 18–65		
No insurance	22%	21%	24%
Public aid	7%	9%	9%
Private insurance	67%	60%	55%
Medicare	4%	11%	12%
Total 18–65	190,781,000	1738	92
	Age 65+		
No insurance	2%	6%	4%
Public aid	0%	1%	1%
Private insurance	5%	11%	9%
Medicare	94%	82%	86%
Total 65+	38,947,000	852	112
Total 18+	229,728,000	2590	204

Note: How multiple insurance coverages (e.g., covered by Medicare and private insurance) are counted may vary from census and hospital data. Because ICU patients are sicker than the general population, some ICU patients less than 65 years of age may be receiving Medicare disability coverage.
Sources: U.S. Census Bureau, "Current Population Survey Tables for Health Insurance Coverage, HI-01. Health Insurance Coverage Status and Type of Coverage by Selected Characteristics: 2009." https://www.census.gov/data/tables/time-series/demo/income-poverty/cps-hi/hi-01.2009.html. ICU insurance data come from documentation in patient charts.

The ICU patients also mirror national trends with respect to access to health insurance (pre-Obamacare). Among those under sixty-five years of age, roughly similar numbers of patients and Americans in general lack health insurance, and the patients are only slightly more likely to receive public aid (probably as a result of previous hospitalizations, where they enrolled). Because ICU patients are more likely to be disabled, higher proportions of those under sixty-five are covered by Medicare. But the proportions with either Medicare or private insurance coverage are comparable for ICU patients and Americans as a whole. Among those over sixty-five, ICU patients are a little more likely to be uninsured, a little less likely to be receiving Medicare (perhaps because of higher proportions of undocumented immigrants in the region), and somewhat more likely to be covered by private insurance. Again, the differences are fairly small, especially given the size of the hospital sample, the number of insurance options available, and the possibility that census takers and hospital billing offices code multiple insurance coverages differently.

As described in the documentation of data sources in table A.5 on the next page, data available on the religious preferences of Americans in general and hospital patients in particular are less rigorous than the other measures. The reasons for reporting or not reporting one's religion in the hospital are undoubtedly reflected in the distribution displayed in the right-hand column of the table. Catholics, Jews, and other religious minorities are probably more likely to respond to questions by hospital staff about religious preference: Catholics to ensure access to rites administered by a priest, and Jews, Muslims, Hmong, and others to avoid Christian interference, to request an appropriate chaplain, or to ensure that their practices are respected. Missing data ("none specified," "don't know") include a number of Protestants who had fewer reasons to disclose, others who are not religiously identified or observant, and a few who did not have capacity to answer and for whom there was no family to ask. It is likely that, if everyone was forced or able to answer, more than half of the ICU patients would report Protestant affiliation. The still smaller number of Protestants in the hospital compared to the United States as a whole reflects its location in a large metropolitan area with greater religious diversity. The disproportionately high number of Jewish patients relative to the U.S. population overall reflects the sizable Jewish population in the metropolitan area as well as greater self-identification in the hospital setting and perhaps our ability to read certain cues.

Overall, then, ICU patients are extremely diverse, their demographic characteristics remarkably similar to the U.S. population as a whole. The

Table A.5   Religion

Religion	United States (2008)	All ICU patients	ICU patients in study
Protestant	64%		44%
Catholic	31%		37%
Jewish	1%		15%
Other	3%		5%
None specified/don't know	(45,984,000)		(58)
Total	228,182,000	2595	147

Data on the religion of ICU patients were only gathered on those observed in the study. These data come from various sources—documentation in patient charts, disclosures by patients or family members, presence of religious icons in the patient's room or on their body, presence or requests for specific clergy or the performance of religious rites (e.g., anointing the sick or last rites), or insisting on or refusing medical procedures (e.g., blood transfusion, nutrition and hydration, organ donation, autopsy) on religious grounds. The meaning of religious preference will be quite different across indicators in the ICU as well as survey respondents reflected in census data and therefore among the least reliable data.
Sources: U.S. Census Bureau, *Statistical Abstract of the United States: 2012*, Table 75. Self-Described Religious Identification of Adult Population: 1990, 2001, and 2008. https://www.census.gov/library/publications/2011/compendia/statab/131ed/population.html. Because the Census Bureau is constitutionally precluded from asking about religion, these data are derived from a university survey. Using random-digit-dialed telephone interviews of a nationally representative sample of 54,461, respondents are asked, "What is your religion, if any?" Barry A. Kosmin and Ariela Keysar, "American Religious Identification Survey (ARIS 2008) Summary Report," March 2009. http://commons.trincoll.edu/aris/files/2011/08/ARIS_Report_2008.pdf.

greatest departures are somewhat higher numbers of blacks and Jews and somewhat lower numbers of Hispanics and Protestants.

The research was set in a large nonprofit secular urban teaching hospital. Clearly a single hospital of any kind anywhere cannot reflect the considerable variation among the thousands of hospitals across the United States—community, religious, for-profit, university, government, VA, and so on. Using the Dartmouth Atlas of Health Care, which relies on Medicare data, one can compare hospital-level measures, mostly of resource use,[26] collected for the hospital in which the research was conducted with hospitals nationally. To protect the anonymity of the research site, I have not listed the actual numbers. However, on all but 16 percent of these measures, the hospital exceeded the national average, on more than a third of them above the ninetieth percentile. This is mostly a reflection of the size of the hospital and of regional norms. Indeed, what the Dartmouth Atlas calls the "hospital referral region" (more than thirty hospitals located in the same metropolitan area) exceeds the national average by more than that of the hospital in which the research was based. The region as a whole exceeded the ninetieth percentile of national data on three-quarters of all measures and fell below the national average on only 5 percent of measures. Unfortunately, specific hospital data from the Dartmouth Atlas is limited to the variables listed in the previous note. Many other datasets that compare hospitals are either proprietary or of much poorer quality.

The location of the research site is relevant in another way as well. As explained in chapter 6, with a few exceptions the laws, regulations, and court cases on surrogate decision making and advance directives in the United States are made at the state level. States differ in their laws, regulations, court opinions, and practices regarding end-of-life decision making, which may percolate down to the ways in which patients, surrogates, institutions, and health care providers anticipate or respond to medical decisions on behalf of those who lack capacity.[27] These differences are addressed in the chapters on law and surrogate decision making. Fortunately, many health care providers are oblivious to legal rules,[28] on the one hand, and Illinois laws and regulations are fairly typical of those of many other states.

This study has several limitations, some noted earlier. Despite a very diverse group of patients and families and observations of more than one thousand interactions between almost three hundred medical staff and more than seven hundred friends and family of patients over more than two years, the resources demanded to conduct observational research significantly limit its breadth. This study was conducted in one state, in one teaching hospital, in only two of its ICUs, about a rather modest number of research subjects. Perhaps other types of ICUs and in other locations face different challenges or have addressed them more effectively than the hospital I studied.

Although intensive care units disproportionately collect patients unable to make their own medical decisions, they represent only one of several venues in which surrogates negotiate end-of-life medical decisions. The findings presented here do not illuminate the experience of everyone nearing the end of life, especially those who eschew aggressive care and stay away from hospitals or ICUs. But they do illuminate the experience of a substantial number of them.

Patient Occupation

Occupation	Number	Percentage of those with known occupations
None	5	5%
Student	1	1%
Farming	3	3%
Manual labor	17	18%
Entertainment	5	5%
Service	3	3%
Sales	7	7%
Clerical	7	7%
Management	8	8%
Business owner	5	5%
Professional	36	37%
Don't know	108	
Total	205	

Note that, with so much missing data, these numbers undoubtedly reflect significant bias.

Patient Age, Gender, and Marital Status

		Never Married*	First marriage	Remarried	Divorced/widowed	Total
<40	Female	4 36%	6 55%		1 9%	11 100%
	Male	10 71%	2 14%		2 14%	14 100%
	Total	14 56%	8 32%		3 12%	25 100%
40–49	Female	3 27%	4 36%	1 9%	3 27%	11 100%
	Male	2 33%	3 50%	1 17%		6 100%
	Total	5 29%	7 41%	2 12%	3 18%	17 100%
50–59	Female	1 6%	10 56%		7 39%	18 100%
	Male	4 27%	8 53%	1 7%	2 13%	15 100%
	Total	5 15%	18 55%	1 3%	9 27%	33 100%
60–69	Female	2 11%	6 32%	2 11%	9 47%	19 100%
	Male	2 12%	9 53%	1 6%	5 29%	17 100%
	Total	4 11%	15 42%	3 8%	14 39%	36 100%
70+	Female	1 2%	17 35%		30 63%	48 100%
	Male	3 7%	29 63%	4 9%	10 22%	46 100%
	Total	4 4%	46 49%	4 4%	40 43%	94 100%
All patients		32 16%	94 46%	10 5%	69 34%	205 100%

*Including unmarried partners of the same or opposite sex. (Same-sex marriage was not legal in Illinois at the time of this study.)

Location and Purpose of Observed Meetings

Meeting location	Meeting addressed consent or goals of care		Total
	No	Yes	
Rounds	(320) 66%	(143) 27%	(463) 46%
Patient room	(95) 20%	(143) 27%	(238) 24%
Conference room	(6) 1%	(134) 25%	(140) 14%
Waiting room/hall	(49) 10%	(76) 14%	(125) 12%
Telephone	(15) 3%	(32) 6%	(47) 5%
Total	(485)	(528)	(1013)

Relationship between Multiple Trajectories Traversed

The table below shows the percentage of each trajectory that was traversed alone or along with an additional trajectory. For example, 21 percent of surrogates who hoped the patient would decide also considered their instructions, and 36 percent stood in the patient's shoes; 43 percent entertained no decision criterion except waiting for the patient to decide. The sum of percentages across the rows exceeds 100 because surrogates sometimes considered several additional criteria.

	Only this criterion	Patient decides	Instruc-tions	Patient's shoes	Benefi-cence	God decides	What we want	Opt out/ denial
Patient decides	43%		21%	36%	14%	0%	14%	14%
Instructions	16%	5%		77%	20%	2%	15%	7%
Patient's shoes	24%	7%	66%		21%	0%	13%	6%
Beneficence	23%	8%	46%	58%		0%	27%	4%
God decides	0%	0%	14%	0%	0%		43%	71%
What we want	43%	5%	24%	24%	19%	8%		19%
Opt out/denial	26%	10%	21%	21%	5%	26%	37%	

Decision Trajectory by Patient and Surrogate Characteristics

The figures below provide more detailed breakdowns of a variety of patient and surrogate characteristics across all of the decision trajectories. Figures present the percentage of persons of a particular trait in each trajectory (compare differences in the size of the different colored bars *within* each trajectory to see which traits are disproportionately present or absent). Because some of the categories presented in the figures are relatively small, some of the differences you will see are not especially reliable or statistically significant.

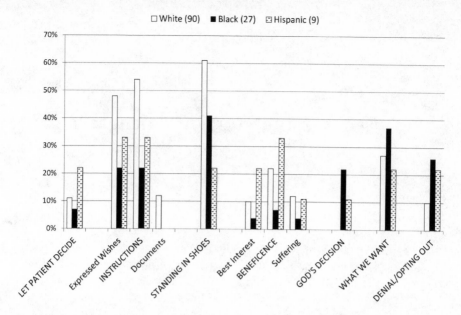

Figure D.1. Decision Trajectory by Patient's Race/Ethnicity

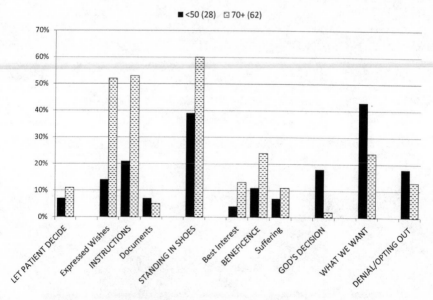

Figure D.2. Decision Trajectory by Patient's Age

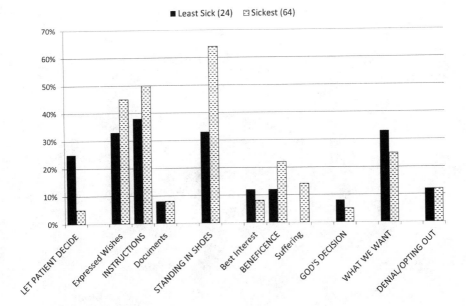

Figure D.3. Decision Trajectory by Severity of Illness

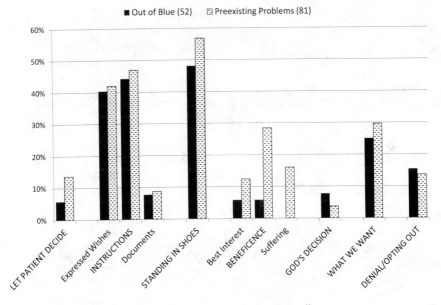

Figure D.4. Decision Trajectory by Preexisting Illness

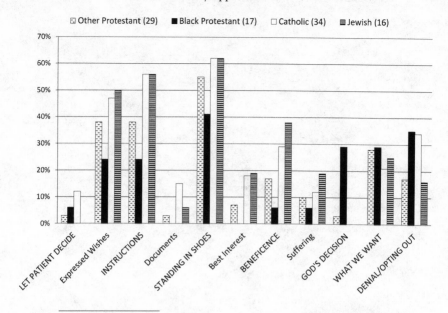

About a quarter of the patients do not disclose their religious preference. This raises concern about selection bias among those who do. If one assumes that many of those who do not disclose are Protestant, this does not substantially alter the findings presented above.

Figure D.5. Decision Trajectory by Patient's Religion

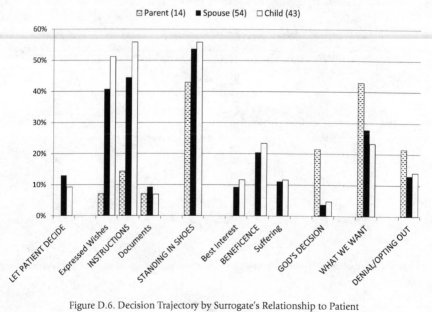

Figure D.6. Decision Trajectory by Surrogate's Relationship to Patient

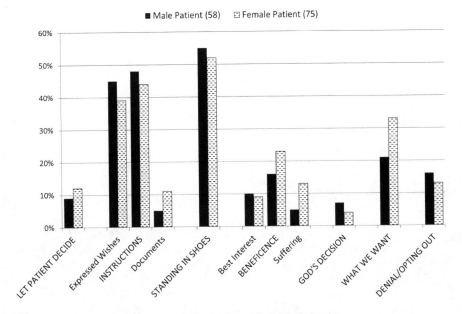

Figure D.7. Decision Trajectory by Patient's Gender

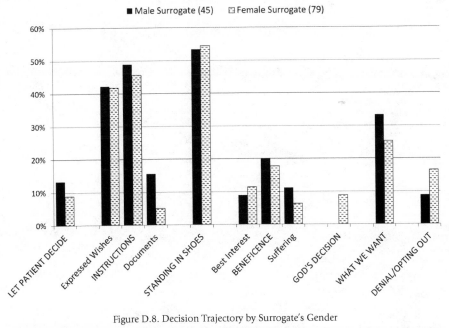

Figure D.8. Decision Trajectory by Surrogate's Gender

Advance-Directive Status and Aspects of the Decision-Making Process, Outcome, and Impact

Attribute/(number of cases)	B	SE
Patient wishes		
Any patient wishes mentioned (120)	.066	.364
Patient's express wishes mentioned (89)	.313	.352
Patient's wishes inferred (51)	.290	.372
Patient's wishes perceived (79)	−.008	.298
Patient's personality described (78)	−.219	.321
Evidence of patient's wishes described (54)	−.084	.352
Family doesn't know patient's wishes (16)	−.040	.549
Discussion of wishes initiated by health care providers		
Any patient wishes mentioned (76)	.377	.334
Patient's express wishes mentioned (51)	.299	.362
Patient's wishes inferred (29)	.422	.450
Patient's wishes perceived (45)	.358	.364
Decision-making process		
Raises goals of care (175)	.257	.436
Family raises goals of care (91)	**.635***	**.309**
Physician raises goals of care (137)	−.326	.329
Who is the decision maker? (52)	−.245	.323
Decision criteria (78)	.124	.357
Best interest (20)	.315	.479
Quality of life (48)	.427	.337
Pain and/or suffering (142)	−.226	.325
Cost (25)	−.405	.435
What I would want for myself (15)	−.693	.567
Needs of self or others (52)	−.441	.330
Family seeks advice (36)	−.168	.409
Physician offers advice (70)	−.280	.329
Conflict between family and physicians (30)	.283	.447
How long it takes to address		
Number of days until patient wishes raised (135)	1.195	1.350
Number of days until goals of care raised (175)	0.658	1.069
Number of days goals of care raised to changed (117)	1.194	1.088
Number of days in ICU (205)	2.190	1.680

(continued)

Table E (*continued*)

Attribute/(number of cases)	B	SE
Outcome measures		
Consults with palliative care (52)	.175	.357
Refuses an intervention (130)	−.698	.429
Do-not-resuscitate (DNR) order (118)	−.801	.417
Withdraws life support (86)	.125	.416
Impact on family		
Conflict within family (20)	−.168	.473
Family emotional burden (103)	−.419	.304

Notes: Reference category is "no advance directive" (N = 105). Logistic and linear regressions control for patient age and ethnicity, severity of illness, and whether illness was preexisting or came out of the blue. Covariates are entered, using a forward stepwise method. B = unstandardized coefficient; SE = standard error. *$p < .05$.

If patients with directives in the hospital are compared with everyone else, weaker though significant differences are also found regarding reprising the patient's express wishes and formulating substituted judgments (Shapiro 2015).

ACKNOWLEDGMENTS

A project of this magnitude can only succeed with the generosity of many individuals and organizations. I am profoundly grateful to medical social worker Rachel Billow Angulo, with whom I shared data-collection and coding responsibilities and whose keen ear is reflected in the transcripts on which this book is built. Her intelligence, insight, and humor made a very grueling enterprise much more rewarding. Thanks also to summer interns Francesca Gibson and Cara McClellan.

Because I am protecting the anonymity of the families and health care providers who welcomed me into their private world, I cannot thank them by name. I owe a great debt especially to the director of the neurological intensive care unit (who helped with both substance and logistics) as well as to the director of the medical ICU; the head of the stroke team; the nurse manager of the neurological ICU; the chair of the hospital ethics committee; the ICU social workers and chaplains; scores of attending physicians, fellows, residents, and nurses; representatives of the regional organ-donation organization; and hundreds of friends and family members of patients, who allowed me to witness one of the most intimate and wrenching journeys of their lives. I hope this book does justice to and honors their experience.

I am grateful as well for generous financial support from the American Bar Foundation and the American Bar Endowment, the M.D. Anderson Foundation, the National Science Foundation (under grant no. SES 0752159), and a 2011 Investigator Award in Health Policy Research from the Robert Wood Johnson Foundation. Any opinions, findings, conclusions, or recommendations expressed in this material are mine and do not necessarily reflect the views of the National Science Foundation or the other foundations.

Chuck Myers has shown me what a great editor can be; his interest, enthusiasm, insight, and feedback have been invaluable. He and Holly Smith of the University of Chicago Press have been a delight to work with.

Many current and former colleagues from the American Bar Foundation and its board of directors provided support and valuable feedback along the way, especially Ajay Mehrotra, Bob Nelson, Traci Burch, Steve Daniels, Shari Diamond, Carol Heimer, Jack Heinz, Bonnie Honig, Camilo Leslie, Beth Mertz, Kathy Pace, Jothie Rajah, Meredith Rountree, Becky Sandefur, Carole Silver, Winni Sullivan, Susan Appleton, Mike Byowitz, Dave Collins, Doreen Dodson, Lauren Edelman, Ellen Flannery, George Frazza, Kay Hodge, David Houghton, Tony Patterson, Ellen Rosenblum, and Mark Suchman.

Rebecca Brashler, Debjani Mukherjee, Teresa Savage, and especially Kristi Kirschner introduced me to the world of disability ethics and helped me get the project off the ground. Over the years, I have also received assistance, advice, or feedback from Larry Magder, Barry Mitnick, Charlie Sabatino, Erica Wood, Mark Kuczewski, David Mechanic, Carl Schneider, Angela Fagerlin, Colleen Grogan, Herschel Nachlis, Susan Hirsch, Sally Merry, Ray Solomon, Nicole Diamond Austin, Polly Edwards, Nancy Shapiro-Pikelny, fellow Robert Wood Johnson Investigator Awardees, many anonymous peer reviewers, and scores of lawyers, doctors, and social scientists with whom I shared preliminary findings along the way.

To those named and those not, and to my loyal and good-natured family and friends, I am so very grateful.

CHAPTER ONE

1. See Appendix A.
2. Buchanan and Brock (1989); Schneider (1998).
3. Luce and Prendergast (2001); Smedira et al. (1990).
4. Silveira, Kim, and Langa (2010), 1214.
5. Roughly one quarter of all Medicare spending pays for patient care in the last year of life (Goodman et al. [2011], 2) and, at least historically, 40 percent of this amount is spent in the last thirty days (Lubitz and Riley [1993]) when it is more likely that surrogates have responsibility for medical decision making.
6. See Teno et al. (2002) and Klingler, in der Schmitten, and Marckmann (2016).
7. Appendix A shows how they compare to the U.S. population as a whole.
8. Centers for Disease Control and Prevention (2017).
9. These statistics come from The Dartmouth Atlas of Healthcare (2014a), (2014b), (2014c), (2014d).
10. U.S. Social Security Administration (2012).
11. Goodman et al. (2011).

CHAPTER TWO

1. In addition to the medical and neurological intensive care units, observed in this study, the hospital provides cardiac and surgical ICUs as well. Other hospitals will not have private ICU rooms or so many beds or as many specialized ICUs as this one.
2. Some of the surgical specialties, such as neurosurgery, will conduct rounds hours earlier before they begin surgery for the day.
3. Lewis et al. (2016); Aviv (2018).
4. Barrett et al. (2014); National Center for Health Statistics (2017). The per patient cost converts 2011 dollars into 2018 dollars, assuming that the underlying cost is the same. It also reflects lower hospital costs incurred before or after the patient was transferred to the ICU during the hospital admission. For both reasons, the estimate is probably low.

CHAPTER THREE

1. Most ICU-based medical research uses physiological measurements—blood count,

heart and respiratory rate, creatinine, arterial pressure, and so on—to rank patients' severity of illness or likelihood of mortality; the most commonly used measure is the so-called APACHE score (Knaus et al. [1985]). Unfortunately, although the ethnographic research reported here collected considerable medical history for each patient, it did not gather detailed clinical information that could generate an APACHE-like score. The measure used here of severity of illness comes from coefficients obtained from logistic regressions of patient medical history, circumstances of admission, and medical status on good (patient goes home or to rehabilitation) or bad (patient dies or is discharged to a facility) outcomes. This gross dichotomy of outcome was chosen because it is generally independent of treatment decisions made by surrogates. For example, no matter how heroic the treatment, a very sick patient will rarely be discharged home directly from the ICU. Similarly, patients on life support typically die if surrogates remove it and either die or end up in a long-term acute care facility if surrogates do not. The best predictors of good or bad outcomes from the logistic regressions are data collected throughout the ICU admission on the patient's ventilation status (i.e., whether on or not on a ventilator) and cognitive responsiveness (Glasgow Coma Score, which is one component of the APACHE score).

2. A quarter of them spent less than 7 days in the ICU; a quarter spent more than 20.5 days.

3. Patients receive a perfect Glasgow Coma Score if they open their eyes spontaneously, obey commands, and are oriented to time, place, and person.

4. The study was conducted before the implementation of the Affordable Care Act.

5. Patients under the age of eighteen are treated in specialized hospitals for children; however, ambulance personnel occasionally misjudge the age of a large, unconscious adolescent.

6. Although one might expect families to disclose that they or the patients have health care experience in the hope of getting more information, respect, or better care; so this is undoubtedly an overrepresentation.

7. The study was conducted before same-sex marriage became legal in Illinois.

8. I ran into the son-in-law of one patient in a department store, shopping for shirts because he had run out of clean clothes and hadn't been home in days to replenish his supply.

9. For example, the family of a young bicycle mechanic, amateur athlete, and musician who suffered a tragic accident reportedly received thousands of calls. The waiting room was continually filled with dozens of friends. It became so overwhelming that at one point the patient's mother asked the organ donor coordinator whether there was any way that she and her son's girlfriend "can go and have a smoke without having to confront all of those people in the waiting room?" The patient's friends also created a website to report on his progress for those unable to visit.

10. One study differentiated participants between those who were "progressing, accommodating, maintaining, struggling, and floundering" (Wiegand, Deatrick, and Knafl [2008]).

11. States have varied names for legally designated and default decision makers, names that sometimes overlap from jurisdiction to jurisdiction. The former include "agents," "proxies," "representatives," "attorneys in fact," "surrogates," and "patient advocates." The latter include "surrogates," "proxies," "next of kin," "family members," "responsible parties," and "appropriate individuals." The most common labels are "agent" or "proxy" for a designated decision maker and "surrogate" for a

default decision maker (American Bar Association Commission on Law and Aging [2016]).

12. Patients who produced a power-of-attorney document were older and more likely to be white. Those who claimed—but never produced—a document were also older and white; they were also more likely to be living in a wealthier neighborhood and to have a preexisting medical problem.

13. Fried et al. (2011).

14. Curlin et al. (2007).

CHAPTER FOUR

1. Donchin et al. (2003).

2. Recall that almost two-thirds of patients arrive in the ICU already intubated.

3. Muppets from the children's television show *Sesame Street*.

4. The critical care fellow met again at 10 P.M. with twenty-five family members and reprised the same information. The family decided that pressors to raise the patient's blood pressure should not be administered.

5. Kaldjian et al. (2009), 501.

6. The protocol has two purposes. First, specially trained facilitators are more effective in communicating with families. Second, the perception that physicians may be more interested in harvesting organs than curing patients is minimized.

7. These findings are derived from logistic regressions. Significant findings reflect p values of < .001 for severity of illness and race/ethnicity and < .05 for age. See chap. 3, n. 1 for an explanation of how severity of illness was measured.

8. Many studies find African American patients less likely to opt for hospice or palliative care (Krakauer, Crenner, and Fox [2002]; Pew Research Center [November 2013]; Phipps et al. [2003]; Shugarman, Decker, and Bercovitz [2009]). Physicians never mentioned these studies in conversations with their team, which, of course, does not mean that they were unfamiliar with them. There is no evidence that physicians consciously avoided certain conversations based on the race or ethnicity of the patient or family. Perhaps their disinclination to discuss these interventions derived from cues they received from family members or from experiences with other African American families that led them to believe that surrogates would decide to stay the course. If this finding was explained by availability of families of color to meet with physicians, the conversations about goals of care or code status would also be significantly less likely for nonwhite patients—which they are not.

9. Katz (1984); Faden, Beauchamp, and King (1986); Meisel and Kuczewski (1996).

10. In some states, including Illinois—the site of the research—physicians are expected to provide information that a reasonable physician would disclose in a similar situation; in others, what a reasonable patient in a similar situation would find material in making a treatment decision.

11. In an emergency situation, when the patient lacks decision-making capacity and a surrogate cannot be found, two physicians typically consent to an intervention, based on what they judge to be in the best interest of the patient.

12. Including neurology, neurosurgery, oncology, orthopedics, infectious diseases, surgery, ENT (ear, nose, and throat), cardiology (heart) hematology (blood), hepatology (liver), nephrology (kidney), pulmonology (lung), gastroenterology (digestion, etc.), immunology, psychiatry, palliative care, and so forth.

13. This number may be slightly exaggerated by inclusion criteria employed by the research design; patients for whom goals of care or consent to a procedure was never

broached and for whom fewer than three interactions were observed were excluded from the study.

14. Although many surrogates stood up to the physicians or refused to accede to their recommendations.

15. See Appendix B.3 for a table showing the location and purpose of the observed meetings.

16. Eight percent of the patients had family members who spoke languages other than English (Spanish, French, Italian, Russian, Greek, Hmong, and Arabic) or who were deaf. Thirty-two observed meetings regarding medical decisions or goals of care involved participants who could not understand the English-language dialogue (there were many more meetings of less consequence). In half of these meetings, there was no translation or interpretation; in 31 percent a family member translated or signed periodically; in 19 percent a professional interpreter played this role. In a few instances, physicians spoke in the foreign language (usually Spanish).

17. Because the neurological ICU did not have critical care fellows, attending physicians conducted more meetings (78 percent) than in the medical ICU, where attendings shared responsibility (59 percent) with fellows (20 percent).

18. The physicians left and the family remained in the conference room for another forty-five minutes, speaking by phone with the primary care physician. When they emerged, they announced tearfully that they would not elect to have the surgical procedure and would instead withdraw care. The patient died later that night.

19. The nurse means that it would cause the heart to stop beating (cardiac death). But of course, the patient is already dead. This demonstrates the awkwardness of speaking about brain death, even by health care providers.

20. Silveira, Kim, and Langa (2010).

CHAPTER FIVE
1. Anspach (1987), 216.
2. Kaufman (2015), 279.
3. Christakis (1999), 92.
4. Enzinger et al. (2015).
5. Christakis (1999).
6. Christakis (1999).
7. Asch (2001), 299, 301.
8. Ubel et al. (2005), S57.
9. Winter, Moss, and Hoffman (2009).
10. Halpern and Arnold (2008).
11. Gertner (2003); Wilson and Gilbert (2005).
12. Igou (2008).
13. Wegwarth (2013); Ghosh, Ghosh, and Erwin (2004).
14. Christakis (1999), 108–9.
15. Anspach (1987).
16. In psychology, bias engendered by the ease with which events come to mind is called the "availability heuristic"; it may lead one to overestimate the likelihood of these recent events (Kahneman [2011]). There will be more on this in chap. 6.
17. Many other studies also report conflicting prognostic information offered by different practitioners (Meeker and Jezewski [2008]).
18. Reasons expressed in the first study included "a belief that God could alter the course of the illness, a belief that predicting the future is inherently inaccurate, prior

experiences in which physicians' prognostications were inaccurate, and experiences with prognostication during the patient's ICU stay" (Zier et al. [2008], 2342). In the second study, this discordance was due to both misunderstanding and surrogate beliefs, including that optimism would improve the patient's outcome or that the patient was stronger than the physician realized (White et al. [2016]).

19. Boyd et al. (2010), 1270.
20. Chiarchiaro et al. (2015).
21. Gawande (2015), 44.
22. Christakis (1999).
23. Christakis (1999), 68.
24. For example, one study of more than 1400 physicians described a treatment effect in several ways: absolute survival (96 percent vs. 94 percent), absolute mortality (4 percent vs. 6 percent), relative mortality reduction (by one-third), and number needed to treat to avoid one death (fifty). Though these formats convey identical information about treatment efficacy, 8 percent of the physicians given the absolute survival percentage said that the treatment was clearly better, 27 percent said so for absolute mortality, 67 percent for mortality reduction, and 34 percent for number to treat. Patterns were similar for patients, though not as strong (i.e., they did better than the physicians) (Perneger and Agoritsas [2011], 1415).
25. Kahneman (2011).
26. Tversky and Kahneman (1981); Kahneman (2011).
27. Tversky and Kahneman (1981), 453.
28. Kahneman (2011), 318–19.

CHAPTER SIX

1. The power of the state to protect those who cannot act on their own behalf.
2. Harmon (1990).
3. Buchanan and Brock (1989); Schneider (1998); Meisel and Cerminara (2008); Beauchamp and Childress (2009).
4. Olick (2001), xiii.
5. Illinois Health Care Surrogate Act (1998).
6. Berlinger, Jennings, and Wolf (2013).
7. Vandenbroucke et al. (2015). These are medical orders, not legal documents.
8. American Bar Association Commission on Law and Aging (2018).
9. Unfortunately, this default ranking does not necessarily correspond with patient preferences, had the patient gone to the trouble of making a choice. One survey suggests that patients do not always get the surrogates they want when they don't name them in advance (Lipkin [2006]). A third of married patients in the survey indicated that they wanted a surrogate other than their spouse (the default decision maker in most jurisdictions). A quarter preferred a surrogate other than the emergency contact person on file in their physician's office. And, although legal default rules are indifferent to gender, most patients preferred their mothers, daughters, and sisters over their fathers, sons, and brothers, respectively. Another study found that patients believed that their children understood their wishes better than their spouses (Hawkins et al. [2005]).
10. American Bar Association Commission on Law and Aging (2015); Wynn (2014); American Bar Association Commission on Law and Aging (2018).
11. As described in chap. 3, states have varied names for legally designated and default decision makers, names that sometimes overlap from jurisdiction to jurisdiction.

The former include "agents," "proxies," "representatives," "attorneys in fact," "surrogates," and "patient advocates." The latter include "surrogates," "proxies," "next of kin," "family members," "responsible parties," and "appropriate individuals." The most common labels are "agent" or "proxy" for a designated decision maker and "surrogate" for a default decision maker (American Bar Association Commission on Law and Aging [2016]).

12. Meisel and Cerminara (2008).
13. Buchanan and Brock (1989), 94–95.
14. Emanuel and Emanuel (1992), 2068.
15. Petersen (2007), 60; Berlinger, Jennings, and Wolf (2013).
16. This discussion draws on Shapiro (2007), with permission of the publisher.
17. Collopy (1999), 39.
18. Beschle (1989); Sabatino (1999), 55.
19. Kim (2014).
20. Emanuel and Emanuel (1992), 2070.
21. Winter, Moss, and Hoffman (2009).
22. Ditto, Hawkins, and Pizarro (2006); Fagerlin and Schneider (2004).
23. Buchanan and Brock (1989).
24. Chochinov et al. (1999); Krumholz et al. (1998); Kirschner (2005); Kim (2014); Fagerlin and Schneider (2004).
25. Kim (2014), 189.
26. Kirschner (2005).
27. Kirschner (2005); Dresser (1986).
28. Dresser (1986), 381.
29. For example, Shalowitz, Garrett-Mayer, and Wendler (2006); Emanuel and Emanuel (1992); Epstein et al. (1989); Hawkins et al. (2005); Magaziner et al. (1988); Ouslander, Tymchuk, and Rahbar (1989); Rubenstein et al. (1984); Tomlinson et al. (1990); Uhlmann, Pearlman, and Cain (1988); Zweibel and Cassel (1989).
30. Shalowitz, Garrett-Mayer, and Wendler (2006). Meta-analysis is a statistical technique that combines data from multiple studies to reach a conclusion with more statistical power.
31. Ditto et al. (2001).
32. See, for example, Lynn (1997); Murphy and Cluff (1990); Pruchno et al. (2006); Pruchno et al. (2008); Bryant et al. (2013).
33. Sharma et al. (2011).
34. Tsevat et al. (1995).
35. Covinsky et al. (2000).
36. Song, Ward, and Lin (2012).
37. Emanuel and Emanuel (1992), 2069.
38. Gutheil and Appelbaum (1983), 10.
39. Kim (2014); Lindemann and Nelson (2014); Ditto and Clark (2014).
40. Blustein (1999); Fins (1999); Powell (1999); Collopy (1999).
41. Collopy (1999).
42. Blustein (1999), 20.
43. Kuczewski (1999).
44. Fagerlin et al. (2001).
45. Kahneman (2011), 318–19.
46. Kahneman (2011), 8.
47. Kahneman (2011), 12.

48. Blumenthal-Barby and Krieger (2015).
49. Fagerlin et al. (2001).
50. Span (2016).
51. This discussion draws on Shapiro (2012b), with permission of the publisher.
52. Shapiro (2002).
53. Hardwig (1992); Sabatino (1999).
54. Rhoden (1988), 438–39.
55. Fentiman (1989), 810–11.
56. King (1989).
57. Friedman and Savage, who examined conservatorship files in California, expressed their suspicion that some conservators "tended to act as if the money belonged to them. After all, they are often the heirs of the ward; they are waiting in the wings and see no harm in treating the money as if it were already theirs" ([1988], 285–86).
58. Chugh, Bazerman, and Banaji (2005).
59. Terry et al. (1999).
60. Schneider (1998).
61. Puchalski et al. (2000).
62. Hawkins et al. (2005); Sehgal et al. (1992); Terry et al. (1999). Hawkins et al. (2005) found slightly less than half, while Sehgal et al. (1992) found slightly more than half.
63. Hardwig (1990), 7,6.
64. Hardwig (1992), 810–11, 16.
65. Kim (2014).
66. Chap. 3 describes higher numbers among the older/sicker patients in the observational study: 22 percent produce an advance directive and another 24 percent claim to have one elsewhere.
67. Karp and Wood (2003).

CHAPTER SEVEN

1. These trajectories mirror somewhat decision criteria described or theorized by others. Swigart (1994) found four methods of deliberation in her study of a medical intensive care unit—deciding "what the patient wanted or would have wanted" (trajectories no. 2 and no. 3), "what was in the patient's best interests" (no. 4), "delegating decisions to a divine power or fate" (no. 5), and concern that a "moral prohibition that withdrawal [of life support] is synonymous with killing." Tunney and Ziegler (2015) described four perspectives that they theorize surrogates consider in decision making: Egocentric (what is best for the surrogate—trajectory no. 6), Projected (what would the surrogate do if he/she were in the patient's position), Benevolent (what is best for the patient—no. 4), and Simulated (what would the patient do—no. 3). Tunney and Ziegler theorize that surrogates consider all four perspectives but then choose among them by weighting the perspectives in light of the surrogate's empathy, their social distance to or intimacy with the patient, the significance of the decision at hand, how accountable they will be for their decision, and their intent. This theory does not draw on empirical evidence, nor does it consider the effect on surrogate decisions of other participants—health care providers as well as significant others—which is sometimes considerable.
2. On average, living wills were five years old and power-of-attorney documents four years old.

3. Illinois changed the wording of these options slightly after the conclusion of the study.

4. One percent of patients expressed their wishes in both a living will and a power-of-attorney form.

5. Fried et al. (2011).

6. As the critical care attending asked: "Her heart is still beating, and she still has blood flowing. Is that what she meant by viable? Or did she mean viable in terms of being able to interact with her environment, being able to eat, things like that?"

7. Ernecoff et al. (2015).

8. Sabatino (1999), 55.

9. Buchanan (1988).

10. King (1989).

11. Research has demonstrated that we face psychological blinders to the recognition of our own conflicts of interest (Chugh, Bazerman, and Banaji [2005]).

12. Rhoden (1988).

13. Marks and Miller (1987).

14. Counterintuitively, there were far more family meetings on average regarding patients on this trajectory than on any other (and more than twice as many overall). However, as shown in the next chapter, patients on the denial, opt-out trajectory stayed in the ICU far longer than those on any other trajectory. As a result, there were considerably fewer meetings for these patients per days in the ICU than for those on any other trajectory (.77 overall). Perhaps this finding represents diminishing returns, but perhaps instead it suggests surrogate-meeting avoidance because of an unwillingness to reconsider the goals of care. Physicians may have played a role in this as well. At least anecdotally, it appeared that, in the face of this resistance, some physicians eventually stopped pressing these surrogates to meet with them.

15. See, for example, Dionne-Odom (2015); Kim et al. (2017); Limerick (2007); Meeker and Jezewski (2008); Swigart et al. (1996); Tilden et al. (2001); and Wiegand, Deatrick, and Knafl (2008).

16. These differences reflect management styles that range from "Progressing" (toward limiting life support) to "Accommodating," "Maintaining," "Struggling," or "Floundering" (Wiegand, Deatrick, and Knafl [2008]).

CHAPTER EIGHT

1. The figure was generated by factor analysis, a statistical technique that seeks to remove redundancy and collapse a number of observed variables into a smaller set of unobserved or latent variables or factors. It looks for patterns in the relationships among the observed variables and determines whether the variables can be explained by a smaller number of underlying factors. Figure 8.2 displays on each axis the three factors that explain the most variation across the trajectories (together, 62 percent). The trajectories are plotted on each axis according to the loadings or correlations between the trajectory and the factor. High positive or negative loadings—where the trajectory is plotted at either extreme of the axis—indicate that the trajectory is highly correlated with the factor. The factor analysis results presented here employ principal component analysis with varimax rotation.

2. See chap. 3, n. 1 for a description of how severity of illness was measured.

3. Decisions attentive to patient suffering were made only for patients with preexisting conditions and those with the most severe medical problems.

4. The median age of patients with a parent as surrogate is thirty-one, versus seventy for patients whose surrogate is not a parent. Fifty-five percent of the patients whose surrogate is their parent are black, compared to 18 percent of patients whose surrogate is not their parent.

5. Analysis employed logistic regression, with the forward LR method.

6. Here beneficence cuts in different directions. Concern about patient suffering is overwhelmingly burdensome (85 percent of them), but determining best interest is not (54 percent of them).

7. Span (2009).

8. Shapiro (2015).

9. This analysis draws on Shapiro (2012a). See the article for more detail.

10. The analysis draws on Shapiro (2015). See the article for more detail on the analytic strategy.

11. Characteristics included age and ethnicity. Preliminary analyses also controlled for gender, income, and whether a family member was in the health care or legal professions, but these variables showed no difference.

CHAPTER NINE

1. The reason this difference is so dramatic is that outcome was one of the factors included in the measurement of severity of illness. (See chap. 3, n. 1 for a description of how severity of illness was measured.) Still, it is clear that, although outcomes are generally unwelcome, some ICU patients do very well.

2. Huynh et al. (2013), 1892.

3. Wendler and Rid (2011).

4. Buchwald (2006).

5. Nor are they always the persons patients prefer to make decisions on their behalf or feel best know their wishes (Hawkins et al. [2005]; Lipkin [2006]).

6. Hickman et al. (2005); Martin, Emanuel, and Singer (2000); Rogne and McCune (2014); Sudore and Fried (2010); McCannon et al. (2012); Volandes et al. (2007).

7. American Bar Association Commission on Law and Aging (2009), (2005).

8. Colaberdino et al. (2016); Gordon (2014).

9. National POLST Paradigm (2018).

10. Teno et al. (2013); Dartmouth Atlas of Healthcare (2014d).

11. Silveira, Kim, and Langa (2010).

12. Emanuel and Emanuel (1993); Cantor (1996); Lindgren (1993); Rid and Wendler (2014a).

13. Shalowitz, Garrett-Mayer, and Wendler (2007); Smucker et al. (2000).

14. Rid and Wendler (2014b).

15. Rid (2014).

16. Levin et al. (2010); Curtis et al. (2002).

17. These include interventions to improve empathy, addressing emotions, active listening, attending to nonverbal cues, giving family members time to speak, providing support, understanding differing interpersonal styles that call for tailored approaches, conflict resolution, and more (Curtis et al. [2012]; Curtis et al. [2013]; Levin et al. [2010]; Scheunemann et al. [2011]).

18. Schwarze et al. (2016), 14.

19. Thaler and Sunstein (2008).

20. Lamas et al. (2018).

21. The 14 percent figure excludes encounters during critical care rounds. As noted in

chap. 3, nurses participated in only 9 percent of total encounters between physicians and family members.

22. Torke et al. (2016); White et al. (2012); Curtis et al. (2016).

23. SUPPORT Principal Investigators (1995), 1591; Scheunemann et al. (2011).

24. Curtis et al. (2016); Khandelwal, Benkeser, Coe, Engelberg, et al. (2016); Khandelwal, Benkeser, Coe, and Curtis (2016).

25. Wolf, Berlinger, and Jennings (2015); Sabatino (2010).

26. Godfrey and Sabatino (2018).

27. Godfrey and Sabatino (2018). Unfortunately, these findings from more than five hundred physicians reflect a 1 percent response rate and therefore may not be representative. But they are nonetheless concerning.

APPENDIX A

1. Shapiro (1987), (2005).

2. See Shapiro (2016).

3. Lynn, Harrold, and Schuster (2011).

4. Critical care physicians in the neurological ICU were mostly anesthesiologists and a few neurologists; in the medical ICU, the critical care physicians were usually pulmonologists or internists.

5. The Glasgow Coma Score is a 15-point scale that measures level of consciousness based on eye, motor, and verbal responses. Individuals receive a score from 3 (deep unconsciousness) to 15 (normal). A perfect score indicates that a patient can follow commands, participate in an oriented conversation, and open eyes spontaneously. Patients with dementia or cognitive impairments may receive scores of 15 along with those with decision-making capacity.

6. Attending physicians asked that we wear white coats like everyone else on the team. Unlike the others, our coats had no hospital insignias or embroidered names or titles, although we wore badges identifying us as researchers. We wore knee-length coats, signifying an advanced degree. Medical students wear waist-length coats.

7. When research began, copies of forms requesting advance-directive and surrogate information, along with copies of the advance directives (living wills and durable powers of attorney for health care) themselves, were collected in a binder for each patient and stored at the nurses' station. Midway through the research, paper forms were replaced with entries in the electronic medical record, and copies of advance-directive documents were scanned into the electronic record.

8. As explained later, encounters were never tape-recorded.

9. Observed meetings are much less common at night (odds ratio = .0975; 95 percent CI = .058–.157; $p < .001$), on weekends (OR = .046; CI = .016–.129; $p < .001$), for white patients (OR = .642; CI = .471–.876; $p = .005$), and more common when attending physicians participate (OR = 1.4; CI = 1.036–1.892; $p = .028$).

10. For example, Shalowitz, Garrett-Mayer, and Wendler (2006).

11. Silveira, Kim, and Langa (2010); Wiegand (2006); Tilden et al. (2001); Swigart (1994); SUPPORT Principal Investigators (1995); Mick, Medvene, and Strunk (2003); Hayes (2003).

12. Torke et al. (2014).

13. Fins et al. (1999); Goodman et al. (2011).

14. Selph et al. (2008); White et al. (2010); Swigart (1994); Anspach (1993); Kaufman (2005).

15. Hayes (2003); Mick, Medvene, and Strunk (2003).

16. Resulting perhaps in cleaner hands and fewer patient infections, but little effect on how physicians interacted with patients, families, and visitors.

17. In one instance, after a particularly obnoxious son suggested that, "as a sociologist, perhaps there is at least something you can say to comfort the family," I responded, blushing, that "I am not the comforting kind of sociologist. I am the research kind."

18. Sometimes, however, the introductions were less than accurate—e.g., "they are here to help us do a better job communicating with families."

19. One told me that he figured I must be pretty important because I never touch the patient.

20. As noted earlier, specialists (neurologists, neurosurgeons, orthopedists, oncologists, etc.) provided primary care for patients in the neurological ICU. Critical care physicians usually served as consultants. But specialists often didn't consult the critical care team for neurological ICU patients whose treatment was not complicated; these patients were excluded from the study. In the medical ICU, the critical care team had primary responsibility for all patients.

21. The proportion is considerably higher in the medical ICU (16 percent) than in the neurological ICU (5 percent) where many patients were not overseen by the critical care team.

22. The certificate of confidentiality protected subjects from disclosure of any information, even by a court subpoena, in any federal, state, or local civil, criminal, administrative, legislative, or other proceeding.

23. Something that physicians who successfully secure consent to risky medical procedures over the phone may not have learned.

24. Secondhand data extracted from medical records and physician accounts also yield 2361 statements allegedly made during unobserved encounters.

25. I use the more general labels "black" and "Hispanic" throughout the book to correspond to census data and hospital records. Rarely is the country of origin of ICU patients known.

26. The following measures from the Dartmouth Atlas of Health Care (http://www .dartmouthatlas.org) were reviewed:

    Hospital Care Intensity Index, Last Two Years of Life, Overall
    Hospital Care Intensity Index, Last Two Years of Life, Number of days spent in the hospital
    Hospital Care Intensity Index, Last Two Years of Life, Number of physician visits as inpatients
    Overall hospital beds/1000 patients in the last 2 years and last 6 months of life
    Total ICU beds/1000 patients in the last 2 years and last 6 months of life
    High-intensity ICU beds/1000 patients in the last 2 years and last 6 months of life
    Inpatient days overall in the last 6 months of life
    ICU inpatient days in the last 6 months of life
    High-intensive ICU inpatient days in the last 6 months of life
    Number of different physicians seen per patient in the last 6 months of life
    Percent of patients seeing 10 or more different physicians in the last 6 months of life
    Percent of deaths occurring in the hospital
    Percent of deaths associated with an ICU admission
    Total Medicare reimbursements per patient in the last 6 months of life
    Medicare reimbursements for inpatient care in the last 6 months of life

Medicare, Part B spending overall in the last 6 months of life

Medicare, Part B spending for evaluation and management in the last 6 months of life

Medicare, Part B spending for imaging in the last 6 months of life

Medicare, Part B spending for procedures in the last 6 months of life

Medicare, Part B spending for tests in the last 6 months of life

Physician labor overall/1000 patients in the last 2 years and last 6 months of life

Medical specialist labor/1000 patients in the last 2 years and last 6 months of life

Primary care physician labor/1000 patients in the last 2 years and last 6 months of life

27. For example, see the materials in the American Bar Association, Commission on Law and Aging, Health Care Decision Making Resources: http://www.americanbar .org/groups/law_aging/resources/health_care_decision_making.html.

28. Godfrey and Sabatino (2018).

REFERENCES

American Bar Association Commission on Law and Aging. 2005. "Consumer's Toolkit for Health Care Advance Planning, Second Edition." Accessed April 13, 2018. http://www.americanbar.org/groups/law_aging/resources/consumer_s_toolkit_for_health_care_advance_planning.html.

American Bar Association Commission on Law and Aging. 2009. "Making Medical Decisions for Someone Else: A How-to Guide." Accessed April 13, 2018. http://www.americanbar.org/content/dam/aba/migrated/Commissions/proxy_guide_generic_final.authcheckdam.pdf.

American Bar Association Commission on Law and Aging. 2015. "Health Care Decision-Making Authority: What Is the Decision-Making Standard?" Accessed April 13, 2018. http://www.americanbar.org/content/dam/aba/administrative/law_aging/What_is_the_Decision_Making_Standard.authcheckdam.pdf.

American Bar Association Commission on Law and Aging. 2016. "Substitute Decision-Maker Terminology under State Law." Accessed April 13, 2018. https://www.americanbar.org/content/dam/aba/administrative/law_aging/SubstituteDecision-Making Terminology.authcheckdam.pdf.

American Bar Association Commission on Law and Aging. 2018. "Default Surrogate Consent Statutes." Accessed April 13, 2018. https://www.americanbar.org/content/dam/aba/administrative/law_aging/2014_default_surrogate_consent_statutes.authcheckdam.pdf.

Anspach, Renée R. 1993. *Deciding Who Lives: Fateful Choices in the Intensive-Care Nursery.* Berkeley and Los Angeles: University of California Press.

Anspach, Renee R. 1987. "Prognostic Conflict in Life-and-Death Decisions: The Organization as an Ecology of Knowledge." *Journal of Health and Social Behavior* 28 (September): 215–31.

Asch, Adrienne. 2001. "Disability, Bioethics, and Human Rights." In *Handbook of Disability Studies*, edited by Gary L. Albrecht, Katherine Seelman, and Michael Bury, 297–326. Thousand Oaks, CA: Sage.

Aviv, Rachel. 2018. "What Does It Mean to Die?" *New Yorker*, February 5.

Barrett, Michael L., Mark W. Smith, Anne Elixhauser, Leah S. Honigman, and Jesse M. Pines. 2014. "Utilization of Intensive Care Services, 2011. HCUP Statistical Brief #185." Agency for Healthcare Research and Quality. Accessed April 24, 2018. http://

www.hcupus.ahrq.gov/reports/statbriefs/sb185-Hospital-Intensive-Care-Units-2011
.pdf.

Beauchamp, Tom L., and James F. Childress. 2009. *Principles of Medical Ethics*. 6th ed. New York: Oxford University Press.

Berlinger, Nancy, Bruce Jennings, and Susan M. Wolf. 2013. *The Hastings Center Guidelines for Decisions on Life-Sustaining Treatment and Care near the End of Life*. Rev. and expanded 2nd ed. New York: Oxford University Press.

Beschle, Donald L. 1989. "Autonomous Decision-Making and Social Choice: Examining the 'Right to Die.'" *Kentucky Law Journal* 77:319–67.

Blumenthal-Barby, Jennifer S., and Heather Krieger. 2015. "Cognitive Biases and Heuristics in Medical Decision Making: A Critical Review Using a Systematic Search Strategy." *Medical Decision Making* 35 (4): 539–57.

Blustein, Jeffrey. 1999. "Choosing for Others as Continuing a Life Story: The Problem of Personal Identity Revisited." *Journal of Law, Medicine & Ethics* 27:20–31.

Boyd, Elizabeth A., Bernard Lo, Leah R. Evans, et al. 2010. "It's Not Just What the Doctor Tells Me: Factors That Influence Surrogate Decision-Makers' Perceptions of Prognosis." *Critical Care Medicine* 38 (5): 1270–75.

Bryant, Jessica, Lesli E. Skolarus, Barbara Smith, Eric E. Adelman, and William J. Meurer. 2013. "The Accuracy of Surrogate Decision Makers: Informed Consent in Hypothetical Acute Stroke Scenarios." *BMC Emergency Medicine* 13:18.

Buchanan, Allen E. 1988. "Principal/Agent Theory and Decisionmaking in Health Care." *Bioethics* 2 (4): 317–33.

Buchanan, Allen E., and Dan W. Brock. 1989. *Deciding for Others: The Ethics of Surrogate Decision Making*. Cambridge: Cambridge University Press.

Buchwald, Art. 2006. "Serious Illness, Serious Choice." *Washington Post*, March 21.

Cantor, Norman L. 1996. "Discarding Substituted Judgment and Best Interests: Toward a Constructive Preference Standard for Dying, Previously Competent Patients without Advance Instructions." *Rutgers Law Review* 48:1193–1272.

Centers for Disease Control and Prevention, National Center for Health Statistics. 2017. "Underlying Cause of Death 1999–2016 on CDC Wonder Database." Accessed March 22, 2018. https://wonder.cdc.gov/ucd-icd10.html.

Chiarchiaro, Jared, Praewpannarai Buddadhumaruk, Robert M. Arnold, and Douglas B. White. 2015. "Quality of Communication in the ICU and Surrogate's Understanding of Prognosis." *Critical Care Medicine* 43 (3): 542–48.

Chochinov, Harvey Max, Douglas Tataryn, Jennifer J. Clinch, and Deborah Dudgeon. 1999. "Will to Live in the Terminally Ill." *Lancet* 354 (9181): 816–19.

Christakis, Nicholas A. 1999. *Death Foretold: Prophecy and Prognosis in Medical Care*. Chicago: University of Chicago Press.

Chugh, Dolly, Max H. Bazerman, and Mahzarin R. Banaji. 2005. "Bounded Ethicality as a Psychological Barrier to Recognizing Conflicts of Interest." In *Conflicts of Interest: Challenges and Solutions in Business, Law, Medicine, and Public Policy*, edited by Don A. Moore, Daylian M. Cain, George Loewenstein, and Max H. Bazerman, 74–95. Cambridge: Cambridge University Press.

Colaberdino, Vincent, Colleen Marshall, Paul DuBose, and Mitchell Daitz. 2016. "Economic Impact of an Advanced Illness Consultation Program within a Medicare Advantage Plan Population." *Journal of Palliative Medicine* 19 (6): 622–25.

Collopy, Bart J. 1999. "The Moral Underpinning of the Proxy-Provider Relationship: Issues of Trust and Distrust." *Journal of Law, Medicine & Ethics* 27 (1): 37–45.

Covinsky, Kenneth H., John D. Fuller, Kristine Yaffe, et al. 2000. "Communication and

Decision-Making in Seriously Ill Patients: Findings of the SUPPORT Project." *Journal of the American Geriatrics Society* 48 (5): S187–S193.

Curlin, Farr A., Ryan E. Lawrence, Marshall H. Chin, and John D. Lantos. 2007. "Religion, Conscience, and Controversial Clinical Practices." *New England Journal of Medicine* 356 (6): 593–600.

Curtis, J. Randall, Anthony L. Back, Dee W. Ford, et al. 2013. "Effect of Communication Skills Training for Residents and Nurse Practitioners on Quality of Communication with Patients with Serious Illness: A Randomized Trial." *Journal of the American Medical Association* 310 (21): 2271–81.

Curtis, J. Randall, Paul S. Ciechanowski, Lois Downey, et al. 2012. "Development and Evaluation of an Interprofessional Communication Intervention to Improve Family Outcomes in the ICU." *Contemporary Clinical Trials* 33 (6): 1245–54.

Curtis, J. Randall, Ruth A. Engelberg, Marjorie D. Wenrich, et al. 2002. "Studying Communication about End-of-Life Care during the ICU Family Conference: Development of a Framework." *Journal of Critical Care* 17 (3): 147–60.

Curtis, J. Randall, Patsy D. Treece, Elizabeth L. Nielsen, et al. 2016. "Randomized Trial of Communication Facilitators to Reduce Family Distress and Intensity of End-of-Life Care." *American Journal of Respiratory and Critical Care Medicine* 193 (2): 154–62.

Dartmouth Atlas of Healthcare, The. 2014a. "Inpatient Days per Decedent during the Last Six Months of Life, by Gender and Level of Care." The Dartmouth Institute for Health Policy & Clinical Practice. Accessed April 11, 2018. http://www.dartmouthatlas.org/data/topic/topic.aspx?cat=18.

Dartmouth Atlas of Healthcare, The. 2014b. "Percent of Decedents Admitted to ICU/CCU during the Hospitalization in Which Death Occurred, by Gender." The Dartmouth Institute for Health Policy & Clinical Practice. Accessed April 11, 2018. http://www.dartmouthatlas.org/data/table.aspx?ind=127.

Dartmouth Atlas of Healthcare, The. 2014c. "Percent of Medicare Deaths Occurring in Hospital, by Gender." The Dartmouth Institute for Health Policy & Clinical Practice. Accessed April 11, 2016. http://www.dartmouthatlas.org/data/table.aspx?ind=131.

Dartmouth Atlas of Healthcare, The. 2014d. "Percent of Medicare Decedents Hospitalized at Least Once during the Last Six Months of Life, by Gender and Level of Care Intensity." The Dartmouth Institute for Health Policy & Clinical Practice. Accessed April 11, 2018. http://www.dartmouthatlas.org/data/table.aspx?ind=133.

Dionne-Odom, J. Nicholas, Danny G. Willis, Marie Bakitas, Beth Crandall, and Pamela J. Grace. 2015. "Conceptualizing Surrogate Decision Making at End of Life in the Intensive Care Unit Using Cognitive Task Analysis." *Nursing Outlook* 63 (3): 331–40.

Ditto, Peter H., and Cory J. Clark. 2014. "Predicting End-of-Life Treatment Preferences: Perils and Practicalities." *Journal of Medicine and Philosophy* 39 (2): 196–204.

Ditto, Peter H., Joseph H. Danks, William D. Smucker, et al. 2001. "Advance Directives as Acts of Communication: A Randomized Controlled Trial." *Archives of Internal Medicine* 161 (3): 421–30.

Ditto, Peter H., Nikki A. Hawkins, and David A. Pizarro. 2006. "Imagining the End of Life: On the Psychology of Advance Medical Decision Making." *Motivation and Emotion* 29 (4): 475–96.

Donchin, Yoel, Daniel Gopher, Miriam Olin, et al. 2003. "A Look into the Nature and Causes of Human Errors in the Intensive Care Unit." *Quality and Safety in Health Care* 12 (2): 143–47.

Dresser, Rebecca. 1986. "Life, Death, and Incompetent Patients: Conceptual Infirmities and Hidden Values in the Law." *Arizona Law Review* 28:373–405.

Emanuel, Ezekiel J., and Linda L. Emanuel. 1992. "Proxy Decision Making for Incompetent Patients: An Ethical and Empirical Analysis." *Journal of the American Medical Association* 267:2067–71.

Emanuel, Linda L., and Ezekiel J. Emanuel. 1993. "Decisions at the End of Life Guided by Communities of Patients." *Hastings Center Report* 23 (5): 6–14.

Enzinger, Andrea C., Baohui Zhang, Deborah Schrag, and Holly G. Prigerson. 2015. "Outcomes of Prognostic Disclosure: Associations with Prognostic Understanding, Distress, and Relationship with Physician among Patients with Advanced Cancer." *Journal of Clinical Oncology* 33 (32): 3809–16.

Epstein, Arnold M., Judith A. Hall, Janet Tognetti, Linda H. Son, and Loring Conant, Jr. 1989. "Using Proxies to Evaluate Quality of Life: Can They Provide Valid Information about Patients' Health Status and Satisfaction with Medical Care?" *Medical Care* 27: S91–S98.

Ernecoff, Natalie C., Farr A. Curlin, Praewpannarai Buddadhumaruk, and Douglas B. White. 2015. "Health Care Professionals' Responses to Religious or Spiritual Statements by Surrogate Decision Makers during Goals-of-Care Discussions." *JAMA Internal Medicine* 175 (10): 1661–69.

Faden, Ruth R., Thomas L. Beauchamp, and Nancy M. King. 1986. *History and Theory of Informed Consent.* New York: Oxford University Press.

Fagerlin, Angela, Peter H. Ditto, Joseph H. Danks, Renate M. Houts, and William D. Smucker. 2001. "Projection in Surrogate Decisions about Life-Sustaining Medical Treatments." *Health Psychology* 20 (3): 166–75.

Fagerlin, Angela, and Carl E. Schneider. 2004. "Enough: The Failure of the Living Will." *Hastings Center Report* 34 (2): 30–42.

Fentiman, Linda C. 1989. "Privacy and Personhood Revisited: A New Framework for Substitute Decisionmaking for the Incompetent, Incurably Ill Adult." *George Washington Law Review* 57:801–48.

Fins, Joseph J. 1999. "Commentary: From Contract to Covenant in Advance Care Planning." *Journal of Law, Medicine & Ethics* 27 (1): 46–51.

Fins, Joseph J., Franklin G. Miller, Cathleen A. Acres, Matthew D. Bacchetta, Lynn L. Huzzard, and Bruce D. Rapkin. 1999. "End-of-Life Decision-Making in the Hospital: Current Practice and Future Prospects." *Journal of Pain and Symptom Management* 17 (1): 6–15.

Fried, Terri R., Colleen A. Redding, Mark L. Robbins, John R. O'Leary, and Lynne Iannone. 2011. "Agreement between Older Persons and Their Surrogate Decision Makers Regarding Participation in Advance Care Planning." *Journal of the American Geriatrics Society* 59 (6): 1105–9.

Friedman, Lawrence M., and Mark Savage. 1988. "Taking Care: The Law of Conservatorship in California." *Southern California Law Review* 61:273–90.

Gawande, Atul. 2015. "Overkill." *New Yorker*, May 11, 42–53.

Gertner, Jon. 2003. "The Futile Pursuit of Happiness." *New York Times Magazine*, September 7.

Ghosh, Amit K., Karthik Ghosh, and Patricia J. Erwin. 2004. "Do Medical Students and Physicians Understand Probability?" *QJM: An International Journal of Medicine* 97 (1): 53–66.

Godfrey, David, and Charlie Sabatino. 2018. "Who Decides if the Patient Cannot and There Is No Advance Directive: Research and Recommendations on Clinical Practice, Law and Policy." American Bar Association Commission on Law and Aging. Accessed April 11, 2018. https://www.americanbar.org/content/dam/aba/administrative/law

_aging/health-care-decision-making-in-critical-care-settings-jan-2018.authcheckdam
.pdf.

Goodman, David C., Amos R. Esty, Elliott S. Fisher, and Chiang-Hua Chang. 2011. "Trends and Variation in End-of-Life Care for Medicare Beneficiaries with Severe Chronic Illness: A Report of the Dartmouth Atlas Project." The Dartmouth Institute for Health Policy and Clinical Practice. Accessed April 13, 2018. http://www.dartmouthatlas.org/downloads/reports/EOL_Trend_Report_0411.pdf.

Gordon, Elana. 2014. "Operator? Business, Insurer Take on End-of-Life Issues by Phone." Kaiser Health News. Accessed April 13, 2018. http://khn.org/news/insurers-new-business-end-of-life-conversations/.

Gutheil, Thomas G., and Paul S. Appelbaum. 1983. "Substituted Judgment: Best Interests in Disguise." Hastings Center Report 13 (3): 8–11.

Halpern, Jodi, and Robert M. Arnold. 2008. "Affective Forecasting: An Unrecognized Challenge in Making Serious Health Decisions." Journal of General Internal Medicine 23 (10): 1708–12.

Hardwig, John. 1990. "What About the Family?" Hastings Center Report 20 (2): 5–10.

Hardwig, John. 1992. "The Problem of Proxies with Interests of Their Own: Toward a Better Theory of Proxy Decisions." Utah Law Review 1992 (3): 803–18.

Harmon, Louise. 1990. "Falling Off the Vine: Legal Fictions and the Doctrine of Substituted Judgment." Yale Law Journal 100:1–71.

Hawkins, Nikki Ayers, Peter H. Ditto, Joseph H. Danks, and William D. Smucker. 2005. "Micromanaging Death: Process Preferences, Values, and Goals in End-of-Life Medical Decision Making." Gerontologist 45 (1): 107–17.

Hayes, Carolyn M. 2003. "Surrogate Decision-Making to End Life-Sustaining Treatments for Incapacitated Adults." Journal of Hospice and Palliative Nursing 5 (2): 91–102.

Hickman, Susan E., Bernard J. Hammes, Alvin H. Moss, and Susan W. Tolle. 2005. "Hope for the Future: Achieving the Original Intent of Advance Directives." Hastings Center Report 35 (6 Supplement): S26–S30.

Huynh, Thanh N., Eric C. Kleerup, Joshua F. Wiley, et al. 2013. "The Frequency and Cost of Treatment Perceived to Be Futile in Critical Care." JAMA Internal Medicine 173 (20): 1887–94.

Igou, Eric R. 2008. "'How Long Will I Suffer?' versus 'How Long Will You Suffer?' A Self-Other Effect in Affective Forecasting." Journal of Personality and Social Psychology 95 (4): 899–917.

Illinois Health Care Surrogate Act (755 ILCS 40/). 1998. http://www.ilga.gov/legislation/ilcs/ilcs3.asp?ActID=2111&ChapterID=60.

Kahneman, Daniel. 2011. Thinking, Fast and Slow. New York: Farrar, Straus & Giroux.

Kaldjian, Lauris C., Ann E. Curtis, Laura A. Shinkunas, and Katrina T. Cannon. 2009. "Goals of Care toward the End of Life: A Structured Literature Review." American Journal of Hospice & Palliative Medicine 25 (6): 501–11.

Karp, Naomi, and Erica Wood. 2003. Incapacitated and Alone: Health Care Decision Making for the Unbefriended Elderly. Washington, DC: American Bar Association, Commission on Law and Aging.

Katz, Jay. 1984. The Secret World of Doctor and Patient. New York: Free Press.

Kaufman, Sharon R. 2005. . . . And a Time to Die: How American Hospitals Shape the End of Life. New York: Scribner.

Kaufman, Sharon R. 2015. Ordinary Medicine: Extraordinary Treatments, Longer Lives, and Where to Draw the Line. Durham, NC: Duke University Press.

Khandelwal, Nita, David C. Benkeser, Norma B. Coe, and J. Randall Curtis. 2016.

"Potential Influence of Advance Care Planning and Palliative Care Consultation on ICU Costs for Patients with Chronic and Serious Illness." *Critical Care Medicine* 44 (8): 1474–81.

Khandelwal, Nita, David Benkeser, Norma B. Coe, Ruth A. Engelberg, and J. Randall Curtis. 2016. "Economic Feasibility of Staffing the Intensive Care Unit with a Communication Facilitator." *Annals of the American Thoracic Society* 13 (12): 2190–96.

Kim, Hyejin, Janet A. Deatrick, and Connie M. Ulrich. 2017. "Ethical Frameworks for Surrogates' End-of-Life Planning Experiences: A Qualitative Systematic Review." *Nursing Ethics* 24 (1): 46–69.

Kim, Scott Y. H. 2014. "Improving Medical Decisions for Incapacitated Persons: Does Focusing on 'Accurate Predictions' Lead to an Inaccurate Picture?" *Journal of Medicine and Philosophy* 39 (2): 187–95.

King, Patricia A. 1989. "Dax's Case: Implications for the Legal Profession." In *Dax's Case: Essays in Medical Ethics and Human Meaning*, edited by Lonnie D. Kliever, 97–113. Dallas, TX: Southern Methodist University Press.

Kirschner, Kristi L. 2005. "When Written Advance Directives Are Not Enough." *Clinics in Geriatric Medicine* 21:193–209.

Klingler, Corinna, Jürgen in der Schmitten, and Georg Marckmann. 2016. "Does Facilitated Advance Care Planning Reduce the Costs of Care near the End of Life? Systematic Review and Ethical Considerations." *Palliative Medicine* 30 (5): 423–33.

Knaus, William A., Elizabeth A. Draper, Douglas P. Wagner, and Jack E. Zimmerman. 1985. "Apache II: A Severity of Disease Classification System." *Critical Care Medicine* 13 (10): 818–29.

Kosmin, Barry A., and Ariela Keysar. 2009. "American Religious Identification Survey (Aris 2008)." Trinity College. Accessed May 8, 2018. http://commons.trincoll.edu/aris/files/2011/08/ARIS_Report_2008.pdf.

Krakauer, Eric L., Christopher Crenner, and Ken Fox. 2002. "Barriers to Optimum End-of-Life Care for Minority Patients." *Journal of the American Geriatrics Society* 50 (1): 182–90.

Krumholz, Harlan M., Russell S. Phillips, Mary Beth Hamel, et al. 1998. "Resuscitation Preferences among Patients with Severe Congestive Heart Failure: Results from the SUPPORT Project." *Circulation* 98 (7): 648–55.

Kuczewski, Mark G. 1999. "Commentary: Narrative Views of Personal Identity and Substituted Judgment in Surrogate Decision Making." *Journal of Law, Medicine & Ethics* 27:32–36.

Lamas, Daniela, Natalie Panariello, Natalie Henrich, et al. 2018. "Advance Care Planning Documentation in Electronic Health Records: Current Challenges and Recommendations for Change." *Journal of Palliative Medicine* 21 (4): 522–28.

Levin, Tomer T., Beatriz Moreno, William Silvester, and David W. Kissane. 2010. "End-of-Life Communication in the Intensive Care Unit." *General Hospital Psychiatry* 32:433–42.

Lewis, Ariane, Aaron S. Lord, Barry M. Czeisler, and Arthur Caplan. 2016. "Public Education and Misinformation on Brain Death in Mainstream Media." *Clinical Transplantation* 30 (9): 1082–89.

Limerick, Michael H. 2007. "The Process Used by Surrogate Decision Makers to Withhold and Withdraw Life-Sustaining Measures in an Intensive Care Environment." *Oncology Nursing Forum* 34 (2): 331–39.

Lindemann, Hilde, and James Lindemann Nelson. 2014. "The Surrogate's Authority." *Journal of Medicine and Philosophy* 39 (2): 161–68.

Lindgren, James. 1993. "Death by Default." *Law and Contemporary Problems* 56 (3): 185–254.

Lipkin, K. Michael. 2006. "Identifying a Proxy for Health Care as Part of Routine Medical Inquiry." *Journal of General Internal Medicine* 21:1188–91.

Lubitz, James D., and Gerald F. Riley. 1993. "Trends in Medicare Payments in the Last Year of Life." *New England Journal of Medicine* 328 (15): 1092–96.

Luce, John M., and Thomas J. Prendergast. 2001. "The Changing Nature of Death in the ICU." In *Managing Death in the ICU: The Transition from Cure to Comfort*, edited by J. Randall Curtis and Gordon D. Rubenfield, 19–29. New York: Oxford University Press.

Lynn, Joanne. 1997. "Unexpected Returns: Insights from SUPPORT." In *To Improve Health and Health Care: The Robert Wood Johnson Foundation Anthology*, edited by Steven L. Isaacs et al., 161–86. New York: Jossey-Bass Health Series.

Lynn, Joanne, Joan Harrold, and Janice Lynch Schuster. 2011. *Handbook for Mortals: Guidance for People Facing Serious Illness*. 2nd ed. New York: Oxford University Press.

Magaziner, Jay, Eleanor M. Simonsick, T. Michael Kashner, and J. Richard Hebel. 1988. "Patient-Proxy Response Comparability on Measures of Patient Health and Functional Status." *Journal of Clinical Epidemiology* 41:1065–74.

Marks, Gary, and Norman Miller. 1987. "Ten Years of Research on the False-Consensus Effect: An Empirical and Theoretical Review." *Psychological Bulletin* 102:72–90.

Martin, Douglas K., Linda L. Emanuel, and Peter A. Singer. 2000. "Planning for the End of Life." *Lancet* 356 (9242): 1672–76.

McCannon, Jessica B., Walter J. O'Donnell, B. Taylor Thompson, et al. 2012. "Augmenting Communication and Decision Making in the Intensive Care Unit with a Cardiopulmonary Resuscitation Video Decision Support Tool: A Temporal Intervention Study." *Journal of Palliative Medicine* 15 (12): 1382–87.

Meeker, Mary Ann, and Mary Ann Jezewski. 2008. "Metasynthesis: Withdrawing Life-Sustaining Treatments: The Experience of Family Decision-Makers." *Journal of Clinical Nursing* 18:163–73.

Meisel, Alan, and Kathy L. Cerminara. 2008. *The Right to Die: The Law of End-of-Life Decisionmaking*. 3rd ed. New York: Aspen.

Meisel, Alan, and Mark Kuczewski. 1996. "Legal and Ethical Myths about Informed Consent." *Archives of Internal Medicine* 156 (22): 2521–26.

Mick, Katherine A., Louis J. Medvene, and Janelle H. Strunk. 2003. "Surrogate Decision Making at End of Life: Sources of Burden and Relief." *Journal of Loss and Trauma* 8 (3): 149–67.

Murphy, Donald J., and Leighton E. Cluff. 1990. "SUPPORT: Study to Understand Prognoses and Preferences for Outcomes and Risks of Treatments, Study Design." *Journal of Clinical Epidemiology* 43:S1–S123.

National Center for Health Statistics. 2017. "Health, United States, 2016, with Chartbook on Long-Term Trends in Health." U.S. Department of Health and Human Services, Centers for Disease Control and Prevention. Accessed April 24, 2018. https://www.cdc.gov/nchs/data/hus/hus16.pdf#094.

National POLST Paradigm. 2018. Accessed April 13, 2018. https://polst.org.

Olick, Robert S. 2001. *Taking Advance Directives Seriously: Prospective Autonomy and Decisions near the End of Life*. Washington, DC: Georgetown University Press.

Ouslander, Joseph G., Alexander J. Tymchuk, and Bita Rahbar. 1989. "Health Care Decisions among Elderly Long-Term Care Residents and Their Potential Proxies." *Archives of Internal Medicine* 149 (6): 1367–72.

Perneger, Thomas V., and Thomas Agoritsas. 2011. "Doctors and Patients' Susceptibility to Framing Bias: A Randomized Trial." *Journal of General Internal Medicine* 26 (12): 1411–17.

Petersen, Abigail. 2007. "Survey of States' Health Care Decision-Making Standards." *BIFOCAL: Bar Associations in Focus on Aging and the Law* 28 (4): 1+.

Pew Research Center. November 2013. "Views on End-of-Life Medical Treatments." Accessed October 8, 2015. http://www.pewforum.org/2013/11/21/views-on-end-of-life-medical-treatments/.

Phipps, Etienne, Gala True, Diana Harris, et al. 2003. "Approaching the End of Life: Attitudes, Preferences, and Behaviors of African-American and White Patients and Their Family Caregivers." *Journal of Clinical Oncology* 21 (3): 549–54.

Powell, Tia. 1999. "Extubating Mrs. K: Psychological Aspects of Surrogate Decision Making." *Journal of Law, Medicine & Ethics* 27 (1): 81–86.

Pruchno, Rachel A., Edward P. Lemay, Jr., Lucy Feild, and Norman G. Levinsky. 2006. "Predictors of Patient Treatment Preferences and Spouse Substituted Judgments: The Case of Dialysis Continuation." *Medical Decision Making* 26 (2): 112–21.

Pruchno, Rachel A., Michael J. Rovine, Francine Cartwright, and Maureen Wilson-Genderson. 2008. "Stability and Change in Patient Preferences and Spouse Substituted Judgments Regarding Dialysis Continuation." *Journals of Gerontology: Series B* 63 (2): S81–S91.

Puchalski, Christina M., Zhenshao Zhong, Michelle M. Jacobs, et al. 2000. "Patients Who Want Their Family and Physician to Make Resuscitation Decisions for Them: Observations from SUPPORT and Help." *Journal of the American Geriatrics Society* 48 (5): S84–S90.

Rhoden, Nancy K. 1988. "Litigating Life and Death." *Harvard Law Review* 102:375–446.

Rid, Annette. 2014. "Will a Patient Preference Predictor Improve Treatment Decision Making for Incapacitated Patients?" *Journal of Medicine and Philosophy* 39 (2): 99–103.

Rid, Annette, and David Wendler. 2014a. "Treatment Decision Making for Incapacitated Patients: Is Development and Use of a Patient Preference Predictor Feasible?" *Journal of Medicine and Philosophy* 39 (2): 130–52.

Rid, Annette, and David Wendler. 2014b. "Use of a Patient Preference Predictor to Help Make Medical Decisions for Incapacitated Patients." *Journal of Medicine and Philosophy* 39 (2): 104–29.

Rogne, Leah, and Susana McCune, eds. 2014. *Advance Care Planning: Communicating About Matters of Life and Death.* New York: Springer.

Rubenstein, Laurence Z., Catherine Schairer, G. Darryl Wieland, and Rosalie Kane. 1984. "Systematic Biases in Functional Status Assessment of Elderly Adults: Effects of Different Data Sources." *Journal of Gerontology* 39:686–91.

Sabatino, Charles P. 1999. "The Legal and Functional Status of the Medical Proxy: Suggestions for Statutory Reform." *Journal of Law, Medicine & Ethics* 27 (1): 52–68.

Sabatino, Charles P. 2010. "The Evolution of Health Care Advance Planning Law and Policy." *Milbank Quarterly* 88 (2): 211–39.

Scheunemann, Leslie P., Michelle McDevitt, Shannon S. Carson, and Laura C. Hanson. 2011. "Randomized, Controlled Trials of Interventions to Improve Communication in Intensive Care: A Systematic Review." *Chest* 139 (3): 543–54.

Schneider, Carl E. 1998. *The Practice of Autonomy: Patients, Doctors, and Medical Decisions.* New York: Oxford University Press.

Schwarze, Margaret L., Toby C. Campbell, Thomas V. Cunningham, Douglas B. White, and Robert M. Arnold. 2016. "You Can't Get What You Want: Innovation for End-of-

Life Communication in the Intensive Care Unit." *American Journal of Respiratory and Critical Care Medicine* 193 (1): 14–16.

Sehgal, Ashwini, Alison Galbraith, Margaret Chesney, Patricia Schoenfeld, Gerald Charles, and Bernard Lo. 1992. "How Strictly Do Dialysis Patients Want Their Advance Directives Followed?" *Journal of the American Medical Association* 267 (1): 59–63.

Selph, R. Brac, Julia Shiang, Ruth Engelberg, J. Randall Curtis, and Douglas B. White. 2008. "Empathy and Life Support Decisions in Intensive Care Units." *Journal of General Internal Medicine* 23 (9): 1311–17.

Shalowitz, David I., Elizabeth Garrett-Mayer, and David Wendler. 2006. "The Accuracy of Surrogate Decision Makers: A Systematic Review." *Archives of Internal Medicine* 166 (5): 493–97.

Shalowitz, David I., Elizabeth Garrett-Mayer, and David Wendler. 2007. "How Should Treatment Decisions Be Made for Incapacitated Patients, and Why?" *PLoS Medicine* 4 (3): 423–28.

Shapiro, Susan P. 1987. "The Social Control of Impersonal Trust." *American Journal of Sociology* 93 (3): 623–58.

Shapiro, Susan P. 2002. *Tangled Loyalties: Conflicts of Interest in Legal Practice.* Ann Arbor: University of Michigan Press.

Shapiro, Susan P. 2005. "Agency Theory." In *Annual Review of Sociology*, edited by Karen S. Cook and Douglas S. Massey, 263–84. Palo Alto, CA: Annual Reviews.

Shapiro, Susan P. 2007. "When Life Imitates Art: Surrogate Decision Making at the End of Life." *Topics in Stroke Rehabilitation* 14 (4): 80–92.

Shapiro, Susan P. 2012a. "Advance Directives: The Elusive Goal of Having the Last Word." *NAELA (National Association of Elder Law Attorneys) Journal* 8 (2): 205–32.

Shapiro, Susan P. 2012b. "Conflict of Interest at the Bedside: Surrogate Decision Making at the End of Life." In *Conflict of Interest in Global, Public and Corporate Governance*, edited by Anne Peters and Lukas Handschin, 334–54. Cambridge: Cambridge University Press.

Shapiro, Susan P. 2015. "Do Advance Directives Direct?" *Journal of Health, Politics, Policy, and Law* 40 (3): 487–530.

Shapiro, Susan P. 2016. "Standing in Another's Shoes: How Agents Make Life-and-Death Decisions for Their Principals." *Academy of Management Perspectives* 30 (4): 404–27.

Sharma, Rashmi K., Mark T. Hughes, Marie T. Nolan, et al. 2011. "Family Understanding of Seriously-Ill Patient Preferences for Family Involvement in Healthcare Decision Making." *Journal of General Internal Medicine* 26 (8): 881–86.

Shugarman, Lisa R., Sandra L. Decker, and Anita Bercovitz. 2009. "Demographic and Social Characteristics and Spending at the End of Life." *Journal of Pain and Symptom Management* 38 (1): 15–26.

Silveira, Maria J., Scott Y. H. Kim, and Kenneth M. Langa. 2010. "Advance Directives and Outcomes of Surrogate Decision Making before Death." *New England Journal of Medicine* 362 (13): 1211–18.

Smedira, Nicholas G., Bradley H. Evans, Linda S. Grais, et al. 1990. "Withholding and Withdrawal of Life Support from the Critically Ill." *New England Journal of Medicine* 322 (5): 309–15.

Smucker, William D., Renate M. Houts, Joseph H. Danks, Peter H. Ditto, Angela Fagerlin, and Kristen M. Coppola. 2000. "Modal Preferences Predict Elderly Patients' Life-Sustaining Treatment Choices as Well as Patients' Chosen Surrogates Do." *Medical Decision Making* 20 (3): 271–80.

Song, Mi-Kyung, Sandra E. Ward, and Feng-Chang Lin. 2012. "End-of-Life Decision-Making Confidence in Surrogates of African-American Dialysis Patients Is Overly Optimistic." *Journal of Palliative Medicine* 15 (4): 412–17.

Span, Paula. 2009. "Why Do We Avoid Advance Directives?" *New York Times*, April 20.

Span, Paula. 2016. "What Doctors Know about How Bad It Is, and Won't Say." *New York Times*, July 1.

Sudore, Rebecca L., and Terri R. Fried. 2010. "Redefining the 'Planning' in Advance Care Planning: Preparing for End-of-Life Decision Making." *Annals of Internal Medicine* 153 (4): 256–61.

SUPPORT Principal Investigators. 1995. "A Controlled Trial to Improve Care for Seriously Ill Hospitalized Patients: The Study to Understand Prognoses and Preferences for Outcomes and Risks of Treatments (SUPPORT)." *Journal of the American Medical Association* 274 (20): 1591–98.

Swigart, Valerie Anne. 1994. "A Study of Family Decision Making about Life Support Using the Grounded Theory Method." Ph.D. diss., School of Nursing, University of Pittsburgh.

Swigart, Valerie Anne, Charles Lidz, Victoria Butterworth, and Robert Arnold. 1996. "Letting Go: Family Willingness to Forgo Life Support." *Heart & Lung* 25 (6): 483–94.

Teno, Joan M., Elliott S. Fisher, Mary Beth Hamel, Kristen Coppola, and Neal V. Dawson. 2002. "Medical Care Inconsistent with Patients' Treatment Goals: Association with 1-Year Medicare Resource Use and Survival." *Journal of the American Geriatrics Society* 50 (3): 496–500.

Teno, Joan M., Pedro L. Gozalo, Julie P. W. Bynum, et al. 2013. "Change in End-of-Life Care for Medicare Beneficiaries: Site of Death, Place of Care, and Health Care Transitions in 2000, 2005, and 2009." *Journal of the American Medical Association* 309 (5): 470–77.

Terry, Peter B., Margaret Vettese, John Song, et al. 1999. "End-of-Life Decision Making: When Patients and Surrogates Disagree." *Journal of Clinical Ethics* 10 (4): 286–93.

Thaler, Richard H., and Cass R. Sunstein. 2008. *Nudge: Improving Decisions about Health, Wealth, and Happiness*. New Haven, CT: Yale University Press.

Tilden, Virginia P., Susan W. Tolle, Christine A. Nelson, and Jonathan Fields. 2001. "Family Decision-Making to Withdraw Life-Sustaining Treatments from Hospitalized Patients." *Nursing Research* 50 (2): 105–15.

Tomlinson, Tom, Kenneth Howe, Mark Notman, and Diane Rossmiller. 1990. "An Empirical Study of Proxy Consent for Elderly Persons." *Gerontologist* 30:54–64.

Torke, Alexia M., Lucia D. Wocial, Shelley A. Johns, et al. 2016. "The Family Navigator: A Pilot Intervention to Support Intensive Care Unit Family Surrogates." *American Journal of Critical Care* 25 (6): 498–507.

Torke, Alexia M., Greg A. Sachs, Paul R. Helft, et al. 2014. "Scope and Outcomes of Surrogate Decision Making among Hospitalized Older Adults." *JAMA Internal Medicine* 174 (3): 370–77.

Tsevat, Joel, Francis E. Cook, Michael L. Green, et al. 1995. "Health Values of the Seriously Ill." *Annals of Internal Medicine* 122 (7): 514–20.

Tunney, Richard J., and Fenja V. Ziegler. 2015. "Toward a Psychology of Surrogate Decision Making." *Perspectives on Psychological Science* 10 (6): 880–85.

Tversky, Amos, and Daniel Kahneman. 1981. "The Framing of Decisions and the Psychology of Choice." *Science* 211 (4481): 453–58.

U.S. Census Bureau. 2009. "Current Population Survey Tables for Health Insurance Coverage, HI-01. Health Insurance Coverage Status and Type of Coverage by Selected

Characteristics: 2009." Accessed May 9, 2018. https://www.census.gov/data/tables/time-series/demo/income-poverty/cps-hi/hi-01.2009.html.

U.S. Census Bureau. 2010. "ACS (American Community Survey) 2006–2010 (5-Year Estimates), Social Explorer Table." Accessed May 9, 2018. https://www.socialexplorer.com/tables/ACS2010_5yr.

U.S. Census Bureau. 2012. "Statistical Abstract of the United States: 2012, Table 75. Self-Described Religious Identification of Adult Population: 1990, 2001, and 2008." Accessed May 9, 2018. https://www.census.gov/library/publications/2011/compendia/statab/131ed/population.html.

U.S. Social Security Administration, Office of the Chief Actuary. 2012. "Actuarial Life Table." Accessed April 13, 2018. https://www.ssa.gov/oact/STATS/table4c6.html.

Ubel, Peter A., George Loewenstein, Norbert Schwarz, and Dylan Smith. 2005. "Misimagining the Unimaginable: The Disability Paradox and Health Care Decision Making." *Health Psychology* 24 (4, Supplement): S57–S62.

Uhlmann, Richard F., Robert A. Pearlman, and Kevin C. Cain. 1988. "Physicians' and Spouses' Predictions of Elderly Patients' Resuscitation Preferences." *Journal of Gerontology: Medical Sciences* 43:M115–M121.

Vandenbroucke, Amy, Susan Nelson, Patricia A. Bomba, and Alvin H. Moss. 2015. "POLST: Advance Care Planning for the Seriously Ill." *Bifocal: A Journal of the ABA Commission on Law and Aging* 36 (4): 91–94.

Volandes, Angelo E., Lisa Soleymani Lehmann, Francis Cook, Shimon Shaykevich, Elmer D. Abbo, and Muriel R. Gillick. 2007. "Using Video Images of Dementia in Advance Care Planning." *Archives of Internal Medicine* 167 (8): 828–33.

Wegwarth, Odette. 2013. "Statistical Illiteracy in Residents: What They Do Not Learn Today Will Hurt Their Patients Tomorrow." *Journal of Graduate Medical Education* 5 (2): 340–41.

Wendler, David, and Annette Rid. 2011. "Systematic Review: The Effect on Surrogates of Making Treatment Decisions for Others." *Annals of Internal Medicine* 154:336–46.

White, Douglas B., Ruth A. Engelberg, Marjorie D. Wenrich, Bernard Lo, and J. Randall Curtis. 2010. "The Language of Prognostication in Intensive Care Units." *Medical Decision Making* 30 (1): 76–83.

White, Douglas B., Natalie C. Ernecoff, Praewpannarai Buddadhumaruk, et al. 2016. "Prevalence of and Factors Related to Discordance about Prognosis between Physicians and Surrogate Decision Makers of Critically Ill Patients." *Journal of the American Medical Association* 315 (19): 1086–94.

White, Douglas B., Sarah Martin Cua, Roberta Walk, et al. 2012. "Nurse-Led Intervention to Improve Surrogate Decision Making for Patients with Advanced Critical Illness." *American Journal of Critical Care* 21 (6): 396–409.

Wiegand, Debra Lynn-McHale. 2006. "Families and Withdrawal of Life-Sustaining Therapy: State of the Science." *Journal of Family Nursing* 12 (2): 165–84.

Wiegand, Debra Lynn-McHale, Janet A. Deatrick, and Kathleen Knafl. 2008. "Family Management Styles Related to Withdrawal of Life-Sustaining Therapy from Adults Who Are Acutely Ill or Injured." *Journal of Family Nursing* 14 (1): 1–32.

Wilson, Timothy D., and Daniel T. Gilbert. 2005. "Affective Forecasting. Knowing What to Want." *Current Directions in Psychological Science* 14 (3): 131–34.

Winter, Laraine, Miriam S. Moss, and Christine Hoffman. 2009. "Affective Forecasting and Advance Care Planning." *Journal of Health Psychology* 14 (3): 447–56.

Wolf, Susan M., Nancy Berlinger, and Bruce Jennings. 2015. "Forty Years of Work on

End-of-Life Care—from Patients' Rights to Systemic Reform." *New England Journal of Medicine* 372 (7): 678–82.

Wynn, Shana. 2014. "Decisions by Surrogates: An Overview of Surrogate Consent Laws in the United States." *Bifocal: A Journal of the ABA Commission on Law and Aging* 36 (1): 10–14.

Zier, Lucas S., Jeffrey H. Burack, Guy Micco, et al. 2008. "Doubt and Belief in Physicians' Ability to Prognosticate during Critical Illness: The Perspective of Surrogate Decision Makers." *Critical Care Medicine* 36 (8): 2341–47.

Zweibel, Nancy R., and Christine K. Cassel. 1989. "Treatment Choices at the End of Life: A Comparison of Decisions by Older Patients and Their Physician-Selected Proxies." *Gerontologist* 29:615–21.

Note: Page numbers followed by "f" indicate figures; page numbers followed by "t" indicate tables.

Acute Respiratory Distress Syndrome (ARDS), 57, 105–6, 113

admission, 26; data on, 267; numbers of patients admitted, 243–44; outcomes of, 234t; out of the blue, 6, 12, 26; for preexisting medical conditions, 221; quality of life after, 233–34; reasons for, 12, 25–26. *See also* ICU stay

advance-care planning, 241–43, 252; about how to improvise, 242; choice of surrogate decision makers and, 242–43; conversations about, 252; goal of, 242; lawyers' role in, 252; physicians' role in, 241; problems with memorializing, 242; programs and resources, 241–43, 252; surrogates and, 242–43; for younger or healthier adults, 243

advance directives, 1, 5, 34, 136, 148, 160, 162, 169, 252; advance-directive status, 258, 289–90t; advocates of, 228–29, 232; ambiguity of, 162; apps to record, 240; characteristics of patients with, 295n12; completed under pressure from family members, 230; discussion of goals of care and, 231; discussions of content of, 229–30; documents in hospital, 34, 148; efficacy of, 11, 229–32, 251; failure of, 230–31; failure to live up to advocates' promises, 232, 237; functional capacity and, 161; history of, 228–29; hydration and, 161; in Illinois, 160–61; logistical discussions of, 229; in medical records, 148, 150, 151, 247; mental capacity and, 161; misunderstanding of, 164–65, 230–31; nonexistent, 34, 148, 161, 229; numbers of patients with and without, 34, 148, 160–62, 229, 231, 251; nutrition and, 161; organ donation and, 161; out-of-date, 230; overriding of, 2, 147–48, 164–65, 199; registries of, 240; role in helping to honor patient's wishes, 230–31; securing of, 16; studies of, 229; surrogate decision makers and, 165–66; that fall on deaf ears, 230; that provide no guidance, 230; undermining patients' wishes, 230–31, 251. *See also* instructional directives; living wills; powers of attorney (for health care); proxy directives

advance-directive status: decision-making process and, 289–90t; impact of, 289–90t; outcomes and, 289–90t

adversity, ability to adapt to, 111

advice, physicians offered or solicited, 39, 43, 100, 101, 183–84

advocates, need for, 248–50, 252

affect, decisions and, 87

"affective forecasting," 111

affluence of residence, 28, 269, 270t; likelihood of discussions about interventions and, 75; in sample, 269, 270t

African American patients. *See* black patients

age, patient, 12, 26, 28, 29, 265, 277t; aggressive care and, 222; decision-making trajectories by, 284f; likelihood of discussions about interventions and, 75; prognosis and, 113

agents, health care. *See* powers of attorney (for health care); proxy directives; surrogate decision makers

aggressive care, 7–8, 105, 159–61, 168, 171, 173–74, 188, 190, 197; age and, 222; conflicts of interest and, 146; conflicts over, 88–92, 95; costs of, 193, 196; decision-making trajectories and, 223–24; decisions about, 47, 59–60, 63–64, 67, 94, 99; denial and, 225; as legal default, 212; length of ICU admission and, 224; outcomes of, 130–32; against patient's will, 194, 213; quality of life and, 108–9; severity of illness and, 223; shift to comfort care, 69. *See also specific interventions*

algorithms, predictive, 244–46

Ambien, 5

ambulation, 110–11

anesthesia, 182

anesthesiologists, 15, 18, 20, 77, 102

aneurysm, 3, 101, 114, 218

anger, 87, 199

angiograms, 56, 177, 218

antibiotics, 89–90

anxiety, 71, 87

APACHE score, 293–94n1. *See also* severity of illness

apnea test. *See* brain-death exams

ARDS. *See* Acute Respiratory Distress Syndrome

Asians, in research sample, 269, 269t, 272

aspiration, risk of, 169

asymmetric relationships. *See* fiduciary relationships

Ativan, 57, 71

attending physicians, 16, 17–19, 20, 42, 256; afternoon rounds and, 20; morning rounds and, 17–19, 256; participation in meetings with surrogate decision makers, 42

audiences of book, 11–13. *See also* lessons learned

autonomy, 137, 151, 152, 153; concept of, 148; constitutional right of, 7; PPP and, 246; protected by legal rules, 252; right of, 135; undermined, 143

"availability" bias, 143

avoidance techniques, family and, 211–12

"bedside manner," 43–44

bedside procedures, 12, 14, 19–20. *See also specific interventions*

bedsores, 90, 100, 186

before it's too late, 238–43

behavioral economics, 132–33, 247

beneficence trajectory, 181–88, 215–17; as last resort, 188; multiple entry points to, 188; written instructions and, 182. *See also* "best-interest" standard; suffering of patient

"best-interest" standard, 137, 141, 152, 181–88, 195

bioethicists, relevance of book to, 13. *See also* bioethics; ethical issues and standards

bioethics, 10–11, 13, 135, 147–48, 183, 194; health care professionals and, 151; "substituted judgment" and, 142. *See also* ethical issues and standards; ethics committees

black patients, 26, 28, 295n8; decision-making trajectories and, 284f, 286f; in sample, 269, 269t, 272

black Protestants, decision-making trajectories and, 286f

bleeding, 21, 56, 257; in the brain, 118, 163

blood pressure, drop in, 59–61, 62, 67, 70, 170, 198, 218–19

blood pressure medications. *See* pressors

bodies, disposition of, 8, 72–73, 177. *See also* organ donation

bodily integrity, right of, 135

body movements, patient, 27, 159

bolts, 56

brain, illness and injury to, 22, 86, 256; procedures to treat, 46; prognosis, 105,

117–18, 132; "substituted judgment" and, 140. See also specific injuries

brain cancer, 82, 85, 155–56, 180–81

brain death, 3–6, 20, 47, 96, 125, 162, 189–90; lay understandings of, 22; in medical vs. neurological ICUs, 22; organ donation and, 22, 72–74, 204–5; recovery from, 22; to steal organs, 95–96; ventilators and, 96–97

brain-death exams, 3–4, 123, 210

brain function, 86, 96, 108, 109, 122, 134, 162, 209

brain-stem, 162, 172

breathing tubes, 48, 56, 218; infection and, 102; removal of, 50, 54, 71, 98, 158, 219. See also intubation

bronchoscopy, 56

Buchwald, Art, 239

cancer, 16, 21, 25, 121, 256–57; brain, 82, 85, 155–56, 180–81; breast, 104, 186, 210–11; comfort care and, 184; esophageal, 122; leukemia, 106–7, 121–22, 202–3; liver, 1–2; lymphoma, 63; prognosis and, 121–22. See also oncologists

capacity. See decision-making capacity

cardiac arrest, 20, 121. See also code (cardiac arrest)

cardiac resuscitation (CPR), 67, 68, 162, 164, 169, 171, 188, 190, 200; decisions about, 99–100; efficacy for older patients, 75. See also code status

cardiology, 16

cardioverting, 20, 67

care: changing, 70; escalation of, 60–61, 63; goals of (see goals of care); withdrawal of, 59–60, 63, 69, 72, 73, 74, 75, 92, 94, 122, 200 (see also withdrawal of life support)

caregivers, 110; costs of, 193. See also caregiving responsibilities

caregiving responsibilities, 146, 193, 197, 201; family members and, 197; surrogate decision makers and, 197

Catholics: decision-making trajectories and, 286f; last rites, 16, 134, 272; in sample, 271, 272t

chaplains, 12, 19, 189; documentation of meetings in medical records, 261; in

family meetings, 247; interfaith, 16; observations of, 261; relevance of book to, 12–13

chemotherapy, 106

chest compression, 67

children, 34, 35; adult, 34, 35, 179; as champions of their parents' values, 179; child custody, 135; daughters, 33; decision-making trajectories and, 286f

"choice architecture," 247

Christakis, Nicholas, 103

class, 28; income, in sample, 269, 270t; likelihood of discussions about interventions and, 75; poverty rates, of sample, 269, 270t

cleaning crews, 20

clear-and-convincing-evidence standard, 138–39. See also evidentiary standards

clergy, 189. See also chaplains

code (cardiac arrest), 15, 18, 20

code status, 47, 64, 66–69, 164, 265; decisions about, 66–69, 99–100; full code, 66–67, 164, 265; likelihood of discussion about, 75. See also cardiac resuscitation (CPR); DNR/DNI (do-not-resuscitate/do-not-intubate orders)

cognitive biases. See heuristic biases

cognitive impairment, 154. See also decision-making capacity

cognitive psychology, 143, 144

cognitive scripts, 142–45

colitis, 121

Collopy, Bart, 138–39

comas, 162; irreversible, 161, 164–65, 168; laypersons' understanding of, 168; medically induced, 56, 100

comatose patients, 123; responsiveness when comatose, 97–98

comfort care, 2, 8, 105, 156, 160, 163, 174, 184, 189–90, 219; conflict over, 88–92, 95; decisions about, 47, 54, 63–64, 69, 99. See also palliative care

communication, 237, 301n17; challenges to, 87; content of, 246–47; facilitating, 156; framing and, 246–47; heuristics and, 246–47; in medical vs. neurological ICUs, 21–22; with patients, 27–28, 97–98, 156, 209–10. See also communication skills communication skills: health care professionals and, 246–47; instruction in, 246; intensive care units (ICUs) and, 246–47; role-playing and, 246; simulation and, 246; training in, 250

confidentiality, research subjects and, 266–67

conflict, interpersonal, 16; decisions and, 88–99; differences between those with advance directives and those without, 232; family dynamics and, 16, 30–31, 38; over goals of care, 95; between medical staff and significant others, 94, 95–99; in neurological intensive care units (ICUs), 95–98; organ donation and, 74, 95–97; prognosis and, 118; rarity of, 88; resolution of, 249; among significant others, 92–95; about speed and rhythms of decision making, 88–92; about trivial issues, 92

conflicts of interest, 193, 201–3, 237, 256; family members/surrogates and, 145–48; religion and, 200–201; source of, 146–48. See also caregiving responsibilities; emotional burden of decision making; financial interests; patient preferences; what the family wants

consciousness: impairments of, 22; loss of, 156; neurological assessment of, 27

consensus: consensus building, 87, 100, 237, 253; consensus seeking, 38, 40; of interested persons, 136

consent, informed, 61, 75–79; deficiencies in, 77–79; to intubation, 1; legal doctrine of, 75–76; solicited face-to face, 80–81; solicited over the telephone, 79–80; statements falling short of, 155, 156, 159; venues for soliciting, 79–81; witnessing of, 79–80; written, 77

consent, research subjects and, 266–67; consent forms, 266; disadvantages of requiring, 267; waiver of, 267

"cows," 15, 17, 258

critical care consultants, vs. primary team, 21, 257

critical care physicians, 15–16, 302n4; encounters with families, 110–11; holistic perspective of, 121

critical care teams, 15–17, 41; afternoon rounds and, 20–21; clothing of, 17; in medical vs. neurological intensive care units (ICUs), 21–22; morning rounds and, 17–19, 258–61; note-taking and record-keeping by, 17, 19; observations of, 258–61; palliative care and, 69. See also specific team participants

Cruzan, Nancy, 135, 252

crying, 87

crystal ball metaphor, 116; examples of, 54, 66, 106, 112, 121

CT scans, 96, 102, 118, 236

custodial care, costs of, 146

CVVH (Continuous Veno-Venous Hemofiltration). See dialysis

Dartmouth Atlas of Health Care, 272, 273, 303n26

data: admission and discharge, 267; advance directives, 267; aggregation of, 268; bounce-back to ICU, 268; characteristics of decision makers, 267; coding of, 268; complexity of, 267; data collection, 256, 257–58, 266; demographic information, 267; diagnosis, 267; generalizability of, 256–57; from physicians' notes, 268; insurance status, 267; medical history, 268; meeting data, 268; outcomes, 268; patient decision-making capacity, 267; recording of, 267; social background, 268; statement data, 268; treatment data, 267–68; on unobserved meetings, 268

data collection, 256–61; by medical social worker, 257–58

death, 7, 224, 225t, 233, 234t; attitudes about, 245; dignified, 91; peaceful, 91; place of, 11, 99, 232, 233, 234t. See also brain death; dying; end-of-life medical decisions

decision makers. See surrogate decision makers

decision making, 1–8, 175; cognitive biases in, 132–33; consensus of interested persons, 136; decision-making criteria, 11; emotional burden of, 193, 199–200, 226–28, 228f, 237; facilitating, 246–47; familial dysfunction and, 38; framing of probabilistic information and, 132–33; improvisation in, 11, 152–213, 242, 252; laws concerning, 34; limits on default surrogate decisions, 136; observations of, 212–13; physicians and, 10, 217–20, 220f; rationale/justification for (*see* decision-making trajectories); in the real world, 152–213; soft recommendations about, 100; speed and rhythms of, 88–92; standards of, 137, 252; time allowed for, 100; venues for, 79–87. *See also* decision-making capacity; decision-making criteria; decision-making process; decision-making standards; decision-making trajectories

decision-making capacity, 7, 26–28, 30, 34; capacity determinations, 27; compromised, 155, 156; impaired, 1–8, 13; lack of, 153, 216, 244, 255–56, 258, 265; in medical vs. neurological intensive care units (ICUs), 22; stroke patients and, 156–57, 256; uncertainty about, 156–58. *See also* Glasgow Coma Score (GCS)

decision-making criteria, 249; alternative, 171; differences made by, 214–15; impact on emotional distress, 239; impact on patient's fate, 239; importance of conversations about, 241–43; interpretation of, 164–66; multiple, 216–17; other studies about, 299n1; prescribed by legal norms, 251; surrogate decision makers' struggles with, 238. *See also* decision-making trajectories

decision-making leeway, 147–48, 204; "substituted judgment" and, 147

decision-making process, 46–48, 47f; advance-directive status and, 289–90t; consensus, 38, 40, 87, 100, 136, 237, 253; ICU improvements and, 246–50; importance of conversations about, 241–43; information considered (*see* decision-making criteria); vs. outcomes, 238; surrogate decision makers' reflections on, 226

decision-making scripts, 134–51; cognitive scripts, 142–45; conflicts of interest and, 145–48; law at the bedside, 148–51; legal script, 135–42

decision-making standards, legal, 137; across states, 137; distress caused by following, 232; evidence regarding, 137–38; hierarchy of, 137; lack of awareness about, 251. *See also* "best-interest" standard; decision-making criteria; patient instructions; patient preferences; "substituted judgment"

decision-making strategy: choice of, 11. *See also* decision-making trajectories

decision-making trajectories, 100, 153–212, 215f; age and, 220, 221, 222, 284f; aggressive care and, 223–24; beneficence, 181–88, 215–17, 215f, 216f, 220–21, 224, 225, 227, 281t; black patients and, 284f, 286f; black Protestants and, 286f; Catholics and, 286f; children and, 286f; denial, 206–12, 215–17, 215f, 216f, 220–21, 224, 228, 281t, 300n14; differences between those with advance directives and those without, 231; ethical standards and, 219–20; expressions of distress across, 227–28, 228f; frequency, 215, 215f; gender (patient) and, 221, 287f; gender (surrogate) and, 221, 287f; God's decision, 189–92, 215–17, 215f, 216f, 220–21, 222, 224, 225, 228, 281t; Hispanic patients and, 284f; impact on family members, 226–28; Jewish patients and, 286f; legal standards and, 219–20; length of ICU stay and, 234–35; life-sustaining treatment and, 223–24; maximizing patient welfare, 181–88, 215–17, 215f, 216f, 220–21, 224, 227, 281t; meeting frequency and, 300n14; for more critically ill patients, 223–24, 223f, 225f; multiple, 153, 215–17; opting for a trajectory, patient characteristics and, 220–22; opting out of decision making, 206–12, 215–17, 215f, 216f, 220–21, 228, 281t, 300n14; outcomes by, 223–28; parents and, 286f; by patient and surrogate characteristics, 283, 283–87t; patient decides, 153–60, 215–17, 215f, 216f, 220–21, 222, 224, 225, 227, 281t; by patient religion, 286f; physicians' role in, 217–20, 220f; post hoc rationalizations and, 225–26; by preexisting illness, 285f; Protestants and, 286f;

decision-making trajectories (*continued*)
race/ethnicity and, 220, 221, 222, 284f;
reassessing choice of, 249; relationships
between, 216f, 281, 281t; religion and,
221, 222 (*see also* God); reprising patient
instructions, 160–71, 215–17, 215f, 216f,
220–21, 222, 224, 227–28, 281t; severity
of illness and, 221, 222, 285f; spouses
and, 286f; standing in the patient's
shoes, 171–81, 215–17, 215f, 216f, 220–
21, 222, 224, 227–28, 281t; "substituted
judgment," 171–81, 215–17, 215f, 216f,
220–21, 222, 224, 227–28, 281t; surrogate decision makers' characteristics
and, 220–22; by surrogate's relationship
to patient, 286f; switching, 215–17, 220;
unknown, 214–15; unsanctioned by law,
251; what family members or surrogates
want, 193–206, 215–17, 215f, 216f, 220–
21, 222, 224, 227, 281t; white patients
and, 284f
decisions, 9, 45–100; affect and, 87; code
status, 66–69; conflict and, 88–99; dialysis, 62–63; differences by intervention,
74–75; end-of-life, 70, 140, 240, 273;
feeding (PEG) tube, 55–56; goals of
care, 63–66; impact on family members
and surrogates, 193–206; intubation,
48–51; "last decisions," 99–100; letting
God decide, 70; letting the body decide,
70; organ donation, 72–74; palliative
care, 69–72; physician framing, 100;
surgical and other interventions, 56–62;
tracheostomy, 51–54. *See also* decision making; decision-making criteria;
decision-making process; decision-
making trajectories
decubitus ulcers. *See* bedsores
default surrogate consent laws, 34–35,
136–37, 149–50, 251, 253
default surrogate decision makers, 34–36,
35t, 148–49, 239, 297n9; compromised, 201; construing their role,
38–40; effectiveness of, 240; end-of-life
decisions and, 240; hierarchy for determining, 148–49, 253; identification
of, 34–36, 35t, 37; limited authority
of in some states, 149, 150, 251, 253;
with poor relations with patients, 201;

self-interest and, 201; taking for granted,
240. *See also* surrogate decision makers
defibrillators, 169
delaying treatments, harm of, 153
dementia, 27, 86, 154, 156
demographic characteristics of patients
compared to U.S. population, 28–30,
44, 268–72, 269t, 270t, 272t
denial, aggressive care and, 225. *See also*
decision-making trajectories
despair, 87, 99
dialysis, 47, 61–63, 70, 100, 108
disability, 111, 122, 130, 245; "the disability
paradox," 111; misunderstanding about
experience of, 111; overestimation of
long-term impact of, 143; quality of life
and, 111; scholarship about, 111; stigma
and stereotypes about the disabled, 111
discharge, 224; data on, 267; discharge
facilities, 196 (*see also specific kinds of
facilities*); discharge planning, 16, 19,
23; to patient's residence, 224
discharge facilities: costs of, 196; health
insurance and, 196
discharge planning, 16, 19, 23
distress, 12, 87, 228, 244; across decision-
making trajectories, 227–28, 228f;
caused by striving for fidelity to patient
wishes and following decision-making
standards, 232; differences between
those with advance directives and those
without, 232; experienced by health
care providers, 5, 40, 212. *See also* emotional burden of decision making
distrust, 87, 209–11
divine intervention, prognosis and, 125.
See also God
DNR/DNI (do-not-resuscitate/do-not-
intubate orders), 1, 5, 64, 67–68, 94,
103, 130, 170–71, 174, 265; intubation
and, 49; rescinding of, 5, 67
Dobhoff tubes, 169
Doe, John or Jane, 30, 149
does any of this matter?, 232
Dopplers, 218
Dresser, Rebecca, 140
driver's licenses: organ donor status
indicated on, 160, 166; possibility of
indicating proxy directives on, 240–41

dying, 59–60, 91, 104–5; artificially prolonged, 163 (*see also* life-sustaining treatment); attitudes about, 245; fear of, 146; naturally, 160, 163

ear, nose, and throat (ENT) specialists (otolaryngologists), 16, 52, 77
economics: billing information, 23; costs of custodial care, 146; costs of discharge facilities, 196; costs of medical care, 8, 146; costs of nursing homes, 193; costs of outpatient therapies, 193; costs of treatment, 23, 43, 79, 86, 193, 195, 196–97; depletion of estates, 194; financial concerns of families and decision makers, 146, 193–97, 201; ICUs and, 22–23, 193, 250; inheritance, 146, 194, 195; interventions delayed for financial reasons, 194–95; lack of discussion about, 22–23; of long-term care facilities, 193; medication costs, 193; of rehabilitation facilities, 193; settling of estates, 201–2, 204; uncovered costs, 194
EEGs (electroencephalograms), 82, 83–84, 86, 87, 96
electric shocks. *See* cardioverting
electronic medical records. *See* medical records
Emanuel, Ezekiel, 139
Emanuel, Linda, 139
embolization, 56, 102, 103
emotional burden of decision making, 12, 87, 193, 198–200, 201, 202–4, 226–28, 228f, 232, 237, 244; differences between those with advance directives and those without, 232; fear of being responsible or blamed for patient's death, 200, 203, 206; fear of loss, 146, 193, 198–99; from following patient wishes, 227–28; guilt, 193, 200; and patient suffering, 227–28
emotions, 11, 199–200. *See also* affect, decisions and
empathy, 87, 152, 299n1, 301n17
encounters. *See* family meetings
end of ICU admission, 233–36
end-of-life medical decisions: changing, 140; surrogate decision makers and, 13, 240; venues for, 273

endotracheal tubes (ETTs). *See* breathing tubes
estates: depletion of, 146, 194; dispute over, 195; settling of, 201–2, 204. *See also* inheritance
ethical issues and standards, 13, 16; decision-making trajectories and, 219–20; encountered by researchers, 264–65; surrogate decision making and, 10–11; withdrawal of life support and, 42
ethics committees, 2, 20, 40, 134, 149, 200–201; in family meetings, 247–48; observations of, 261; withdrawal of life support and, 42
ethics consults, 203
ethics programs, observations of, 261
ethnicity. *See* race/ethnicity
EVDs (drain from brain). *See* external ventricular drains (EVDs)
evidence, prognosis and, 112–16
evidence of patient preferences, 137–39
evidentiary standards, 138–39, 152
exhaustion, 87, 99
experimental treatments, costs of, 193, 196
external ventricular drains (EVDs), 56, 98, 194–95
extubation, 50, 54, 71, 98, 158, 219

facilitators, in ICUs, need for, 247–50
Fagerlin, Angela, 142–43
faith, 189
"false consensus effect," 143, 206
families, 30–40; conflict and, 88; distress of, 227–28; distrust of health care professionals, 210–11; encounters with physicians, 31, 36–38, 40–43, 110–11 (*see also* family meetings); extended family, 32; familial dysfunction, 38; family dynamics, 16; fractured, 30–31, 88; hybrid, 30–31; locating of family members, 16; nontraditional, 30–31; nuclear, 30; patient wishes and, 1–3; physician deference to, 150; resistance of, 2–4; structures of, 237, 253; supporting, 246–47. *See also* family members; significant others; surrogate decision makers
family doctors. *See* primary care physicians
family meetings, 31, 36–38, 40–43, 110–11; attending physicians and, 42; data on

family meetings (*continued*)
  unobserved, 268; discussion of advance
    directives and living wills in, 230; ethics
    and palliative care specialists attend-
    ing, 247, 248; fellows and, 42; health
    care professionals and, 40–42; meeting
    participants, 32–33; multidisciplinary,
    248; neurologists and, 41; neurosur-
    geons and, 41; nurses and, 40, 247, 248;
    observations of, 259–60; oncologists
    and, 41; palliative care physicians and,
    41; with regional organ-transplant
    agency, 261; residents and, 42; surrogate
    decision makers and, 40, 41–42; sur-
    rogate decision makers unavailable for,
    211; tape recording of, 262
family members: befriending other
    families, 32; characteristics of, 30–33;
    comprehension of medical information
    and, 33; conflicts of interest and, 145–
    46; decisions based on what they want,
    193–206, 215–17, 215f, 216f, 220–21,
    222, 224, 227, 281t; fear of loss and,
    198–99; financial interests of, 193–97;
    impact of decision-making trajectories
    on, 226–28, 228f; impact of medi-
    cal decisions on, 193–206; language
    spoken, 33; legal training of, 33; medi-
    cal background of, 33; participation
    in meetings, 32; preexisting research
    about, 261–62; pressure from others,
    193; self-interest and, 193–206. *See also*
    specific relationships
fate: belief in, 5. *See also* God
fates worse than death, 111, 233–34, 235
fear, 87; of being responsible or blamed for
    patient's death, 200, 203, 206; of loss,
    146, 193, 198–99
feeding (PEG) tubes, 47, 55–56, 91, 94,
    100, 102, 159, 168–69, 218; decisions
    about, 55–56; risk of aspiration and,
    169
fellows, 16, 18, 19; in medical vs. neurolog-
    ical intensive care units (ICUs), 21–22;
    participation in meetings with surrogate
    decision makers, 42
fentanyl, 71, 211
fidelity, 8, 37, 151, 152, 170, 244, 246, 254
fiduciary relationships, 145, 255–56

financial interests, 146, 194; of family
    members, 193–97; goals of care and,
    194; of surrogate decision makers,
    193–97
"floor," the, 20
fluids, procedures to drain, tap, or measure,
    56. *See also* hydration
food: quality of life and, 55; symbolic
    meaning of, 55. *See also* feeding (PEG)
    tubes
food service workers, 20
framing: communication and, 246–47;
    framing effects, 143–44
"framing" bias, 132–33
friends, 30–40; close, 34
functional status: advance directives and,
    161; difficulty of predicting, 237; goals
    of care and, 167; interpretation of,
    168; underestimation of, 141. *See also*
    prognosis
futility, 235–36

gastroenterology, 16
Gawande, Atul, 129
gender: of family members at bedside, 35–
    36; of patients, 28, 29, 268–69, 269t,
    287f; of surrogate decision makers,
    268–69, 269t, 287f; of visitors, 32–33,
    35–36
Glasgow Coma Score (GCS), 27, 258,
    294n1, 294n3, 302n5
goals of care, 47, 63–66, 157, 163; changes
    in, 174; conditional, 167; decisions
    about, 63–66; definition of, 63; dis-
    agreement over, 95; financial interests
    and, 194; functional status and, 167;
    length of ICU stay and, 235; likelihood
    of discussion about, 75; meetings to dis-
    cuss, 46; for more critically ill patients,
    223–24, 223f; patient wishes and, 167;
    presence of advance directives and, 231;
    prognosis and, 104, 167; quality of life
    and, 167; in sample selection, 265;
    surrogate decision makers refusing to
    reconsider, 211. *See also* aggressive care;
    code status; comfort care; palliative care
God, 189; in God's hands, 5, 189, 190,
    192; role in decision making, 191–92;
    signs from, 191; will of, 189–92, 215–

17, 215f, 216f, 220–21, 222, 224, 225, 228, 281t
grandchildren, 34
grief counseling, 16
guardians, 34, 35
guilt, 12, 146, 193, 200

hand washing, 18, 263
Hardwig, John, 147–48
health care institutions, 8; likelihood of dying in, 11. *See also* hospitalization; hospitals
health care policy, 13, 229, 234, 244–46. *See also* legal policy
health care professionals, 12–13, 40–44; barred from ingesting food or beverages in ICU, 19; "best-interest" standard and, 182; bioethics norms and, 151; communication skills and, 246–47; conflict with significant others, 94, 95–99; distrust of, 210–11; legal norms and, 151; meetings with surrogate decision makers, 40; as patient advocates, 39, 40; preexisting relationships with patients and families, 41; religion and, 41–42; training of, 247, 252; trust in, 97–99. *See also specific roles*
health care proxies. *See* proxy directives
health insurance, 19, 194; co-payments, 194; coverage ceilings, 194; coverage exclusions, 194; coverage of advance-care planning, 241; coverage of treatments, 196; deductibles, 194; discharge facilities and, 196; health insurance status, 23, 28; lifetime maximums, 196; limited numbers of days of treatment, 194; resolution of issues, 16; status among sample, 270t, 271. *See also* Medicaid enrollment; Medicare; public aid
hematology, 16
hematoma, 172
hemorrhage, 21, 22, 26
hemorrhagic conversion, 163
hemorrhagic stroke, 218
hepatology, 16
herniation, 73, 172
heroic measures. *See* aggressive care
heuristic biases, 143–44, 237, 245, 249; "affective forecasting," 111; "availability"

bias, 143; cognitive biases, 11, 132–33, 143, 237; "false consensus effect," 143, 206, 222; "framing" bias, 132–33; framing effects, 143–44; "hindsight" bias, 213; "impact" bias, 111; inaction, preference for, 237; "Lake Wobegon effect," 144; "omission" bias, 144; "optimism" bias, 144; projection, 143–44, 206, 222, 237; risk aversion, 132, 143; sunk cost, 144
heuristics, 143–44; "choice architecture," 247; communication and, 246–47; heuristic shortcuts, 143–44. *See also* behavioral economics; psychology
"hindsight" bias, 213
Hispanic patients, 28; decision-making trajectories and, 284f; in sample, 269, 269t, 272
Hmong patients, 271
hope, 87
hospice care, 89; black patients and, 295n8; costs of, 193; at home, 69. *See also* palliative care
hospitalists, 41
hospitalization: length of, 11; likelihood of, 11
"hospital referral region," 272
hospitals: deaths in, 11; dramatic depictions of, 20, 27, 48, 68; federal regulations and, 34, 72, 148, 150; generalizability of research, 268, 272–73; improvements to, 246–50; protocols, 76, 79, 96, 168; research in, 8, 256; staying out of, 232. *See also* economics
house staff, 16
hydration: advance directives and, 161; artificially supplied, 163
hypothetical scenarios, 179–80, 245; patient preferences and, 179–80, 245, 261. See also *Newlywed Game* research design

ictal scans, 83–84
ICU. *See* intensive care units (ICUs)
ICU admission. *See* admission
ICU discharge. *See* discharge
ICU nurse managers, 15; observation of rounds of, 261
ICU stay: decision-making trajectories and, 234–35; end of, 233; goals of care

ICU stay (*continued*)
and, 235; length of, 26, 224, 234–35,
265; of most critically ill patients, 234;
severity of illness and, 234–35; suffering
and, 234–35; survival and, 233–34;
unforeseen, 12
Illinois, 253; advance directives in, 160–61;
laws in, 34–35, 134–37, 149; limited
authority of default surrogate decision
makers in, 149, 150; living wills in,
160–61; POLST and, 136; powers of
attorney in, 34, 161; research site in,
256, 273
Illinois Health Care Surrogate Act, 134,
135–36, 149
imaging, 19. *See also specific types of imaging*
immunology, 16
"impact" bias, 111
impairment: misunderstanding about
experience of, 111; overestimation of
long-term impact of, 143. *See also* "affective forecasting"; disability; "impact"
bias
implications of the study, 236–54
improvisation, in decision making, 11,
152–213; discussions about, 242; preference for, 252
inability to speak, 7, 27, 135, 156
inaction, preference for, 237
income, patient. *See* affluence of residence
incompetent patients: forced treatment of,
135; rights of, 135–36
infections, breathing tubes and, 102. *See
also* sepsis
infectious diseases, 16, 121
informed consent. *See* consent, informed
inheritance, 146, 194, 195. *See also* estates
institutional review board (IRB), 256, 264,
266, 267
instructional directives, 136, 228, 239. *See
also* living wills
intensive care, expense of. *See* economics
intensive care units (ICUs), 10, 11–12,
14–24; admission out of the blue, 6,
12, 25–26; communication skills and,
246–47; critical care physicians in,
15–16; deaths in, 11, 233; differences
among, 21–22; economics of, 22–23,
193, 250; facilitators and, 247–50;
as ground zero for surrogate medical
decision making, 7; improvements to,
246–50; medical specialists in, 15–16;
nurses in, 15; open vs. closed units,
21–22, 257; outsiders passing through,
17; personal items in, 15; personnel in,
15–17 (*see also specific roles*); pessimism
in, 130; prognosis in, 130; realism
about outcomes, 233–34; reasons for
admission to, 25–26, 26t, 46; resources
in, 247; rhythms of, 17–22; steps to improve decision-making process, 246–50;
technological improvements in, 247;
technology in, 14–15; time spent by
patients in, 26; visiting hours in, 20–21;
visitors to, 20–21; vulnerable principals
in, 255–56. *See also* medical intensive
care units (MICUs); neurological intensive care units (ICUs)
internists, 15
interpreters, 33. *See also* language; non-
English-speaking significant others
interventional radiology, 16
interventions, 19, 20, 56–62, 100; decisions
about, 56–62; delayed for financial
reasons, 194–95; differences about decisions by, 74–75; different kinds of, 46–
47, 47f, 99; likelihood of discussions
about, 75; most common contemplated
in ICUs, 46–47, 47f; number performed
per patient per day, 46. *See also* treatment; *and specific interventions*
interviews, in preexisting research, 261;
biases in, 212; retrospective, 212–13,
261–62
intubation, 20, 46–48, 65, 91, 121, 158,
164; dangers of prolonged, 52, 53;
decisions about, 1, 48–51; medications
for, 49; resuscitation and, 67; tracheostomies and, 76–78. *See also* breathing
tubes; extubation; reintubation
intuitive thinking, 143
IVC filters, 56

jargon, medical, 168, 230
Jewish patients: decision-making trajectories and, 286f; in sample, 271, 272, 272t

Kahneman, Daniel, 132–33, 143
kidney disorders, 61–63, 131, 134, 257. *See also* dialysis

"Lake Wobegon effect," 144
language: language difficulties, 296n16 (*see also* non-English-speaking significant others); meaning and, 129. *See also* jargon, medical
law(s), 253; across states, 251; at the bedside, 148–51; efficacy of, 11, 13, 229–32, 251; evolving, 250–51; health care professionals and, 150–51; irrelevance of in ICU, 251; policy reform, 142, 240, 250–54; relying on, 228–32; role of, 250–54; timelines, of law vs. critical care, 252. *See also* advance directives; default surrogate consent laws; evidence of patient preferences; legal rules, norms, and standards; state differences; *and specific laws*
lawsuits, 194; compensation from, 146; physician disinterest in, 43
lawyers. *See* legal practitioners
legal developments, evolving, 250–51
legal documents, accessibility of, 240
legal policy, 142, 240, 250–54
legal practitioners, 5; as counselors, 252–53; in the ICU, 5, 88, 237, 250; lessons for, 250–54; relevance of book to, 13
legal rules, norms, and standards, 10–11, 247; consequences of, 252; decision-making trajectories and, 219–20; disincentives for complying with, 151; role of health care professionals in implementing, 150–51; unforeseen consequences of, 253–54. *See also specific standards*
legal script, 135–42; evidentiary challenges, 138–42
length of life, quality of life and, 8
lessons learned, 236–54
leukemia, 106–7, 121–22, 202–3
life-and-death decisions, 132–33. *See also* end-of-life medical decisions
life insurance, 194
life's end: how we die, 8
life support: withdrawal of, 1–3, 42, 47, 69, 72, 128, 130, 134–36, 149, 150, 163,

168. *See also* life-sustaining treatment; palliative care; *and specific interventions*
life-sustaining treatment, 161, 163, 164–65, 167; decision-making trajectories and, 223–24; limiting of toward end of life, 223–24. *See also specific interventions*
limitations, of study, 273. *See also* research, preexisting
liver disorders, 1–2, 56, 59–60, 198, 257
living wills, 16, 136, 148, 160, 161, 163, 164–65, 168, 178, 200; completed under pressure from family members, 230; discussions of content of, 229–30; efficacy of, 11, 229–32, 251; failure of, 230–31; history of, 228–29; honoring, 199; in Illinois, 160–61; logistical discussions of, 229; misunderstanding of, 164–65, 230–31; out-of-date, 230; role in helping to honor patient's wishes, 230–31; studies of, 229; surrogate decision makers and, 165–66; that fall on deaf ears, 230; that provide no guidance, 230. *See also* advance directives
locked-in state, 105, 156–57
long-term care facilities, 53, 54, 157, 187–88, 196, 234t; costs of, 193; discharge to, 224
loss: fear of, 146, 193, 198–99; risk seeking to avoid, 237
love, 146
loved ones. *See* significant others
lumbar puncture, 56
lunacy, law of, 135

making a difference, 214–32; impact of directives, 228–32; outcomes by decision-making trajectories, 223–28; role of physicians, 217–20
manipulativeness, 38, 79, 158, 170
McMath, Jahi, 135
M.D. Anderson Foundation, 257
Medicaid enrollment, 23. *See also* public aid
medical charts, 258. *See also* medical records
medical crises: denial about possibility of future, 243; impossibility of anticipating, 237–38; as levelers, 32

medical equipment, costs of, 193
medical intensive care units (MICUs), 45, 46, 257; brain death in, 22; closed units, 21, 257; conditions treated in, 21; decision-making capacity of patients in, 22; differences from neurological intensive care unit, 21–22; meetings with health care professionals observed in, 42; personnel in, 15–16; rounds in, 18–19, 21–22
medical orders, portable, 241. *See also* Physician Orders for Life-Sustaining Treatment (POLST)
medical records, 14, 17, 18, 19, 23, 258; advance directives in, 150; documentation of chaplains' meetings in, 261; documentation of planning and directives in, 247; electronic, 14, 17–19, 23, 247, 248, 258, 261, 268, 302n7; insurance status and, 23; studies of, 261, 262; treatment costs and, 23. *See also* physicians' notes
medical specialists: in ICUs, 15–16. *See also* specific specialists
medical specialties: prognosis and, 121–22. *See also specific specialties*
medical students, 16; morning rounds and, 256
Medicare, 86; advance-care planning and, 241, 253; participants in sample, 270t, 271; studies of claims data, 261, 262
medications, 56; to alleviate pain, 49, 54, 60, 71; to cause to forget, 49, 71; for comfort, 59, 71, 80, 89, 219; costs of, 23, 79, 193; to reduce anxiety, 59, 60, 71; for resuscitation, 67. *See also specific medications*
meetings: length of, 81; meeting participants, 32–33; multidisciplinary, 81–87; number of participants in, 81. *See also* family meetings
memorial services, 16
memory, 71, 109, 110, 131, 218
mental capacity, advance directives and, 161
methodology. *See* research, the
miracles, 112–13, 130–32, 189; belief in, 3; "miraculous" outcomes, 113, 130–32, 233, 235; prognosis and, 125

mixed messages, 237; about prognosis, 119–23, 124, 133
mobility, 110–11
moral responsibilities toward others, "substituted judgment" and, 147–48
morphine, 71, 80, 88, 219
MRA (scan of blood vessels), 218
MRIs, 82–84, 86, 218; brain function and, 86
Muslims, in sample, 271

National Healthcare Decisions Day, 228
National Institutes of Health, 266
National Science Foundation, 257
negotiation: pleading for more time, 153; prognosis and, 124–29
nephrology, 16
neurological function. *See* brain function
neurological impairment, 25, 156. *See also* brain, illness and injury to
neurological intensive care units (ICUs), 15–16, 256–57; brain death in, 22; conditions treated in, 21; conflict in, 95–98; data collection in, 266; decision-making capacity of patients in, 22; delayed prognosis in, 117–18; differences from medical intensive care units, 21–22; meetings with health care professionals observed in, 42; multidisciplinary meetings in, 81–87; open units, 21, 257; opportunities for communication with critical care teams in, 21–22; personnel in, 15; rounds in, 21–22
neurologists, 4, 15, 17, 21, 82–87, 101–3, 121, 122, 257; participation in meetings with surrogate decision makers, 41
neuromuscular blockers, 57
neurosurgeons, 3–5, 15, 21, 66, 82–87, 101–3, 122, 132, 257; participation in meetings with surrogate decision makers, 41
Newlywed Game research design, 140–42, 147–48, 213, 244–45; in the real world, 179–80
night float. *See* residents
non-English-speaking significant others, 94; consent forms and, 266; likelihood of discussions about interventions and, 75
nuclear flow studies, 3–5

nurses, 12, 15; backstage role of, 40; ICU
nurse managers, 261; morning rounds
and, 256; night nurses, 17; participation
in encounters between physicians and
families, 40–41, 247, 248; as patient
advocates, 39, 40, 247–50; relationships
with family members, 39, 40; relevance
of book to, 12–13; role in surrogate
decision making, 40–41; unflappability
and skill of, 40; workload and schedule
of, 15, 17, 40
nursing homes, 175, 176, 196; costs of,
193; discharge to, 224; willingness to
live in, 128, 141, 175
nutrition: advance directives and, 161;
artificially supplied, 163; withdrawal of,
200. See also feeding (PEG) tubes

observational research, 212–13; risk of
reactivity (changing situation observed),
263–64; strengths of, 262–63; weaknesses of, 263–64
observations, of family meetings, 259, 279t
obstetrician-gynecologists, 16
"omission" bias, 144
oncologists, 16; optimistic prognosis and,
121–22; participation in meetings with
surrogate decision makers, 41; preexisting relationships with families, 41, 121
optimism, 237; prognosis and, 121–22,
129–30
"optimism" bias, 144
orderlies, 20
organ donation, 20, 47, 72–74, 160, 201,
206–7; advance directives and, 161;
brain death and, 22, 204–5; conflict
over, 74, 95–97; decisions about,
72–74; donor status, 161, 166; driver's
license, and, 166; evaluation for, 72; in
medical vs. neurological intensive care
units (ICUs), 22; organ donor cards, 72,
73, 160
organ-donation organizations, 20, 72–73,
family meetings with, 261
organ failure, 25, 61–63, 65
orthopedics, 16
outcomes, 223–28; advance-directive
status and, 289–90t; decided before
rationalization to support it, 225;

vs. decision-making process, 238; by
decision-making trajectory, 224–25,
225f; differences between those with
advance directives and those without,
231; of ICU admission, 233–35, 234t;
for more critically ill patients, 225f; realism about, 234; severity of illness and,
234–35; survival vs. recovery, 234
out of the blue. See suddenness of illness
outpatient therapies, costs of, 193

pain, 182; alleviation of, 163; avoiding,
210–11; beneficence and, 185–86, 188.
See also medications
palliative care, 16, 47, 69–72, 94, 265;
black patients and, 295n8; decisions
about, 69–72, 99; likelihood of discussion about, 75. See also comfort care;
hospice care
palliative care specialists, 69, 71, 72; in
family meetings, 41, 247–48
palliative care teams, 19–20, 90–92
paracentesis, 56
paralytic drugs, administration of, 56–57
parens patriae, 135
parents, 34, 35; decision-making trajectories and, 221–22, 286f; as surrogate
decision makers, 301n4 (chap. 8)
patient instructions: absolute vs. contingent, 238; addressing outcome rather
than decision-making process, 238;
conditional, 167, 171, 238; body language shows, 27, 125, 159; dismissed by
surrogates, 170; to give priority to needs
and interests of others, 204; imprecise,
168–69; inauthentic, 171; inconsistent
with patient wishes, 238; incorrect jargon used, 238; lack of, 171; limitations
of, 237–38; no longer appropriate, 169–
70; privileged by law in most states, 160;
recollection and retelling of, 170–71;
reprising, 160–71, 215–17, 215f, 216f,
220–21, 222, 224, 227–28, 281t; too
general or do not apply, 138, 169, 230,
237; verbal, 166–71; written, 160–66
patient interests, 8–11. See also conflicts of
interest
"patient preference predictor" (PPP),
244–46

patient preferences, 8, 10–11, 152; changing, 111, 139–40, 176, 230, 245; compared with "substituted judgment," 179; distress caused by striving for fidelity to, 232; documentation of, 151; evidence of, 137–39; evidentiary standards for, 138–39, 152; family pressure on, 171; fidelity to, 170–71; general agreement of significant others about, 180; goals of care and, 167; hypothetical scenarios and, 179–80, 245, 261; impairment affecting, 139–40; inability to know future preferences, 139, 142; inferred, 171–81; inferred from personality, 174; inferred from values, 174; misunderstanding of, 141; predicting, 244–46; putting interests of others first, 146–48; quality of life and, 174–75; sources for understanding, 137–39; standing in the patient's shoes, and, 171–81; uncertainty about, 237, 251; when patients' minds are literally changed, 140. See also patient instructions

patients, 25–30; age of, 26, 28, 29, 75, 113, 222, 265, 277t; aliases for, 31, 93; Asian, 269, 269t, 272; black, 26, 28, 269, 269t, 272, 284f, 286f, 295n8; Catholic, 271, 272t, 286f; children of, 29, 32; class of, 28; comatose, 26–27; communication with, 27–28, 97–98, 209–10; daughters of, 33; demographic characteristics of, 28–30, 44, 265, 268; diversity of, 28–30, 44; family of, 30–40 (see also families; family members); friends of, 30–40; gender of, 28, 29, 268–69, 269t, 277t; Hispanic, 28, 269t, 272, 284f; income of, 269, 270t; insurance status of, 28; Jewish, 271, 272, 272t, 286f; marital status of, 29, 277t; in medical vs. neurological intensive care units (ICUs), 22; nonwhite, 28; occupations of, 29, 275t; parents of, 32, 301n4 (chap. 8); with preexisting medical conditions, 26, 221, 285f; poverty rates of, 269, 270t; Protestant, 271, 272t, 286f; race/ethnicity of, 26, 28, 29, 75, 268–69, 269t, 272, 284f, 286f, 295n8; reasons for admission, 12, 25–26, 26t; relevance of book to would-be, 12, 13; religion of, 29, 189, 221, 222, 271, 272t, 286f; residence, 29; responsiveness of, 26–28, 65, 159, 209–10; siblings of, 32; time spent in ICU, 26; unidentified, 30, 149; unmarried partners of, 29; white, 26, 269, 269t, 284f. See also sample, the

Patient Self-Determination Act of 1990, 148
patients' rights, 135
patient welfare, 137; maximizing, 181–88. See also beneficence trajectory
patient wishes. See patient preferences
pentobarbital, 82, 84
percutaneous endoscopic gastrostomy (PEG) tube (sometimes called a G-tube), 55. See also feeding (PEG) tubes
personal experience, prognosis and, 115
pessimism, in intensive care units (ICUs), 130
pharmacists, 16
physiatrists, 16
physical therapy, 90, 182
Physician Orders for Life-Sustaining Treatment (POLST), 136, 241, 252. See also advance directives
physicians, 15–16, 41–44; advice offered or solicited, 39, 43, 100, 101, 183–84; age of, 41; attending, 16, 17–19, 20, 42, 256, 263–64; "bedside manner" of, 43–44; "best-interest" standard and, 182, 183; coat length and, 16; communication skills of, 43, 246–47; confusion about identity or legal status of decision makers, 36–38, 151; consultants, 21, 41, 42, 69, 257; crying, 87; deference to patients' surrogates, 43; differences in engagement across trajectories, 219–20, 220f; encounters with families, 31, 36–38, 40–43, 110–11 (see also family meetings; surrogate decision makers); fellows, 16, 18, 19, 21–22; fractured families and, 31; gender of, 43; general observations about, 42–43; heuristic biases and, 11, 132–33, 143; hospitalists, 41; legal issues, awareness of, 43, 149–50, 152; legal norms and, 151; legal rules, role in implementation of, 150–51, 165; participation in meetings with surrogate decision makers, 42; personal experience and, 115; pragmatism of, 43;

primary care, 17, 41; professionalism of, 42; prognosis discomfort with, 103, 115; race/ethnicity and, 41; relevance of book to, 12–13; religion, 41–42; residents, 16, 18, 19; role in decision making, 217–20, 220f; rotations of, 42, 44; statistical illiteracy/innumeracy of, 112; "substituted judgment" and, 152; success in persuading course correction for trajectories, 220; treatment costs, awareness of, 23, 43. *See also specific specialties*

physicians' notes, 17–19, 76, 150, 259–60, 268

pneumonia, 26, 89–90, 113

policy makers, 11, 229, 237, 240, 244, 252–53

post hoc rationalizations, decision-making trajectories and, 225–26

poverty rates, of sample, 269, 270t

powers of attorney (for health care), 1, 16, 34–36, 101, 134, 136, 148, 149–50, 160–61, 164, 169, 182, 202–3, 227–28, 251, 266; challenges from unorthodox choices, 37–38; differences from default surrogate decision makers, 149, 150; documents in hospital, 34, 35, 148; effectiveness of, 238; identities of, 35; in Illinois, 161; names for in different states, 294–95n11; numbers of, 34, 35, 148, 161; responsibility of serving as, 173. *See also* advance directives

preemptive actions to improve end-of-life decisions, 238–43

preexisting medical conditions, 6, 25–26, 221, 243, 285f

"present preferences," 140. *See also* patient preferences

pressors, 56, 59–61, 64, 100, 121, 163, 218, 223

pride, 87, 74

primary care physicians, 17, 41

principals, 255–56

privacy, right of, 135

private insurance: in sample, 270t, 271. *See also* health insurance

probabilities: difficulty of processing, 237; framing of, 132–33; misunderstanding of, 112; prognosis and, 112–13; weighing, 238

prognosis, 10, 101–33, 157; about functional status, 108–11; about likelihood of survival, 104, 105–6, 117; about quality of life, 107–11, 117–18; about remaining time, 106–7; accuracy and, 117, 129–32; after building up trust, 116; age and, 113; avoidance of, 115; changes in, 99; conflict and, 118; conveying, 116; crystal ball metaphor, 116, 121; for different medical issues of same patient, 120–21; differing perspectives on, 121; difficulty of giving, 101–4; by disease, 117–18, 121–22; divine intervention and, 125; elusive, 237; evidence and, 112–16; exceptions to, 130–32; goals of care and, 104, 167; imperfection of, 130–32; medical specialties and, 121–22; miracles and, 125; mixed messages about, 119–23, 124, 133, 237; multiple sources of, 119; negotiation and, 124–29; neurological, 117–18; norms regarding, 103; optimism and, 121–22, 129–30; personal experience and, 115; physicians' dread of, 103; probabilities and, 3, 112–13; prognostic framing, 132–33; self-fulfilling prophecy and, 129–30; statistics and, 112–13; surrogates' disagreement with, 124; timing and, 116–18, 237; uncertainty and, 117; weighing prognostic uncertainty, 238; withdrawal of care and, 122; "zero" prognosis, 114. *See also* functional status; probabilities; quality of life; survival

projection, 143–44, 206, 222, 237

Protestants: decision-making trajectories and, 286f; in sample, 271, 272t

proxy decision makers. *See* surrogate decision makers

proxy directives, 136, 228, 251; apps to record, 240; consequentiality of, 239; documents in hospital, 34, 35, 148; ease of completing in most jurisdictions, 240; effectiveness of, 238; names for in different states, 294–95n11; numbers of, 34, 35, 148, 161; policies that would facilitate completion of, 240–41; rarity of, 238–39; role of, 238. *See also* advance directives; powers of attorney (for health care)

psychiatrists, 16
psychology, 132–33, 143, 144; cognitive psychology, 143, 144; social psychology, 143
public aid, 194, 270t, 271
pulling the plug, 1–3, 178. *See* life support
pulmonologists, 15, 127

quality of life, 161, 172, 178, 179, 202–3; after ICU stay, 233–34; aggressive care and, 108–9; beneficence and, 185–88; difficulty of predicting, 237; disability and, 111; food and, 55; goals of care and, 167; heuristic bias and, 111, 143; length of life and, 8; negative assumptions about, 111; patient wishes and, 174–75; prognosis about, 107–11, 117–18; subjectivity of, 187–88; surrogate decision makers' assessment of, 141; survival and, 107–11; views about, 245
Quinlan, Karen Ann, 135

race/ethnicity, 26, 28, 29, 295n8; decision-making trajectories and, 220, 221, 222, 284f, 286f; likelihood of discussions about interventions and, 75; patients and, 26, 28, 29, 75, 268–69, 269t, 272, 284f, 286f, 295n8; physicians and, 41; in sample, 268–69, 269t, 272
radiology, interventional, 16
reasonable-person standard, 183, 185. *See also* "best-interest" standard
recovery: meaning of, 129; vs. survival, 234. *See also* prognosis
rehabilitation, 182
rehabilitation facilities: costs of, 193; discharge to, 224
reintubation, 50, 158, 196
religion and religious beliefs, 203; conflicting between surrogate and patient, 200–201; decision making and, 189–92; of families, 192; health care professionals and, 41–42, 191–92; of patients, 29, 189, 221, 222, 271, 272t, 286f; ventilators and, 152. *See also* chaplains; God; *and specific religious groups*
remorse, 12, 87, 234, 236, 244
renal failure. *See* kidney disorders

research, the, 255–73; confidentiality, 266–67; consent, 266–67; the data, 267–68; data collection, 258–65; demographics of sample compared to U.S. population, 269, 270t; ethical dilemmas, 264–65; generalizability of, 268–73; limitations of, 273; methodology, 8–9; research question, 255–56; research sites, 256–58; sampling, 265 (*see also* sample, the); strengths and limitations of observational research, 261–64; transcripts of meetings, 8–9, 46, 258–61
research, preexisting: on surrogate decision making, 8, 99, 212–13, 261–62, 299n1
research site: anonymity of, 272; characteristics of, 272–73; compared to other health care settings, 272–73, 303–4n26; in Illinois, 273; location of, 272–73
research subjects, 264, 265; confidentiality and, 266–67; consent and, 266–67; privacy of, 266, 267
residents, 16, 18, 19; afternoon rounds and, 20; communication skills of, 43; morning rounds and, 17–19, 256; night-float residents, 16, 17, 19, 20; participation in meetings with surrogate decision makers, 42
resources, for teaching families in intensive care units (ICUs), 247
respirators. *See* ventilators
respiratory distress, 26, 50, 57, 102
respiratory therapists, 16
responsiveness: of comatose patients, 97–98; sedation and, 65–66
resuscitation, 5, 20, 66–67; consent to, 1. *See also* cardiac resuscitation (CPR); DNR/DNI (do-not-resuscitate/do-not-intubate orders)
Rhoden, Nancy, 145–46
right to die, 135
risk aversion, 132, 143
risk(s): difficulty of processing, 237; level of, 8; presented absolutely or relatively, 132–33; presented as frequencies or percentages, 132–33; survival vs. death, 132–33; weighing, 238
role-playing, communication skills and, 246

rounds: afternoon, 20–21; critical care teams and, 258–61; entering patient room, 18–19; length, 19, 259; morning, 17–19, 256, 258–61; observations of, 258–61; structuring of, 18

sadness, 87
sample, the: affluence of residence in, 28, 75, 269, 270t; Catholics in, 271, 272t; class in, 269; comparison with U.S. Census, 28, 268–72, 269t, 270t, 272t; demographic trends mirrored in, 268–72, 269t, 270t, 272t; diversity of, 268, 271–72; economic diversity of, 269, 270t; gender distribution in, 268–69, 269t; health insurance status in, 270t, 271; income in, 269, 270t; Jews in, 271, 272, 272t; Medicare participation in, 270t, 271; patient religion in, 271, 272t; poverty rates of, 269, 270t; proportion of blacks and Hispanics in, 269, 269t, 272; proportion of whites and Asians in, 269, 269t, 272; Protestants in, 271, 272t; public aid in, 270t, 271; race/ethnicity in, 269, 269t; selection bias of, 267
scans, 15, 18, 20, 81. See also specific types of imaging
Schiavo, Terri, 135, 252
scholars, relevance of book to, 13
security guards, 20
sedation, 27, 51, 52, 55, 57, 65, 74, 78, 84, 96, 120, 154, 156–57; with feeding tubes, 55; responsiveness and, 65–66; stopping of to aid communication, 156–57; tracheostomy and, 78–79; vacation from, 65–66
seizures, 82, 84, 86, 87; brain damage and, 86
selection bias, 260, 262, 265, 267
self-censorship of meeting participants, 205, 213
self-determination, 152; constitutional right of, 7, 135, 136; legal norms of, 148; PPP and, 246; privileging of, 137
self-fulfilling prophecy, prognosis and, 129–30
self-interest: default surrogate decision makers and, 201; family members and,

193–206; surrogate decision makers and, 146–47, 193–206, 215. See also conflicts of interest
sepsis, 26, 90, 121
severity of illness, 212, 265; advance directives and, 229, 231; aggressive care and, 223; decision-making trajectories and, 221, 222, 285f; length of ICU stay and, 234–35; likelihood of discussions about interventions and, 75; measurement of, 293–94n1; outcomes and, 233–35, 301n1; withdrawal of life support and, 150
siblings, adult, 34
significant others, 30–40; conflict among, 92–95; emotional distress of, 11; general agreement about patient wishes and, 180. See also families; family members; and specific relationships
simulation(s), 247; communication skills and, 246
social psychology, 143
social workers, 12, 16, 19, 23; in family meetings, 247; observations of, 261; relevance of book to, 12–13
Span, Paula, 229, 232
speaking for the patient, 7, 9, 10, 12, 30, 173, 232, 255
specialty teams, 16, 19. See also specific specialties
speech, impaired, 156
spouses, 30–40, 286f
standards of proof, 251. See also evidentiary standards
standing in the patient's shoes, 3, 171–81, 215–17, 215f, 216f, 220–21, 222, 224, 227–28, 281t; decision making, 171–81. See also "substituted judgment"
state differences, 273; advance directives, 34, 136, 160, 240; decision-maker names, 294–95n11; decision-making standards, 136–37, 160, 171–72; default surrogate authority, 34–35, 149, 253; default surrogate consent laws, 34–35, 253; evidentiary standards, 138–39; forms, 136; informed consent, 75, 295n10; POLST (Physician Orders for Life-Sustaining Treatment), 136, 241

statistical illiteracy/innumeracy, physicians and laypersons and, 112

statistics: numbers, power of, 114; prognosis and, 112–13

step-down units, 20

stroke patients, 26, 66, 105, 109–10, 129, 156–57, 163, 218; decision-making capacity and, 156–57, 256; prognosis and, 117–18

"substituted judgment," 137, 139–42, 152, 171–81, 215, 245–46, 251; alternatives to, 244–46; assumptions underlying, 140–41; based on consensus of friends and family, 178; based on consistency of patient's statements, 178; based on knowledge of patient's wishes and values, 177–78; based on patient's prior decisions, 176; based on patient's reactions to misfortune of others, 177; bioethicists and, 142; brain injury/illness and, 140; challenges getting it right, 138–42, 179–80; conflicts of interest and, 146–47; decision-making leeway and, 147–48; evidentiary standards for, 137–38, 176–77, 251; heuristic bias and, 142–43; hypothetical studies of, 179–80; as imaginative narrative ideal, 142; judgmental bias and accuracy and, 143; moral responsibilities toward others and, 147–48; *Newlywed Game* research design and, 179–80; offered by adult children, 179; offered by health care providers, 175–76; and standing in the patient's shoes, 172, 175, 180, 215. *See also* algorithms, predictive; *Newlywed Game* research design

suddenness of illness, 6, 12, 26, 26t, 38, 221. *See also* preexisting medical conditions

suffering of patient, 104, 146; avoiding, 89–90, 198, 210–11, 219, 225; beneficence and, 185–86, 188; change of decision-making trajectory and, 215–16; effect on health care staff, 212; length of ICU stay and, 234–35; level of, 8, 11; limiting of care toward end of life and, 224; limiting source of, 225; perceptions of, 99. *See also* pain

"sunk-cost" effects, 144

surgery, 47, 56–62, 100; decisions about, 56–62; types of, 16

surrogate facilitators and advocates: cost of, 250; need for, 248–50, 252

surrogate consent laws. *See* default surrogate consent laws

surrogate decision makers, 1–8, 34–38, 294–95n11; advance-care planning and, 242–43; caregiving responsibilities and, 197; conflicts of interest and, 145–48, 201–3; construing their role, 38–40; as critical black box at end of life, 13; demographics and, 266–67; emotional burden of decision making and, 236–37, 244, 248; emotional needs of, 198–200; fear of loss and, 198–99; financial interests of, 193–97; gender of, 34–36, 268–69, 269t, 287f; identities of, 35t; impact of medical decisions on, 193–206; obligations to others, 147–48, 237; observations of, 214–15, 255–56; parents as, 301n4; pressure from others, 193, 201–3; relationship with patient, 286f; responsibility of serving as, 239; role of, 142, 239; self-interest and, 146–47, 193–206, 215; support needed for, 248–49; unaware of self-interest conflicting with patient interests, 205–6; universal need for, 7, 12, 244. *See also* default surrogate decision makers; powers of attorney (for health care)

surrogate decision maker selection: challenges in determining appropriate, 36–38; characteristics of effective, 239–40; consequentiality of choosing well, 239–41; default, 34–36, 35t, 37, 38–40, 136, 251, 253; difficulty finding effective, 238–41; displacement of, 36–37; documenting choice, 240, 242–43; legally appointed vs. default, 253; legally designated, 34, 238, 240, 242–43; need for guidance on how to select, 243; reassessing choice of, 240, 241; role of lawyers in finding, 252; trusted by patient, 147–48

surrogate decision making, 8; algorithm predictions for, 245; bioethical norms about, 10–11; characteristics and trajectories chosen, 286f, 287f; cognitive biases of, 11; confidence in ability to make end-of-life decisions, 141; difficulties of, 12, 237–38; drawing on own experience, 152–53; facilitating, 247–48; as guesswork, 142; hiding behind documents, 231; ignoring patient instructions, 180–81; invoking advance directives, 165–66; legal norms about, 10–11; legal requirements and, 247; legal script and, 135; limitations of legal framework, 251–52; medical history and, 41; preexisting research about, 8, 99, 212–13, 261–62, 299n1; preparation for decision-making role, 241, 249; prognosis and, 124–29; refusing to reconsider goals of care, 211; uncertainty about patient wishes, 237; what surrogates would want for themselves, 175

surrogate meetings with health care professionals, 40, 41–42; avoiding encounters with health care team, 211–12; decision-making trajectories and, 300n14; distrust of health care professionals, 210–11; self-censorship by surrogates, 205, 213; surrogate availability for family meetings, 211

surrogates. *See* surrogate decision makers

survival, 130; likelihood of, 11, 104–6; prognosis about, 104–6, 117; quality of life and, 107–11; vs. recovery, 234

swallowing, difficulty, 55–56

symptom control, 90

TB (tuberculosis), 122

tears, 87

technology, 14–15, 168, 247. *See also specific technologies*

"terminal candor," 116

thoracentesis, 56

"time trade-off scores," 141

"tincture of time," 117

tracheostomy, 47, 51–54, 94, 98, 100, 102, 109, 116, 157, 158, 183, 186; decisions about, 51–54; and feeding (PEG) tube, 55; intubation and, 76–78; scars due to, 51, 53; sedation and, 78–79; as symbolic turning point, 53; talking with, 52; window to decide whether to insert, 252

tracheotomy. *See* tracheostomy

trajectories. *See* decision-making trajectories

transcripts of meetings. *See* research, the

transfers, 5–6

transplant candidacy, 1–2, 127, 188, 198, 206–7

trauma patients, 26; traumatic brain injury, 131–32, 209

treatment: benefits of, 182–83; burdens of, 182–83; costs of, 23, 79, 86, 193, 195, 196–97; cutting-edge interventions, 8; futile, 235–36; harm of delaying, 153; risks of, 182; side effects of, 182; treatment plans, 19. *See also* aggressive care; *and specific interventions*

trust: building up, 116; in medical staff, 97–99. *See also* distrust

trust, relationships of. *See* fiduciary relationships

"truth dumping," 116

uncertainty: decision-making capacity and, 156–58; patient preferences and, 237, 251; prognosis and, 117, 238

uninsured patients, in sample, 270t, 271

urinary tract infection (UTI), 89, 90

values (patient), 44, 239, 245, 246; advance-care planning and, 241; changing, 111, 139–40; conflicting with those of surrogate, 163, 200–201; family values and, 145–46, 179; "patient preference predictor" (PPP) and, 245; "substituted judgment" and, 142, 173, 174, 177. *See also* "false consensus effect"; patient preferences; projection; "substituted judgment"

vasospasm, 218

vegetative states, 162, 167, 169, 184, 189–90

ventilation, 47, 48, 49–50, 52–53, 67

ventilators, 48, 54, 57, 71, 100, 108, 109, 121, 152, 156, 165, 168, 186; brain death and, 96–97, 189–90; dialysis and, 61–63; management of, 16; palliative care and, 70; religious beliefs and, 152; removal of, 114, 156, 157, 189–90; weaning patients from, 52–53, 97–98, 106

ventriculoperitoneal (VP) shunts, 56
venues, for decision making, 79–87
verbal instructions, 166–71. *See also* patient instructions
visiting nurses, costs of, 193
visitors, 12, 15, 20–21, 30–32; demographics of, 33; gender of, 32–33, 35–36; non-English-speaking, 33; numbers of, 6, 30; suffering from serious illnesses, 33; vigils, 4, 10; visitation patterns, 30–31; visiting hours, 20–21; in waiting rooms, 32

waiting rooms, 32
what the family wants, 193–206, 215–17, 215f, 216f, 220–21, 222, 224, 227, 281t. *See also* conflicts of interest
when it's too late, 243–54
when "this" happens to me, 254
white patients, 26; decision-making trajectories, 284f; in sample, 269, 269t

withdrawal of care. *See* withdrawal of life support
withdrawal of life support, 7, 59–60, 94, 135–36, 149; conflict over, 92; legal requirements for, 150; likelihood of discussion about, 75; organ donation and, 72, 73, 74; powers of attorney and, 134–35; prognosis and, 122. *See also* goals of care
women, patient preference for as surrogate, 35–36; preponderance of at bedside, 35–36. *See also* gender
written instructions, 160–66; beneficence and, 182; limiting of care toward end of life and, 223–24; numbers of patients with and without, 160–62, 229, 231. *See also* patient instructions

X-rays, 50, 97, 211; technicians, 19

"zero" prognosis, 114. *See also* statistics

THE CHICAGO SERIES IN LAW AND SOCIETY
Edited by John M. Conley and Lynn Mather

Series titles, continued from front matter:

Failing Law Schools
by Brian Z. Tamanaha

Everyday Law on the Street: City Governance in an Age of Diversity
by Mariana Valverde

Lawyers in Practice: Ethical Decision Making in Context
Edited by Leslie C. Levin and Lynn Mather

Collateral Knowledge: Legal Reasoning in the Global Financial Markets
by Annelise Riles

Specializing the Courts
by Lawrence Baum

Asian Legal Revivals: Lawyers in the Shadow of Empire
by Yves Dezalay and Bryant G. Garth

The Language of Statutes: Laws and Their Interpretation
by Lawrence M. Solan

Belonging in an Adopted World: Race, Identity, and Transnational Adoption
by Barbara Yngvesson

Making Rights Real: Activists, Bureaucrats, and the Creation of the Legalistic State
by Charles R. Epp

Lawyers of the Right: Professionalizing the Conservative Coalition
by Ann Southworth

Arguing with Tradition: The Language of Law in Hopi Tribal Court
by Justin B. Richland

Speaking of Crime: The Language of Criminal Justice
by Lawrence M. Solan and Peter M. Tiersma

Human Rights and Gender Violence: Translating International Law into Local Justice
by Sally Engle Merry

Just Words, Second Edition: Law, Language, and Power
by John M. Conley and William M. O'Barr

Distorting the Law: Politics, Media, and the Litigation Crisis
by William Haltom and Michael McCann

Justice in the Balkans: Prosecuting War Crimes in the Hague Tribunal
by John Hagan

Rights of Inclusion: Law and Identity in the Life Stories of Americans with Disabilities
by David M. Engel and Frank W. Munger

The Internationalization of Palace Wars: Lawyers, Economists, and the Contest to Transform Latin American States
by Yves Dezalay and Bryant G. Garth

Free to Die for Their Country: The Story of the Japanese American Draft Resisters in World War II
by Eric L. Muller

Overseers of the Poor: Surveillance, Resistance, and the Limits of Privacy
by John Gilliom

Pronouncing and Persevering: Gender and the Discourses of Disputing in an African Islamic Court
by Susan F. Hirsch

The Common Place of Law: Stories from Everyday Life
by Patricia Ewick and Susan S. Silbey

The Struggle for Water: Politics, Rationality, and Identity in the American Southwest
by Wendy Nelson Espeland

Dealing in Virtue: International Commercial Arbitration and the Construction of a Transnational Legal Order
by Yves Dezalay and Bryant G. Garth

Rights at Work: Pay Equity Reform and the Politics of Legal Mobilization
by Michael W. McCann

The Language of Judges
by Lawrence M. Solan

Reproducing Rape: Domination through Talk in the Courtroom
by Gregory M. Matoesian

Getting Justice and Getting Even: Legal Consciousness among Working-Class Americans
by Sally Engle Merry

Rules versus Relationships: The Ethnography of Legal Discourse
by John M. Conley and William M. O'Barr